THE BIG BO[...]MERICAN HUMOR

P9-DHM-921

"Ken, Martha—please don't feel you have to entertain me."

THE BIG BOOK OF
NEW AMERICAN
HUMOR

THE BEST OF THE PAST 25 YEARS

EDITED BY

WILLIAM NOVAK•MOSHE WALDOKS

WITH DONALD ALTSCHILLER

HarperPerennial

A Division of HarperCollinsPublishers

OTHER BOOKS BY WILLIAM NOVAK AND MOSHE WALDOKS
The Big Book of Jewish Humor

OTHER BOOKS BY WILLIAM NOVAK
High Culture: Marijuana in the Lives of Americans
The Great American Man Shortage
  and Other Roadblocks to Romance

OTHER BOOKS WITH WILLIAM NOVAK
Iacocca: An Autobiography, by Lee Iacocca
Goodbye to the Low Profile, by Herb Schmertz
Mayflower Madam, by Sydney Biddle Barrows
Man of the House, by Tip O'Neill
My Turn, by Nancy Reagan

THE BIG BOOK OF NEW AMERICAN HUMOR. Copyright © 1990 by William Novak and Moshe Waldoks. All rights reserved. Printed in the United States of America. No part of this book may be used or reproduced in any manner whatsoever without written permission except in the case of brief quotations embodied in critical articles and reviews. For information address HarperCollins Publishers, 10 East 53rd Street, New York, NY 10022.

FIRST EDITION

Designed by Adrianne Onderdonk Dudden

LIBRARY OF CONGRESS CATALOG CARD NUMBER 90-55004
ISBN 0-06-096551-7

90 91 92 93 94 CG/MPC 10 9 8 7 6 5 4 3 2 1

CONTENTS

ATTACHMENTS

PART THREE

I WOULDN'T WANT TO PAINT IT

I WOULDN'T WANT TO PAINT IT

EVOLUTION'S BEEN GOOD TO YOU, SID

TOASTERS FROM GOD

REAL PEOPLE

I DON'T LIKE YOUR SIGN

PART FOUR   # MATTERS OF TASTE

MATTERS OF TASTE

THERE'S LADIES HERE

PRIVATE PARTS

I'LL EAT IT HERE

WE'LL BE RIGHT BACK

with drawings by (in alphabetical appearance):

Ron Barrett, Lynda Barry, Simon Bond, George Booth, Charles Bragg, Ken Brown, M. K. Brown, John Caldwell, Roz Chast, Tom Cheney, Leo Cullum, Nick Downes, Mort Drucker, Jules Feiffer, Shary Flenniken, Frascino, John Gallagher, Kate Gawf, Bill Griffith, Matt Groening, S. Gross, Cathy Guisewite, Nicole Hollander, Bob Johnson, Charlie Kadau, B. Kliban, Kornblum, Gary Larson, Lee Lorenz, Robert Mankoff, Don Martin, Joe Martin, Michael Maslin, Steve Moore, Skip Morrow, Martin Murphy, Lou Myers, Andrew Newman, Mark O'Donnell, C. F. Payne, Dan Piraro, Leigh Rubin, Mick Stevens, Ed Subitzky, Garry Trudeau, P. C. Vey, Bill Watterson, Gahan Wilson, Jill Wright, Jack Ziegler.

and quickies by:

Woody Allen, Joy Behar, Mary Bly, Victor Borge, Dennis Bruce, Rodney Dangerfield, Jules Feiffer, Lewis Grizzard, Abbie Hoffman, Nicole Hollander, Jonathan Katz, Brian Kiley, Bill Maher, Jackie Mason, Dennis Miller, Martin Mull, Michael O'Donoghue, Robert Orben, Joan Rivers, Mike Royko, Drake Sather, Ronnie Shakes, Carol Siskind, Judy Tenuta, Gore Vidal, Robin Williams, Steven Wright.

PREFACE

Comedy is the art of making people laugh without making them puke.   *—Steve Martin*

To compile this book we hunted in libraries, bookstores, record shops, humor archives, and joke collections. We barreled through hundreds of books that were reputed to be funny. We devoured back issues of humor magazines and fed countless coins into photocopiers. We considered more than eleven thousand cartoons. We sought advice from editors, literary agents, columnists, clairvoyants, and collectors. We inspected the bulletin boards and refrigerator doors of our neighbors and friends. We wrote to hundreds of writers and cartoonists, inviting them to nominate their funniest work. We rounded up the best jokes and one-liners we could find and sent them on to be evaluated by our International Society of Wits, Wags, and Raconteurs (ISWWR). In our spare time, we watched movies, rented videos, listened to records, and visited comedy clubs. This relentless pursuit of levity continued for two years, until we just couldn't take it anymore.

Throughout our search, we kept reminding each other that the only criterion that really mattered was *funny*—a concept we defined rather narrowly. As a result, we had to eliminate many well-crafted items that were primarily entertaining, intriguing, brilliant, unusual, arcane, insightful—or the kiss of death: amusing.

We also had to ask ourselves whether a particular selection would still seem funny in five years, or ten. This guideline forced us to rule out political and topical humor, although we did make an exception for Richard Nixon, who has become an enduring (and, for some, endearing) target.

Like many close friends, the two of us share a similar sense of humor. Even so, in a book of this size there are bound to be differences of opinion. We had a few affable arguments, and when no easy resolution was forthcoming, a certain amount of horse-trading ensued. If anyone takes issue with our choices, we'll always be able to blame the other guy.

By choosing to focus on contemporary humor (by which we mean material written and performed since 1965), we had to exclude many time-honored American humorists—not only the legendary Mark Twain, but also outstanding names from the past couple of generations, including the Marx Brothers, Dorothy Parker, S. J. Perelman, Robert Benchley, and Damon Runyon, to name just a few. While we recognize their influence on many of the contributors to this book, their work has filled other collections.

It was somewhat more frustrating to omit humor from the early years of television, including the shows we grew up on during the 1950s: "The Honeymooners," "Sergeant Bilko," "The Jack Benny Show," and "Burns and Allen." But rules are rules, and out they went—along with "Your Show of Shows," whose writers included Woody Allen, Mel Brooks, Carl Reiner, and Neil Simon, all of whom are represented in these pages.

Even Lenny Bruce belongs to an earlier era. Although he opened the door for much of what you are about to read, he retains his outsider status even here. We wonder: If Lenny Bruce were still alive, what would he make of the recent proliferation of comedy clubs, where performers are allowed—even encouraged—to say *anything*?

In making our selections, we resisted the temptation to be encyclopedic, to include certain authors or performers primarily on the basis of their fame and popularity. Some are individuals whom we like and respect, but whose work just didn't seem to fit the spirit we were looking for—a sensibility in large measure shaped and created by the baby-boom generation's coming-of-age.

Like so many of our contemporaries, we grew up on *Mad* magazine, with its less-than-subliminal messages about the hypocrisy of adult society. Many of our contributors were shaped by this attitude, and their humor retains an edge that's often risk-taking, cynical, and even offensive.

But here our book parts company with one recent trend in American culture: offensiveness for its own sake. We mean, of course, that rash of "tasteless," aggressive, and victimizing jokes that were so prevalent in the eighties, and which gave rise to the popularity of several obnoxious stand-up performers. But rest assured, you will find occasional lapses of taste in these pages, too.

There are a few other imbalances and omissions. Due to copyright restrictions, we were unable to present some of our favorite comedy routines and film scripts. And while women are amply represented in these pages, gays are not. Nor is the humor of most regional cultures and minority groups, which isn't always appreciated by a general audience. While a few minority performers, like Richard Pryor, have been able to reach a wider public, Pryor's routines, like those of that other great stand-up performer of our time, Robin Williams, simply defy transcription.

But then, as Steven Wright likes to say, you can't have everything. Where would you put it?

Many of the selections in this book first appeared in magazines. We have mentioned *Mad,* whose explosive visuality we continue to admire. There is, of course, *The New Yorker,* which continues to publish some of the best comic writing and cartoons. But the magazine that most deserves mention here is the underappreciated *National Lampoon.* The *Lampoon* is typically dismissed as "sophomoric," and often it is. But at its best it has been clever, sophisticated, and very funny.

Most of our jokes and one-liners appear in the margins, forming a kind of commentary on the longer selections. We found our jokes the old-fashioned way: We stole them. After rewriting the jokes, we submitted them to ISWWR, whose members are listed in the acknowledgments. Although certain patterns did emerge, the responses of our panel were rarely unanimous, especially when it came to determining which jokes were "old." We hoped to feature jokes that were relatively recent, but since nobody really knows where jokes come from in the first place, this wasn't always easy. When it came to dirty jokes, we tried to avoid the lewd without ruling out the lascivious. We generally avoided profanities and expletives, as these often aren't necessary to convey the essential comedy of sex. We were, however, more tolerant of the language of some of our contributors.

Throughout our work, we had this goal in mind: to produce an anthology you could dip into and savor again and again. Essentially, we wanted a book that was contemporary without being topical; cynical, but not contemptuous; literate, but not obscure. We also wanted a book that was more concerned with personal and social affairs than with public events. But above all, we wanted a book that would make the reader feel good.

But you'll be the judge of that.

—William Novak and Moshe Waldoks

ACKNOWLEDGMENTS

Lots of people helped us in many different ways, and we greatly appreciate all they did. Thank you Brenda Abramovich, David Allender, Larry Ashmead, James Atlas, Mel Berger, Ken Bernard, Eugene Brissie, Lora Brody, Michael Brooks, Jean Burling, Allan Burns, Christopher Cerf, Ann Close, Lela Cocoros, Aaron Cohen, Sherry Suib Cohen, Charles Conrad, Hillel Cooperman, Geoffrey Cowan, Frank Curtis, Grace Darvey, Joelle Delbourgo, Paul Dickson, Alec Dubrow, Chuck Distler, Barbara Drucker, Nora Ephron, Joni Evans, David Feldman, Roger Feldman, Gary Fisketjon, Robert Fogarty, Lewis Frumkes, Casey Fuetsch, Deborah Futter, Veronica Geng, Peter Gethers, Reg Gibbons, Alfred Gingold, Hayim Goldgraber, Jeffrey Goldstein, Michael Hammer, DeWitt Henry, Fred Hills, David Hirshey, Jane Isay, Ronda Jacobson, Josh Jacobson, Mort Janklow, Jon Karp, Jonathan Katz, Deborah Kram, Karen Kramer, Paul Krassner, Ellen Levine, Paul Lewis, Greg Lovern, Matthew Martin, Norma Martin, Jordan Moffet, Colleen Mohyde, Susan Moldow, Don Nilsen, Keith Osher, Robert Pisani, Marjorie Pomerantz, Mimi Pond, Victor Raskin, Rich Ross, Mordecai Richler, Susan Richman, Linda Safran, Ann Sandhorst, Tim Sarkes, George Shapiro, Bill Shinker, Mark Singer, Arthur Slutsky, Ron Smith, Robert Taylor, Ted Solotaroff, David Strauss, James Thomas, Calvin Trillin, Amanda Urban, Helen Vendler, Paul Wesolowski, Jim Webber, Wendy Weil, Stephen Whitfield, Robert Wyatt, and Jack Ziegler.

Special thanks to the International Society of Wits, Wags, and Raconteurs (ISWWR), who evaluated our jokes: Steven Axelrod, Daniel Bial, Steven and Amy Broder, Marcia Ely, Leonard Fein, David Feldman, Alan Handler, Jon Karp, Gail Kaufman, Larry Kushner, Arthur Magida, Gwen Mayers, Andy McKey, Ralph and Taren Metson, Colleen Mohyde, Scott O'Malley, Gary Rosenblatt, Elsie and Bob Summit, Jeffrey Summit, Ira Teich, Donald and Tess Witchel, and Anne Pomerantz Waldoks.

Extra-special thanks to Bill Franzen, William Gaines, Sam Gross, Linda Selsman-Jones, Gail Sicilia, and Mary Suggett for their advice and generosity.

We regret that for reasons of space we were unable to include many fine contributions that we had originally planned to use.

We are indebted to Arthur Samuelson, who initiated this book, and to Daniel Bial, our editor, whose assiduousness and close attention to detail were enormously helpful. Dan has an excellent sense of humor, which means that he usually agreed with us as to what was funny. When he didn't, he was generally convincing, especially when it came to the difficult task of bringing this book down to its current size.

Eileen Campion, Dan's assistant, remained remarkably cheerful in the face of our many requests. Donald Altschiller helped with the research, and Tom Mellors handled the labyrinth of permissions with great aplomb.

Steve Axelrod, our agent, was helpful and supportive, as was our designer, Adrianne Onderdonk Dudden.

Finally, a word of thanks to our wives, Anne Pomerantz Waldoks and Linda Manaly Novak, who laughed along with us (and occasionally at us), and to our children—Shula, Brina, and Risa Waldoks, and Ben and Jesse Novak.

PART ONE

RICH AND FAMOUS

Rich and Famous
How to Write Good

Used to be a joke had two parts: the set-up and the punchline. Not with today's comedians! To see what we mean, just imagine...

IF DIFFERENT COMEDIANS TOLD THE SAME JOKE

(There's a fly in my soup...)

ARTIST: MORT DRUCKER   WRITER: RUSS COOPER

ROBIN WILLIAMS

What's this fly doing in my soup? Wow! Fly in my soup? What a concept! (*Peter Lorre voice*) Oooh myyy! Tere's a flyyy een my sooop, massster! (*Herve Villechaize voice*) Ze fly, Boss! Ze fly! (*Elmer Fudd voice*) Kill du fwy…Kill duh fwwwy… (*Regular voice*) Fly in my soup! I want to DIE! (*High-pitched voice, as in the movie "The Fly"*) Help me! Help meee! (*Liz Taylor voice*) There's a what in my soup..? A fly? Only one? (*Panicky voice*) BEEP BEEP! MAYDAY! MAYDAY! (*Unintelligible*) I mean…it's crazy… fly in my soup… I mean, it's like Nancy Reagan on steroids! Just say NO! (*Incoherent babbling*)

GEORGE CARLIN

Went to a restaurant…weird, man. Got a fly in my soup. Why do they call flies "flies," man? Ever wonder? I mean birds fly too, right? The weird thing is that flies don't fly that much. The flies I see, they crawl all the time. (*New York voice*) "Gee, Martha, dere's a crawl in my soup." Why do they call fleas "fleas"? What are they running from? Are they fleeing the soup? Then don't order scary soup, man…After all, what is soup but just a bowl of wet food…right? I don't trust soup anyway. Soup is food right before you throw it away… Soup is food's last chance to get eaten…I figure, if it ain't been eaten by now, let the flies have it, man! (*Makes a real goofy face, then leaves stage*)

DAVID LETTERMAN

But you know...Ye-ah! What's next? What are we doin'? Oh, a joke? Do we have time for this, Paul? Hey, Paul...are you paying attention, Paul? Should we do this one or not? It's up to you, Paul. (*Audience groans, annoyed*) Okay... Uh oh! (*Goes bug-eyed*) I been hyp-mo-tized!! Don't know why I said that, I just like saying the word "hyp-mo-tized." Ye-ah! But you know... (*silence*) Did you hear that, Paul? Silence. Sort of a "comedy lull"...We're just coasting, right Paul? A little breather between jokes. Just saving our energy for the...you know, Paul, I went to a restaurant the other day, don't want to name the restaurant, but it was (*NBC lawyers bleep out name*), and I don't want to say anything, just...don't order the soup, okay? That's all I'm saying. So here he is, you know him, you love him...

RODNEY DANGERFIELD

Hoo...heh...I'm tellin' ya...Went to a restaurant. Tough place, really tough...the black-eyed peas had real black eyes! (*Tugs on tie, rolls eyes, starts to perspire*) I asked the waiter what was on the menu. He said he thought it was tomato sauce...Like I tell ya, I get no respect. (*Thunderous applause*) I asked for the chicken soup. Big mistake. There was a fly in it. (*Yanks tie, eyes bulge, sweats heavily*) I asked the waiter why there was a fly in my soup. He said it wasn't a fly, it was a very small chicken... No respect, no respect at all. (*Wrenches tie, eyes spin wildly, sweat sprays onto audience*)

SAM KINISON

Yeah...I went to this restaurant the other day...ordered some soup...there was a fly in it. Waiter asks me what's wrong. I say, "Ooooh, nothing. Just that there's this FLY IN MY SOUP! I CAN'T BELIEVE IT! A FLY IN MY SOUP!!! AAARRGHGHGH! I'm sorry if I seem a little upset, but excuse me if I'd rather not be served a meal with LIVE MEMBERS OF THE ANIMAL KINGDOM SWIMMING AROUND IN IT! AARRRRRGHGHGH! Call me crazy, but if I wanted to consume insects as part of my daily diet I'D GET MARRIED AGAIN! I WAS IN 'NAM! I WAS MARRIED FOR TWO YEARS! I WAS A HOSTAGE IN HELL FOR TWENTY-FOUR MONTHS! AAARRRRGHGHGH-GHGHGH!" Thank you. You've been great.

DANA CARVEY
(As the Church Lady)

So...I went to the restaurant from hell and ordered soup...and there was this teensy weensy little teeny tiny fly in my soup...and I said, "Oooh...a fly in my soup...isn't that CON-VEEN-IENT!" I went up to the waiter and I said, "My, my, my...a fly in my soup...a little beastiality buffet for the customers, hmmm? A little sin soufflé, eh? Gee, I wonder who could have put that fly in my soup...hmmm, I wonder...the chef, maybe?...No...the Campbell's Kids, perhaps. I wonder...who could it possibly be...Oh, I don't know...maybe...SATAN!?!" So then I said, "You look a bit nervous, Mr. Waiter...feeling a little prickly heat in your bulbous tipping region? Hmmm? Why do you call yourself a 'waiter,' anyway? What exactly is it you're waiting for? Could it be, oh, I don't know...let's see...let me guess...oh...perhaps...SATAN?! Isn't that special!" So I said a little prayer against the restaurant and did my little superiority dance just like this...Hit it, Pearl! (*Music begins, he/she dances weirdly off stage*)

YAKOV SMIRNOFF

What a country! Went to American restaurant. There was a fly in my soup. In Russia, fly in soup is considered two-course meal! What a country! Restaurants are nice here. It's different in Russia. Russian restaurant doesn't have waiters. Customers are the waiters. Waiting for food! What a country! In America, it's great. American people are lucky to have enough soup for fly to get wet in. In Russia, fly is lucky to get damp! What a country! You leave tips here in America...In Russia, you don't want to leave tips...you just want to leave! What a country! What a country! What a (*etc...*)

STEVEN WRIGHT

*...mumblemumblemoan...*I heard about this restaurant...had reservations...but I went anyway. I ordered soup...they brought it to me, and it had a fly in it. I was so depressed...I had ordered moth...*mumble*...I wonder if flies hate it when they order soup and they get a human in it...I know I do. Of course, I couldn't eat him, so I took him home as a pet...named him "Buzz"...funny thing is, he named me the same thing...*mumblemumble*...I feel bad, though...he wears glasses, and my friends always make fun of him...call him "400 eyes"...*mumble*...he got so depressed he tried to commit suicide...came home one day, found him with his head stuck in a no-pest strip...But they do make great pets...they just need a litterbox...and one piece of litter...I love my pet fly...he makes me so happy...I almost had a facial expression...*mumblemoanmumblemumble...*

DEANNE STILLMAN

Dean Martin Roasts Alexander Solzhenitsyn

10:00 **4** DEAN MARTIN—COMEDY SPECIAL: Nobel Prize winner Alexander Solzhenitsyn takes the verbal punches as he is roasted on the third anniversary of his emigration to the Free World by Dean Martin, Bernard Malamud, Svetlana Alliluyeva, Rudolph Nureyev, Henny Youngman, Charo, Muhammad Ali, Howard Cosell and Sammy Davis, Jr.

Dean Martin (*staggering to podium*): Tonight, ladies and gentlemen and esteemed members of the dais, we are honoring a wonderful human being. He's taken a lot of hard knocks like the rest of us. (*Pauses and surveys guests on dais.*) He's gotten his chops busted at almost every bend in the road. But, as we all know, *nothing has stopped him,* because he is a man endowed with courage . . . and a lifetime supply of Russian vodka. (*Sneers.*) Ladies and gentlemen, for our salute to this unbelievable individual, this human being who is as great a man as he is a writer, I'd like to call on my good friend and terrific human being, *Henny Youngman!*

Henny Youngman (*assumes aggressive stance at podium*): Man walks into a bar and says to the bartender, "Gimme a drink." Bartender says, "Why should I? You're so drunk your breath gives me a nosebleed." You know, Dean, I bet you could get loaded on Scotch tape! Folks, Dean's been thrown out of so many bars that he wears gray suits so he'll match the sidewalk! But seriously folks, Dean's a wonderful person. And speaking of wonderful people, I'd like to give my regards to Alexander Sells-a-lot-of-novels—I mean, Solzhenitsyn. You know, Al, you're beautiful and I love you. I love your books, too. Folks, there's nothing better than settling down in front of a fireplace with a couple of great Russian novels. They make great logs! And Al, I really admire suffering. My wife will kill me for this but she's taught me a lot about suffering. I mean she's so cold her side of the waterbed's frozen. But all kidding aside, folks, my wife's a beautiful person. And so are you, Al. Even though your books are lousy! Frankly, I can't wait till you're deported! I mean you've got a lot of nerve calling yourself a writer! You think it was bad in the Gulag archipelago? Back in—

Dean Martin: Henny, that was a beautiful and moving statement. Ladies and gentlemen, our next distinguished member of the dais to honor Mr. Solzhenitsyn (*slurs name drunkenly*) is that fabulous Coochie-Coochie Girl, *Charo!* Whew! What a hunk of woman!

Charo: Hey coochie coochie! Alexander, you are bery cute! Your beard is bery sexy! You like to coochie coochie? I coochie all the time with Cugat! Hey coochie—

Dean Martin: Whew! There's really a lot of woman there! Charo, you better sit down before Mr. Solzhenitsyn has to make a very tough decision. Now, I'd like to turn the podium over to my good friend and heavyweight champion of the world, Muhammad Ali. Muhammad, I see you've taken some time off from the Uncle Ben's rice box to add something to tonight's proceedings.

Muhammad Ali: Roses are red, Russia is blue, 'cause Solzhenitsyn is here, and I am too!

Dean Martin (motions to waiter for refill): Muhammad, you break me up. Wasn't that great, folks? Please say yes—I'd like to live a few more years. I think it's time to call on one of our honored guest's fellow countrymen, Rudolph Nureyev. Rudy, howzabout it?

Rudolph Nureyev (assumes first position at podium): Thank you very much, Dean. You're a beautiful person. Aren't I a beautiful person? And don't I have a beautiful body? (*Walks in front of podium, executes a flawless grand plié.*) Alexander, if you want to meet some beautiful women, just let me know. Jackie, Lee, Bianca, I know them all. Or if you want to meet some beautiful men, I can arrange that too. I'll even introduce you to Truman Capote if you like. Do not fear, comrade—you will not get arrested for hooliganism like at home. You can do anything you want in the West. Isn't it a wonderful place?

Dean Martin: Now, that's what I call a right-on testimonial to freedom! Rudy, you're a wonderful human being and it's been a real privilege for the Free World to get to know you. And speaking of privileges and the Free World, it is my privilege to introduce Svetlana Alliluyeva, who proves without a doubt how great it is to be an American!

Svetlana Alliluyeva: Mr. Solzhenitsyn, if my father were here today, you would not be very popular. Nobody would read your books. They would read only mine—

Dean Martin: She's only kidding, folks. Right, Svetlana? What a sense of humor those Russians have! I bet her father was a real card. I think it's time to hear from the most beloved member of the dais, Howard Cosell.

Howard Cosell: Dean, you're cute. Real cute. Folks, I wouldn't say that Dean Martin has a drinking problem, but if a mosquito bit him, it would die of alcohol poisoning. (*Laughs.*) But we're not here to talk about Dean Martin. We're here to pay homage to Alexander Solzhenitsyn. The greatest writer of our time. Mr. Big. Mr. Brains. Mr. Typewriter. And, if I may paraphrase myself, the Killer from Siberia. He's taken guff from no one. He's a real champ. Even Ali couldn't K.O. the likes of the Soviet Politburo. I'd like to thank you, Mr. Solzhenitsyn, for many thrilling moments in the fast-moving and action-packed world of sports—I mean literature. You've really got the crowd on your side. And if you'd like to go a few rounds with Mailer, let me be the first to know.

Dean Martin: Thanks, Howard. That was about as stimulating as a mouthful of sawdust and water. Which paves the way for a tribute from the well-known man of letters, Bernard Malamud. Say, Bernie, didn't I see you the other night with a good-lookin' blonde?

Frank was a man who believed in the deeper meaning of numbers. He was born on May 5, 1905, and was fifty-five years old. He had five children, and he lived at 555 East 55th Street. For the past five years, he had earned $55,000 as an executive at Sak's Fifth Avenue.

On his fifty-fifth birthday, Frank went to the track and was astonished to find that a horse named Numero Cinquo was running in the fifth race that afternoon. Five minutes before the race began, he went to the fifth window and put down five thousand dollars in five-dollar bills on Number Five.

Sure enough, the horse finished fifth.

Bernard Malamud (*with stern expression on his face*): I don't think it's necessary to make remarks like that, Mr. Martin. This is a very solemn occasion. I mean it isn't every day that a chronicler of oppression such as myself gets to meet another such writer whose works have depressed and saddened even more readers! Alex—you don't mind if I call you that, do you?—you have profoundly influenced me. Especially the way you describe prison gruel—

Dean Martin (*sipping from martini glass*): Very poignant, Bernie. It's been an honor to hear from you. And now, ladies and gentlemen, I'd like to introduce Golda Meir's favorite entertainer, Sammy Davis, Jr.

Sammy Davis, Jr.: Too much, Dean. Like too much. You really break me up . . . *pizza* face. Folks, I kid Dean. Like, I really love him. My wife and I had him over to the pad the other day and it was really beautiful. We rapped about a lot of things. Like why we love this country. We love this country because it has been so good to us. I mean where else could a black man such as myself become a Jew and still get to hang out with Peter Lawford? But seriously, folks, there is nothing more moving than the sight of Alexander Solzhenitsyn on this dais. Because this dais sits on *free soil,* man. Think about it. It's too groovy for words. Al, I know this sounds crazy, but I feel like I'm your brother. Your *soul brother.* Can you dig it? Like, I'm a Jew, man, and there are a lot of Jewish cats in Russia who are in a lot of trouble. And I know you left because of *them.* Al, my man, I know where you're coming from and I can really get behind it. Like, I've just got to *hug you,* man—

Dean Martin (*hurriedly staggering to podium*): Sammy, thank you from the bottom of my heart. You are truly a beautiful human being. Well, I guess that about wraps it up, folks. I'd like to congratulate our honored guest, Alexander Solzhenitsyn (*slurs name*), and offer our heartfelt—

Jerry Lewis (*runs up to podium from wings, grabs microphone*): Dean, excuse me. Ladies and gentlemen, all of you know that Dean and I aren't exactly on speaking terms, but I just had to be here. I mean this occasion is so beautiful and I felt that God wanted me to be here for this blessed and wonderful event I mean I just had to meet this marvelous human being I'll just be here a minute Dean I just gotta ask Al one question so let me just say how humbled I am to be in the presence of this *modern saint,* this remarkable human being who has done more for America than anybody, even more than the President, this truly amazing little man who stood up to those *shmoes* in Russia I cry whenever I think about it Dean I've just gotta ask him *one question* so just give me another minute of your time, ladies and gentlemen. IS THAT TOO MUCH TO ASK, FOLKS? Al, if you say yes to this question I'll be the luckiest guy in the whole world. I'll know that my life has been *full of meaning!* I'll know that I have followed the *right path!* I'll know that my fans in France haven't been wrong! PLEASE SAY YES! Al, would you appear next year on my Muscular Dystrophy Telethon?

SEAN KELLY

Kā-si Atta Bat

Not brilliant was the outlook for the Yokohama Prawn—
The score stood four to two, with eight and one-half innings gone.
But the fans loved *basa boru*, and so in the stands they sat,
And hoped for one more chance to watch Kā-Si-*san* come to bat.
Go, Nagasaki Goldfish! Yokohama Prawn, hurrah!
Hot saki here! Cold Kirin! Sushi, get it while it's raw!
With stoic calm they watched two hitters pop to shallow short.
Of scorn they gave no raspberry, nor of disgust a snort,
Although they knew Frin (who was small) and Burake (who was fat)
Would have to stay alive to bring Kā-Si-*san* to the bat.
But with Zen patience Frin just stood, and somehow drew a walk.
And after Burake and the third-base coach had had a talk
Concerning kamikaze, Bushido, and loss of face,
The fat man caught a fastball in the ear, and took his base.
Now the Kabuki cheerleader, a white-faced acrobat,
Leapt up and led a chorus of "Kā-Si-*san* atta bat!"
You may well wonder (while they give their neat, preprogrammed cheer)
Just how that diamond superstar came to be playing here:
Men's motives may be many, but the yen to win is why
The vaunted slugger had become a Rent-a-Samurai.
The Mudville owners wouldn't pay the wages he was worth,
So Casey took his glove and bat halfway around the earth.
By geishas he was entertained, and on tempura dined,
He was honored, he was worshiped, and eventually signed,
To play his nation's pastime in the nation of Nippon,
As the round-eyed gate attraction of the Yokohama Prawn,
Where the scoreboards and the stadiums and the bullpens look the same,
But just a little *smaller*—a scale model of The Game.
He strode out of the dugout, swinging half a dozen bats,
Through a blizzard of kimono belts and meditation mats.
His muscles flexed, his knuckles white, his visage set and grim,
He dug in with his cleats, and then—the umpire *bowed* to him!
A pause. The umpire bowed again. How formal. How discreet.
Our hero sent a gob of Red Man splashing at his feet.
"Ah, so!" the umpire murmured, and he signaled to the mound.
The pitcher nodded, stooped, and rolled the ball along the ground!
While Casey watched, amazed, it reached the plate, and there stopped
    dead.
"Hey, what the hell . . ." said Casey. "Stlike one!" the umpire said.
Now Casey stepped out of the box, and looked up at the stands.
Not a single soul was shouting. They were sitting on their hands.

The players in the dugout, the coaches down the lines
Were quiet as the bodhisattvas in their roadside shrines.
Once more the umpire smiled and bowed, and once more Casey spat.
He grabbed his crotch and crouched and sneered and twitched his mighty
    bat . . .
This time, the pitcher lobbed the ball somewhere not far from third.
And Casey shook his head, because the only thing he heard
Was the umpire saying, "Stlike two!" and no other sound at all,
For the silence was so perfect, you could hear a lotus fall.
Now Casey threw his helmet. Now Casey lost his cool.
He called the ump a dog's child, out of wedlock born, a fool;
Set out upon a stomping, spitting, shouting, swearing spree;
And stopped to catch his breath, and heard the umpire say, "Stlike thlee!"
Two hits. Two left. No runs. O shame! O terrible disgrace!
O awful loss of ball game! More awful loss of face!
Now, Casey thinks, "Can't win 'em all . . . wait 'til next . . . *what the hay?!*"
For the coach is looking at him in the most peculiar way.
Not a fan has left the bleachers, and his teammates gather 'round.
Looking sad and kinda solemn, and nobody makes a sound . . .
And just now Casey notices the batboy coming toward
Home plate, where Casey's still standing, and . . . he's carrying a *sword!*
It's raining in the Favored Land. They've had to call the game.
But there's joy in Yokohama, where they honor Kā-Si's name,
For there's nothing more exciting to the fans of old Nippon
Than an executed sacrifice, when the suicide squeeze is on!

WELL, BOY, YOUR LIFE'S COURSE HAS TAKEN A DANGEROUS, HAIRPIN TURN. LIKE IT OR NOT, YOU NOW HAVE TO ANSWER TO AN AWESOME NEW MASTER—MONEY!

NO WAY, UNCLE DUKE. MONEY DOESN'T CHANGE A THING. I'M CONTINUING TO STUDY TO BE A DOCTOR!

NEPHEW, THINK FOR A MOMENT. WHY IS IT YOU WANTED TO BE A DOCTOR?

WELL, TO MAKE..

GOOD POINT.

ZONKER, DON'T BE AFRAID TO ASK FOR HELP IN THE DAYS AHEAD.

ZONKER! HOW DID YOU FEEL WHEN YOU HEARD THE GOOD NEWS?

YEAH, WHAT WERE YOUR FEELINGS?

COULD YOU DESCRIBE THEM?

WELL, AT FIRST I DIDN'T FEEL ANYTHING. I JUST WENT NUMB.

THEN I FELT A RUSH OF GIDDINESS, FOLLOWED BY FEELINGS OF DISORIENTATION, QUEASINESS, SHORTNESS OF BREATH..

.. HUNGER, RAGE, SEXUAL LONGING, VERTIGO, BOREDOM, AND FINALLY, A TINGLING SENSATION.

WHAT ABOUT AFTER THE NEWS SUNK IN?

LADIES AND GENTLEMEN, THE BOTTOM LINE HERE IS THAT NO AMOUNT OF MONEY COULD EVER INTERFERE WITH MY DREAM OF ESTABLISHING A PRIVATE MEDICAL PRACTICE IN SOUTHERN CALIFORNIA.

WHAT ABOUT CHARITY, ZONKER?

HOW DOES YOUR FAMILY FEEL?

WHAT'S THE TAX BITE?

HEY, HEY, YOU NETWORK BOYS HAVE BEEN HOGGING ALL THE QUESTIONS. LET'S LET THE SUPERMARKET MEDIA GET IN A FEW, OKAY?

ZONKER, ABOUT YOUR LOVE-CHILD WITH MRS. GORBACHEV..

ZONKER, WILL YOU BE SLAYING MOM, CO-ED, SELF?

THAT'LL HAVE TO BE THE LAST QUESTION, BOYS! I HAVE TO GET BACK AND HIT THE BOOKS!

SO SAID LOTTERY WINNER ZONKER HARRIS THIS MORNING AS HE RETURNED TO CLASSES HERE AT THE ACADEMICALLY GRUELING BABY DOC COLLEGE OF PHYSICIANS.

$23 MILLION JUST DOESN'T SEEM TO HAVE CHANGED THIS UNAFFECTED YOUNG MAN AND HIS BOYHOOD DREAM OF BECOMING A DOCTOR.

YO, BABE! I'LL GIVE YOU TEN GRAND TO TAKE MY BIO-CHEM EXAM!

OKAY.

IAN FRAZIER
Thanks for the Memory

Two years ago I was driving to Pebble Beach from Palm Springs to play in Bing's pro-amateur tournament at Pebble Beach. I got into my car with Freddie Williams, and we started for Los Angeles. Between Beaumont and Riverside I was pushing it along at about seventy-two. The highway was wide open, nobody in sight, but it was raining a little and I went into a skid.

We turned around, bounced into a ditch, rolled into an orchard and ended up against a tree. Both of us were thrown out. I felt that there was something wrong with my left shoulder, so I stood ankle-deep in mud and practiced my golf swing. The swing wasn't so hot. We left the car and hitch-hiked back to Riverside, and I went to see a doctor. He stretched me out on an X-ray table and took some pictures.

When he'd looked at them, he said, "You're not going to play any golf for eight weeks. You've got a fractured clavicle."

Following that layoff, I went back East, stopping off at the Bob-O'-Link Golf Club in Chicago, where I'm a nonresident member, to have a crack at the course. I got together three friends, Dick Snideman, Dick Gibson and Hugh Davis, and we teed off.

I had a seventy-four for the eighteen holes. It's one of my best scores. The payoff was that on the eighth hole—158 yards—I had a hole in one. You may think that a busted clavicle is a hard way to improve a score, but if you're willing to try it, it could work. It did for me.

—*"Have Tux, Will Travel: Bob Hope's Own Story," by Bob Hope as told to Pete Martin (1954), pp. 225–26.*

It was 1950, and I was making the movie *Fancy Pants* with Lucille Ball. Dick Gibson and I had planned to play after the day's shooting had been completed at Paramount. I had one scene left, in which I was riding a horse.

These were close-up shots, so instead of a real horse they used a prop horse, a mechanical gadget. The director wanted more action, so they loosened the straps on the horse and speeded up the action. I was flipped backwards off the horse, head over teakettle. They carried me off the lot in a stretcher, and as they put me into a car, I said, "Right to Lakeside, please." I wound up in Presbyterian Hospital for eight weeks. It was a long time to be away from golf.

The next time I played was at Bob O' Link, a men's club in Chicago. The others in the group were Dick Gibson, Hugh Davis and Dick Sniderman. We had started on the back 9, so by the time we reached the 8th hole, which was our 17th, the bets were rolling. I hit a little faded 5-iron on the hole, which measured 150 yards, and knocked it into the cup for an ace. There is still a plaque on that tee commemorating that feat. I also shot 74 that day, which wasn't bad for a refugee from the hospital.

—*"Bob Hope's Confessions of a Hooker: My Lifelong Love Affair with Golf," by Bob Hope as told to Dwayne Netland (1985), p. 112.*

People always seem surprised when I tell them that Dan Quayle was the man who introduced Coca-Cola to Asia in 1906. But it's true. I was touring the Far East at the time for Underwood Deviled Ham, in a group that included Stella Stevens and the late President Ike Eisenhower's father, Dick Snideman. We stopped to play a little jewel of a course in Burma, which is what they used to call Ceylon, and there I met the now Vice-President, who told me of his accomplishments for the soft-drink industry and American business in general. He and I were in a foursome which included Pearl Bailey, the humanitarian Albert Schweitzer, and the chairman of the American Can Company (now Primerica), Mr. William Howard Taft. I had either just been run

An avid golfer hits his ball into the woods. As he goes to look for it, he stumbles upon a leprechaun who is brewing a mysterious concoction.

"What are you making?" asks the golfer. "It smells wonderful."

"This is a magic brew," says the leprechaun. "If you drink it, your golf game will improve remarkably, and you'll never be defeated."

"Well, then, let me have some," says the golfer.

"Have as much as you like," says the leprechaun. "But I must warn you, there is one serious side effect. It will almost certainly diminish your sexual desire."

"I can live with that," says the golfer, and gulps down a full cup.

The brew works. Just as the leprechaun predicted, the golfer defeats all challengers and within six months he's the undisputed local champion.

The golfer is delighted, and one day he goes back into the woods to thank his benefactor.

"It worked," says the golfer. "It really worked! I'm the best golfer this club has ever seen."

"Yes, but about your sex life?" asks the leprechaun.

"Pretty good," says the golfer. "I've had sex three or four times in the past six months."

"That doesn't sound so great to me," says the leprechaun.

"Actually," says the golfer, "it's not bad at all for a Catholic priest in a small parish."

over by a car or had just run over someone else in a car. Albert Schweitzer—who by the way is one of the nicest guys you'd ever want to meet—and I had a side bet going: dollar a stroke, quart a hole, winner does the loser's yard. By the time we reached the seventh, which was our sixteenth, the bets were rolling pretty good. Pearl Bailey, who can hit a golf ball farther than any person I've ever seen, made a perfect little shank shot off a cow or bull of some kind, directly at the flag, which was beyond a group of people hired specially for the occasion, which included Dick Gibson from Paramount and the gals from Air-India publicity. Tee to green, the distance was 18,000 meters—about 20,000 yards. TV's Ned Beatty, the only man in the American military to predict the Japanese attack on Pearl Harbor, noticed that I'd broken a spike on my left golf shoe, and he offered to take me up in his reconnaissance helicopter so that I could have better traction for my swing and wouldn't have to walk so far. We took off, and when I was above the flag, I lifted a gentle chip shot, meaning to put enough backspin on it to stop it just by the hole. Instead I knocked the ball into the whirling rotor blades, which chopped it into eighteen little pieces. Somehow, each one of those little pieces went into a different hole around the course. I not only had a one on that hole, I had a one for the whole course! Today there is a plaque on top of something commemorating this event.

That was 1926. 1927 I worked for the phone company. Ditto 1928. In 1929 came the Crash, and everything changed. I was working as a hoofer for Zwieback Toast in the old Palace Theatre on Broadway when I got a call from William Lear, chairman of Lear Jet Corp.: would I like to come out and make a movie? Would I! I ran over myself with my car, hopped in, and drove straight to Hollywood.

In my life I have been blessed with a fabulous bunch of friends who love the game just as much as I do, and I put Bill Lear at the very top of that list. He was just a nice, nice man, and a day doesn't go by that I don't think of him. Bill met me at the airport with Dick Sniderman, Freddie Williams, and the people from Cannon Towel, and the next day we started production on a picture called "The Bear," by William Faulkner, starring the wonderful Mexican comedian Cantinflas, Dorothy Lamour, and yours truly. They had a great big prop bear which was motorized and which I was supposed to box with in the climactic scene. The stunt director, Dick Gibson and Hugh Davis, wanted more realism, so for the last scene the Hamm's Breweries people loaned us their real grizzly. He sure went to town on me. By the time the scene was over, pieces of my scalp and cheekbone were AWOL, and I had a fractured clavicle. Weak with loss of blood, I practiced my golf swing. When I came to, I was hitchhiking to Chicago, where I'm a nonresident member. A doctor there strapped me to a mechanical X-ray table and turned up the juice until I glowed like the marquee at Caesars Palace. Then he slapped me into a men's hospital for eight weeks.

The next time I played was in Bing's Nabisco Pro-Amateur sponsored by Johnson's Wax at a golf course someplace. I was in a

Just as Dale entered the clearing and discovered, standing together, the Loch Ness monster, Bigfoot, and Jackie Onassis, his camera jammed.

foursome that included Lt. Dan Quayle, Pearl Bailey, Dick Sniderman, and what's-his-name, the fat guy. Even though it was frowned on, we had a bet going, a reverse Nassau, where the player with the lowest last number on his card pays the opposite of what everybody else pays him, and by the time we reached the seventh, which was our fourteenth, all the wallets were out. As a gag, the guys from Sperry Rand had substituted an electric golf ball which went right into the cup no matter where you hit it, and I teed up with the thing and it went into the hole and then just kept on going into a lot of other holes around the course, I believe.

I make it a point to get out on the links three hundred and sixty-five days a year, no matter what. I don't know anyone else in the entertainment industry who can say the same. I've played in England where it was so foggy that even the seagulls were flying on instruments, and in Africa where it was so hot that.

I was visiting Syria in 1967 as a guest of the Arab-Israeli war with Freddie Williams, Ariel Sharon, Lucille Ball, and University of Texas Longhorns' football coach Darrell Royal, and someone suggested we go play this little course about four miles from the front lines. Well, I'm a sucker for sand—I've been in it most of my golfing life—and that whole region of the world is one big sand trap, if you ask me. So I said sure, and pretty soon we were barrelling along in a converted half-track troop carrier Ariel had found somewhere. I was driving, and the vehicle registration was in a coffee can on the dashboard, and suddenly it rolled off and then out the open front door, and we went into a skid, bounced over Dick Gibson from Paramount, and ended up in a pond. I stove up my neck pretty good.

Lucille Ball, a terrific gal who I loved as if she were a friend, immediately put me in her car and took me to a hospital where they were filming "Fancy Pants," starring Lucille Ball. They had an X-ray table with straps on it, and the doctor buckled me in and turned up the juice. The thing started bucking and prancing around, and the next I knew it flipped me onto my back like an insect. The doctor took one look at me lying there and said, "You've got a fractured clavicle." Then he stretched me out on an X-ray table for eight weeks. Lucy, God bless her, did not play golf, but she sympathized with my predicament: on the following afternoon I was scheduled to play in the Sam Giancana– Underalls Palm Springs Open. Yet here I was, half a world away and laid up in a hospital to boot. Lucy sat down and thought for a while, and then she came up with a solution that was pure Lucy.

Ten years passed. My Desert Classic Tournament, excuse me, my *Chrysler* Classic Tournament was drawing a good crowd and sensational ratings, and the Timex people had agreed to sponsor me. I was playing every day, don't forget. I generally teed up with a Dean Martin's– drinking joke. The guys from Jimmy Dean Pork Sausage always brought a camera crew, and I kidded around, pretending like my putter was a pool cue. This one particular time I sort of remember happened either in California or someplace else. I was with people I had played with before or knew from another context. Dick somebody. We decided to start at the last hole and then play the previous one, and so on. We got all ready, and then we teed off.

The payoff was over half a billion dollars, just for me. It's one of the largest amounts of money there is. To give you some idea, the average professional golfer votes Republican his entire life for scores which work out to far less. On top of all that I got the houses, the cars, the dough from Texaco, and an international recognition factor that can't be measured in dollars and cents. You should try it yourself sometime. Bust a clavicle and lie around a German P.O.W. hospital for eight weeks and then escape to the West and play thirty-six holes at Inverness with nothing for breakfast but a Clark Bar. Fall from a plane, hit a fir tree, bust a clavicle, and play Winged Foot with some of the top-ranking daytime stars and the guys from the Village People. Play

Pebble Beach: try and hit straight drives in that wind off the Pacific with 5,000 sailors on the U.S.S. Coral Sea two miles offshore and a whole lot of water hazard beyond them, while Stella Stevens (as a shapely Wac) saunters by and your buddies hoot and whistle and comment on your club selection. You might do better than you think.

SANDRA BERNHARD

My Date with Isaac Bashevis Singer

On a recent trip to New York, I found myself with some time on my hands, and I realized how lonely I was. Friends sensed it and urged me to try and meet a nice guy, just for an evening out. I felt resistant. All those Wall Street types just turned me off; younger men were becoming a bore.

A really close girlfriend called me up one day and said, "Honey, what are you doing tonight? I think I've got someone you're going to like a lot. I don't want to tell you too much, but does Isaac Bashevis Singer ring a bell?"

"Cheryl, you're kidding me! He's every girl's dream! I would kill to go out with Isaac. I've had a thing for him ever since he autographed my copy of *The Magician of Lublin*. He's fabulous, and I really picked up on a great vibe from him. Is this for real, because if it is, I've got to start pulling it together. I look like hell!"

"Yes, baby, it's definitely for real. He loves your work and wants to take you to Memphis for dinner."

"Oh, I think I'd rather stay in town—only kidding. Gosh, he sounds very cool."

"He is, darling, and he'll be by in a car at nine-thirty for drinks. I'll call you tomorrow. Oh, by the way, just be yourself. Love you!"

He picked me up a half hour late and apologized profusely; he'd had an overseas call and couldn't get off. He hated what I was wearing and rushed me over to Comme Des Garçons to buy me a man-tailored suit. He said he liked his women butch. Who was I to argue? Dinner was incredible. He kept whispering sexy things in Yiddish in my ear, running his hand across my thigh, barking orders to the waiters to bring more Cristal and to make it snappy, he didn't have time to waste, couldn't they see he was with a beautiful woman! He kept getting up and going to the bathroom. "Isaac honey, I think you'd better wipe off your nose." He laughed and kissed me hard, dribbling champagne into my throat.

We left and went dancing at Palladium, where every gorgeous woman in the place was all over him like cheap perfume, but he laughed it off and swung me around the dance floor like Sterling St. Jacques. He introduced me to some model he'd gone out with and kept pushing for a three-way, but I started getting jealous at that point and told him I wanted to go home. He finally figured it out that I wanted to be alone with him and that he was close to blowing it, so he grabbed my hand and we ran up those stairs into the limo, and it all started right then and there.

By the time we got back to his place, a penthouse at Trump Tower, he slapped on a pair of handcuffs and told me to put on this black teddy he'd bought for me. He smacked me across the face and screamed something in Russian, a throwback to his childhood. He cried and told me he was tired of playing the intellectual, that he really wanted to experience life now. I held him in my arms until the sun came up. After finding the key to the handcuffs, I kissed him gently on the cheek and left.

He called me for weeks on end, but I told my maid to pretend I was out on the Coast. He was just too needy, and I felt I couldn't be there for him. It broke my heart when the necklace from Cartier arrived, with a note reading: "In all my years of magic, never have I been as bewitched. Keep the necklace forever. Say nothing and I will know how much you care. Such a *shayne maydl*. With love and loneliness, Isaac." I wept in the bathtub. Cheryl told me I was insane, but I knew I would destroy him eventually, so I went back to my quiet days and empty New York nights.

VERONICA GENG

My Mao

"Kay, would you like a dog? . . ." Ike asked.
  "Would I? Oh, General, having a dog would be heaven!"
  "Well," he grinned, "if you want one, we'll get one."
  —*Past Forgetting: My Love Affair with Dwight D. Eisenhower*

"I don't want you to be alone," he said after a while.
  "I'm used to it."
  "No, I want you to have a dog."
  —*A Loving Gentleman: The Love Story of William Faulkner and Meta Carpenter*

Why this reminiscence, this public straining of noodles in the colander of memory? The Chairman despised loose talk. Each time we parted, he would seal my lips together with spirit gum and whisper, "Mum for

Mao." During our ten-year relationship, we quarreled only once—when I managed to dissolve the spirit gum with nail-polish remover and told my best friend about us, and it got back to a relative of the Chairman's in Mongolia. For one month the Chairman kept up a punishing silence, even though we had agreed to write each other daily when it was not possible to be together. Finally, he cabled this directive: "ANGRILY ATTACK THE CRIMES OF SILLY BLABBER-MOUTHS." I knew then that I was forgiven; his love ever wore the tailored gray uniform of instruction.

Until now, writing a book about this well-known man has been the farthest thing from my mind—except perhaps for writing a book about someone else. I lacked shirts with cuffs to jot memorandums on when he left the room. I was innocent of boudoir electronics. I failed even to record the dates of his secret visits to this country (though I am now free to disclose that these visits were in connection with very important official paperwork and high-powered meetings). But how can I hide while other women publish? Even my friends are at it. Betty Ann is writing *Konnie!: Adenauer in Love*. Cathy and Joan are collaborating on *Yalta Groupies*. And my Great-Aunt Harriet has just received a six-figure advance for *"Bill" of Particulars: An Intimate Memoir of William Dean Howells*. Continued silence on my part would only lead to speculation that Mao alone among the greatest men of the century could not command a literate young mistress.

That this role was to be mine I could scarcely have foreseen until I met him in 1966. He, after all, was a head of state, I a mere spangle on the midriff of the American republic. But you never know what will happen, and then it is not possible to remember it until it has already happened. That is the way things were with our first encounter. Only now can I truly see the details of the Mayflower Hotel in Washington, with its many halls and doors, its carpeted Grand Suite. I can feel the static electricity generated by my cheap nylon waitress's dress, the warmth of the silver tray on which I hoisted a selection of pigs-in-blankets.

Chairman Mao was alone. He sat in the center of the room, in an upholstered armchair—a man who looked as if he might know something I didn't. He was round, placid, smooth as a cheese. When I bent over him with the hors d'oeuvres, he said in perfect English but with the mid-back-rounded vowels pitched in the typical sharps and flats of Shaoshan, "Will you have a bite to eat with me?"

"No," I said. In those days, I never said yes to anything. I was holding out for something better.

He closed his eyes.

By means of that tiny, almost impatient gesture, he had hinted that my way of life was wrong.

I felt shamed, yet oddly exhilarated by the reproof. That night I turned down an invitation to go dancing with a suture salesman who gamely tried to date me once in a while. In some way I could not yet grasp, the Chairman had renewed my sense of possibility, and I just wanted to stay home.

> **Prince Charles. Those ears? He could play Ping-Pong without a paddle. The royal family? A bunch of dogs. Go out on the street and call their names: Queenie, Duke, and Prince. See what shows up!**
> Joan Rivers

Broder walks into a bar with a dog on a leash. "Bartender," he says, "I'll have a scotch on the rocks, and a whiskey sour for my dog."

"I'm sorry, sir, but we don't allow dogs in here."

"Just a minute," the dog says. "I'm not used to being treated this way. Maybe you've never seen a talking dog."

"Don't give me no talking dog, mister," the bartender tells Broder. "You're not the first ventriloquist we've had in here."

"Wait, you've got it all wrong," says Broder. "I'll go across the street to get a newspaper, and I'll leave the dog here. Then you'll see."

When Broder is gone, the dog says, "Hey, pal, what happened to my whiskey sour?"

The bartender is astonished. "Sure, right away. It's on the house. I can't believe this. Say, would you do me a favor? Here's ten bucks. My wife works in the restaurant next door. Would you mind going in and ordering a coffee to go? This will make her day, and you can keep the change."

"Fine," says the dog, who takes the money and leaves.

A moment later, Broder returns to the bar. "Hey, where's Oliver?"

"He *can* talk," says the bartender. "I gave him ten bucks to surprise my wife. Here, I'll go with you."

As they leave the bar, they see Oliver in an alley, having his way with an attractive French poodle.

"Oliver, I can't believe it," says Broder. "You've never done this before."

"Hey," says the dog, "I've never had money before."

One evening about six months later, there was a knock at my door. It was the Chairman, cheerful on rice wine. With his famous economy of expression, he embraced me and taught me the Ten Right Rules of Lovemaking: Reconnoiter, Recruit, Relax, Recline, Relate, Reciprocate, Rejoice, Recover, Reflect, and Retire. I was surprised by his ardor, for I knew the talk that he had been incapacitated by a back injury in the Great Leap Forward. In truth, his spine was supple as a peony stalk. The only difficulty was that it was sensitive to certain kinds of pressure. A few times he was moved to remind me, "Please, don't squeeze the Chairman."

When I awoke the next morning, he was sitting up in bed with his eyes closed. I asked him if he was thinking. "Yes," he said, without opening his eyes. I was beginning to find his demeanor a little stylized. But what right did I have to demand emotion? The Cultural Revolution had just started, and ideas of the highest type were surely forming themselves inside his skull.

He said, "I want to be sure you understand that you won't see me very often."

"That's insulting," I said. "Did you suppose I thought China was across the street?"

"It's just that you mustn't expect me to solve your problems," he said. "I already have eight hundred million failures at home, and the last thing I need is another one over here."

I asked what made him think I had problems.

He said, "You do not know how to follow Right Rule Number Three: Relax. But don't expect me to help you. Expect nothing."

I wanted to ask how I was supposed to relax with a world figure in my bed, but I was afraid he would accuse me of personality cultism.

When he left, he said, "Don't worry."

I thought about his words. They had not been completely satisfying, and an hour after he had left I wanted to hear them again. I needed more answers. Would he like me better if I had been through something—a divorce, a Long March, an evening at Le Club? Why should I exhaust myself in relaxation with someone who was certain to leave? Every night after work I studied the Little Red Book and wrote down phrases from it for further thought: "woman . . . certain contradictions . . . down on their knees . . . monsters of all kinds . . . direct experience."

My life began to feel crowded with potential meaning. One afternoon I was sitting in the park, watching a group of schoolchildren eat their lunch. Two men in stained gray clothing lay on the grass. Once in a while they moved discontentedly from a sunny spot to a shady spot, or back again. The children ran around and screamed. When they left, one of the men went over to the wire wastebasket and rifled the children's lunch bags for leftovers. Then he baited the other man in a loud voice. He kept saying, "*You* are not going downtown, Tommy. *We* are going downtown. *We* are going downtown."

Was this the "social order" that the Chairman had mentioned? It seemed unpleasant. I wondered if I should continue to hold out.

As it happened, I saw him more often than he had led me to expect. Between visits, there were letters—his accompanied by erotic maxims. These are at present in the Yale University Library, where they will remain in a sealed container until all the people who are alive now are dead. A few small examples will suggest their nature:

My broom sweeps your dust kittens.
Love manifests itself in the hop from floor to pallet.
If you want to know the texture of a flank, someone must roll over.

We always met alone, and after several years *dim sum* at my place began to seem kind of hole-in-corner. "Why don't you ever introduce me to your friends?" I asked. The Chairman made no reply, and I feared being pushy. We had no claims on each other, after all, no rules but the ones he sprang on me now and then. Suddenly he nodded with

MICKEY MAO

© 1987 by Ken Brown

"Excuse me for interrupting, madam, but before you go on allow me to make these comments: one, I have no desire for you to do my cooking; two, I neither want nor need you to pay my rent; three, I'm very sorry you cried the whole night long; and four, and perhaps most important, I think you've called the wrong Bill Bailey."

vigor and said, "Yes, yes." On his next trip he took me out to dinner with his friend Red Buttons. Years later, the Chairman would often say to me, "Remember that crazy time we had dinner with Red? In a restaurant? What an evening!"

Each time we met, I was startled by some facet of his character that the Western press had failed to report. I saw, for instance, that he disliked authority, for he joked bitterly about his own. No sooner had he stepped inside my bedroom than he would order, "Lights off!" When it was time for him to go, he would raise one arm from the bed as if hailing a taxi and cry, "Pants!" Once when I lifted his pants off the back of a chair and all the change fell out of the pockets, I said, "This happens a lot. I have a drawer full of your money that I've found on the floor."

"Keep it," he said, "and when it adds up to eighteen billion yuan, buy me a seat on the New York Stock Exchange." He laughed loudly, and then did his impersonation of a capitalist. "Bucks!" he shouted. "Gimme!" We both collapsed on the bed, weak with giggles at this private joke.

He was the only man I ever knew, this pedagogue in pajamas, who did not want power over me. In conversation, he was always testing my independence of thought. Once, I remember, he observed, "Marxism has tended to flourish in Catholic countries."

"What about China?" I said.

"Is China your idea of a Catholic country?"

"No, but, um—"

"See what I mean?" he said, laughing.

I had learned my lesson.

To divest himself of sexual power over me, he encouraged me to go dancing with other men while he was away. Then we held regular critiques of the boyfriends I had acquired. My favorite, a good-looking Tex-Mex poet named Dan Juan, provided us with rich material for instruction and drill.

"What is it you like about Dan Juan?" the Chairman asked me once.

"I'd really have to think about it," I said.

"Maybe he's not so interesting," said the Chairman.

"I see your point," I said. Then, with the rebelliousness of the politically indolent, I burst into tears.

The Chairman took my hand and brooded about my situation. I think he was afraid that helping me to enter into ordinary life—to go out with Dan Juan and then to learn why I should not be going out with him and so forth—might not be very much help at all.

Finally, he said, "I don't like to think you're alone when I'm not here."

"I'm not always alone."

"I'd like to give you a radio."

The radio never reached me, although I do not doubt that he sent it. His only other gifts we consumed together: the bottles of rice wine, which we drank, talking, knowing that while this was an individual solution, it was simple to be happy. Now other women have pointed out to me that I have nothing to show for the relationship. Adenauer gave Betty Ann a Salton Hotray. Stalin gave Cathy a set of swizzlesticks with little hammer-and-sickles on the tops. William Dean Howells gave my Great-Aunt Harriet a diamond brooch in the form of five ribbon loops terminating in diamond-set tassels, and an aquamarine-and-diamond tiara with scroll and quill-pen motifs separated by single oblong-cut stones mounted on an aquamarine-and-diamond band. That I have no such mementos means, they say, that the Chairman did not love me. I think they are being too negative.

The Chairman believed that the most revolutionary word is "yes." What he liked best was for me to kiss him while murmuring all the English synonyms for "yes" that I could think of. And I feel to this day that I can check in with him if I close my eyes and say yes, yeah, aye, uh-huh, indeed, agreed, natch, certainly, okeydoke, of course, right, reet, for sure, you got it, well and good, amen, but def, indubitably, right on, yes siree bob, sure nuff, positively, now you're talking, yep, yup, bet your sweet A, O.K., roger wilco over and out.

A tractor salesman is driving up to a farm when he is startled to see the farmer lifting a large pig up to the branch of an apple tree. As the salesman watches in amazement, the pig bites a large apple off the branch, whereupon the farmer gently puts the animal down and picks up another pig, who gobbles up his own apple. This goes on for quite a few pigs, until the salesman can no longer restrain himself.

"Excuse me," he says to the farmer, "but wouldn't it be easier to pick all the apples yourself and let the pigs eat them off the ground?"

"Might be," allows the farmer as he reaches for yet another pig. "But what's the advantage?"

"For one thing," says the salesman, "it would save a lot of time."

"Could be," says the farmer, "but what's time to a pig?"

Licorice is the liver of candy.   —*Michael O'Donoghue*

Some Famous Couples Discuss Their Divorces

DICK & JANE

Jane: When Dick left me, I got depressed. I mean really depressed. But now I'm going to a therapist and it's been incredible. In my first session, he said, "What do you want?" It was so brilliant because you know what I realized? I didn't know! I mean it was always Dick and Jane, Dick and Jane, never just Jane. My shrink says I was intimidated by Dick. Like even though it was my money too, I never felt it was. When I bought a pair of shoes, I always told Dick the price minus two dollars so it wouldn't seem as much. I mean, even though it was Dick and Jane, it was like Dick was in capital letters and Jane was in lower case. Also, though Dick denies it, he always acted as if what I said wasn't as important as what he said. If he said, "Look, look," I always looked. But if I said, "Look, look," he didn't pay any attention.

Spot is living with me and visits Dick on alternate weekends. I got the house and pretty much all the furnishings because Spot needs continuity.

Dick: It's true I was having an affair with Eloise, but I don't think she was the reason the marriage broke up per se. Jane and I never should have been married in the first place. We'd been going together since we were kids, and she said it wasn't going anywhere and we had to break up or get married. So we got married.

It's been rough being without Spot. What I miss most is the dailiness—the walks, the feedings. My watching the football game in one room, while Spot scratched himself in another. When we're together now, it seems like we're always doing things. I'm either throwing a ball or a bone. We never just hang out.

What makes it really hard is that Eloise's dog, Weenie, is living with us. I don't get to be Spot's master but I have to be stepmaster to Weenie. Luckily, when Spot visits, he and Weenie get along great. The problem is Eloise and I have different rules for raising dogs. She lets Weenie sleep at the bottom of our bed. Spot has always slept on the service porch. I can tell from how he whimpers at night he doesn't think it's fair that Weenie gets to be in the bedroom. Eloise says if she moves Weenie out of the bedroom now he'll feel rejected, and he's feeling insecure these days as it is. Well, so is Spot. I don't know. The only thing Eloise and I ever fight about is the dogs.

MINNIE MOUSE & MICKEY MOUSE

Minnie: I was the one who did it. I kicked him out. But he made my life so miserable I had to. That's always been Mickey's game—passive aggression. It really pisses me off. He acts like a bastard, then gets to be the victim.

What an infant! His priorities are completely screwed up. Like if I was about to be eaten by a cat and Mickey ran into a lost mouse, he'd spend an hour making sure the mouse got where he was supposed to, and to hell with me. Mickey's always wanted to be loved—by the masses, by the studio, by everyone but his wife. Well, he says I'm supposed to love him no matter what. I told him he's got me mixed up with his mother.

I gave up my career for Mickey. I was going to be just as famous as he, but, no, Mickey wanted me to stay home with the kids. The only time I had any fun was when the company trotted me out for a stockholders' meeting. And then they always wanted me to wear the same damn thing—a polka-dot dress and those ridiculous high heels. Do you know what it feels like to wear shoes that are too large for you? Mickey couldn't stand it when I complained. He said he didn't mind the shorts with large buttons, why should I mind the polka dots and the shoes? Doesn't he realize he's just a figurehead, a glorified P.R. man? Maybe he does. Maybe he feels empty and that's why he screws anything that squeaks. Whatever. It's not my problem anymore.

It's really strange how everything changes. Mickey and I were together fifty years, and now when I see him, I think, Who is this mouse? How was I ever attracted to him?

Mickey: Everything I have to say about this I've already said through my agent.

ARCHIE & VERONICA

Archie: I guess I just don't get it. I always thought we were the perfect couple, but when I told Betty, Reggie, and Jughead that Veronica and I were splitting, they said they'd been expecting it for years. Veronica says we're just not in the same place anymore. She says we never really were, it just seemed like it because, in high school, we were both popular. Anyway, I'm holding her back. She says I never take anything seriously, even California wines, and my idea of a good time is to go to a high school basketball game with the old crowd. I told her I'd change. I'll root for the NBA. She said, "Great," like really sarcastically. It seems like nothing's ever enough for her.

Betty's been really helpful through this, pointing out all the ways Veronica hasn't been there for me. Betty's a family therapist now so she knows a lot about this stuff. At first we just met for coffee and talked, ya know, kinda informally. But I'm going to have my first real session Saturday night. It's the only time she can see me.

Searching for a cheap fare to Europe, Charles and Carol Baxter see an ad for a ten-day cruise at the astonishing price of $200 per person. Arriving at the pier, they are surprised to find an exact replica of an ancient Roman galleon. Even the stewards are dressed in ancient Roman garb.

"Isn't this romantic?" says Carol as they board the ship and are shown to their room.

As the gangplank is lifted, they hear their names being called through a megaphone by one of the stewards. "Baxters. Charles and Carol Baxter, please report to the lower deck!"

When they get to the deck, a steward checks them in. "Baxters? It's your turn at the oars."

"Oars?" says Charles, "What oars?"

"Just come with me."

He leads them to the bottom of the ship, where the Baxters are immediately chained along with forty other couples, all of whom are rowing steadily to the rhythm of an enormous kettledrum played upon by a ferocious armored guard. Whenever the pace slows, a midget centurion walks down the aisle flailing a whip.

They row for ten days, receiving only meager rations of bread and water.

Finally, at the end of the tenth day, they arrive in Marseilles. As they stagger back to their rooms to pick up their luggage, Charles turns to Carol and whispers, "By the way, how much are we supposed to tip the drummer?"

Veronica: That was my best friend, Betty, on the phone. She has been so great to me through this you wouldn't believe it—calling every day. Friends are so important, aren't they? But it's really strange. Aren't you supposed to be depressed when you get divorced? I've never felt better. Because of this divorce, I've found a career. I'm going to be a consultant to divorcing couples on splitting up their belongings. Isn't that fantastic? I always knew Archie was holding me back, but until I got divorced, I never knew from what.

I made up all these rules. They worked so well for me and Archie that I just know they'll work for everyone else. For one thing, they're based on fairness. That's the most important part. Do you want to hear them? Great.

First of all, whatever you inherited, you keep. In the case of Archie and me, that meant I got the china, silver, flatware, and crystal. Anything that was your hobby, you also keep. Furnishing the house was my hobby, so I kept the house and the furniture. Archie kept his collection of high school yearbooks and his sixteen letter sweaters. If you both collected something together, you split the collection in half unless one of you put in much more time collecting than the other. Then that person gets more, proportionate to the amount of time put in. For example, since I was the one who was pregnant and gave birth, I got to pick two children for Archie's one. We have two kids so I kept them both. When I tried to discuss this with Archie so he would understand my reasoning, he said, "Do whatever you want." And that brings up another thing I discovered: In order for the splitting up of things to work, both people don't have to participate. The only thing Archie contributed was his saying that if one person made fun of an object, the other should get it. Well, fine, that's his loss because he thinks everything is a big joke and I have no sense of humor.

Wait, there's more. Anything that your parents paid for, you get. For instance, Daddykins gave us the money for the stereo and the car so I got them. Record collections should be divided in half—rock 'n' roll selected by performer, classical by composer. But—and here it gets a little complicated—if you have nothing on which to use something, then you don't get the thing because what would you do with it? So I ended up taking all the records because I had the stereo.

You see, it's important to be fair, but you must also be practical at the same time.

NANCY DREW & NED NICKERSON

Ned: Quite seriously, Nancy needs help, has for years. She's a workaholic. For the longest time, I just didn't realize it. Before we were married I thought she was so—I guess you'd say, cool. The other girls were boring debutantes, and Nancy was always disappearing in a rowboat with a foreigner named Romano. Of course, in those days her sleuthing was less frequent. She had about one mystery a year. But then all of a sudden she was up to one a month, then one a week. Sleuthing

became compulsive. If the car wouldn't start, it became "The Clue in the Carburetor." If the refrigerator went on the blink, it became "The Secret of the Melting Ice." The maid quit, and it was "The Clorox Conspiracy." I tried to get her into a treatment program but she refused. In fact, she won't discuss her neurosis. She won't even admit her sleuthing *is* a neurosis. I think she has a problem expressing her feelings. That fits, doesn't it? If you spend all day sleuthing, it's a way to avoid yourself.

I've done a considerable amount of reading now that I'm alone. *I'm OK—You're OK; Living, Loving, and Learning; When Bad Things Happen to Good People.* I don't think I was held enough as a child, and that's why I was attracted to someone cold and distant like Nancy. I'm working on hugs now and dating someone who's Jewish.

Nancy: I only have a minute because I'm working on "The Clue in the Out-of-Court Settlement." The problem with Ned and me in a nutshell: He's jealous. While we were going together he always acted as if he liked it that I sleuthed. We got married and overnight it was, "Can't you just sleuth part-time?"

What's really bothering me is that Ned thinks he's entitled to fifty percent of the proceeds from my books. Ned says if it weren't for him, I wouldn't have been as successful as I was. Having a boyfriend made me more appealing to the public, and if he hadn't been holding down the fort—providing me with a secure relationship to come home to—I couldn't have had all my adventures. That's easy for him to say. He's not the one who was kidnapped by a gypsy violinist or poisoned by a sword doll. Besides, I was always encouraging him to sleuth, but he didn't want to.

Daddy's handling the divorce for me. He says not to worry.

OLIVE OYL & POPEYE

Popeye: I hate to think of Swee'pea growing up with that woman as his mother (or should I say, as her mother? I've never been absolutely sure what sex Swee'pea is. I think a boy). Olive is a complete control freak. Just get a load of the poor kid's schedule. Monday, clarinet; Tuesday, computer class; Wednesday, soccer; Thursday, scouts; Friday, gymnastics. I don't think he has any fun when he's with her. And she's always acting like I'm not a responsible person. Just because I don't have a job. When I take Swee'pea sailing, she always says, "Don't forget to put sun block on him." She claims I once brought him back as red as a lobster, which isn't true. "Oh, Popeye," she shrieked. "Look what you've done!" Somebody should do something about that voice. I thought when we got married it would lower a few octaves, but I found out marriage doesn't change anything.

I think Swee'pea's going to want to live with me when he's older. I wish he did right now. If he's a boy, he'd be better off with his father.

Olive: Okay, so he rescued me a few times when we were younger. Popeye always liked to put on a big show when everyone was watching. Most of the time, he just lay around on that boat with a pipe

"MY WIFE DOESN'T UNDERSTAND ME."

in his mouth. I suppose I shouldn't complain. The truth is, I don't need him anymore because, now that I've taken karate, I can rescue myself.

Popeye's always been pretty good to Swee'pea considering we never did know who his father is and I'm not sure I'm his mother. Though I wish Popeye would grow up already. When I first met him, I thought it was so cute the way he flipped the tops off tin cans and poured the contents down his throat. We all did things like that when we were kids. But now he's forty and it's time to use a knife and fork. Popeye says I'm so uptight. Just because Swee'pea has Monday, clarinet; Tuesday, computer class; Wednesday, soccer; Thursday, scouts; Friday, gymnastics. I'm not uptight; he's irresponsible. Once he brought Swee'pea back from sailing as red as a lobster. Men have it so easy. Doesn't he realize what it's like being a single mother? He takes Swee'pea out, buys him whatever he wants, and drops him off. I'm the real parent—I'm the one who makes sure he studies, gets enough sleep, and talks to him about his feelings about androgyny. I guess when it comes to Swee'pea, you could say that I'm the lettuce, Popeye's the dressing, which is pretty ironic if you think about it.

> **My wife thinks I'm too nosy. At least that's what she scribbles in her diary.**
>
> —Drake Sather

SNOW WHITE & THE PRINCE

Snow White: Off the record, he's a pervert. He only wanted to do it if I was drugged. I had to take a 'lude, pass out, and then he'd wake me with a kiss. At first I thought it was sort of sweet—re-creating the first time we met and all. But then it turned out, if I wasn't unconscious, he couldn't get it up. That's sick. It's only logical I began to look for comfort elsewhere. What would you expect?

To be honest, I suppose it was inevitable. There was always this unresolved thing between me and Doc (he's so take-charge), and me and Bashful (secretly he's a tiger), and me and Happy (such a compelling laugh), and me and Grumpy (it's just an act, he's really tender), and me and Sneezy (God bless him), and me and Dopey (I finally found out where his brain is located), and me and . . . and . . . wait a second, there's one more, that's only six. Who is it? Who is it! Dammit.

The Prince: My lawyers have advised me to say nothing, but not-for-publication I can tell you I was appalled. I thought she had just cooked and cleaned for those dwarfs, and the relationship was, shall we say, avuncular. I had no idea. But when Snow White began disappearing every afternoon and I became concerned, her stepmother suggested I engage a private detective. It turned out there were goings-on in that cottage quite unbefitting my wife, the future queen. I have been informed that she was actually having relations with all seven— Doc, Bashful, Grumpy, Sneezy, Happy, Dopey, and wait, let me think, there's one more. Who's the seventh? Rudolph?

GREETINGS, NAMES

(1986)

Once again the season lowers,
Slushy streets and snowball throwers;
Carols where you least expect 'em,
Halls that pall 'cause you ain't decked 'em.
Christmas specials spawned in summer,
One more time, "The Little Drummer."
Obligations pounding at you,
Screaming kids demanding that you
Name eight reindeer, plus or minus.
Dasher? Let's see. Snoopy? Linus?
Partridges once more in pear trees,
Skaters, hope their derrières freeze.
Blaring trumpets, crashing cymbals,
Joy to Bloomie's, Macy's, Gimbels.
Frantic shoppers, cards at ready,
Make believe they're J. Paul Getty,
Out of sorts and out of cash . . .
Now's the time to have a bash;
A good old blowout, nothing arty,
Everyone can join this party.
Before you drop, before you wear down,
Come on over, let your hair down!
Friends and neighbors, glad to see you!
Barbara Jordan, Nick Fotiu
Bon soir, Bergens! Edgar, Polly,
Hi, Picasso, Hello, Dali,
Put your coats down by Madonna
(Uh-oh, hope that's Sean Penn on her),
Thrilled to have you here, we mean it,
Mr. Mister, Mister Peanut,
Dragon, Carmen; Dragon, Ollie,
Steinberg, Saul and Goldberg, Molly.
Arthur Prysock, Arthur Frommer,
Curt LeMay, our favorite bomber.
Yuppies, yahoos, Yurts and *yentas,*
Mingle with the de la Rentas.
Richard Simmons, fey *aerobiste,*
Euell Gibbons, who eats no beast.
Charo's pregnant; who beguiled her?
Cornell's Wilde but Thornton's Wilder.
Dance the samba, do the hustle,

Helga Testorf, Bertrand Russell.
Richards, Mss. Renée and Mary,
One so straight, one quite contrary.
Major Deegan, General Tire,
Bernie Goetz, *please* hold your fire.
Rajneesh Baghwhan, exiled swami,
Milton Berle, *beaucoup* salami.
Arthur Treacher in a bowler,
Sydney Greenstreet, Sidney Toler,
Sylvia Sidney, Sylvia Fine,
Arlene Francis, what's *her* line?
Beauteous women, men of parts,
All our fave non-martial Arts:
Farmer, Shamsky, Carney, Deco,
Say hello to José Greco.
Solzhenitsin and Yvonne,
Gulag-guy, meet Goolagong.
Come in from the snow and hailstorm,
Charlie Farrell, Margie (Gale Storm).
Shecky Greene, a born-to-clown guy,
Caryl Chessman, *"Don't sit down, guy!"*
Brothers Grimm and brothers Mayo,
Hail the Wolfe boys, Nero, Beo.
Channing, Carol; Channing, Stockard,
One and all are getting snockered.
Horton Foote, who wears no socks.
Timothy Bottoms, Wally Cox.
Fill the glass, this night shows promise,
Someone wake up Dylan Thomas.
Tallulah says it's too, too thrilling,
Dancing slow with Lionel Trilling.
Beer for Beattys Clyde and Zelmo,
Grog for Admiral Zumwalt (Elmo),
Toast the Dons (Ameche? Fagen?),
And the Rons (McDonald? Reagan?).
Emile Verban, Stanley Hack,
Zooey, Franny, Mabel, Mack,
Charlie Chaplin and his Oona,
Charlie Weaver, Charlie Tuna.
That reminds me, check the pantry,
Food for Elmers Fudd and Gantry,

Snacks for Max and Marlin Perkins,
Holding out on slaw and gherkins,
Goose and turkey, stuffing, sauce.
Eat like Kate Smith, eat like Hoss;
The less that's left, the less to clean up.
Eat the pâté and terrine up,
'Til you're stuffed up to the gills, son,
'Til you look like old Don Wilson.
Bring the Cheddar, slice the Stilton
(Taylor-made for Nicky Hilton),
Crackers with the Camembert
(Ginger Snaps for Fred Astaire),
Goat and Gouda, head, Havarti,
For Rachel Carson, Rico Carty.
Fill your plate with curd and rennett,
Benny Bengough, Constance Bennett.
Noël Coward's a mozzarell' man,
Laughing Cow for Lillian Hellman.
What's the matter, feel *facochte?*
Not to worry, pick a doctor:
Gooden, Mengele, or Schweitzer.
One's no fun, the others nicer.
Idi Amin, how they hanging?
No, don't answer. Who's that banging
On the roof, is it Kriss Kringle,
Sack a-bulge and bells a-jingle?
Give the old roué a toddy,
One more round for everybody!
One more time, a little drink-o;
Hemingway is good and stinko.
He did *what* into the punchbowl?!?
Pardon me, here comes my lunch, whole.

What's the ruckus? Who's the red-ass?
Just benign but crusty Ed As-
Ner, but trouble could be starting;
Time for friends to be departing.
Alfred Gingold's nurse is coming,
Johnny Buskin's hugging plumbing.
Rambo's shooting all the Asians
(Really, some guests try one's patience).
Hope you wake up home and thriving
(Monty Clift should not be driving).

Morning comes, *amis* and *paisans,*
Heads pikestaffed and breath like bisons.
Gone the raconteur, the funster;
Mirror's showing Herman Munster.
Whom did I insult, let's think now;
What I need's a little drink now.
Somewhere Dottie P. is smiling,
S.J., E.B., A.J. filing
Copy that I wish I'd written,
Funny stuff galore befittin'
Days of dash, panache, and élan,
Of Lefty Grove and Grover Whelan.
What the hell, this Yule is finished,
Mon odeur un peu diminished.
Light the fire, hope this log'll
Clear the air of suspect dogg'rel.
What's the chance of one more pun?
Pickens? Trevor? (Slim to Nunn).

–ROGER DEVILL

DAVID BUSKIN

JOE QUEENAN
A 'Who's Who' Whodunit

With the possible exceptions of the Sons of Peter Abelard, the Friends of Idi Amin, and the League of Scintillating Philadelphia Conversationalists, there is probably no fraternity smaller than People Who Aren't in *Who's Who*. Just about everyone I interview as a journalist is listed in *Who's Who*, as are most of the people I admire, virtually everyone I despise, and more than a handful of the people I foul in our Saturday afternoon pick-up basketball games at the YMCA. R. C. Webster is in *Who's Who* this year too, even though R. C. Webster doesn't exist.

A few years ago, when I started editing *American Business*, Ralph Ginzburg's offbeat business publication, R. C. Webster had been a fixture on the masthead for some time. Though he may have started out as somebody's nom de plume, by the time I got there he was turning up as managing editor, staff writer, and general office help—wherever we needed to fill a space on the masthead. Mostly "R. C. Webster" was a handy name people at the magazine used to get rid of persistent salesmen, dunners, or flacks. "Send it to R. C. Webster," our receptionist would say. "The only person who would know about that is R. C. Webster, and he's in Houston" was another familiar comment, as was "I'll have to ask Mr. Webster to get back to you on that one." In about 500 years.

In any case, R. C. Webster, like half the other people on the planet, eventually turned up on *Who's Who*'s mailing list, and was duly sent an application form inviting him to become a biographee. So was Joe Queenan. This in itself was a trifle unusual, given that *American Business* had always given inordinate editorial priority to stories about floating brothels, burial in outer space, computerized solar doghouses, and the investment value of haunted houses, carrying such headlines as: "COCKY BULL BREEDER HORNS IN ON SEED MONEY"; "NEVADA GAMBLES ON SLIME"; and "CAFETERIAS EAT IT RAW." But heck, these things happen. In any case, Joe Queenan sent in a reasonably legitimate application, though it is not true that he has published a book called *Only the Good Stay Dead*. Then Joe Queenan sent in a bogus application for Mr. Webster, just to see how rigorous the screening process is at *Who's Who*.

Not so rigorous. The people there didn't blink when they received a biography from a man who had supposedly been born on September 1, 1939, in Arcis-sur-L'Abattoir; whose wife's name is Trish Abigail Boogen; whose children include Cassette, Lothar, Skippy, and Boo-Boo; and who holds a Master of Fine Arts degree from F&M T&A University. They didn't think it odd that Mr. Webster should hold a bachelor's degree from Holy Indigents High School, doctorates from the University of Ron (Ron, France) and Quaker State University, and claim to be the author of such books as *Mars and Menials*, *Jake and Pete*, and *Mr. Sleazy in Zion*. They didn't find anything unusual about a man whose professional associations include being treasurer of the Association of Men, the Bureau of People, and the Christian Managing Editor Association; secretary of the Better Club Association; and who has served as an officer of the North Bronx Dog Club and the Christian Dog Club. They didn't find it at all strange that Mr. Webster should list "managing editing" as one of his hobbies, or that his career should have included stints as editor of *American Business*, *Latin-American Business*, *The Business of Business*, *Your Business*, and *Our Business Monthly*.

WEBSTER, ROLAND CHANSON, magazine editor; b. Arcis-sur-L'Abattoir, France, Sept. 1, 1939; s. Jean-Luc and Jeanne-Lucie (Simone) W. m. Trish Abigail Boogen, Nov. 3, 1956; children—Skippy, Clay, Lance, Duane, Lothar, Cassette, Alice. B.A., Green Bay Coll., 1962; M.F.A., Houston Poly. Inst., 1964; Ph.D. (hon.), Quaker State U., 1978, U. Ron., France, 1982. Writer Our Bus. Monthly, Cleve., 1966–67; editor, writer Your Bus., Cleve., 1967–68; mng. editor, editor The Bus. of Bus., Chgo., 1969–73; mng. editor Latin-Am. Bus., N.Y.C., 1973–77, Am. Bus., N.Y.C., 1977— Author: (textbook) Mars and Menials, 1978; (novel) Jake and Pete, 1968; Causes of World War II, 1964; Mr. Sleazy in Zion, 1966. Treas., Bur. People, Dobbs Ferry, N.Y., 1980–81. Assn. Men., Irvington, N.Y., 1981–82. Served as sgt. U.S. Army, 1956–58. Recipient Bronze Phoenix award Gray Found., 1982. Mem. Am. Assn. Mng. Editors (Golden Stylus award 1983), Am. Mng. Editors Assn., Westchester Assn. Editors, North Tarrytown Literacy Club, Christian Mng. Editor (treas. 1983–85). Better Club Assn. (sec. 1979–80), Tarrytown Dog Club (pres. 1980), Westchester Dog Club (sec. 1978), North Bronx Dog Club, Christian Dog Club. Republican. Lutheran. Home: 33 Kendall Pl. North Tarrytown NY 10591 Office: Am Bus Mag 1775 Broadway New York NY 10019.

And they didn't ask what a "Low Lutheran" is. (If you must know, it's a sect of very short Protestants who have been given an ecclesiastical dispensation to preach that God the Father only stands four feet six inches, and that his son Christ couldn't have much more than an inch on him.) The *Who's Who* people took it all in and put it in their computer.

Did anyone from *Who's Who* ever contact Mr. Webster to check for authenticity? Yes, once he got a letter asking what year he'd gotten his master's degree. At this point, I changed F&M T&A to Houston Polytechnical Institute, to see if anyone was paying attention. Nobody was.

However, this was not the last time *Who's Who* contacted me or Mr. Webster. Actually, we got a steady stream of correspondence. A warning that the Deluxe Edition was going fast, so order soon. A galley proof warning that this was the last time we would be offered prepublication prices. A warning that this was our last chance to get a copy, period. An offer of a mahogany wall plaque. An urgent verification request. An invitation to be listed in *Who's Who in U.S. Writers, Editors & Poets*, followed by the same barrage of come-ons, though this time the wall plaque was made of sturdy, handsome walnut.

I did not respond to any of these overtures, and must say that the *Who's Who* people deserve credit for not cutting Mr. Webster or me out of the book simply because we failed to order a copy. In any case, the 1986–87 edition of *Who's Who* is on library bookshelves everywhere, and I'm listed, as is my non-existent sidekick, most of whose pertinent accomplishments appear in print. Actually, his entry is no longer than mine; of course, his accomplishments are considerably more noteworthy.

Mr. Webster's listing seems to suggest that the *Who's Who* people don't do a whole lot in the way of fact checking. This being the case, my advice is: If you get an invitation to submit your biography, embellish the hell out of it. Next year, God willing, I'm bailing out of this outfit and moving over to the editorship of *Time*. I'm going to say I not only graduated from Yale, but founded it. I'm going to give myself eight Golden Gloves, two Wimbledon championships, and the NBA slam-dunk title. And when they ask for employment history, I'm going to list my previous jobs as Secretary of Defense, Senate Majority Leader, Director of the KGB, Assistant Pope, president of the Fraternal Order of Iranian Moderates, and ex-husband of Wallis Simpson. It'll all look good on my résumé.

> **On a New York subway train, you get heavily fined if you spit. On the other hand, you're allowed to throw up for nothing.**
> —Lewis Grizzard

A narcissist is someone better looking than you are.   —*Gore Vidal*

MICHAEL O'DONOGHUE
How to Write Good

"If I could not earn a penny from my writing, I would earn my livelihood at something else and continue to write at night."

—Irving Wallace

"Financial success is not the only reward of good writing. It brings to the writer rich inner satisfactions as well."

—Elliot Foster, Director of Admissions, Famous Writers School

Introduction

A long time ago, when I was just starting out, I had the good fortune to meet the great Willa Cather. With all the audacity of youth, I asked her what advice she would give the would-be-writer and she replied:

"My advice to the would-be-writer is that he start slowly, writing short undemanding things, things such as telegrams, flip-books, crank letters, signature scarves, spot quizzes, capsule summaries, fortune cookies and errata. Then, when he feels he's ready, move up to the more challenging items such as mandates, objective correlatives, passion plays, pointless diatribes, minor classics, manifestos, mezzotints, oxymora, exposés, broadsides and papal bulls.

And above all, never forget that the pen is mightier than the plowshare. By this I mean that writing, all in all, is a hell of a lot more fun than farming. For one thing, writers seldom, if ever, have to get up at five o'clock in the morning and shovel manure. As far as I'm concerned, that gives them the edge right there."

She went on to tell me many things, both wonderful and wise, probing the secrets of her craft, showing how to weave a net of words and capture the fleeting stuff of life. Unfortunately, I've forgotten every bit of it.

I do recall, however, her answer when I asked "If you could only give me one rule to follow, what would it be?" She paused, looked down for a moment, and finally said, "Never wear brown shoes with a blue suit."

There's very little I could add to that except to say "Go to it and good luck!"

Lesson 1—The Grabber

The "grabber" is the initial sentence of a novel or short story designed to jolt the reader out of his complacency and arouse his curiosity, forcing him to press onward. For example:

"I've got an idea for a story: Gus and Ethel live on Long Island,
on the North Shore. He works sixteen hours a day writing fiction. Ethel never goes out,
never does anything except fix Gus sandwiches, and in
the end she becomes a nympho-lesbo-killer-whore. Here's your sandwich."

"It's no good, Alex," she rejoined, "Even if I did love you, my father would never let me marry an alligator."

The reader is immediately bombarded with questions, questions such as: "Why won't her father let her marry an alligator?" "How come she doesn't love him?" and "Can she learn to love him in time?" The reader's interest has been "grabbed"!

Just so there'll be no misunderstanding about grabbers, I've listed a few more below:

"I'm afraid you're too late," sneered Zoltan. "The fireplace has already flown south for the winter!"

Sylvia lay sick among the silverware . . .

"Chinese vegetables mean more to me than you do, my dear," Charles remarked to his wife, adding injury to insult by lodging a grapefruit knife in her neck.

One morning Egor Samba awoke from uneasy dreams to find himself transformed into a gigantic Volkswagen.

"I have in my hands," Professor Willowbee exclaimed, clutching a sheaf of papers in his trembling fingers and pacing in circles about the carpet while I stood at the window, barely able to make out the Capitol dome through the thick, churning fog that rolled in off the Potomac, wondering to myself what matter could possibly be so urgent as to bring the distinguished historian bursting into my State Department office at this unseemly hour, "definitive proof that Abraham Lincoln was a homo!"

These are just a handful of the possible grabbers. Needless to say, there are thousands of others, but if you fail to think of them, feel free to use any or all of these.

Lesson 2—The Ending

All too often, the budding author finds that his tale has run its course and yet he sees no way to satisfactorily end it, or, in literary parlance, "wrap it up." Observe how easily I resolve this problem:

Suddenly, everyone was run over by a truck.
                            —The End—

If the story happens to be set in England, use the same ending, slightly modified:

Suddenly, everyone was run over by a lorry.
                            —The End—

If set in France:

Soudainement, tout le monde était écrasé par un camion.
                            —Finis—

You'll be surprised at how many different settings and situations this ending applies to. For instance, if you were writing a story about ants, it would end "Suddenly, everyone was run over by a centipede." In fact, this is the only ending you ever need use.*

Lesson 3—Choosing a Title

A friend of mine recently had a bunch of articles rejected by the *Reader's Digest* and, unable to understand why, he turned to me for advice. I spotted the problem at a glance. His titles were all wrong. By calling his pieces such things as "Unwed Mothers—A Head Start on Life," "Cancer—The Incurable Disease," "A Leading Psychologist Explains Why There Should Be More Violence on Television," "Dognappers I Have Known and Loved," "My Baby Was Born Dead

_____
*Warning—If you are writing a story about trucks, do *not* have the trucks run over by a truck. Have the trucks run over by a *mammoth* truck.

and I Couldn't Care Less" and "Pleasantville—Last of the Wide-Open Towns," he had seriously misjudged his market. To steer him straight, I drew up this list of all-purpose, surefire titles.

> _____ *at the Crossroads*
> *The Case for* _____
> *The Role of* _____
> *Coping with Changing* _____
> *A Realistic Look at* _____
> *The* _____ *Experience*
> *Bridging the* _____ *Gap*
> *A* _____ *for All Seasons*

Simply fill in the blanks with the topic of your choice and, if that doesn't work, you can always resort to the one title that never fails:

South America, the Sleeping Giant on Our Doorstep

Lesson 4—Exposition

Perhaps the most difficult technique for the fledgling writer to master is the proper treatment of exposition. Yet watch the sly, subtle way I "set the scene" of my smash play, The Last to Know, *with a minimum of words and effort.*

(The curtain opens on a tastefully appointed dining room, the table ringed by men in tuxedos and women in costly gowns. There is a knock at the door.)

Lord Overbrooke: Oh, come in, Lydia. Allow me to introduce my dinner guests to you.

This is Cheryl Heatherton, the madcap soybean heiress whose zany antics actually mask a heart broken by her inability to meaningfully communicate with her father, E. J. Heatherton, seated to her left, who is too caught up in the heady world of high finance to sit down and have a quiet chat with his own daughter, unwanted to begin with, disposing of his paternal obligations by giving her everything, everything but love, that is.

Next to them sits Geoffrey Drake, a seemingly successful merchant banker trapped in an unfortunate marriage with a woman half his age, who wistfully looks back upon his days as the raffish Group Captain of an R.A.F. bomber squadron that flew eighty-one missions over Berlin, his tortured psyche refusing to admit, despite frequent nightmares in which, dripping with sweat, he wakes screaming, "Pull it up! Pull it up, I say! I can't hold her any longer! We're losing altitude! We're going down! Jerry at three o'clock! Aaaaaaaaaaaaaaaaagggh!", that his cowardice and his cowardice alone was responsible for the loss of his crew and "Digger," the little Manchester terrier who was their mascot.

The empty chair to his right was vacated just five minutes ago by Geoffrey's stunning wife, twenty-three-year-old, golden-tressed Edwina Drake, who, claiming a severe migraine, begged to be excused that she

> I went to a bookstore today. I asked the woman behind the counter where the self-help section was. She said, "If I told you, that would defeat the whole purpose."
>
> —Brian Kiley

BETH, YOU ARE MY WOMAN
Now, by Melva Toast (Fjord
and Peckerwood; $19). Yet
another sweeping novel of
the Babylonian captivity, this
one with a romantic twist.
Kalifa, wealthy "even beyond
dreams of avarice," falls in
love with Beth, a young
maiden with "lips so red
they were as berries." He
pursues her relentlessly and
finally purchases her, only to
find that he cannot really
possess her unless he is nice.
Desperate to win her soul, he
sells all his other females
(except his cook and cleaning
women) and, in a somewhat
less than unexpected role
reversal, pledges himself in
service to her. She laughs at
him, and he cuts out her
heart, cooks it in a casserole,
and serves it to company.
Nothing new here. There are
several effective descriptions
of what it must have been
like to walk up all those
steps on the ziggurats, but
someone should tell Miss
Toast that they didn't have
designer jeans then.

BLOOMSBURY KIND OF GUY, by
Guy Fusspot (Dipsy Doodle
Books; $12.95). Guy Fusspot
is a distant cousin of Lytton
Strachey and a nephew of
Vanessa Bell, lived two

might return home and rest, whereas, in reality, she is, at this moment, speeding to the arms of another man, convinced that if she can steal a little happiness now, it doesn't matter who she hurts later on.

The elderly servant preparing the Caviar *en Socle* is Andrew who's been with my family for over forty years although he hasn't received a salary for the last two, even going so far as to loan me his life's savings to cover my spiraling gambling debts but it's only a matter of time before I am exposed as a penniless fraud and high society turns its back on me.

The dark woman opposite me is Yvonne de Zenobia, the fading Mexican film star, who speaks of her last movie as though it was shot only yesterday, unwilling to face the fact that she hasn't been before the cameras in nearly fifteen years; unwilling to confess that her life has been little more than a tarnished dream.

As for her companion, Desmond Trelawney, he is an unmitigated scoundrel about whom the less said, the better.

And, of course, you know your father, the ruthless war profiteer, and your hopelessly alcoholic mother, who never quite escaped her checkered past, realizing, all too late, that despite her jewels and limousines, she was still just a taxi-dancer who belonged to any man for a drink and a few cigarettes.

Please take a seat. We were just talking about you.

This example demonstrates everything you'll ever need to know about exposition. Study it carefully.

Lesson 5—Finding the Raw Material

As any professional writer will tell you, the richest source of material is one's relatives, one's neighbors and, more often than not, total strangers. A day doesn't go by without at least one person, upon learning that I'm a professional writer, offering me some terrific idea for a story. And I'm sure it will come as no shock when I say that most of the ideas are pretty damn good!

Only last week, a pipe-fitter of my acquaintance came up with a surprise ending guaranteed to unnerve the most jaded reader. What you do is tell this really weird story that keeps on getting weirder and weirder until, just when the reader is muttering, "How in the heck is he going to get himself out of this one? He's really painted himself into a corner!" you spring the "mindblower": "But then he woke up. It had all been a dream!" (which I, professional writer than I am, honed down to: "But then the alarm clock rang. It had all been a dream!") And this came from a common, run-of-the-mill pipe-fitter! For free!

Cabdrivers, another great wealth of material, will often remark, "Boy, lemme tell ya! Some of the characters I get in this cab would fill a book! Real kooks, ya know what I mean?" And then, without my having to coax even the slightest, they tell me about them, and they *would* fill a book. Perhaps two or three books. In addition, if you're at all interested in social science, cabdrivers are able to provide countless examples of the failures of the welfare state.

blocks away from Leonard and Virginia Woolf, and met E. M. Forster once at a jumble sale. An inveterate stroller, the young Fusspot liked to take the air in all weathers, and the routes he favored are described here in more detail than one might wish. What makes these dimly recalled memoirs of more than passing interest is the fact that Fusspot did not know that many of the people he glimpsed through the windows of their homes were writers, even though whenever he saw them they were hunched over desks.

THE ICE CUBE BOOK, By Sherry Friddleman (Rubber House; $26.95). Do not be deceived by the title; ice cubes are merely the starting point for this entertaining collection of photographs, drawings, essays, poems, and recollections about frozen water. Blocks of ice and crushed ice are here, in addition to a well-researched and provocative section on novelty ice such as the topless mermaid ice-cube mold and the classic horsefly-in-the-plastic-ice-cube trick. With an introduction by Dick Button.

To illustrate just how valid these unsolicited suggestions can be, I shall print a few lines from a newly completed play inspired by my aunt, who had the idea as far back as when she was attending grade school. It's called *If an Old House Could Talk, What Tales It Would Tell:*

> *The Floor:* Do you remember the time the middle-aged lady who always wore the stiletto heels tripped over an extension cord while running to answer the phone and spilled the Ovaltine all over me and they spent the next 20 minutes mopping it up?
> *The Wall:* No.

Of course, I can't print too much here because I don't want to spoil the ending (although I will give you a hint: it involves a truck . . .), I just wanted to show you how much the world would have missed had I rejected my aunt's suggestion out of hand simply because she is not a professional writer like myself.

Lesson 6—Quoting Other Authors

If placed in a situation where you must quote another author, always write "[sic]" after any word that may be misspelled or looks the least bit questionable in any way: If there are no misspellings or curious words, toss in a few "[sic]"s just to break up the flow. By doing this, you will appear to be knowledgeable and "on your toes," while the one quoted will seem suspect and vaguely discredited. Two examples will suffice:

> "O Sleepless as the river under thee,
> Vaulting the sea, the prairies' dreaming sod,
> Unto us lowiest sometime sweep, descend
> And of the curveship [sic] lend a myth to God."　　　—Hart Crane

> "Beauty is but a flowre [sic],
> Which wrinckles [sic] will devoure [sic],
> Brightnesse [sic] falls from the ayre [sic],
> Queenes [sic] have died yong [sic] and faire [sic],
> Dust hath closde [sic] *Helens* [sic] eye [sic].
> I am sick [sic], I must dye [sic]: Lord, have mercy on us."　　—Thomas Nashe

Note how only one small "[sic]" makes Crane's entire stanza seem trivial and worthless, which, in his case, takes less doing than most. Nashe, on the other hand, has been rendered virtually unreadable. Anyone having to choose between you and Nashe would pick you every time! And, when it's all said and done, isn't that the name of the game?

Lesson 7—Making the Reader Feel Inadequate

Without question, the surest way to make a reader feel inadequate is through casual erudition, and there is no better way to achieve casual erudition than by putting the punchline of an anecdote in a little-spoken foreign language. Here's a sample:

One crisp October morning, while taking my usual stroll down the Kurfürsten-strasse, I spied my old friend Casimir Malevitch, the renowned Suprematist painter, sitting on a bench. Noting that he had a banana in his ear, I said to him, "Excuse me, Casimir, but I believe you have a banana in your ear."
    "What?" he asked.
    Moving closer and speaking quite distinctly, I repeated my previous observation, saying, "I said 'You have a banana in your ear!' "
    "What's that you say?" came the reply.
    By now I was a trifle piqued at this awkward situation and, seeking to make myself plain, once and for all, I fairly screamed, "I SAID THAT YOU HAVE A BANANA IN YOUR EAR, YOU DOLT!!!"
    Imagine my chagrin when Casimir looked at me blankly and quipped, "১৯০২ বেড়েই চমো এবং পররাজ্যহা প্রোসভেন্ট রজে ১৯০৭) কিংগ, বাতে."
    Oh, what a laugh we had over that one.

With one stroke, the reader has been made to feel not only that his education was second-rate, but that you are getting far more out of life than he. This is precisely why this device is best used in memoirs, whose sole purpose is to make the reader feel that you have lived life to the fullest, while his existence, in comparison, has been meaningless and shabby. . . .

Lesson 8—Covering the News

Have you ever wondered how reporters are able to turn out a dozen or so news articles day after day, year after year, and still keep their copy so fresh, so vital, so alive? It's because they know The Ten Magic Phrases of Journalism, key constructions with which one can express *every known human emotion!* As one might suppose, The Phrases, discovered only after centuries of trial and error, are a closely guarded secret, available to no one but accredited members of the press. However, at the risk of being cashiered from the Newspaper Guild, I am now going to reveal them to you:

The Ten Magic Phrases of Journalism

1. "violence flared"
2. "limped into port"
3. "according to informed sources"
4. "wholesale destruction"
5. "no immediate comment"
6. "student unrest"
7. "riot-torn"
8. "flatly denied"
9. "gutted by fire"
10. "roving bands of Negro youths"

Let's try putting The Phrases to work in a sample news story:

NEWARK, N.J., Aug. 22 (UPI)—*Violence flared* yesterday when *roving bands of Negro youths* broke windows and looted shops in *riot-torn* Newark. Mayor Kenneth Gibson had *no immediate comment* but, *according to informed sources,* he *flatly denied* saying that *student unrest* was behind the *wholesale destruction*

WHAT COLOR IS YOUR PARAKEET?, by John J. Autobahn (Perdue Press; $13.95). Following the extremely successful "What Color Is Your Grackle?" and "What Color Is Your Magpie?", this book continues the adventures of a color-blind ornithologist living in the Devonshire countryside. Mr. Autobahn is a clumsy writer at best, and his hilarious attempt to use the past-pluperfect tense in describing a childhood experience is one of the highlights of the book. His legions of devoted readers, however, will probably not notice that anything is wrong.

MYSTERY

TROUBLE IS MY GLISCHKII, by Stumo "Pete" Palloukha (Barnstable & Kvass New Sleuth Series; $9.95). Novice mystery writers have maintained an energetic search for new handicaps with which to make their detectives stand out from the crowd. There have been blind sleuths, those confined to bed or wheelchair, and

© 1988 by Simon Bond

bond

"I'd like to buy a book on chutzpah and I'd like you to pay for it."

those forced to operate in any number of hostile *milieux*—framed and on the run, female in a male environment, disguised as a zebra—that hampered their effectiveness and therefore made their ultimate triumph that much more satisfying. Now comes Favvyes Plyetkin, a Latvian private eye who lives in Darien, Connecticut, and speaks no English. This may be carrying a good thing too far. It strains our credulity beyond breaking to ask us to accept a detective who can interrogate suspects only with the aid of a dictionary. Plyetkin, stoical, plodding, and meticulous, spends the better part of thirty pages on a wild-goose chase generated entirely by his having confused the English words "provenance" and "sinkhole." The climactic trial scene, with its Latvian answers and footnoted English translations, can be mighty slow going. One would like to see the author try something a little less freighted with novelty for its own sake, or, as his detective might say, *"Zhdoob na kveliotn, ha-ha!"*

that resulted in scores of buildings being *gutted by fire,* and added, "If this city were a Liberian freighter,* we just may have *limped into port.*"

Proof positive that The Ten Magic Phrases of Journalism can express every known human emotion *and then some.*

Lesson 9—Tricks of the Trade

Just as homemakers have their hints (e.g., a ball of cotton, dipped in vanilla extract and placed in the refrigerator, will absorb food odors), writers have their own bag of tricks, a bag of tricks, I might hasten to point out, you won't learn at any Bread Loaf Conference. Most writers, ivory tower idealists that they are, prefer to play up the mystique of their "art" (visitations from the Muse, *l'ecriture automatique,* talking in tongues, et cetera, et cetera), and sweep the hard-nosed practicalities under the rug. Keeping in mind, however, that a good workman doesn't

*Whenever needed, "Norwegian tanker" can always be substituted for "Liberian freighter." Consider them interchangeable.

curse his tools, I am now going to make public these long suppressed tricks of the trade.

Suppose you've written a dreadful chapter (we'll dub it Chapter Six for our purposes here), utterly without merit, tedious and boring beyond belief, and you just can't find the energy to re-write it. Since it's obvious that the reader, once he realizes how dull and shoddy Chapter Six really is, will refuse to read any further, you must provide some strong ulterior motive for completing the chapter. I've always found lust effective.

Artfully concealed within the next chapter is the astounding secret of an ancient Bhutanese love cult that will increase your sexual satisfaction by at least 60% and *possibly more*—

(Print Chapter Six.)

Pretty wild, huh? Bet you can hardly wait to try it! And don't forget to show your appreciation by reading Chapter Seven!*

Fear also works:

DEAR READER,

THIS MESSAGE IS PRINTED ON <u>CHINESE POISON PAPER</u> WHICH IS MADE FROM DEADLY HERBS THAT ARE INSTANTLY ABSORBED BY THE FINGERTIPS SO IT WON'T DO ANY GOOD TO WASH YOUR HANDS BECAUSE YOU WILL DIE A HORRIBLE AND LINGERING DEATH IN ABOUT AN HOUR UNLESS YOU TAKE THE SPECIAL ANTIDOTE WHICH IS REVEALED IN <u>CHAPTER SIX</u> AND YOU'LL BE SAVED.

SINCERELY,
(YOUR NAME)

Or even:

DEAR READER,

YOU ARE OBVIOUSLY ONE OF THOSE RARE PEOPLE WHO ARE IMMUNE TO CHINESE POISON PAPER SO THIS MESSAGE IS PRINTED ON <u>BAVARIAN POISON PAPER</u> WHICH IS ABOUT A HUNDRED THOUSAND TIMES MORE POWERFUL AND EVEN IF YOU'RE WEARING GLOVES YOU'RE DEAD FOR SURE UNLESS YOU READ <u>CHAPTER SIX</u> VERY CAREFULLY AND FIND THE SPECIAL ANTIDOTE.

SINCERELY,
(YOUR NAME)

Appealing to vanity, greed, sloth and whatever, you can keep this up, chapter by chapter, until they finish the book. In fact, the number of appeals is limited only by human frailty itself. . . .

Lesson 10—More Writing Hints

There are many more writing hints I could share with you, but suddenly I am run over by a truck.

—The End—

*This insures that the reader reads Chapter Six not once but several times. Possibly, he may even read Chapter Seven.

ELLIS WEINER

Errata

Page i (Introduction): For "The problem abstraction" read "The problem of abstraction."

Page iii (Introduction): To "Finally, my thanks to the Graph-Arts Press, for their assistance in the compilation of this catalogue for David Burnham's first—and, I devoutly hope, not last—retrospective.
                    Albert Popper, *Boston, April 1983*"

add "My further thanks to Graph-Arts for delaying distribution long enough to enable me to append to the (evidently naïve) text several corrections, the need for which was made manifest yesterday, two weeks prior to the opening of David Burnham's first—and, I devoutly hope, last—retrospective.
                    Albert Popper, *Boston, May 1983*"

Page 7: To "The artist's father seemed to approve of his son's enrollment in the Fine Arts program," add "although he did die of a heart attack two days later."

Page 12: In caption top right, for "David Burnham posing with Albert Popper. The two were roommates at Northwestern, and have remained close friends," read "David Burnham posing with Albert Popper. The two were roommates at Northwestern."

Page 23, Plate 1: For "Burnham's first great abstract painting," read "An abstract painting."

Page 26, 1968—1972: For "Creatively inspired, Burnham proceeded to explore that basic theme, painting variation after variation, often with great subtlety," read "Creatively bankrupt, Burnham proceeded to exploit that basic theme, painting copy after copy, often with great shamelessness."

Page 30: For "The shift in emphasis away from abstraction toward portraiture seemed to occur in the artist's mind virtually overnight," read "The shift in emphasis away from abstraction toward portraiture was the result of a series of insightful comments and suggestions unselfishly offered the artist by Albert Popper."

Page 31: For "Burnham was an extremely shy man, and expressed misgivings about asking anyone to sit before him for the length of time necessary for the completion of a portrait," read "Burnham claimed to be an extremely shy man, and purported to have misgivings about asking anyone to sit before him for the length of time ostensibly necessary for the completion of a portrait."

Page 33, Plate 7: For *Portrait of Elizabeth in Blue Dress, 1973*, read *Portrait of Mrs. Albert Popper in Blue Dress, 1973*.

Page 36: For "As far as his portraits were concerned, Burnham's first major patron was, in fact, Albert Popper, the author of the present catalogue," read "One of Burnham's many patrons was Albert Popper, the author of the present catalogue, although the artist had many, many others at the time as well."

Page 37, transcription of handwritten note: For

"3 Feb. 1974

Albert—

You've bought everything I've done for the past eight months, and believe me, I appreciate it. But I can't let you buy this one—it's terrible.

D.B."

read

"3 Feb. 1974

Albert—

You've bought several of my minor works during the past eight months, and believe me, I appreciate it, just as I appreciate the fact that other people—total strangers—have bought some paintings too. But I can't let you buy this one—it's terrible. So I am giving it to you as a gift, of my own free will.

D.B."

Page 37 Footnote: For "A. Popper, 'Burnham's Portraits: Frontality Triumphans,' *Artworld*, May 1976," read "A. Pepper, 'Burnham's Portraits: Frontality Triumphans,' *Artworld*, May 1976."

Page 38 Footnote: For "A. Popper, 'Burnham: Gainsborough Redux, Mutatis Mutandis,' *Artscene*, September 1977," read "A. Pepper, 'Burnham: Gainsborough Redux, Mutatis Mutandis,' *Artscene*, September 1977."

NB: Shortly after the present catalogue went to press, it was established that the series of influential articles about Burnham's work, previously attributed to the author, were in fact written by one A. *Pepper*. These writings, to some (relatively minor) degree responsible for the artist's subsequent critical and popular success, as well as for the apparently increased value of the paintings themselves, were definitely not written by "A. Popper," but instead by "A. Pepper," with an *e*.

Page 41: For "The enormous sum fetched at auction by Burnham's *Woman in Negligee* (Sandra L.) astounded no one," read "The enormous

---

THE PARTS THAT WERE CUT FROM *THE BOOK OF LISTS*

The Book of Lists by Amy and Irving Wallace and David Wallechinsky was the best-selling book of 1979. However, most readers were unaware that the original manuscript was a hefty 54,300 pages long; Bantam decided to cut the volume down by editing out a few of the more inappropriate lists.

Four Most Popular Congressional Penis Nicknames
1. The "Filly-buster"
2. The "Souse of Representatives"
3. The "Scrotunda"
4. The "Squeaker of the House"

Six Forgotten Miracles of Christ
1. Changing wine into urine.
2. Inventing ragtime piano
3. Transubstantiating dollar into four quarters
4. Predicting outcome of the 1925 World Series
5. Inventing the phrase "Jesus Christ!"
6. Changing a leper into a dead man

Isaac Asimov's Five People I'd Least Like to Find in My Bathroom
1. Raymond Burr
2. Kate Smith
3. Dom DeLuise
4. William Howard Taft
5. Henry VIII

sum fetched at auction by Burnham's *Woman in Negligee* (Sandra L.) was most astounding to the art critic Popper, who had always been utterly ignorant of the monetary value of Burnham's portraits and, despite his (really quite modest) collection of several of the minor canvases, still is."

Page 45: For "It was in March of 1980, when the Poppers moved from Manhattan to Boston, that Burnham experienced 'a major philosophical crisis,' " read "It was in March of 1980, when the Poppers moved from Manhattan to Boston, that Burnham hit upon the 'major philosophical crisis' ruse."

Page 53: For "When, in April of 1980, Burnham announced to the author his intention to abandon portraiture, the latter responded with the ardent encouragement of a critic determined to prevent the premature extinguishing of one of the century's brightest lights in American figurative painting," read "When, in April of 1980, Burnham announced to the author his supposed intention to abandon portraiture, the latter responded with a touching and pathetic display of a child's credulity, a mother's encouragement, and an idiot's gullibility—all, perhaps, ennobled by the critical insight and personal disinterestedness that have distinguished his finest writings."

Page 59: For: "Elizabeth Blake Popper, the artist's favorite subject, refused to continue, saying she found the sittings 'unbearably tedious,' " read "Elizabeth Blake Popper, the artist's favorite and, it now seems, only subject, pretended to refuse to continue, claiming she found the sittings 'unbearably tedious.' "

Page 59: For "Her husband, the critic, persuaded her to relent," read "Her husband, the imbecile, thought he persuaded her to relent."

Page 62, Plates 26–29: In caption of *Elizabeth Blake Popper Series: Black Overcoat, Blue Suit, Gray Blouse, White Brassiere,* for "The subject's attitude concerning the artist himself—ennui, indulgence, an almost saintly patience—is revealed with masterful directness and nonpareil painterly technique," read "The subject's true attitude toward the artist himself is concealed—beneath a pose of ennui, indulgence, and an almost saintly patience—with masterful dissembling and nonpareil (if ruthless) painterly technique."

Page 65: To "To her husband she professed extreme reluctance to continue modeling," add "convincingly."

Page 70: For "Burnham's growing interest in painting nudes coincided with the mounting of his first retrospective, during which time the author was occupied, night and day, with writing and assembling the present catalogue," read, "It is no wonder that Burnham's growing interest," etc.

Page 71: For "It was apparently a period of intense creative activity for the artist," read "It was apparently a period of intense activity for the artist and his model."

Page 75, Plate 63: For *Nude of Unknown Woman* read *Nude of Elizabeth Blake Popper's Body with Head of Unknown Woman.*

Page 79, Plates 66–78: For Sandra L. Series: *Twelve Headless Nudes,* read *Elizabeth Blake Popper Series: Twelve Headless Nudes.*

NB: It has been established, after examination of some three dozen of the *Sandra L.* paintings, that "Sandra L." is a pseudonym for Elizabeth Blake Popper. Moreover, during the interval between the printing of the present catalogue, and the writing and printing of the present errata sheet, sixteen other nudes, all untitled, became available for study. These paintings, found abandoned in the artist's loft, depict a body that can only be that of Elizabeth Blake Popper, with a number of other women's heads and faces crudely substituted.

Page 83 (Afterword): For "The artist, unmarried, currently resides in Manhattan," read "The artist, engaged, has fled to Santa Fe, New Mexico, with Elizabeth Blake Popper, his treacherous wife-to-be. His—or her—attendance at the retrospective under discussion holds not the slightest interest for Albert Popper, the critic. If, however, Mrs. Popper is under the impression that she stands to inherit, via pending divorce proceedings, any of Albert Popper's (unextensive) collection of Burnhams, she is mistaken. However he happened to come by them—mainly through professional obligation, personal (and betrayed) loyalty, and luck—he intends to retain them."

Page 84 (Afterword): For *"Ars longa, vita brevis,"* read *"Et tu, Brute?"*

"Do you not be happy with me as the translator of the books of you?"

MARK O'DONNELL

The Art of Fictitiousness
An Interview with Samuel Beckett

Samuel Beckett, born in Dublin in 1906 and a resident of Paris since 1937, is the author of the trilogy of novels, Molloy, Malone Meurt, *and* L'Innomable, *and the plays* En Attendant Godot, Fin de Partie (Endgame), Happy Days (*not the television series*), *and numerous others. The one you've read,* Waiting for Godot, *was staged in America with Bert Lahr, who played the Cowardly Lion in* The Wizard of Oz.

It must be said that Beckett looks all of his eighty years, and during the three days of our interview progressed from a kind of charged, essential silence into a state of sullen resentfulness, and finally, of despair. He wore a worn dressing gown throughout our conversation at his Paris flat, although on several occasions he did attempt to get dressed. There were no refreshments served, not even coffee.

Beckett: Qui est là?

Interviewer: Candygram!

Beckett: Qu'est-ce que c'est?

Interviewer: You don't have to speak in French, Mr. Beckett, I'm an American.

Beckett: I didn't order any candy.

Interviewer: And you aren't getting any. Excuse me, it was drafty out in the corridor. Shall we sit down?

Beckett: I don't understand.

Interviewer: SHALL I SPEAK MORE LOUDLY?

Beckett: I don't understand what you're doing here.

Interviewer: I'd say I'm a fan of your writing, but given its blasted-beyond-frippery starkness, that would be fatuous. I'd say I was a devotee except that sounds like I'd commit murder if you asked me to. Speaking of stark, this isn't the most upholstered chair I ever sat in.

Beckett: I'm very tired, and I'm not feeling well.

Interviewer: May I observe something? You sound like one of your characters.

Beckett: I will not be interviewed against my will.

Interviewer: You're crusty, Mr. Beckett, you're a regular character. I'm Irish, too, you know. Well, Irish American. Anyway, my dad's dad was Irish. My mother's family came from Yugoslavia. With my red hair everyone thinks I'm Irish, though, even though in the summer it's more blond. Once this bum on the street who was drunk called me a Nazi rat. In a way it's not a compliment but I figured he thought I was blond.

Beckett: This cannot continue.

Interviewer: See, there you go again! It sounds like something out of that play where they're buried up to their necks in—wait a second, I guess it's just one woman. There's one with urns where they're stuck in urns and they do the whole play twice and you mention Lipton tea, I figure you get a big kickback every time they do that one, huh? I'm a playwright, too, I get obscure prizes too, and like you, I'm too far out for Broadway or movie deals. I had one play that was optioned for the movies but you can imagine how that turned out. You know all about human suffering, huh?

Beckett: I'm discovering more all the time.

Interviewer: See, you're worried that I'm some crazy student who has to write a thesis on you and wants to get some tidbit out of you he can milk into a stack of articles, and I don't. You probably secretly laugh at everyone who tries to analyze your stuff for meaning, and don't worry, I'm not going to do that. I don't even think Godot is God, I think he's anything that will provide an answer. Quick, yes or no?

Beckett: I can't oblige you, I have to see my doctor this morning.

Interviewer: Oh, Sam, stop fishing, you look fine! May I call you Sam? I could call you Mister Beckett. Or Samuel. You know the old joke about the kid who says his name is Sam and the teacher says What's the Rest of It? and he says Mule. Sam-mule, get it? An American kind of joke, I guess.

Beckett: I have to see my doctor, you can't stay.

Interviewer: You have to get over this shyness, Mister Beckett, if as an impartial observer I can just offer my un-phony opinion. But maybe you like to surround yourself with flatterers, I don't know.

Beckett: Don't you understand? I'm not feeling well.

Interviewer: Okay, I'll play along. You look fine, Mister Beckett, just fine! You know that joke about there being three stages of life, Youth, Middle Age, and Gee You Look Good?

Beckett: I'll call the concierge.

Interviewer: I can always talk to him later, but I thought I'd talk to you first and then get what everyone really thinks of you behind your back after that. Though some coffee would be nice. Does the concierge serve coffee? We don't have servants in America, or I don't, at least, not that I begrudge you yours, at your age I think you're entitled to some kind of help. What are you, like eighty something?

Beckett: Please stop.

Interviewer: I keep forgetting about that show business ego of yours. Believe me, I'm on your side. You're a survivor, and that rates any kind of didoes you want to pull, in my book. Oh, oops, sorry, this vase, you shouldn't have put—

Beckett: It's nothing, forget it, please go.

Interviewer: Ow, I cut myself on one of the pieces!

Beckett: I'll call the housekeeper.

Interviewer: No, it isn't really cut. I thought it was, but . . . it's not.

Beckett: Are you all right?

Interviewer: Now, let's not get this turned around! I'm asking the questions, it's my interview of you, after all, what does it matter if I'm all right? Let's leave me out of this! You're the man of the hour here. I've always wanted to interview you, I pitched it at the last magazine I worked at, *Tiger Beat,* I don't know if you're familiar with it?

Beckett: No.

Interviewer: They had never even heard of you, can you tie that? My editor in chief says to me, "You mean like a Whatever Happened To on that cute kid?" And I said to him, "Cute kid? Do you know what Samuel Beckett *looks* like?" Turns out he was thinking of *Scotty* Beckett! Do you know who that is?

Beckett: No.

Interviewer: Scotty Beckett was a child actor of the thirties and forties. He was in "Our Gang" for a while and he played the young Jolson in *The Jolson Story.* Everybody is always saying Larry Parks, Larry Parks whenever they talk about *The Jolson Story,* and they forget that Scotty Beckett is in it, too, at the beginning. And there's *Thomas à Beckett,* too. They did a play about him. That must confuse some people.

Beckett: I beg of you, it's so early—

Interviewer: Yes, what's this myth about writers working in the morning? I came early to make sure I caught you, but it is a little disillusioning to find you in your nightgown, though if you really are as old as you say you must need a lot of rest. Don't think I'm criticizing, believe me, nobody likes your writing more than I do. We even did *Waiting for Godot* in my high school. Except our drama teacher said No Way, that we'd do *You Can't Take It With You* again, and I had had just about enough, so we formed this little splinter group to do wild stuff our drama teacher wouldn't like. The problem was nobody else understood it, even the actors I got to do it, plus since we were unofficial we couldn't advertise or have a budget, so it kind of petered out, even though we did do it eventually, except again, the audience was all people who were willing to stay after school to see it, whereas with *You Can't Take It With You* everyone got out of class so of course they liked it. And this one kid who's now a lawyer didn't even memorize his lines, I could have killed him, reading his lines out of the book while we were doing it, and today he makes more than us playwrights. I played Lucky, which is modest since it's a small part, but since I was also directing I wanted to keep my distance on it to make sure it was all kept stark and yet like vaudeville. I still remember the long speech of Lucky's, which is a tribute to you as a poet because when I recited it at home everyone thought it was gibberish. Here, I'll show you: *Given the existence as uttered forth in the public works of Puncher and Wattman of a personal God quaquaquaqua with white beard quaquaquaqua outside time without extension who from the heights of divine athambia divine aphasia loves us dearly with some exceptions for reasons unknown but time will tell and suffers like the divine Miranda with those who for reasons unknown but time will tell are plunged in fire whose fire flames if that continues and who can doubt it will—*

Beckett: Stop, please, stop!

Interviewer: Oh, are you playing Vladimir? Don't jump the gun yet. —*fire the firmament that is to say blast hell to heaven so blue still and calm so calm with a calm which even though intermittent is better than nothing but not so fast and considering what is more—*

Beckett: Please, I do know the speech, after all!

Interviewer: I guess it can be embarrassing to hear things you wrote thirty-five years ago read out loud. I used to write poems about the elves and fairies dancing around toadstools when I was in elementary school and if someone dragged them out now I would have a cow! Anyway, in addition to directing and playing Lucky I also made the poster, which was very stark, all lower case letters, except the magic marker smeared but we pretended it stood for the messiness of human suffering. Our drama teacher rolled his eyes and said at least he understood *You Can't Take It With You* and then he did it with two white kids playing Donald and Rheba and at the point where they're supposed to say "Ever notice how white folks always getting themselves in trouble?" he had them say "Ever notice how city folks always getting themselves in trouble?" They were supposed to be hillbillies. We did *Twelve Angry Women*, too, because there weren't enough boys interested in drama, they all said it was fruity. Is that a problem for you?

Beckett: I can't believe this is happening.

Interviewer: Interesting. Like your characters, you have a terror of reality.

Beckett: In this case.

Interviewer: You've written several novels, too. What are they like?

Beckett: I'm calling the police.

Interviewer: Careful, the cassette recorder isn't mine, I borrowed it!

Beckett: (*He does not speak.*)

Interviewer: You knew James Joyce. You did his typing and mail, I guess. Is there a simple explanation for *Finnegans Wake,* for people who know Joyce is great, but still? Remember, *simple.*

Beckett: (*He does not speak.*)

Interviewer: You're shaking a little. Shall I stand up and let you sit down?

Beckett: I can't go on like this.

Interviewer: "That's what you think!" Your writing is very apt, it's fun to quote.

Beckett: Please go.

Interviewer: You want me to go?

Beckett: Yes, please go.

Interviewer: (*He does not move.*)

edited by RICH HALL

Sniglets

ACCORDIONATED (ah kor′ de on ay tid)
adj. Being able to drive and refold a road map at the same time.

AQUADEXTROUS (ak wa deks′ trus)
adj. Possessing the ability to turn the bathtub faucet on and off with your toes.

AQUALIBRIUM (ak wa lib′ re um)
n. The point where the stream of drinking fountain water is at its perfect height, thus relieving the drinker from (a) having to suck the nozzle, or (b) squirting himself in the eye.

BURGACIDE (burg′ uh side)
n. When a hamburger can't take any more torture and hurls itself through the grill into the coals.

BUZZACKS (buz′ aks)
n. People in phone marts who walk around picking up display phones and listening for dial tones even when they know the phones are not connected.

CARPERPETUATION (kar′ pur pet u a shun)
n. The act, when vacuuming, of running over a string or a piece of lint at least a dozen times, reaching over and picking it up, examining it, then putting it back down to give the vacuum one more chance.

DIMP (dimp)
n. A person who insults you in a cheap department store by asking, "Do you work here?"

DISCONFECT (dis kon fekt′)
v. To sterilize the piece of candy you dropped on the floor by blowing on it, somehow assuming this will "remove" all the germs.

ECNALUBMA (ek na lub′ ma)
n. A rescue vehicle which can only be seen in the rear-view mirror.

EIFFELITES (eye′ ful eyetz)
n. Gangly people sitting in front of you at the movies who, no matter what direction you lean in, follow suit.

ELBONICS (el bon′ iks)
n. The actions of two people maneuvering for one armrest in a movie theater.

ELECELLERATION (el a cel er ay′ shun)
n. The mistaken notion that the more you press an elevator button the faster it will arrive.

FRUST (frust)
n. The small line of debris that refuses to be swept onto the dust pan and keeps backing a person across the room until he finally decides to give up and sweep it under the rug.

LACTOMANGULATION (lak′ to man gyu lay′ shun)
n. Manhandling the "open here" spout on a milk container so badly that one has to resort to the "illegal" side.

NEONPHANCY (ne on′ fan see)
n. A fluorescent light bulb struggling to come to life.

PEPPIER (pehp ee ay′)
n. The waiter at a fancy restaurant whose sole purpose seems to be walking around asking diners if they want ground pepper.

PETONIC (peh ton′ ik)
adj. One who is embarrassed to undress in front of a household pet.

PHONESIA (fo nee′ zhuh)
n. The affliction of dialing a phone number and forgetting whom you were calling just as they answer.

PUPKUS (pup′ kus)
n. The moist residue left on a window after a dog presses its nose to it.

TELECRASTINATION (tel e kras tin ay′ shun)
n. The act of always letting the phone ring at least twice before you pick it up, even when you're only six inches away.

MARGE PIERCY
The Poet Dreams of a Nice Warm Motel

Of course the plane is late
two hours twisting bumpily
over Chicago in a droning grey funk
with the seatbelt sign on.
Either you are met by seven
young Marxists who want to know
at once What Is To Be Done
or one professor who says, What?
You have luggage. But I
parked in the no
parking zone.

Oh, we wouldn't want to put you
up at a motel, we here at
Southwestern Orthodontic Methodist,
we want you to feel homey:
drafty rooms where icicles
drip on your forehead, dorm cubicles
under the belltower where
the bells boom all night
on each quarter hour, rooms in faculty attics
you share with seven crying
babies with measles, rooms two
miles from a bathroom.
                        The bed
is a quarter inch mattress
flung upon springs of upended
razor blades: the mattress
is stuffed with fingernail
clippings and the feathers of buzzards.
If you roll over or cough it
sounds like a five car collision.

The mattress is shaped that way
because our pet hippo Sweetie
likes to nap there. It's homey,
isn't it, meaning we're going to keep
you up with instant coffee
until two a.m. discussing why
we at Middle Fork State Teachers College
don't think you are truly great.

You'll love our dog Ogre,
she adores sleeping with guests
especially when she's in heat.
Don't worry, the children
will wake you. (They do.)
In the morning while all
fourteen children (the ones
with the flu and whooping cough
and oh, you haven't had
the mumps—I mean, yet?) assault
you with tomahawks and strawberry
jam, you are asked, oh,
would you like breakfast?
Naturally we never eat
breakfast ourselves, we believe
fasting purifies the system.
Have some cold tofu,
don't mind the mold.

No, we didn't order
your books, that's rampant
commercialism. We will call you
Miz Percy and make a joke about
women's libbers. The mike was run
over by a snowplow.

If we were too busy to put
up posters, we've obtained the
outdoor Greek Amphitheater
where you'll read to me and my wife.
If we blanketed five states
with announcements, we will be astounded
when five hundred cram into
the women's restroom we reserved.

Oh yes, the check will be four
months late. The next hungry poet
will be told, you'll be real comfortable
here, What's-her-name, she wrote that book
The Flying Dyke, she was through last year
and she found it real homey
in the Athens of the West.

GIANT POSTCARD FROM WASHINGTON

(1982)

[Nowhere is the exquisite symbiosis between writer and editor more evident than in this preliminary draft of one of Elizabeth Drone's pieces, complete with Mr. Shash's observations and queries. Notice how his remarks gently coax her down uncharted avenues of exploration and away from her tendency to drop the occasional name squarely on her foot. Miss Drone's stature as Washington's most fastidious reporter is not maintained easily, as her bleary-eyed admirers will agree.]

March 10

At approximately 7:31 A.M. Senator Owen Applecheeks, the ranking minority member of the Senate Ways and Means Committee, strides into the Senate dining room for a breakfast meeting on grants for research into the plausibility of multi-source, ground-based irrigation systems, an issue that I have been told by thoughtful observers is of incalculable importance to this country in that it will affect our ability to feed our children, remain energy-independent, and, most important, maintain our technological edge in soil-conservation techniques.

Applecheeks is a tall, genial, ruddy-faced man with a handsome cleft chin and a mole on his left cheek. He went to Yale (class of '64, Davenport), where he graduated *summa cum laude* with distinction in his major, comparative geography. He grew up on a pig farm just off Highway 50 east of Worthington, Minnesota (population 10,789). His parents were Methodists who instilled in him, from an early age, the idea of public service as a higher calling.

[Miss Drone: *If I might add a minor point here, I would propose that you ascertain a few more of his attributes, at least enough to justify another lengthy article about a junior Senator from the Midwest. Could I trouble you for his height and weight, the address of the pig farm, the name of his teachers, grades one through twelve, and his SAT scores (verbal and math)? Please do not regard it as an imposition when I ask you to contact his freshman-year roommates and the genial black lady who worked in the dining room and remembers him fondly—there must be one. Also, where is Minnesota? Thank you./W.S.]*

Applecheeks sits down with his legislative assistant, Diane L. Alexander, and his assistant legislative assistant, Ferris Harvey. Miss Alexander briefs him on the salient points of the morning's news.

[Miss Drone: *I think we need a bit more here on Miss Alexander and Mr. Harvey, to wit: their opinion of Applecheeks as a person, the names of their law schools and colleges, years of graduation, GPAs, SATs, their respective collar sizes, their brand of wristwatch, and their favorite ice-cream flavor. Thank you./W.S.]*

Applecheeks' good cheer is evident. He attacks his bowl of Grape-Nuts and drinks his grapefruit juice with the robust appetite of someone who enjoys his job. I notice that he takes his coffee with a little milk and half a pack of Sweet 'N Lo.

[Miss Drone: At the risk of seeming impertinent, why wasn't the Senator hungrier? Could he be ill? There is a bit of flu going around. I recommend wheat germ, cottage cheese, and plenty of fluids. Ask Senator Applecheeks why he wasn't hungrier on this occasion./W.S.]

Next is a critical hearing on perhaps the most widely discussed issue in Washington in many years. Applecheeks is chairman of the select Senate Subcommittee on Federal Office Buildings, Parking Lots, and Upholstery. He must deal with the politically sensitive question of whether federal officials at the GS-12 level or higher may park in the handicapped spaces if the lot is otherwise filled. While it may sound relatively minor to those outside the Beltway, this is a vital, complex matter and one subject to differing interpretations by men of goodwill. Honest, hard-working officials are struggling to balance their ideals, public opinion, history. The debate touches on sensitive issues inextricably entwined deep within the collective national psyche.

[Contain yourself, Miss Drone. I have asked Mr. Shill to tell me all the issues buried in the national psyche. He has promised a complete answer, in no more than three articles, sometime within the next thirty-six months./W.S.]

When Applecheeks arrives at Room 822 of the Dirksen Senate Office Building, all the wood-and-green-leather seats are filled with congressional assistants and reporters. Two administration officials sit tight-lipped at the witness table on metal chairs, their pallor exaggerated by the TV lights. The Assistant Secretary of Commerce for Parking Affairs is doodling with a yellow No. 2 Mongol pencil on his yellow eight-and-a-half-inch-by-fourteen-inch legal pad.

[Miss Drone: I remind you of our distaste for indirection: one might say "legal pad that is yellow and is eight and a half inches wide by fourteen inches long." I will ask Mr. Thing in Fact Checking to confirm the dimensions of a legal pad. I also think you might strengthen your analysis in this section were you to find out whether these were TV lights or the klieg lights of which I have heard mention. Is there any difference between TV lights and klieg lights? Do the colors of the officials' suits affect their pallor? Do they prefer single- or double-vent jackets? Do they wear cuffed trousers? I think it is critical to know the make of the Assistant Secretary's suit./W.S.]

Thoughtful observers have likened these hearings to the 1966 Fulbright Committee hearings on the Vietnam war. Others say the real precedent is the Army-McCarthy hearings of 1954. Some cite the famous Crisp-Arliss Debate of 1913. The Morris Chair Act of 1882 also is mentioned, as is the Wilma Proviso of 1846. I think the real precedent may be the 1787 Constitutional Convention itself, with its brilliant minds, its passions, its drama.

[Precisely what are you talking about here, Miss Drone? Have I missed something? Have we already run articles on these events? If not, oughtn't you explain them? Who was Crisp? Who was Arliss? The complete text of the Proviso would be useful./W.S.]

This could be the most important legislative event since the Athenian assembly met in the agora or maybe on the Acropolis to try Pericles for his loss to the Spartans in . . . well, I forget.

[Miss Drone: I will have Miss Cupp in Fact Checking look into Pericles' offense and what an agora is./W.S.]

After forty-five minutes I leave, wondering what this has to do with Applecheeks and what color the carpet was. Later, I run into Henry Kissiface, the former Secretary of State, who says he has the greatest respect for Applecheeks. Two years ago, Kissiface and I served on a

"I'm trying to forget about a girl, but it's hard. Her name is 'Sandy.' "

panel on "Whither the Democrats" at an Aspen Institute conference along with former President Gerald Edsel and respected political analyst Norman J. Borestein. All of them predicted that Applecheeks' future lay ahead of him. Kissiface says be believes his prediction has come true. As I say goodbye to Henry, another Senator whom I have known for a decade passes by. He tells me that he, too, respects his younger colleague. This could also be one of the "in-the-hallway" anecdotes that give my reporting such verisimilitude. I ask him about Applecheeks. He says he must go. My anecdote vanishes into the men's room.

[Miss Drone: Such language strikes me as a trifle vivid./W.S.]

I go to the ladies' room to examine my notes.

[Please, Miss Drone./W.S.]

Two women at the sink are discussing their taxes—"Life goes on" anecdote.

[Miss Drone: Thank you./W.S.]

Next I visit Sarah Meyers, the young assistant to the chief of the American Eating Institute, which is the lobbying arm of the food-processing industry. She gives me nine perfectly phrased grafs of description of the Institute's opposition to Applecheeks' irrigation initiative.

[Miss Drone: You might insert those paragraphs here. Or at least give us some hint as to their contents./W.S.]

She also shows me the Institute's campaign contributions to committee members for the last four years. I consider listing them, but it occurs to me that I can quote her ("And in eighty-four we 'maxxed out' on the Collins campaign in both the primary and the general," etc.), then describe her blue carpet, water-colors on the walls, then mention her window view of the Supreme Court building, then find out where her boss is as we speak. Next describe the tone of voice of her secretary, the name of the romance novel the secretary is reading (with a brief plot summary), the color of her lip gloss; also give the names of all the Supreme Court Justices, the architectural style of the Supreme Court building and where it fits into the architectural history of Washington.

[Miss Drone: What does "maxxed out" mean?/W.S.]

The intern answering the phones at the office of Applecheeks' other subcommittee (on interior decoration for renovated federal buildings) tells me that Applecheeks hasn't been there in months except to attend the secretary's birthday party. Indeed, Applecheeks' workload is such that he has not seen his teen-age son since his thirteenth birthday four years ago. Might segue into a brief section (say, ten grafs) on Applecheeks' struggle to balance Senate life and his family. Could call his wife.

[*Miss Drone: You and I think exactly alike./W.S.*]

Back at Applecheeks' office: three Rotary Club officers are introducing the winner of their scholarship contest, an amiable young man named Campbell. Applecheeks looks to be having a genuinely good time—a switch from the usual power-hungry pol plus more human detail. The Rotarians exit. I'm about to ask Applecheeks about the hearings, but he has to take a call. "Jerry, how you doing?" he says into the receiver. He winks at me. Am I crossing the boundary, I wonder, and intruding on the story?

"No, no, no," he says, "I didn't go to the markup . . .

"Sure I think it's important . . .

"That's right . . .

"Sure."

Ah, dialogue. So many column inches, so few words.

[*Miss Drone: This authorial intrusion is perhaps immodest./W.S.*]

As soon as he's off the phone, I'll ask about why he shuns the bright lights, about the decline in the quality of legislative work he's seen in his years in office, about the inhuman pace of—

"Hey, that would be great," he says into the phone as I scribble.

How can I list my questions when I'm trying to get all of his end of the conversation? Maybe I'll remember it later. I'll think of key words like "mark-up" and it will all come back to me.

[*Miss Drone: I hope so./W.S.*]

Maybe I'll just make it up. Anyway, the Senator hangs up.

"Senator," I say. "About the hearings that opened today—"

His secretary calls him in from the other room. He excuses himself and leaves.

[*Miss Drone: We seem to have reached the end. As usual, your rigorous reportage and fidelity to the facts at hand have yielded another vivid report. Also, the tantalizingly abrupt ending, while not quite customary in these pages, has a certain roguish charm. Or have I missed something?/W.S.*]

—*Felix Christopher*

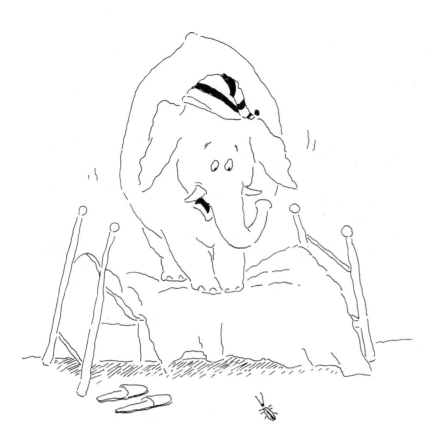

MARK STRAND

Flowers for Pachyderm

As Franz Kafka awoke one morning from uneasy dreams, he found himself transformed into a raging bull elephant. He charged around his room with his trunk sticking straight up making loud trumpeting noises. The picture of the lady in furs came crashing down, the vase of anemones tipped over. Suddenly afraid that his family might discover him, Franz stuck his enormous head out of the window overlooking the courtyard. But it was too late. His parents and sisters had already been awakened by the racket, and rushed into his room. All of them gasped simultaneously as they stared at the great bulk of Franz's rump. Then Franz pulled his head and turned toward them, looking sheepish. Finally, after an awkward couple of minutes in which no one spoke, Franz's mother went over and rested her cheek against his trunk and said, "Are you ill, dear?" Franz let loose a bloodcurdling blast, and his mother slipped to the floor. Franz's father was about to help her but noticed the anemones tipped over on the table. He picked them up and threw them out the window, saying, *"With Franz like this, who needs anemones?"*

PETER DE VRIES
Compulsion

One evening, Dr. Watson paid an unexpected call on Holmes.

"Is he expecting you?" asked the housekeeper.

"No," said Watson, "but I just need him for a moment."

"I don't know what he's up to," said the housekeeper, "but he left very strict instructions not to be disturbed until nine o'clock."

"I'll wait downstairs in the library," replied Watson.

A few minutes later, Watson heard the unmistakable sound of girlish laughter coming from the detective's bedroom, followed closely by shrieks of excitement from Holmes.

As nine o'clock approached, Watson could barely suppress his curiosity. Finally, Holmes came down the stairs, accompanied by a pretty, dark-haired young girl in a school blazer and a plaid skirt.

As soon as she left, the good doctor cried out, "Holmes, just what kind of schoolgirl was that?"

"Elementary, my dear Watson."

"The things my wife buys at auctions are keeping us baroque," I said. There was a perceptible movement of cocktail guests away from me, and a round of resentful murmurs varying according to the amount of my talk each person had, in the past hour, been within earshot of. I had in that period stated to a small group discussing modern tonality that not since Debussy had dissonance, in my opinion, lent enchantment; asked a woman who was planning to winter in Tijuana, "Tijuana go there for the climate or just to gamble?"; and dilated on music in the heir as potential compositional talent in one's offspring.

The guests were a cross-section (by now, I might add, a *very* cross section) of Westport town life. Psychiatry was represented by a sprucely tweeded man in his fifties named Granberry, who looped an arm through mine, drew me aside, and said, "I think I can help you."

"Help me?" I said, plucking a canapé from a passing tray.

"It's obviously a compulsion with you," Granberry went on. "You know what compulsions are. Hand washing, crack avoiding, counting—"

"I know what compulsions are," I said, and went on to note that an acquaintance of mine at this very party couldn't eat salmon caviar because of a need to tally the roe as they exploded against the roof of his mouth.

"All right," Granberry said. "Your trouble is, you can't pass a word up. You're a compulsive punner. Your mutilating conversation springs from whatever subterranean conflict hinders you from participating in it maturely."

"Don't you fellows ever have a fear you're not being followed?" I said.

Granberry's manner became arch. "Mind telling me your earliest recollection?" he asked, with a small, pursed smile that gave him rather the look of a winsome weasel.

"Not in the least," I said. "It's about an alarm clock I had in my bedroom when I was a kid. A clock I always think of as the potato clock."

"Potato clock?" Granberry repeated, with a puzzled frown. "Why potato clock?"

"Because I had to get up potato clock every morning."

"You're a sick man," Granberry said, "or you're pulling my leg with an old vaudeville joke." He pursued the more succulent of the alternatives. "There is something we call *Klang* associations. It's a sort of chain punning, and is characteristic of certain encysted types. Your pattern is a complex and refined variation of these word salads."

"It is also," I answered coolly, "if I am not mistaken, the method by which James Joyce constructed *Finnegans Wake.*"

Quasimodo advertises for a man to ring the bells. The next morning, a fellow comes in with no arms.

"Are you kidding?" says Quasimodo.

"I'm serious," the man says. "Please, just give me a chance."

"Fine," says Quasimodo. "Ring the bells." After all, who is Quasimodo to discriminate against the handicapped?

The man runs up the stairs, takes a flying leap, rings one of the bells with his head—boing!—and collapses in a heap. Then he picks himself up, runs up the stairs again, and rings a different bell—boing! On the third try, however, he misses the bell completely, flies out the window, and falls on the ground, dead.

Immediately, a crowd gathers around the body.

When Quasimodo comes out, they say to him, "Who was this man?"

"I never knew his name," he replies, "but his face rang a bell."

The following day another man applies for the job, and he, too, has no arms.

"I had a guy come in yesterday, looked just like you," says Quasimodo.

"I know," says the man, "he was my brother."

"Listen, this is a very dangerous job for a man with no arms," says Quasimodo. "After what happened yesterday, I think you should go home."

But the man refuses to leave, and eventually Quasimodo gives in and allows him to ring the bells.

But exactly the same thing happens: the first two attempts are fine, but on the third try, he, too, goes flying out the window and falls dead on the ground.

When Quasimodo comes out, they say, "Who was this man?"

"I never knew his name," comes the reply, "but he's a dead ringer for his brother."

I turned and walked off.

For some days, however, I was unable to get Granberry's impromptu observations out of my mind. I sedulously derided his phrase "mutilating conversation" in talking the encounter over with my wife, aware that I was doing so because that quill had gone home. One aspect, in particular, of my habit tended to bear Granberry out—the fact that these rejoinders of mine did not arise principally out of a wish to play the wag, and not infrequently fell as drearily on my own ears as on those of my hearers. Perhaps I was indeed driven by some subcutaneous need to sabotage dialogue. Since Granberry had put his finger on that much, why not, I thought, let him try to uncover the cause of my compulsion, which was really so much sand in the gears of my social relations and repeatedly cost me my wife's good graces? So I took up the genial challenge, "Come see me sometime," which Granberry had flung over his shoulder—or, rather, over mine—as I walked away from him, and made an appointment for the first of what was to be a series of interviews, in his midtown office.

Granberry's headway with me may be inferred from the way matters stood at the end of one month. As my fourth weekly consultation drew to its close, he leaned across his desk and asked, "Do you feel, now, that you're acquiring a better grasp of your symptoms?"

"Symptoms I do," I answered, "and then again, symptoms I don't."

"*Don't be discouraged,*" Granberry said, with a smile that tendered me every good wish. "*I'm not.*"

Granberry remained, throughout the proceedings, the soul of patient industry, never doubting that we were burrowing steadily toward the root of my *volonté*. His confidence buoyed me. Then, suddenly, my responses became completely phonetic. When, in some illustrative reference of Granberry's to his own formative years, he mentioned that he was born in Oklahoma, I threw out "Oklahoma tell your mother she wants you."

I wet my lips nervously and slid up in my chair. "Good God," I said, "I was never *that* bad before. What's happened? Now I even dream in puns. Like last night I dreamed of a female deer chasing a male deer in the mating season."

"?"

"A doe trying to make a fast buck."

"!"

I was vexed to see Granberry, while I was visualizing ostracism from all but the most undiscriminating circles, rise and rub his hands.

"We're muddling the disease, so to speak—the way medication sometimes stirs up an infection before it can get to correcting it," he said. "Your white count, as it were, is way up."

"Well, let's get it down," I said.

But up it stayed. I now not only refrained from mingling in society—I didn't dare leave the house (except, of course, to visit Granberry). During this period, only my wife knew that I was "worse." I wouldn't care to give any detailed evidence of my white count other than the above ramshackle instances. Granberry, on the other hand, had never been so optimistic; he said that nothing proved so much as the intensification of my condition how close we were to uncovering the traumatic incident that undoubtedly lay at the heart of it. But weeks went by and still no traumatic incident.

So finally, resentful of Granberry and the pass to which he had brought me, I made up a traumatic incident that I felt would, preparatory to my bailing out on the whole business, caricature both him and the calling he professed.

I sprang it on him midway of an interview.

"Say," I said, pausing in a train of reflections on my early school days, "I just remembered something. Something that comes back to me now, after all these years."

"What's that?" Granberry said alertly.

"I was in fifth or sixth grade," I said. "We were being asked to use words in a sentence. When it came my turn, the teacher gave me the word 'ominous.' 'Let's hear you use "ominous" in a sentence,' she said. I got up and stood in the aisle." I hesitated in my narrative, as though the strain of resurrection were a taxing one.

"Go on," Granberry said.

"I groped desperately for a way to use the word assigned me," I resumed. "As I did so, I heard the kid in the seat behind me—a kid who was always razzing me in the schoolyard—I heard him whisper something to somebody and snicker. Burning with anger, I turned and said, 'If he doesn't shut his mouth, ominous sock him one!'"

"Actually, I'm not even a real Modo. I'm only a Quasimodo."

Granberry set down a letter knife he had been bending back and forth in his hands. He coughed into his fist and rose.

"It's impossible, you see, to cheat," he said. "I mean a hoax is just as significant as a bona fide memory. More so, in what it reveals of you, because it's an act of *conscious* selection, whereas memory is an *unconscious* one."

Embarrassed for me, he walked to the window and tugged at the cord of a Venetian blind. "I can never seem to adjust this thing," he said. "Why, I have no choice but to take your little charade at face value. And I think that what it constitutes is nothing less than an X-ray of your personality."

The thought seemed to steep him momentarily in a gloom as great as my own; Granberry, that is, had the same sense as I of being stuck with this very corny case history.

"Couldn't it be part of the white count?" I asked, trying to renege.

Granberry shook his head. "It would still be just as revelatory," he said.

Returning to the chair behind his desk, he plunged into an interpretation of the data I had given him.

"It confirms and crystallizes what I have felt about you all along," he said. "You are fundamentally afraid of people. I said from the start, this habit of yours was a way of mutilating conversation, and now we know why you mutilate it. You do so in order to escape the risks of engaging in it on an adult level, because you're afraid you won't stand up to the test of social comparisons it constitutes. Everybody you meet is that boy in the schoolyard—oh, I don't doubt that there *was* one, or many—and you ought to recognize that, in trying to grasp why you deflate people." He paused, then went astringently but sympathetically on. "Freud has explained that humor is a denial of anxiety, so you must understand that these puns of yours arise from one of the most intense forms of belligerence—the belligerence of the insecure."

He let this sink in a moment. "Let that do for today," he concluded. "Think over what I've said, and we'll talk about it some more next time."

There weren't many more next times. At first I was piqued, but soon I came to feel that Granberry was probably right. With this new insight into myself, I determined to control my tendency, and, slowly, I succeeded. Success came somewhat faster once Granberry had stressed this important point: "Always bear in mind that the other fellow is just as afraid of you as you are of him."

At length, my habit cleared up. When, for example, some friends of my wife's and mine named Pritchett phoned to invite us to come listen to a record they had just acquired, adding that it was "the new long-playing *Godunov*," I did not reply, as once I might have, "That's Godunov for me." Nor, when a dinner companion exclaimed that she had glimpsed three wedges of southbound geese over her rooftop in one day, did I succumb to the temptation to murmur, "Migratious!"

Granberry dismissed me as arrested. "I think it'll stick," he said. "Your adjustment should last indefinitely. Unless, of course, you have

DO IT'S

Anesthesiologists do it unconsciously.
Bigots do it intolerably.
Cardiologists do it heartily.
Drummers do it differently.
Engineers do it mechanically.
Frankenstein did it monstrously.
Gillespie does it dizzily.
Hairdressers do it permanently.
Ivan did it terribly.
Jacob and Wilhelm did it grimly.
King Arthur did it nightly.
Louisianians do it bayoutifully.
Masturbators do it singlehandedly.
Nudists do it barely.
(Nixon did it trickily.)
Oil refiners do it crudely.
Procrastinators do it later.
Reporters do it sensationally.
Shriners do it conventionally.
Thespians do it playfully.
Undertakers do it gravely.
Venetians do it swimmingly.
Wagnalls does it funkily.
Yentas do it nosily.
Zen Meditators do it thoughtlessly.

some experience sufficiently unsettling to jar loose your old resentment and antagonism. But I think that unlikely. I can't imagine what it could be."

Nor could I. Matters seemed to have been resolved.

Then, one Saturday morning a month or so after Granberry and I had shaken hands and bade one another farewell, I was drinking midmorning coffee at home with my wife when I saw the mailman drive up.

"I'll get it," I said, and rose and went out to the mailbox.

There were three pieces of mail—one, I saw by the return address on the envelope, from Granberry's office. I had not opened it by the time I rejoined my wife.

"This is from Granberry," I said, giving her the two others, which were addressed to her. "Probably his bill."

"Well, whatever it is, it's worth it," she said, abstractedly perusing the other things. "There's nothing whatever left of that awful habit of yours. Not one iota."

I opened the envelope and peered inside. I uttered a cry of genuine shock.

"How do you like that!" I exclaimed. "Fifteen calls and iota bandit seven hundred and fifty dollars!"

GILDA RADNER as EMILY LITELLA

The Deaf Penalty

Chevy: Here, in reply to a Weekend Update editorial, is Miss Emily Litella.

Gilda: What is all this fuss I hear about the Supreme Court decision on a deaf penalty? It's terrible. Deaf people have enough problems as it is. I know I myself occasionally have difficulty with my hearing, but I know I wouldn't want to be punished for it. And what do they do to them, anyway? Would they have to pay a fine? Or would they wait till the poor souls turn their backs and then shout nasty things at them? You mark my words! If we start punishing deaf people, they'll get back at us. They'll close their eyes when we talk to them and they won't be able to see a thing we're saying. Instead of making deafness a penalty, we ought to start doing nice things for them . . . like talking louder. (SHOUTING) *You hear me!!! We should help these people!!!*

Chevy: Miss Litella.

Gilda: What?

Chevy: That's death penalty. The editorial was about the Supreme Court's decision about the death penalty. Not deaf penalty.

Gilda: Death penalty. Hmm. That's entirely different. (TO CAMERA) Never mind.

The baby was so ugly they had to hang a pork chop around its neck to get the dog to play with it.

—*Rodney Dangerfield*

PART TWO

LIFE AFTER BIRTH

S.GROSS

DAVE BARRY

To See Your Child Being Born Is to Know the Meaning of Yucky

For thousands of years, only women had babies. Primitive women would go into huts and groan and wail and sweat while other women hovered around. The primitive men stayed outside. When the baby was born, the women would clean it up as best they could and show it to the men, who would spit appreciatively and go into the forest to hurl sharp sticks at animals. If you had suggested to primitive men that they should watch women have babies, they would have laughed and tortured you for three or four days.

At the beginning of the 20th Century, women started having babies in hospital rooms. Often males were present, but they were doctors who were paid large sums of money and wore masks. Civilian males stayed out of the baby-having area; they remained in waiting rooms reading old copies of *Field and Stream.*

What I'm getting at is that for most of history, baby-having was in the hands (so to speak) of women. Many fine people were born under this system. Things changed in the 1970's. The birth rate dropped sharply. Women started going to college and driving bulldozers and carrying briefcases and using words like "debenture." They didn't have time to have babies. For a while there, the only people having babies were unwed teenage girls, who can get pregnant merely by standing downwind from teenage boys.

Then young professional couples began to realize that their lives were missing something: a sense of stability, of companionship, of responsibility for another life. So they got Labrador retrievers. A little later they started having babies again, mainly because of the tax advantages. Now you can't open your car door without hitting a pregnant woman. But there's a catch. *Women now expect men to watch them have babies.* This is called natural childbirth.

At first, natural childbirth was popular only with granola-oriented couples who named their babies things like Peace Love World Understanding Harrington Schwartz. The males, their brains badly corroded by drugs and organic food, wrote smarmy articles about what a Meaningful Experience it is to see a New Life Come into the World. None of the articles mentioned the various fluids and solids that come into the world with the New Life, so people got the impression that watching somebody have a baby was fun. Now innocent males are required by law to watch females have babies.

I recently had to watch my wife have a baby in our local hospital. First we had to go to ten childbirth classes with fifteen other couples consisting of women who were going to have babies and men who

> My wife and I went to natural childbirth classes. Great place to meet chicks, by the way, if you're into the full-figured gal. You can be reasonably sure these girls put out.
>
> —Jonathan Katz

were going to have to watch them. Some of the couples were wearing golf and tennis apparel and were planning on having wealthy babies. The classes consisted of openly discussing, among other things, the uterus. In high school I would have killed for reliable information on the uterus. But having discussed it at length and having seen full-color diagrams, I must say that it has lost much of its charm, although I still respect it a great deal as an organ.

Our instructor also spent some time on the ovum, which is near the ovaries. What happens is that the ovum hangs around until along comes this big crowd of spermatozoa, which are tiny, stupid, one-celled organisms. They're looking for the ovum, but most of them wouldn't recognize it if they fell over it. They swim around for days trying to mate with the pancreas or whatever other organs they bump into. Eventually one stumbles into the ovum, and the happy couple parades down the fallopian tube to the uterus.

In the uterus, the Miracle of Life begins, unless you believe the Miracle of Life doesn't begin there, and if you think I'm going to get into that you're crazy. Anyway, the ovum starts growing rapidly and dividing into lots of specialized parts, not unlike the federal government. Within six weeks it has developed all the organs it needs to drool; by ten weeks it has the ability to cry in restaurants. The class was shown photographs of a fetus developing inside the uterus. We weren't told how the photos were taken, but I suspect it involved a lot of drinking.

One evening we saw a movie of a woman we didn't even know having a baby. I am serious. She was from California. Another time we were shown slides of a Caesarian section. The first slides showed a pregnant woman cheerfully entering the hospital. The last slides showed her holding a baby. The middle slides showed how they got the baby out of the cheerful woman. I can't give you a lot of details here because

Kate Gawf © 1987 by Carol Wilson Fine Arts, Inc.

Unwittingly, the Stanleys have invited a total stranger to come live in their home and mooch off their finances for 18 years.

I had to leave the room fifteen or twenty times. I do remember that at one point our instructor observed that there was "surprisingly little blood." She evidently felt this was a real selling point.

When we weren't looking at pictures or discussing the uterus we practiced breathing. In the old days, under President Eisenhower, doctors gave lots of drugs to women having babies. They'd knock them out during the delivery and the women would wake up when the kids were entering the 4th grade. The idea with natural childbirth is to avoid drugs so the mother can share the first intimate moments after birth with the baby and the father and the obstetrician and the standby anesthesiologist and the nurses and the person who cleans the room.

The key to avoiding drugs, according to the natural childbirth people, is for the woman to breathe deeply. Really. The theory is that if she breathes deeply, she'll get all relaxed and won't notice that she's in a hospital delivery room wearing a truly perverted garment and having a baby. So in childbirth class we spent a lot of time on pillows and little mats while the women pretended to have contractions and the men squatted around them with stopwatches and pretended to time them. The golf and tennis couples, who had pillows with matching pillowcases, didn't care for this part as they were not into squatting. They started playing backgammon when they were supposed to be practicing breathing. I imagine they had a rough time in childbirth, unless they got the servants to have contractions for them.

My wife and I traipsed along for months, breathing and timing. We were a terrific team and had a swell time. The actual delivery was slightly more difficult. I don't want to name names, but I held up my end. My stopwatch was in good order and I told my wife to breathe. She, on the other hand, was unusually cranky. She almost completely lost her sense of humor. At one point, I made an especially amusing remark and she tried to hit me.

The baby came out all right, which is actually pretty awful unless you're a big fan of slime. The doctor, who up to then had behaved like a perfectly rational person, said, "Would you like to see the placenta?" *Nobody* would like to see a placenta. It's like a form of punishment:

Jury: We find the defendant guilty of stealing from the old and crippled.
Judge: I sentence the defendant to look at three placentas.

Without waiting for an answer, the doctor held up the placenta as he might hold up a bowling trophy. I bet he didn't try that with the people who had matching pillowcases.

We ended up with a healthy, organic, natural baby, who immediately demanded to be put back in the uterus.

I understand that some members of the flatworm family simply divide in two.

My idea of natural childbirth is no eye makeup and no lipstick. —Joy Behar

MARK DROP & STEVEN SPIEGEL

My Dad the Observational Humorist

(*Music is heard: sappy family sit-com music. Then a voice is heard singing:*)

Voice: You're looking around the world you're in
Laughing at the things you see
Where do missing socks go in the dryer?
Are free things really free?

You're a satirical guy . . .
Analyzin', trivializin', anesthetizing . . .
All of us.
You're *our* . . . sat-ir-ic-al guy . . .

Voiceover: *My Dad The Observational Humorist* is filmed before a live audience.

(*Open on a typical sit-com living room. Mother enters and begins to dust. Daughter enters through the front door. She seems worried.*)

Mother: Hello, darling. How was school?
Daughter: Fine, Mom. Is Dad home?
Mother: Not yet. Why?
Daughter: Wilber's asked me to go to the movies with him.
Mother: When?
Daughter: Tonight.
Mother: You know the rules; your dad and I have to meet whoever you go out with.
Daughter: Can't you just meet him and tell Dad what you think?
Mother: Are you ashamed of your father?
Daughter: No. It's just that every boy I introduce to Dad is driven stark raving mad.
Mother: I think you're exaggerating just a little.
Daughter: What about Tommy Smithers?
Mother: It was only coincidence that Tommy came down with that degenerative nerve disease the day he met your father. Now be nice, I hear his car pulling up.

(*The door opens and Dad enters. He looks and talks exactly like Andy Rooney. He is carrying a grocery bag and a briefcase.*)

Mother: Hello, Honey. Did you go grocery shopping?
Andy: (*He empties the contents of the bag onto a table. It is twelve different boxes of cereal.*) Did you ever wonder why there are so many different kinds of cereal?
Mother: Honey, I told you that I just needed some milk and broccoli . . .

My mother said, "You won't amount to anything because you procrastinate!" I said, "Just wait."

—Judy Tenuta

Andy: Look at all the different kinds of bran: Raisin Bran, All Bran, Bran Flakes . . .

Daughter: Who cares, Dad?

Andy: (Ignores her.) Look at this . . . some of them offer prizes so you'll pick their cereal over the others. Do I really want to buy a box of Alpha-bits just to get a roll of Life-Savers for nothing? I could just pay 35 cents and buy a roll of Life-Savers. I'm not going to eat the Alpha-bits anyway . . .

Mother: Andy, your daughter wants to ask you a question.

Andy: Did you ever wonder why kids ask so darn many questions?

Daughter: Daddy, I want to go to the movies.

Andy: Oh, you do? With who?

Daughter: Wilber.

Andy: Did you ever wonder what makes parents choose the names they do? Sometimes I think they have it in for the kid before he's even born. I mean, what did any kid ever do to deserve the name Wilber or Gertrude? And why name kids after someone else and then assign them a number? Like Arnold Bartholomew the Second? Aren't they good enough for their own name?

Daughter: Do you want to meet him or not?

Mother: Yes, we do.

(Daughter opens the kitchen door and brings in Wilber, a good-looking young man.)

Wilber: It's a pleasure to meet you, Mr. and Mrs. Rooney.

Mother: It's nice to meet you, Wilber.

Andy: Do you mind if we have a little man to man talk?

Daughter: Daddy . . .

Wilber: Not at all, sir.

(Andy takes Wilber over to a corner.)

Andy: Wilber, did you ever wonder why women go to the bathroom in pairs? Is the bathroom that scary that they feel they can't go in there alone?

Wilber: I never thought about it.

Andy: Come here Wilber. I want you to see something. *(He empties a pocket of his coat and it contains numerous bars of used soap.)* Did you ever wonder why there are so many different types of soaps?

Wilber: No.

Andy: Look at this one . . . *(Holds up small blue one.)* It's scented. I don't want my soap to smell. Isn't that what I use soap to get rid of?

Wilber: Do you collect used soap?

Andy: I collect everything, young man. *(Holds up a bar of black soap.)* Look at this. Who wants to wash themselves with black soap? Or green? Personally, white has always been my favorite color for soap. After all, I'm not choosing soap to go with my shirt. I just want to be clean. Understand?

> **I had dinner with my father last night, and I made a classic Freudian slip. I meant to say, ''Please pass the salt,'' but it came out, ''You prick, you ruined my childhood.''**
>
> —Jonathan Katz

"Poor daddy, off on another business trip."

Wilber: I . . . think so . . .

Andy: (*He empties his pants pocket of change.*) And did you ever wonder who uses pennies anymore? Is there anything that still costs a penny? Why bother minting them? Can't we just round everything to the nearest tenth? It would certainly make my pockets a little less bulky.

Wilber: I . . . understand . . .

Andy: (*Empties the contents of another pocket, pens of all types and sizes.*) Look at all these pens. Who needs this many pens, Wilber? Do I?

Wilber: Yes?

Andy: Of course not! No one needs this many pens! Most of them don't even work. This one writes in four colors. Why don't I just buy four pens? After all, they're not that expensive. And why do people who manufacture four color pens think *anyone* wants to write in green?

Wilber: God help me, I don't know!

Daughter: Dad, you've had Wilber long enough. It's time for us to go.

Andy: Just a second, I haven't even shown him my sock drawer yet.

Wilber: I really have to get going. We'll do the movie some other time . . .

Daughter: But, Wilber . . .

Wilber: I'll call you, Debbie. *(He runs out.)*

Daughter: I can't take it anymore!

Mother: He seemed like an awfully nervous young man. *(Daughter pulls out a big gun.)* What are you doing, Sweetheart?

Daughter: I've had it with Dad and his meaningless insights and his unanswerable questions and his stupid collections of trivial garbage.

Mother: It may be trivial to you and me and the rest of humanity, but it's your father's life.

Daughter: Not anymore. *(She fires and Andy falls backward onto a chair.)*

Mother: My God . . . What have you done?

Daughter: I've finally freed us! That's what I've done!

Andy: *(From the chair, clutching his wounds)* Did you ever realize that when bad guys are shot on television, they usually fall forward through a glass window, when, in reality, you fall backward? I guess it's more dramatic that way. And I think people in movies bleed more than is really necessary. I mean, I've just been shot with a large caliber weapon, but there really isn't much blood, is there? *(Andy continues as the daughter collapses and the mother resumes her dusting.)*

JOHN UPDIKE

On the Inclusion of Miniature Dinosaurs in Breakfast Cereal Boxes

A post-historic herbivore,
I come to breakfast looking for
A bite. Behind the box of Brex
I find *Tyrannosaurus rex.*

And lo! beyond the Sugar Pops,
An acetate *Triceratops.*
And here! across the Shredded Wheat,
The spoor of *Brontosaurus* feet.

Too unawake to dwell upon
A model of *Iguanodon,*
I hide within the Raisin Bran;
And thus begins the dawn of *Man.*

MARILYN SUZANNE MILLER

Slumber Party from Saturday Night Live

CAST

> Jane Curtin
> Madeline Kahn
> Laraine Newman
> Gilda Radner

(A darkened living room, with single lantern-type light of type used for camping. Girls huddled around Madeline on the floor with pillows, blankets, sleeping bags, etc. Assorted old pizza boxes, Coke bottles strewn around them.)

Madeline: (Enormously confidential) . . . so then, the man gets bare naked in bed with you and you both go to sleep which is why they call it sleeping together. Then you both wake up and the man says, "Why don't you slip into something more comfortable?"—no, wait, maybe that comes before—it's not important—and then the man says . . .

(Light goes on at top of staircase)

Mother's Voice: Gilda, it's five A.M. When does the noise stop?
Gilda: We're just going to sleep, Mother.
Mother's Voice: What are you talking about at this hour?
Gilda: School!
Mother's Voice: Well, save it for the morning.

(Door slams. Lights out.)

Jane: (To Madeline, as if nothing has happened) And then the man . . .
Madeline: Anyway . . . *(Brings girls closer, whispers something inaudible. We finally hear:)* . . . then the man . . . *(Whispers)* . . . in you and then you scream and then he screams and then it's over.

(Moment of silence. The girls sit there, shocked and horrified.)

Laraine: (Making throwing-up sounds, pulling blanket up over her head) That's disgusting!
Gilda: You lie, Madeline.
Madeline: Cross my heart and hope to die. My brother told me in my driveway.
Gilda: Your brother lies, Madeline.
Madeline: No, sir.
Jane: Come on. Isn't he the one who said if you chew your nails and swallow them, a hand will grow in your stomach?
Madeline: Well, it's also true because I read it in this book.
Jane: What'd it say?

Madeline: It said, "The first step in human reproduction is . . . the man . . . (*Whispers*)

Laraine: (*Hysterical, coming out from under covers*) It's disgusting!

(*Laraine, Gilda, and Jane all do fake throwing up*)

Madeline: It's true.

Jane: Well, I just know it can't be true, because nothing that sickening is true.

Madeline: Boogers are true.

(*The girls all consider this for a moment*)

Gilda: Well, I mainly don't believe it because I heard from my sister about this girl who this guy jumped out from the bushes and forced to have a baby.

Madeline: (*Smugly*) How?

Gilda: I don't know. I think he just said, "Have a baby right now."

Madeline: Oh, sure, Gilda. And you think that would work if I tried it on you?

Gilda: (*Scared*) Hey, don't. O.K.?

Madeline: Well, don't worry. It wouldn't because that's not how it's done. How it's done is . . . the man . . .

Laraine: Don't say it again, O.K.? I just ate half a pizza, O.K.?

Gilda: (*Thoughtfully*) So that's why people were born naked.

Jane: Yeah.

Laraine: But how could you face the man after? Wouldn't you be *so embarrassed*?

Jane: I'd have to kill myself right after. I mean, I get embarrassed when I think how people standing next to me can see inside my ear.

Madeline: Well, that's why you should only do it after you're married. Because then you won't be so embarrassed in front of your husband after, because you're in the same *family*.

Laraine: Oh, well, I really want to get married now. *Now.*

Madeline: But the worst thing is—your *parents* do it, you know?

Gilda: Come on!

Madeline: Gilda, think: none of us would be here unless our parents did it *at least once.*

(*Moment of silence. They all consider the horror of this.*)

Jane: (*Horrorized*) My parents did it at least twice. I have a sister.

Gilda: (*Greater horror*) And my parents did it at least three times. I have a sister *and* a brother.

(*They all turn to give her a "you're dirt" look*)

Gilda: But, like, I know they didn't do it because they *wanted* to. They did it because they *had* to. To have children.

Madeline: (*Accusing*) They could have adopted children.

Gilda: Yeah, but adopted children are a pain. You have to teach them how to look like you.

Laraine: Well, my father would never do anything like that to my mother. He's too polite.

Madeline: My father's polite, and we have six kids.

Laraine: He's obviously not as polite as you think.

(*They glare at each other*)

Jane: I wonder whose idea this was.

Madeline: (*Offhand*) God's.

Jane: Oh, come on. God doesn't go around thinking up sickening things like this for people to do.

Gilda: Maybe God just wants you to do it so you'll appreciate how good the *rest* of your life is.

Jane: Maybe.

Laraine: (*To Madeline*) How long does it take?

There are still double standards. A man can sleep around and sleep around and nobody asks any questions. A woman makes nineteen, twenty mistakes, right away you're a tramp.

Joan Rivers

Madeline: Stupid! That depends on how big the girl's stomach is and how fast she can digest.

Gilda: Oh.

Jane: Can you talk during it?

Madeline: You have to hold your breath or else it doesn't work.

(Various vomit-sounding shrieks, screams, etc.)

Jane: Well, I'm just telling my husband I'm not going to do it. *(To heaven)* Tough beansies.

Madeline: What if he says he'll get divorced from you if you didn't do it?

(The girls consider this.)

Jane: I would never marry someone like that.

Madeline: What if you did by accident? What if . . . *(making up story)* . . . you met him in a war and married him real fast because you felt sorry for him since he'd probably get killed only he didn't and then you were stuck with him?

Gilda: *(Moved by emergency)* Look—let's make this pact right now that after we get married, if our husbands make us do it, we'll call each other on the phone every day and talk a lot to keep our minds off it, like our mothers do.

Jane: Right.

Madeline: Right.

Laraine: Right, because it's *disgusting.*

(Laraine makes same throw-up sound. Ducks under covers.)

Jane: Well, don't worry, we'll never have to keep this pact, because I'll never do it.

Gilda: Me, neither.

Madeline: Me, neither.

(There is a beat)

Laraine: *(Quietly)* I might.

(Fade)

DOONESBURY *by Garry Trudeau*

DELIA EPHRON
A Mom's Life

Take your plate into the kitchen, please.

Take it downstairs when you go.

Don't leave it there, take it upstairs.

Is that yours?

Don't hit your brother.

I'm talking to you.

Just a minute, please, can't you see I'm talking?

I said, don't interrupt.

Did you brush your teeth?

What are you doing out of bed?

Go back to bed.

You can't watch in the afternoon.

What do you mean, there's nothing to do?

Go outside.

Read a book.

Turn it down.

Get off the phone.

Tell your friend you'll call her back. Right now!

Hello. No, she's not home.

She's still not home.

She'll call you when she gets home.

Take a jacket. Take a sweater.

Take one anyway.

Someone left his shoes in front of the TV.

Get the toys out of the hall. Get the toys out of the
    bathtub. Get the toys off the stairs.

Do you realize that could kill someone?

Hurry up.

Hurry up. Everyone's waiting.

I'll count to ten and then we're going without you.

Did you go to the bathroom?

If you don't go, you're not going.

I mean it.

Why didn't you go before you left?

Can you hold it?

What's going on back there?

Stop it.

I said, stop it!

I don't want to hear about it.

Stop it, or I'm taking you home right now.

That's it. We're going home.

Give me a kiss.

I need a hug.

Make your bed.

Clean up your room.

Set the table.

I need you to set the table!

Don't tell me it's not your turn.

Please move your chair in to the table.

Sit up.

Just try a little. You don't have to eat the whole thing.

Stop playing and eat.

Would you watch what you're doing?

Move your glass, it's too close to the edge.

Watch it!

More, what?

More, *please*. That's better.

Just eat one bite of salad.

You don't always get what you want. That's life.

Don't argue with me. I'm not discussing this anymore.

Go to your room.

No, ten minutes are not up.

One more minute.

How many times have I told you, don't do that.

Where did the cookies go?

Eat the old fruit before you eat the new fruit.

I'm not giving you mushrooms. I've taken all the
    mushrooms out. See?

Is your homework done?

Stop yelling. If you want to ask me something, come here.

STOP YELLING. IF YOU WANT TO ASK ME
    SOMETHING, COME HERE.

I'll think about it.

Not now.

Ask your father.

We'll see.

Don't sit so close to the television, it's bad for your eyes.

Calm down.

Calm down and start over.

Is that the truth?

Fasten your seat belt.

Did everyone fasten their seat belts?

I'm sorry that's the rule. I'm sorry that's the rule. I'm
    sorry, that's the rule.

MEL BROOKS & CARL REINER
Two Thousand Year Old Man

By the way, sir, are you still married?

I've been married several hundred times.

Several hundred times! Do you remember all your wives?

One I remember well.

Which one was that?

The third one, Shirley, I remember her, a redhead.

I'm afraid to ask the next question. You've had many hundreds of wives—

Hundreds and hundreds of wives.

How many children do you have?

I have over forty-two thousand children. And not one comes to visit me!

Having a family is like having a bowling alley installed in your brain.   —*Martin Mull*

© 1990 by S. Gross

DAVID LLOYD

Chuckles Bites the Dust

from THE MARY TYLER MOORE SHOW

CAST

Mary Richards	Mary Tyler Moore
Lou Grant	Edward Asner
Ted Baxter	Ted Knight
Murray Slaughter	Gavin MacLeod
Georgette Franklin	Georgia Engel
Sue Ann Nivens	Betty White
Reverend Burke	John Harkins
Louise Thomas	Helen Kleeb

SETS

Newsroom
Mary's Living Room
Lou's Office
Mortuary Chapel
Small Area off Chapel

Act One

Fade In:
Autumn in Minneapolis:
Interior newsroom—day
Murray is at desk. Mary is returning from teletype carrying tearsheet.

Mary: Murr, have you noticed anything funny with the teletype machine this morning? I sure hope there's something wrong with it.
Murray: Why?
Mary: Because if there isn't President Ford just held up a liquor store with a water pistol.

Sue Ann sticks her head through the door.

Sue Ann: Hello, people.
Mary: Hi, Sue Ann.
Sue Ann: Mary, I want you to close your eyes. Now, no arguments—close them.
Murray: It's all right, Sue Ann. She's seen you without makeup before.
Sue Ann: (*Laughs*) Oh Murray, I just hope *my* mind's still active when I'm your age . . . C'mon, Mary, close them.
(Mary shrugs and closes her eyes. Sue Ann enters carrying a huge mobile made entirely of food and holds it right in front of Mary.)

*"Butchie's asleep, you should have no trouble with him. The first switch is the porch light.
The one in the middle's for the living room, and this one will suck the face
right off your skull. There's pizza in the fridge; we'll be home by eleven."*

Now you can open your eyes.

(Mary opens eyes.)

Well, what do you think?

Mary: Is it all right if I close them again? . . . What is it?

Sue Ann: It's a free-form mobile showing the four basic food groups. I used it for a special I did last week called: "What's All This Fuss About Famine?" . . . And I thought it would be just the thing to brighten up your new apartment.

Mary: Oh, Sue Ann, you . . . shouldn't have. Of course, I'll have to check my lease. I mean, just to make sure there isn't any regulation against . . . you know, hanging food . . .

Sue Ann: I think it would go beautifully in your kitchen—don't you?

Mary: Well I think the kitchen might be a little too small for it.

Sue Ann: Well I'm sure you'll find the perfect place for it. *(Starts to exit)* I know, why don't you put it in your bedroom? I'm sure you must need something in there to relieve the tedium.

Sue Ann exits, passing Ted, who enters.

Ted: Hello Sue Ann. Hello Murray. Hello Mary.

Mary is on her way to hang the mobile on the hat rack.

(*To mobile*) Hello whatever you are. This is Ted Baxter saying: Happy days are here again!

Mary: Did you make that up, Ted?

Ted: Naw, it's from some song. (*Thinking*) I forget the name of it.

Murray: And what are you so happy about?

Ted: The circus is in town and they want me.

Murray: That's terrific, Ted. Do you have to bring your own shovel?

Ted: It so happens they want me to ride at the head of the parade. I'm this year's Grand Marshall. It's something I've always wanted. (*Bitterly*) I should have had it *last* year—but they gave it to that stupid weather girl from Channel Six. Well it served them right what happened . . .

Murray: What happened?

Mary: It . . . rained on their parade.

Ted: (*Still bitter*) And the year before that, when they chose that big, dumb basketball player who does the sports on Channel Eight. Made a fool of himself!

Murray: I don't remember that, either.

Mary: He got in the wrong car. He . . . squeezed into the little tiny one with all the clowns in it and . . . wedged them in. They eventually had to take the car apart. It kind of spoiled the effect.

Murray: Gee. It sounds as if the Grand Marshall's job has a history of disaster.

Ted: Yeah, well—this year they've got me.

Murray: I rest my case.

Ted: Ha-ha. You can't bug me, Murr. Nothing can spoil my day now that I'm going to be Grand Marshall of the circus parade.

Lou enters from his office on Ted's last line.

Lou: Forget it, Ted! You aren't.

Ted: (*Staggered*) W-what, Lou?

Lou: I said forget it. My anchorman isn't marching down the street with a chimp. It tends to give him an undignified image!

Lou keeps right on walking, but Ted stops him at door.

Ted: Lou, please! It *won't* give me an undignified image.

Lou: (*To Ted*) I was talking about the chimp.

Lou exits and Ted follows him out.

Ted (*O.S.*): Lou!

Dissolve to:
Int. Mary's living room—night
Door opens. Mary enters, turns on light and closes door. She is carrying the mobile Sue Ann gave her. She looks for some place to set it down, and the doorbell rings. She goes to door and opens it. Georgette enters.

Mary: Georgette, hi, what brings you here?

We used to terrorize our babysitters when we were little, except for my great-grandfather, because he used to read to us. From his will.

—Brian Kiley

Georgette: Ted. He's parking the car. He's looking for a meter that still has some time left on it.

Mary continues to look for place to set mobile down.

Mary: Would you like some coffee?

Georgette: Okay. Mary, when Ted gets here you've got to talk to him, he's very upset.

Mary: About what?

Georgette: I don't know. He's too upset to talk about it.

Mary: So what makes you think he'll tell *me* about it?

Georgette: He will, Mary. He said to me, "I'm not going to burden you with my troubles, because it's just a bore to burden people with your troubles. Let's go see Mary" . . . Mary, can I ask you a question?

Mary: Sure.

Georgette: (*Indicating mobile*) What's this?

Mary: What's what? . . . Oh that. It's a gift from Sue Ann. It's a mobile. I'm just trying to find a place for it.

Georgette: Why don't you put it in a mobile home? (*They both laugh.*) I think it's really beautiful.

Mary: You do?

Georgette: Yes, all this food—it looks good enough to—look at. What do you want me to do with it?

Doorbell rings.

Mary: Oh just put it anywhere.

Georgette shrugs and puts it into freezer. Mary is about to open door; Georgette stops her.

Georgette: Oh, Mary. Whatever it is that's bothering Ted, you'll have to worm it out of him—he never likes to show his true feelings.

Mary opens door and Ted enters, smiling.

Mary: Hi, Ted.

Ted: (*Brightly*) Hiya, Mary . . .

(Face falls and he gives a strangled sob)

Mary: (*Dryly*) Something wrong, Ted?

Ted: I never could hide anything from you. All right. I'll tell you. I'm quitting WJM.

Mary: (*Now concerned*) Quitting? Ted, why?

Ted: Because I'm not appreciated, that's why. Because after seven years of giving the station the best I had, Lou still treats me like dirt.

Mary: Oh come on, Ted!

Ted: He treats me like a little child, Mary. He bosses me around as though I were ten years old.

Mary: Ted that isn't true. He may boss you around but he doesn't think you're a kid. He respects you as a mature adult.

Ted: (*Anguished*) Then why won't he let me go to the circus?

(Kettle whistles. Mary crosses to kitchen.)

DOONESBURY *by Garry Trudeau*

I mean, it's an honor being asked to be Grand Marshall. A very *great* honor. *(Beat)* The Grand Marshall rides ahead of the elephants!

Mary: Ted, for what it's worth, I think Mr. Grant was unfair about the circus.

Ted: Then why don't you talk to him, Mary. He listens to you. Maybe he'll change his mind.

Mary: I'm afraid it's a little late for that, Ted. Just before I left the office, I heard the circus had chosen a new Grand Marshall.

Ted: *(Resentful)* Already. Boy they didn't waste any time did they? Who'd they get to replace me, the Mayor, the Governor?

Mary: Chuckles the Clown.

Georgette: Oh. How'd they ever get him?

Ted: *(Incredulous)* Chuckles? Our Chuckles? A kiddie show host? Grand Marshall of the circus? A clown? Well, I hate to say this but I hope they laugh at him.

Dissolve to:
Int. newsroom—day
Ted is on the air. Murray and Mary are watching at their desks.

Ted (On the air): *(Grimly throughout)* . . . leaving twenty-eight people condominiumless. Now for the lighter side of the news. A cocker spaniel named Skippy who had been left behind by the Hargrove family when they moved from San Jose, California, two years ago, today showed up at the Hargrove's new home in Westport, Connecticut . . . *(ad lib)* Big deal. And now a word from one of our sponsors . . . Big deal.

Murray: What's the matter with him?

Mary: He's still angry with Lou about that circus thing and you know something, Murray? I don't blame him.

Murray: Aw Mair! You're gonna be reasonable now, aren't you? You're going to be fair, and look at both sides of things, and see Ted's point of view. If you're in *that* kind of mood I don't even want to talk to you!

LIFE AFTER BIRTH   83

Mary: I mean it. Do you know how close Ted came to quitting his job over this?

Murray: Not close enough!

Lou enters, genuinely stricken.

Lou: (*Mutters*) Oh my! Oh, dear . . . !

Mary: Mr. Grant . . . ?

Lou: (*Really shaken*) Something terrible has happened.

Murray: (*Sober*) What is it, Lou?

Lou: Someone we all know is dead.

Mary: What! Mr. Grant—who?

Lou: (*Getting control*) No . . . I won't tell you about it now . . . I don't want to upset you . . .

Mary: (*Frantic*) Mr. *Grant!!* . . .

Lou: Where's Ted? I gotta tell Ted . . .

Murray: He's on the air, Lou. What happened? Who died? Tell us!

Lou: (*Still dazed*) Chuckles. Chuckles the Clown is dead. It was a freak accident. He went to the parade dressed as Peter Peanut . . . and a rogue elephant tried to shell him.

They are both stunned.

Mary: Oh Mr. Grant . . .

Lou (*Moving to door*): I gotta get this on the air. You start working on the formal obituary, Murray. Chuckles' real name was George . . . his wife's name is Louise . . .

Lou starts out, then turns in the doorway, with an afterthought.

. . . The elephant's name is Jocko . . .

Ted (*On the air*): (*Still glum*) And in St. Paul today, when stopped for going through a traffic light a woman gave this excuse to a police officer: "It's a new car. I'm trying not to wear out the brakes" . . . (*sarcastically*) Ha ha. We'll be back after this commercial.

Lou dashes in from the side.

Lou: Ted, listen closely. Chuckles the Clown was just killed. He was dressed as a peanut and an elephant crushed him.

Ted: Stop trying to cheer me up, Lou. I mean, it's funny but it's in bad taste.

Lou: Ted, it's not a joke.

Ted: You mean it? . . . Good Lord.

Lou: Look, Murray's writing a formal obituary for tomorrow. You'll just have to ad lib something for now.

Ted: (*Panicking*) What'll I say? I mean, I hardly knew the man.

Lou: Sure you did. You knew him. You were on his show.

Ted: It's hard to get to know a man when he's chasing you with a rubber chicken.

Lou: Ted, just say something short and simple and warm. You can do it, Ted. We're counting on you.

Ted: Don't worry. I won't let you down.

Stage manager gives Ted "on the air" cue.

Ted (*On the air*): (*Reverently*) Ladies and gentlemen—sad news . . . one of our most beloved entertainers and a close personal friend of mine is dead. Chuckles the Clown died today of—(*flounders, can't think how to put it*) . . . um, died today a broken man! Chuckles . . . um, leaves a wife. At least I assume he was married . . . he didn't seem like the other kind . . . I don't know his age, but I'd say he was probably in his early sixties . . . of course, it's hard to judge by a guy's face—especially when he's wearing big lips and a lightbulb for a nose . . . Anyhow, he had his whole life in front of him—except the sixty years he'd already lived . . . I remember . . . Chuckles had a motto he used to recite at the end of his shows. It was called "The Credo of a Clown." I'd like to offer it now, in his memory . . . (*religiously*) "A little song—A little dance—A little seltzer down your pants." That's what it's all about, folks . . . that's what he stood for—that's what gave his life meaning . . . (*Ted is winging now*) Chuckles liked to make people laugh. And you know what I'd like to think? I'd like to think that somewhere up there tonight (*eye heavenward*)—behind those pearly gates . . . in the Great Beyond, where some day all must go . . . somewhere up there tonight, in honor of Chuckles, a celestial choir of angels . . . (*his big finish*) . . . is sitting on whoopie cushions. (*Quickly*) Ted Baxter, good night and good news!

And on Lou's face, we:
Fade Out.

END OF ACT ONE

Act Two

Fade In:
Int. Lou's Office—Next Day
Lou is pouring coffee, talking to Murray.

Lou: Chuckles worked at this station for twenty years. The least we can do is put together some kind of tribute to him.
Murray: I think I got a title for it. "Requiem For A Peanut."

Murray immediately regrets having said it, and covers his face. Lou gives him a reproachful look.

Lou: That isn't very respectful, Murray.
Mary: Then why *are* you laughing?
Sue Ann: Mary, dear—don't the circumstances strike you as being the least little bit . . . bizarre?
Lou: After all, the guy died wearing a peanut suit, killed by an elephant.
Murray: Yeah—born in a trunk, *died* in a trunk!
Mary: Okay. *Forget* what he was wearing! Suppose he *hadn't* been dressed as a peanut—would it still be funny?

There is a pause while they all consider that. Then Murray, very somberly, says:

> **My daughter has me totally wrapped around her little finger. I don't even try to win anymore. I just try and save face. I say things to her like, ''Go to your room at your earliest convenience. O.K. Daddy's going to count to fifteen hundred.''**
>
> —Jonathan Katz

Drawing by M. Stevens. © 1985 The New Yorker Magazine, Inc.

CHILD FROM ANOTHER PLANET

Murray: . . . It could have been worse . . . he could have gone as Billy Banana—and had a gorilla peel him to death.

Without a word, Mary tosses clipboard on desk and exits, as we:
Dissolve to:

Murray: I'm sorry, Lou, but I can't stop. I've been doing it ever since you gave us the news yesterday afternoon.
Lou: Me, too. It was some shock.
Murray: (*Very serious*) It sure was.
Lou: A real tragedy.
Murray: (*Ditto*) Terrible thing.
Lou: Lucky *more* people weren't hurt. Lucky that elephant didn't go after anybody else.
Murray: (*Solemnly*) That's right. After all, you know how hard it is to stop after just one peanut . . .

Murray goes to pieces. Can't help it. Breaks up completely.

Lou: (*Going fast*) That's not funny, Murray . . . (*He breaks up too*)

As they are both in stitches Ted enters, gradually starts laughing with them.

Ted: What are we laughing at?
Murray: Chuckles.

Ted gives them scathing look and exits. A beat, then he re-enters.

Ted: That's not nice.

Murray: (Guilty) I know. Why do I say things like that, Lou?

Lou: It's a release, Murray. A kind of defense mechanism. It's like whistling in a graveyard. You try to make light of something because it scares you. We laugh at death because we know death will have the last laugh on us.

Ted: (Impressed) Hey, Lou, that's good! It's not only good, it's heavy.

Lou: "Ask not for whom the bell tolls: It tolls for thee."

Ted: "It tolls for thee." Movingly put, Lou. *(Beat)* Why does it toll for me?

Lou: Because this could have happened to any of us, Ted.

Murray: (Philosophically) Somewhere out there there's an elephant with your name on it.

There is a beat. Then an awful thought suddenly hits Ted.

Ted: Lou! That's right. It could have been me!

Lou: No it couldn't Ted—

Ted: I wanted to go! You wouldn't let me!

Lou: Ted, it doesn't work that way—

Ted: (Clutching Lou's hand) You saved my life, Lou! You saved my life.

Lou: Please, Ted, I feel bad enough today.

Ted exits.
Int. newsroom
Ted exits as Mary enters and crosses to her desk.

Mary: Oh, Ted . . . My car is being fixed—could I possibly ride with you and Georgette to the funeral tomorrow?

Ted: Sure. The more the merrier.

Ted crosses and exits. As he does so, he passes Sue Ann, who enters.

Sue Ann: Mary, dear—there's no point in duplicating efforts. I'll do the tribute to Chuckles on *my* show this afternoon. I have to peel onions anyhow—my eyes will be too puffy for anything else.

Mary: (Annoyed) Sue Ann! Why is everybody being so callous about this?

Sue Ann: (Hurt) Callous? I'll have you know, dear, that Chuckles and I were very close. I made the first custard pie he ever sat on.

Mary: All right. Maybe callous isn't what I mean. But the man is dead, and it seems to me that Mr. Grant and I are the only ones in this whole place who are showing any reverence.

Lou and Murray enter from Lou's office. Lou is laughing.

Lou: (Still laughing) Cut it out, Murray.

Murray: Can you imagine the insurance claim? "Cause of death: a busted goober."

They both laugh. Sue Ann joins them.

It's been a tough year for the Katz family. My aunt passed away two weeks ago. She was cremated. We think that's what did it.
—Jonathan Katz

Sue Ann: I don't know what you two are laughing at but I'll take a chance it's dirty.

Mary: (Upset) Murray! You're not still making jokes about . . . about that?

Murray nods his head, ashamed.

Murray: Sorry, Mair.

Lou: It's a release, Mary. People need that when dealing with a tragedy. Everybody does it.

He smiles apologetically at her. She looks him in the eye, unsmiling.

Mary: I don't.

Gradually the other three wipe the smiles off their faces. When all are serious again, Mary picks up a clipboard.

Mary: Shall we discuss the tribute, now.

Lou: Right. Good idea.

Mary: As you suggested, Mr. Grant, I screened a number of Chuckles' old shows this morning. His best known characters were . . . "Mr. Fee-Fi-Fo," "Billy Banana," "Aunt Yoo-Hoo," and . . . um, of course . . . *(quickly)* "Peter Peanut."

She looks up. All three of them have covered their faces. Mary stands and stares at them. Lou is the first to recover.

Lou: Sorry, Mary.

Mary: (Cool) Oh, that's all right, Mr. Grant. This tribute was your idea—if you think it's funny . . .

Lou: No, no. You're absolutely right. The guy deserves a dignified farewell.

Mary: Exactly. Now I thought we might open with some film of him at work, and maybe just the words, "As We Remember Him."

Sue Ann: Oh, Mary, that's beautiful.

Murray: Yeah, that's nice—really nice.

Lou: Great idea. As we remember him. *(Checking list)* Who was Aunt Yoo-Hoo?

Mary: (Embarrassed, quickly) Oh, well, I don't think we'd want to use Aunt Yoo-Hoo . . .

Lou: Why not? What did he do as Aunt Yoo-Hoo?

Mary: Nothing much. He'd just . . . put on a dress and scream "Yoo-Hoo."

Lou: I don't want to remember him that way . . .

Mary: . . . T-then at the end of the show he'd . . . you know, bend over . . . um, with his little back to the camera . . . and on the seat of his—his bloomers, ah, would be written . . . "the end."

Murray: (Beat) Maybe they should bury him that way.

Sue Ann and Lou break up. Mary turns and looks right at Murray, really disappointed. Murray can't look at her.

Mary: (*Tight*) Okay, Murr. I give up. You win. Chuckles' death was a scream.

Murray: Aw come on, Mair. We're not laughing at his death. We all liked him and we're sorry.

Int. Mortuary Chapel—Day
We don't actually see a casket. We see two or three rows of people, facing a small lectern where the minister will speak. Two of the rows are strangers: one is WJM people. Sue Ann is there. After a beat, Ted, Georgette and Mary enter, make their way up the aisle, and slide into the WJM row. Organ music plays faintly. They exchange hellos.

Sue Ann: You're looking very nice, Ted.

Ted: Thanks, Sue Ann. I just paid half a buck to have my shoes done. Cream shine. I think that's what he would have wanted.

LIFE IN HELL   *by Matt Groening*

Georgette: (*Looking around*) Why do people always send flowers when someone passes on?

Sue Ann: What would you suggest, dear, fruit?

Georgette: It's so sad. Funerals always come too late.

Mary: Ah, I'm . . . not sure I understand that, Georgette.

Georgette: Well I mean, we take people for granted while they're with us. Then, when they're gone, we wish we'd been nicer to them. So we dress in black and cry our eyes out. Why don't we ever think to do that while they're still alive?

Mary: Good question.

Ted: I wish I'd been nicer to Chuckles when I had the chance. I always kind of looked down on him—you know, him being a clown. I was prejudiced against him just because his skin was different colors than mine.

Lou and Murray enter. They all exchange hellos.

Lou: (*Looking around*) Not much of a crowd.

Ted: I know. If it were my funeral this place would be packed.

Murray: That's right, Ted. It's just a matter of giving the public what they want.

Lou: (*Still looking around*) I wonder which ones are the other clowns?

Murray: You'll know soon. They're all going to jump out of a little hearse.

Mary: (*Sharply*) Murray—enough is enough. This is a funeral. Somebody has died. It's not something to make jokes about. We came here to show respect—not to laugh.

Murray: I'm sorry, Mary, you're right. No more jokes.

Organ music stops and Reverend Burke steps to the lectern.

Burke: My friends . . . "Any man's death diminishes me, because I am involved in mankind. Therefore, ask not for whom the bell tolls—it tolls for thee."

Ted: (*Sotto: scandalized*) Hey, Lou, he stole your poem!

Burke: Chuckles the Clown gave pleasure to millions. The characters he created will be remembered by children and adults alike: Peter Peanut, Mr. Fee-Fi-Fo, Billy Banana, and my particular favorite, Aunt Yoo-Hoo.

(Mary stifles a laugh.)

And not just for the laughter they provided—there was always some deeper meaning to whatever Chuckles did. Remember Mr. Fee-Fi-Fo's little catch phrase, remember how when his arch rival Senor Caboom would hit him with the giant cucumber and knock him down? Mr. Fee-Fi-Fo would always pick himself up, dust himself off and say, "I hurt my foo-foo."

(Mary again stifles a laugh. The others in the row glare at her.)

> I had plenty of pimples as a kid. One day I fell asleep in the library. When I woke up, a blind man was reading my face.
> —Rodney Dangerfield

"I'm sorry you saw me, Timmy. Now I'll have to kill you."

Life's a lot like that. From time to time we all fall down and hurt our foo-foo's.

(Mary again has to stifle a laugh. Other people turn to look at her.)

If only we could all deal with it as simply and bravely and honestly as Mr. Fee-Fi-Fo. And what did Chuckles ask in return? Not much—in his own words—"A little song, a little dance, a little seltzer down your pants."

(Mary has great difficulty in stifling herself here. Many people turn to look at her.)

(Looking right at Mary) Excuse me, young lady . . . yes you . . . would you stand up please?

(Mary, with no alternative, stands up.)

You feel like laughing, don't you?

Don't try to stop yourself. Go ahead, laugh out loud. Don't you see? Nothing could have made Chuckles happier. He lived to make people laugh. He found tears offensive, deeply offensive. He hated to see people cry. Go ahead, my dear—laugh.

(As Mary bursts into tears, we:)
Fade Out.

END OF ACT TWO

"Mrs. Hammond! I'd know you anywhere from little Billy's protrait of you."

Tag

Fade In:

Int. Mary's apartment—immediately following funeral

Mary, Lou, Murray, Georgette, Ted, and Sue Ann enter.

Mary: (*To Lou*) But I just felt so dumb standing there like that.

Lou: Mary, forget about it. Everybody else did. All in all it was a very nice funeral.

Georgette: Right. All's well that ends well . . .

Mary: Everybody just make yourself at home. I'll put some coffee on.

Georgette: You know. It's just the sort of funeral I would want.

Sue Ann: Not me. I want to be cremated and have my ashes thrown on Robert Redford.

Murray: What about you, Lou?

Lou: I don't want anybody to make any fuss. When I go, I just want to be stood outside in the garbage with my hat on.

Murray: What kind of funeral do you want, Mary?

Mary: Do we have to talk about this?

Sue Ann: C'mon, Mary, everyone else has.

Mary: Oh, I don't really care. I just don't want an organ playing sad music.

Murray: What do you want them to play—"Everything's Coming Up Roses"?

Ted: I'd like a real fancy funeral if I were going to die.

Lou: What do you mean "if"?

Ted: I'm not going to die.

Murray: Why not? How else are you going to be reunited with your brain?

Ted: No, I'm not going to die. See, I'm into this thing where if I ever get sick—real sick—like I'm about to go—they take me away and freeze me. Then, two or three hundred years from now when they find a cure for whatever it was that was wrong with me then they'll just unfreeze me.

Georgette: That's terrific, Ted. Maybe when you come back you won't complain so much about my cold feet.

Fade Out

THE END

It's no longer a question of staying healthy.

It's a question of finding a sickness you like.   —*Jackie Mason*

M.I.T. Graduate Qualifying Examination

Instructions   Read each question thoroughly. Answer all questions. Time limit—four hours. Begin immediately.

History   Describe the history of the papacy from its origins to the present day; concentrate especially but not exclusively on the social, political, economic, religious, and philosophical impact on Europe, Asia, America, and Africa. Be brief, concise, and specific.

Medicine   You have been provided with a razor blade, a piece of gauze, and a bottle of Scotch. Remove your own appendix. Do not suture until your work has been inspected. You have fifteen minutes.

Public Speaking   2,500 riot-crazed aborigines are storming the classroom. Calm them. You may use any ancient language except Latin or Greek.

Biology   Create life. Estimate the differences in subsequent human culture if this form of life had developed 500 million years earlier, with special attention to the probable effects on the English parliamentary system. Prove your thesis.

Music   Write a piano concerto. Orchestrate it and perform it with flute and drum. You will find a piano under your seat.

Psychology   Based on your knowledge of their works, evaluate the emotional stability, degree of adjustment, and repressed frustrations of each of the following: Alexander of Aphrodisias, Ramses II, Hammurabi. Support your evaluation with quotations from each man's work, making appropriate references. It is not necessary to translate.

Sociology   Estimate the sociological problems that might accompany the end of the world. Construct an experiment to test your theory.

Management Science   Define management. Define science. How do they relate? Why? Create a generalized algorithm to optimize all managerial decisions. Assuming an 1130 CPU supporting 50 terminals, each terminal to activate your algorithm, design the communications interface and all the necessary control programs.

Economics   Develop a realistic plan for refinancing the national debt. Trace the possible effects of your plan in the following areas: Cubism, the Donatist controversy, the wave theory of light. Outline a method from all points of view. Point out the deficiencies in your point of view, as demonstrated in your answer to the last question.

Political Science   There is a red telephone on the desk beside you. Start World War III. Report at length on its socio-political effects, it any.

Epistemology   Take a position for or against the truth. Prove the validity of your position.

Physics   Explain the nature of matter. Include in your answer an evaluation of the impact of the development of mathematics on science.

Philosophy   Sketch the development of human thought; estimate its significance. Compare with the development of any other kind of thought.

General Knowledge   Describe in detail. Be objective and specific.

DOONESBURY *Class Reunion by Garry Trudeau*

PETER CHERCHES
Problems

1. Johnny wants to buy a bicycle, which costs $200. He has only $120 in his savings account, but he knows of a way to earn the rest of the money he'll need for the bicycle: In his neighborhood there is a man who will pay $15 apiece to have certain individuals bumped off. Johnny goes to see the man, and that day he is given $45 and 3 names. He successfully pulls off all 3 murders, but somehow slips up and leaves a clue. The police catch him and he spends 3 years in a juvenile detention home. When he gets out he still has the money in his savings account and the $45 hit money, but due to inflation the cost of the bicycle has gone up.

    If the annual rate of inflation is 8%, and Johnny has been earning 5³/₄% interest on his savings account, compounded quarterly, how many more people will he have to kill before he can buy the bicycle?

2. Mr. Smith wants to get from Plainville to Anytown. He can take either the train, the bus, or a plane. The plane is the quickest way. The plane will take Mr. Smith from Plainville to Anytown in 2 hours. But the plane is the most expensive of the 3 choices. The plane costs $200. The cheapest way to get from Plainville to Anytown is by bus. The bus costs only $35. But the bus is also the slowest and least comfortable of the 3 choices. The bus takes 24 hours to get from Plainville to Anytown. The train, on the other hand, is relatively comfortable yet still moderately priced. The train costs $75 and gets from Plainville to Anytown in 15 hours. Mr. Smith decides to take the train.

    Mr. Smith kisses his wife in Plainville goodbye. Mr. Smith is going to Anytown to see his other wife. Mr. Smith is a bigamist. Mr. Smith has 2 wives.

    Mr. Smith leaves his house in Plainville at 2:00 P.M. His train leaves at 4:00 P.M. It takes Mr. Smith 45 minutes to get from his house to the train station. When he arrives at the train station Mr. Smith is propositioned by a hooker. Since he has some time to kill, and since he has saved $125 by taking the train instead of the plane, he decides to go with her. They go to the Paradise Motel, which is a 5 minute walk from the station. A room at the Paradise Motel costs $10, a room with a clean sheet costs $12. Mr. Smith gives the desk clerk $10. They get to the room and the hooker explains her schedule of fees. Her basic rate is $50, with an additional charge of $15 for "Greek," and she doesn't get into S & M. Mr. Smith decides to pay the extra money for Greek since neither of his 2 wives allow him that particular outlet. . . . After he is through he asks the hooker if she'll marry him. The hooker declines, explaining that she doesn't get involved with her clients.

Mr. Smith stays in the room with the hooker until 3:30, when he decides it is time to start heading back to the station. He gets to the station at 3:35 and is informed that his train will be 15 minutes late.

The train is actually 20 minutes late, and when it finally comes Mr. Smith gets on and takes a seat.

On the train Mr. Smith meets Miss Doe. They talk for 22 minutes, then Miss Doe tells Mr. Smith that she has a sleeper, which costs an extra $20, but that two can sleep as cheaply as one, as long as they're discreet. Mr. Smith, never one to pass up a bargain, goes with Miss Doe to her sleeper, an upper berth. They do not sleep.

The train pulls into Anytown the next morning at 7:20 A.M. Mr. Smith takes a cab from the station to his house in Anytown. The cab ride takes 18 minutes and costs $3.65, plus a 75¢ tip. When Mr. Smith enters his house he discovers that his wife is not there. She has left a note on the kitchen table explaining that she has turned gay and gone off to live with a woman in Plainville.

Where does that leave Mr. Smith?

3. Mr. Green has been working for Mr. Cod for 10 years. Mr. Green is upset that after working for the same outfit for 1 decade he earns only $3.50 an hour. Mr. Green has resented his employer for some time, but he has just now gotten up the courage to ask for a raise. Mr. Cod denies Mr. Green a raise on the grounds that he is retarded. When Mr. Green counters by saying that handicapped people deserve a liveable wage just like everybody else, Mr. Cod accuses him of ingratitude and fires him. Mr. Green, unable to face having to tell the bad news to his wife and 3 children, takes his own life by jumping off a bridge. Mr. Cod now has to find a replacement for Mr. Green, another token handicapped individual. He interviews people with all sorts of handicaps, but they all turn the job down based on 2 factors: 1. The job, which entails nothing more than the individual sitting in the firm's reception room wearing a placard that says: MR. COD HIRES THE HANDICAPPED, is wholly undignified, and 2. The pay is too low. Unable to find a bona fide handicapped person, Mr. Cod instead hires his cousin Phil, who is to all appearances completely normal, though he has been unemployed for 2 years. Mr. Cod offers Phil $3.25 an hour, which Phil gladly accepts since any wage, however small, is preferable to the indignity of unemployment. However, several months later, Phil learns that his predecessor had been paid at a higher rate. When he complains to Mr. Cod of this discrepancy, Mr. Cod explains that Mr. Green was retarded, and therefore was entitled to more money.

Assuming the validity of Mr. Cod's argument, what would Phil have to do to earn a raise?

LARRY SLOMAN & DAVE HANSON

The Yearning Annex
Greater Pittsburgh Edition

011 How to Successfully Own and Operate a Dehumidifier in Your Own Home

You've heard and read about the benefits of owning a dehumidifier—you may even have friends or loved ones who've owned one. Now, thanks to hands-on Yearning Annex workshop, you too can have the confidence and know-how to own and operate a dehumidifier in your home, and to live in the dehumidified comfort and luxury you've always dreamed of. You'll be instructed in the various methods and techniques of emptying and cleaning your dehumidifier, and we'll even help you establish a personal maintenance timetable. Don't miss this chance to learn about dehumidifiers, and to meet other people interested in household appliances.

Vic Barnes is a graduate of Mercy College. He has had two dehumidifiers operating simultaneously in his home for 11 years, and is the author of Coping with a Dehumidifier: A Guidebook for Singles and Couples. *Materials Fee $2.*

Downtown		Course fee $57
Sec. M____Mon. Nov. 2, 9, 16, 23, 30_____		5:30–9:30pm
Sec. N____Tue. Nov. 3, 10, 17, Dec. 1, 8____		5:30–9:30pm
Sec. O____Wed. Nov. 4, 11, 18, 25, Dec. 2___		5:30–9:30pm
Sec. P____Sat. Nov. 7, 14, 21, 28, Dec. 5___		5:30–9:30pm
Sec. Q____Sun. Nov. 8, 15, 22, 29, Dec. 6___		5:30–9:30pm

051 How to Tell Orientals Apart

Gone are the days when any of them was as good as another as long as you didn't lose your laundry ticket. Orientals have become a crucial part of today's business world, working right alongside many of us white people, and every motivated businessperson owes it to him or herself to acknowledge their individuality. With this Yearning Annex seminar you'll learn easily memorizable math formulas about the angles of eye slants, shades of yellow, height tables, and more, so you'll know who not to rehash memorable scenes from M*A*S*H with, who not to talk gleefully about Pearl Harbor with, and who will be most helpful when your calculator is on the fritz. And not only will you learn to distinguish nationalities, you'll learn to tell individuals from each other. You'll be able to tell the one from the second floor from the one down the hall, even if they're dressed the same. By the end of this fascinating seminar, you'll know Fong from Wong, Kim from Nim, Chin from Chan, and will your human resources department be proud of you!

Rod Horvath is a professor of variegation at Carnegie Mellon University and is the author of Different Shades of Yellow *and* Different Sizes of Wang.

Chinatown		Course fee $37
Sec. V____Tues. Dec. 1, 8, 15_____		7–9:30pm
Sec. W____Thurs. Dec. 3, 10, 17_____		7–9:30pm
Sec. X____Sat. Dec. 5, 12, 19_____		7–9:30pm

602 The Joys of Eastern Bloc Cuisine

You don't have to be a professional Eastern European chef to surprise your guests with exotic dishes of the Eastern bloc nations of Hungary, Bulgaria, Rumania, Czechoslovakia, and Poland. Under the guidance of Bulgarian master chef Lugamiv Bartok, once a personal chef to Leopold XVIII, you'll learn how to prepare mouth-watering dishes like blood pudding, brains in purple gravy, cabbage tarts, goat bucket soup, and the Czech version of pâté, a rich frothy mousse made from the marinated spleen of a musk ox. You'll sip a glass of Hglechz, the legendary Hungarian turnip-skin wine, while you watch Chef Lugamiv prepare Iron Curtain favorites like Bulgarian bowel cakes, jellied calves' feet, goatwurst, fungus derma, and a magical Rumanian casserole containing the entrails of animals not allowed in American zoos. And finally, you will sit down with your classmates and dine in northern Balkan splendor on these unique and sensuous delights. Bring your appetite, and $10 for materials fee.

Lugamiv Bartok was among Varna's most sought-after brothmeisters, having been declared a national treasure by the Bulgarian king in 1963. He came to America in 1976.

Midtown		Course fee $37
Sec. J____Thurs. Dec. 3, 10, 17_____		6:30–9:30pm
Sec. K____Fri. Dec. 4, 11, 18_____		6:30–9:30pm
Sec. L____Sat. Dec. 5, 12, 19_____		6:30–9:30pm
Sec. M____Mon. Dec. 7, 14, 21_____		6:30–9:30pm

222 Walking Crosstown

Maybe you're new in town. Maybe you just don't have occasion to walk crosstown that much. Maybe you're intimidated, maybe you don't have the necessary confidence. Chances are, if you don't walk crosstown, you're missing out on much of the splendor Pittsburgh has to offer. Well, now, for the first time, you'll be able to walk crosstown just like the cosmopolitan natives you see doing it with such ease and savvy. You'll go on an actual walk along Forbes Avenue and then swing up to Murray with Joel Medford, who has been walking across town in such major cities as Atlanta, Philadelphia, Dallas, and Boston for over 16 years. He'll peel away the mysteries of walking crosstown, take you behind the scenes as you walk across both odd- and even-numbered streets. You'll learn the safest routes and the best places to pause for coffee, clean telephones, and comfort stops. You'll see brownstones, family-owned delicatessens, and many, many people.

Joel Medford hosted the Cable TV special entitled Know Your Side Streets *and has written several pamphlets on the subject. He has walked crosstown in numerous cities and has been a resident of Pittsburgh for five years. Materials fee $3.*

Forbes & Vine		Course fee $37
Sec. M____Tues. Nov. 10, 17, 24_____		5–8:30pm
Sec. N____Wed. Nov. 4, 11, 18_____		5–8:30pm
Sec. O____Fri. Nov. 6, 13, 20_____		5–8:30pm

DOCTOR-LAWYER!

 FIRST OF A BOLD NEW BREED!

BY ED SUBITZKY

ORIGINS:

AT HARVARD IN 1968, A YOUNG MAN GRADUATES!

I CAN'T BELIEVE IT! A LIFELONG DREAM FULFILLED! HERE I STAND, A DOCTOR AT LAST, ABOUT TO EMBARK ON A SACRED CAREER OF HEALING... OF HELPING... OF EARNING...

DID YOU SAY "DOCTOR"?

WHY, THIS IS HARVARD LAW SCHOOL! YOU DON'T HAVE A DEGREE IN MEDICINE! THE MEDICAL SCHOOL IS ACROSS THE QUADRANGLE! SON, YOU'RE A LAWYER NOW!

NO WONDER THERE WERE NO BODIES TO DISSECT!

QUICKLY, HE CHECKS THE ALMANAC!

WHY... WHY... DOCTORS EARN 14% MORE THAN LAWYERS! DRAT... NOW I HAVE TO SPEND ANOTHER EIGHT YEARS IN MEDICAL SCHOOL!

HOW DO I GET ACROSS THE QUAD-RANGLE, ANYHOW?

EIGHT MORE YEARS LATER, THERE EMERGES A WHOLE NEW BREED OF PROFESSIONAL!

A MAN WITH THE EARNING POWER OF A DOCTOR AND A LAWYER COMBINED!

A MAN WHO, THROUGH GROSS INCOMPETENCE AND NEGLECT, CAN DESTROY HUMAN LIVES IN TWO ENTIRELY DIFFERENT WAYS!

A MAN SO MAGNETIC TO WOMEN THAT WHOLE SINGLES BARS DEVELOP WHEREVER HE WALKS!

BUT THIS IS THE APPLIANCE SECTION OF A DEPARTMENT STORE!

THUS WAS BORN DOCTOR-LAWYER! SOMEDAY, AS THE FIELDS OF MEDICINE AND LAW CONTINUE TO MERGE, THERE WILL BE MANY LIKE HIM! BUT FOR NOW THERE IS ONLY ONE, AND YOU ARE ABOUT TO WITNESS HIS TYPICAL GREATEST ADVENTURE OF THEM ALL THAT HAPPENS EVERY WORKDAY!

HEY, BUY YOU A DRINK?

BUY YOU A DRINK?

BUY YOU A DRINK?

THE NEXT DAY, ON THE SAME NEW YORK SIDEWALK

...AND HE DIED OF A MASSIVE CORONARY DUE TO YOUR TOTALLY INCOMPETENT DIAGNOSIS! I'M GOING TO FIND ME A GOOD LAWYER AND SUE YOU FOR MALPRACTICE! THIS IS EVEN BETTER THAN WINNING THE LOTTERY!

MY GOOD WOMAN, THERE'S NO NEED TO TROUBLE YOURSELF SEARCHING FOR ANYONE! YOU SEE, I'M A LAWYER TOO, AND I TAKE THE CASE!

WHAT'S MORE, I'LL DO IT FOR JUST 90% OF THE AWARD, IF ANY, PLUS EXPENSES!

BUY YOU A DRINK?

THE DAY OF THE TRIAL ARRIVES!

BAILIFF, BE SURE TO KEEP OUT ALL THE HORDES OF EAGER YOUNG WOMEN WHO WANT TO MARRY THIS MAN BEFORE THE TRIAL IS OVER!

YES SIR, YOUR HONOR!

AS A LAWYER, HE CALLS HIMSELF AS HIS FIRST WITNESS! HIS QUESTIONS FLY RAPIDLY, HARD-HITTING AND DIRECT!

AND WHAT MADE YOU DECIDE THAT A MASSIVE CORONARY WAS MERELY A CASE OF PASSIVE INDIGESTION?

AS A DOCTOR, HE ANSWERS TIMIDLY, BUT TO THE BEST OF HIS MEDICAL KNOWLEDGE!

HE JUST DIDN'T LOOK THAT SICK TO ME!

TELL ME, DID YOU TAKE ANY TESTS THAT WERE CONSISTENT WITH ACCEPTED CURRENT STANDARDS OF MEDICAL PRACTICE?

TEST HIM? LISTEN, I'M A DOCTOR, NOT A SCHOOLTEACHER!

DID YOU ATTEMPT TO OBSERVE THE PATIENT AFTERWARDS TO MAKE SURE YOUR DIAGNOSIS WAS CORRECT?

I WOULD HAVE, EXCEPT I WANTED TO BEAT THE LUNCH-HOUR CROWD AT THE BANK!

AS A LAWYER, HE ELOQUENTLY SUMS UP HIS CASE!

YOUR HONOR...

LADIES AND GENTLEMEN OF THE JURY...

THIS MAN IS OBVIOUSLY GROSSLY INCOMPETENT AND NEGLIGENT AND SIMPLE JUSTICE REQUIRES THAT YOU AWARD HIS INNOCENT VICTIM'S WIDOW THE FULL SUM OF $10,000,000!

AS A DOCTOR, HE GASPS!

WHY... THAT'S ALMOST ONE WEEK'S PAY!

AS A LAWYER, HE DECIDES ON A SUDDEN, LAST-MINUTE STRATEGIC MOVE... A GRANDSTAND FINALE THAT BRINGS A HUSH TO THE COURTROOM!

YOUR HONOR, BY LAW XV-407-6 OF THE SOVEREIGN STATE OF NEW YORK, I DEMAND THAT YOU INSTRUCT THE JURY THAT THEY HAVE NO LATITUDE BUT TO RULE IN FAVOR OF THE PLAINTIFF!

LAW XV-407-6 APPLIES TO AUTO THEFT! SINCE YOU'RE EVEN MORE INCOMPETENT AS A LAWYER THAN AS A DOCTOR, I RECOMMEND TO THE JURY THAT YOU LOSE AS LAWYER AND THEREFORE WIN AS DOCTOR!

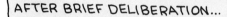
AFTER BRIEF DELIBERATION...

YOUR HONOR, WE WANT TO GET HOME IN TIME TO WATCH "DALLAS" RERUNS, SO WE CONCUR!

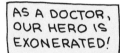
AS A DOCTOR, OUR HERO IS EXONERATED!

ANOTHER GREAT VICTORY FOR MODERN MEDICINE!

THEN, AS A LAWYER...

SINCE YOU LOST, I GUESS THE LAUGH'S ON YOU! YOU GET 90% OF NOTHING!

UH, THERE IS THIS LITTLE MATTER OF EXPENSES...

OH, MY LATE HUSBAND'S BROTHER, AL, WILL PAY FOR THEM!

CERTAINLY!

DOCTOR-LAWYER AGAIN WHIPS OUT HIS LIGHTNING-SPEED BILL PAD...

YOUR COOPERATION IS APPRECIATED IN UNDERSTANDING THAT PAYMENT IS REQUIRED AT THE TIME SERVICES ARE RENDERED!

GULP! THIS AMOUNT... IT CAN'T BE...

WHY NOT? MY COLLEGE EDUCATION WAS CERTAINLY PART OF MY EXPENSES, WASN'T IT?

GASP!

AL! WHAT'S WRONG!

THIS SUDDEN PAIN IN MY CHEST! IT FEELS LIKE A THUNDERING HERD OF ELEPHANTS STAMPEDING OVER ME!

SOMEONE GET A DOCTOR, QUICK!

BUT I'M A DOCTOR, SIR! HARVARD '76!

WHAT'S THE MATTER WITH ME, DOC?

WHY, NOTHING TO WORRY ABOUT! IT'S OBVIOUSLY JUST A LITTLE INDIGESTION! PROBABLY THE TENSION OF THE TRIAL! TAKE TWO ASPIRINS AND YOU'LL FEEL A LOT BETTER IN THE MORNING!

THANKS, DOC! WHAT A RELIEF!

AND SO DOCTOR-LAWYER'S TYPICAL GREATEST ADVENTURE COMES TO AN END! OR DOES IT? THAT HAS TO AWAIT ANOTHER EPISODE— AND ANOTHER DAY'S WORK!

PHILIP ROTH
Doctor Schmuck

Sherman gets a call from his doctor with the results of his blood test.

"I've got bad news and some worse news," says the doctor. "The bad news is that you've only got twenty-four hours to live."

"Oh, no," says Sherman. "That's terrible. How can it get any worse than that?"

"I've been trying to reach you since yesterday."

Pianist! Oh, that's one of the words they just love, almost as much as *doctor*, Doctor. And *residency*. And best of all, *his own office. He opened his own office in Livingston.* "Do you remember Seymour Schmuck, Alex?" she asks me, or Aaron Putz or Howard Shlong, or some yo-yo I am supposed to have known in grade school twenty-five years ago, and of whom I have no recollection whatsoever. "Well, I met his mother on the street today, and she told me that Seymour is now the biggest brain surgeon in the entire Western Hemisphere. He owns six different split-level ranch-type houses made all of fieldstone in Livingston, and belongs to the boards of eleven synagogues, all brand-new and designed by Marc Kugel, and last year with his wife and his two little daughters, who are so beautiful that they are already under contract to Metro, and so brilliant that they should be in college—he took them all to Europe for an eighty-million-dollar tour of seven thousand countries, some of them you never even heard of, that they made them just to honor Seymour, and on top of that, he's so important, Seymour, that in every single city in Europe that they visited he was asked by the mayor himself to stop and do an impossible operation on a brain in hospitals that they also built for him right on the spot, and—listen to this—where they pumped into the operating room during the operation the theme song from *Exodus* so everybody should know what religion he is—and that's how big your friend Seymour is today! *And how happy he makes his parents!*"

"This, Mr. Carlisle, is what we found lodged in your skull."

Your witness.

"Objection."

LAWYER JOKES

A man asked a lawyer what his fee was.

"I charge $50 for three questions," the lawyer replied.

"That's awfully steep, isn't it?" the man asked.

"Yes," replied the lawyer. "Now what's your final question?"

Why was the shipwrecked lawyer allowed to swim safely through shark-infested waters?
Professional courtesy.

A lawyer arrives at the Pearly Gates and is greeted by St. Peter.

"There must be some mistake," says the lawyer. "I'm only fifty-four. I'm too young to die."

"That's odd," says St. Peter. "Because according to your time sheets, you're eighty-nine."

Why is it that California has the most lawyers and New Jersey has the most toxic waste dumps?
New Jersey had first choice.

The gate breaks down between heaven and hell. St. Peter comes to examine the damage, and then he calls the devil. "That darn gate broke again," he says. "It's your turn to fix it."

"Forget it," says the devil. "My people are too busy."

"But we had a deal," says St. Peter, "and if you don't honor it, I'll have to sue you for breach of contract."

The devil laughs. "Sure you will. And just where do you expect to find a lawyer?"

Insurance Claim #233

Dear Sirs:

I am writing in response to your request for additional information. In block #8 on the accident form, I put "Trying to do the job alone" as the major cause of my accident.

You said in your letter that you needed a more detailed report, and I trust the following will be sufficient.

I am an air conditioning/heating service person by trade. On the date of the accident, I was working alone on the roof of a new six-story building.

When I completed my work, I found that I still had about 500 pounds of tools on the roof. Rather than carry these tools down six flights of stairs by hand, I then decided to lower them from the roof in a barrel by rope and pulleys.

Securing the rope at ground level, I then went up to the roof and swung the barrel out and loaded the tools into the barrel. Then I went back down to ground level and untied the rope, holding it tightly to insure a slow descent of the 500 pounds of tools.

You will note in block #11 of the accident report that I weigh 135 pounds. You can imagine my surprise when suddenly I was jerked off the ground, lost my presence of mind, and forgot to let go of the rope.

Needless to say, I proceeded at a rather alarming rate up the side of the building. In the vicinity of the third floor, I met the barrel coming down the side of the building. This will explain the fractured skull and broken collarbone.

Slowed only slightly, I continued my rapid ascent, not stopping until my knuckles on my right hand were buried two inches deep into the pulley.

Fortunately at this time, I regained my presence of mind and was able to hold onto the rope in spite of the pain.

At approximately the same time, the barrel hit the ground and the bottom fell out of the barrel, dumping the tools into a pile on the ground.

With the barrel now empty—and again I refer you to the block #11 on my weight—I began a rapid descent down the side of the building.

Again in the vicinity of the third floor, I met the barrel coming up. This will explain the two fractured ankles and lacerations on my legs.

When I hit the barrel, it slowed me down enough so that when I fell on the tools, I only sustained three broken vertebrae in my back.

I am sorry to report that as I lay on the ground in pain, I again lost my presence of mind and let go of the rope. The barrel came down and broke my hip.

I hope that this is sufficient information for the insurance company. Please send the check to me.

MORE LAWYER JOKES

Two scientists are discussing their latest research in behavior modification.

"We've started something new," said the first man. "For some of our more dangerous experiments, we've started using lawyers."

"Lawyers?" says his colleague. "We've always used rats. I've never heard of using lawyers."

"Well, you know how it is," says his friend. "You get so attached to rats."

What's the difference between a dead snake lying in the road and a dead lawyer lying in the road?

There are skid marks in front of the snake.

How can you tell when a lawyer is lying?

His lips are moving.

Two lawyers are having a drink after work. "The most amazing thing happened to me last night," said the first one. "I was working, and suddenly the devil was standing before me, right there in my office! He told me that in exchange for my soul, I could become a United States Senator!"

"Great!" says his friend. "But what's the catch?"

HEY! NO PROBLEM!

© 1987 M. Stevens

LIFE WITHOUT LAWYERS

Drawing by Gahan Wilson. Reproduced by special permission of *Playboy* Magazine; © 1971 by *Playboy*.

MARSHALL BRICKMAN
The Analytic Napkin

Recent work by Frimkin and Eliscu has brought to light valuable new material about the origin and development of the analytic napkin. It is not generally realized outside of psychoanalytic circles that the placement by the analyst of a small square of absorbent paper at the head of the analysand's chair or couch at the start of each session is a ritual whose origins are rooted in the very beginnings of analysis, even predating the discovery of infant sexuality. Indeed, references to a "sticky problem" ("*eines Entführung bezitsung*") appear as early as 1886, in a letter the young Freud wrote to his mentor Breuer:

I am convinced that "hysterical symptoms," so-called, are nothing but the emergence of long-buried psycho-neurotic conflicts [bezitsunger Entführung]. Does that sound crazy? More important, how can I keep the back of the patient's chair from becoming so soiled [ganz geschmutzig]? They come in, they put their heads back—one week and already my upholstery has a spot the size of a Sacher Torte.

With warm regards,
FREUD

Breuer's reply is not known, of course, because of the curious manner in which he conducted his correspondence. (Breuer was unreasonably afraid that samples of his handwriting might fall into the hands of his "many powerful enemies"; therefore, upon receiving a letter, he would carefully draft a reply, take it to the addressee's home, read it aloud to him, and then tear it to shreds. He claimed that this behavior saved him a fortune in postage, although Mrs. Breuer opined that her husband's head was lined with "wall-to-wall kugel.") Breuer's only public statement on the napkin question was made during a demonstration of hypnosis, when he remarked that "a patient in a trance can be induced to stand on his feet for an entire treatment and never know the difference."

It is perhaps ironic—or, as Ernest Jones put it, "not ironic at all"—that the napkin problem should have emerged at a time when the anti-macassar was attaining universal acceptance by the East European intelligentsia. Freud, however, abhorred simplistic solutions, and sought more profound answers. Failing to find these, he sought more complicated questions. In any event, he rejected the use of antimacassars as "Victorian, confining, and repressive—everything I am fighting against. Besides, they are too bumpy." The extent of the problem, however, can be inferred from a perusal of Freud's professional expenses incurred for April, 1886, his first month of private practice:

WAITING ROOM

3 coat hooks @ 5 kreuzer	15 kr.
2 chairs @ 20 gulden	40 fl.
1 ashtray	8 kr.
16 issues *Viennese Life* magazine, 1861–77 period	2 fl., 8 kr.
1 framed Turner reproduction, "Cows in a Field"	16 fl.

CONSULTING ROOM

3 doz. medium-hard pencils	18 kr.
9 writing tablets, unlined, in "easy-eye green"	2 fl., 14 kr.
Certificates & diplomas, framing and mounting	7 fl.
"Complete Works of Goethe" (18 vols.)	40 fl.
"Works of Nietzsche" (abridged, 20 vols.)	34 fl.
"Simple Card Tricks You Can Do" (pocket edition)	20 kr.
1 clock	8 fl.
Dry-cleaning and spotting upholstery	240 fl.

"At this rate," Freud wrote to Koller, "every neurasthenic I treat this year should set me back in the neighborhood of four hundred gulden.

The Pope dies and goes to heaven. As he enters the gates, he sees a sign explaining that everybody there will be treated equally, without regard to his position on earth. The Pope smiles. He's a modest man, and this, he thinks, is just as it should be.

Later, as he is standing in line at the cafeteria, a man in a white coat with a stethoscope hanging out of his pocket suddenly cuts in front of him and grabs a tray.

The Pope is horrified. He rushes over to St. Peter and points to the offender. "I don't understand," he says, "I thought everyone was supposed to be equal."

"Oh, don't worry about *him*," says St. Peter. "That's God, and every now and then he thinks he's a doctor."

Pretty soon, *I'll* be needing some treatment, eh? Ha, ha." On the advice of Charcot, Freud had his housekeeper apply a solution of nux vomica and lye to his consulting chair after each session—a remedy that was hastily abandoned when a patient, Theo F., brought a legal complaint of massive hair loss directly traceable to consultations with the young neurologist. Freud managed to mollify the unfortunate man with a sampler of marzipan and a warm fur hat, but his reputation in Vienna had been shaken.

The early practitioners of psychoanalysis devised artful stopgap solutions to the problem of the napkin. For a time, Jung met his patients at a furniture store, where, under the pretext of inspecting a couch, he would conduct an analytic session. After fifty minutes, patient and doctor would depart, Jung explaining to the salesman that they wanted to "shop around a little more." By contrast, Ferenczi required his patients to lie face down on the consulting couch—a procedure that eliminated all stains but a small nose smudge. However, the patients' constant mumblings into the upholstery caused Ferenczi to become enraged, and he finally abandoned this technique. Klein, claiming that he was only trying to "lighten up" what was "an already dreary enough business," asked his patients to wear cone-shaped party hats during their session hours. The real reason, of course, was to protect Klein's couch, a flamboyant chesterfield covered in pale-lemon bombazine.

Freud launched his own systematic research program by scouring Vienna for fabric samples, which he placed on the upper portion of his couch, a different sample being assigned to each patient. One case, that of a man who was analyzed on a folded barbecue apron, became the subject of an extended monograph of Freud's on hallucinations and

hysteria. The apron had been presented to Freud by Charcot, and bore the legend *"König von die Küche"* ("King of the Kitchen"). An apparently severe olfactory hallucination (old cabbage) reported by the patient during his analysis eventually proved to have its source in the apron, and Freud was forced to withdraw his paper. To conceal his disappointment, he invited the man to a coffeehouse, but at the last moment changed his mind and instead sent Adler to meet him. Unfortunately, Adler became distracted in the process of flattening kreuzer on the trolley tracks and arrived a day late. (This episode was often referred to sarcastically by Freud, and provided the basis for the later break between him and Adler.)

In a series of unattended lectures (May, 1906), Freud crystallized the need for a resolution of the "sofa problem," as he termed it. "Something small and protective, yet flexible," he wrote in his notes, "ought to be placed beneath (or possibly wrapped around) the patient's head. Perhaps a small rug or some sort of cloth." It was several decades before the notion of a napkin would surface, but during a summer visit to Manchester, England, during which Freud presented his half-sister with a bookend, he purchased a bolt of Japanese silk, which he sent to Vienna and caused to be cut up into small squares. The new material seemed to be working admirably, until an unexpected occurrence shattered his illusions. From his notebook:

OCTOBER 8. Especially crisp fall day. Treating Otto P., a petty official of the Bureau of Wursts. Classic psycho-neurosis: inability either to go to sleep or remain awake. Patient, while recounting significant dream, thrashed about on the couch. Because of the extremely cool climate, extensive static electricity caused the silk to cling to the patient's hair when he rose to leave at the end of the session. Analytic propriety, plus the delicacy of the transference, prevented me from mentioning the situation and I merely bade him good day.

Upon reaching home, Otto P. was mortified to find a square of cloth adhering to the back of his head, and he publicly accused Freud of insensitiveness and willful japery. An anti-Semitic journalist claimed that Freud had attempted to impose his own ethnic customs on a patient. The outcry raged for months, severely taxing Freud's energies, and only after it had abated could he enter in his journal, with wry insight: "Clearly, silk is not the answer—unless perhaps it is first dampened."

Freud's tentative moves in the direction of an all-purpose analytic napkin inspired others to ponder the matter. At the Weimar Congress, Bleuler called for a standardization of napkin technique. A lively debate ensued, with a variety of shapes, sizes, and materials finding ready champions. Abraham favored classical antimacassars, while Jung was partial to jute placemats, which he imported from a private source in Africa. The purist Holtz (it was he who in 1935 criticized Freud for not being Freudian enough) ridiculed the whole notion of a napkin and advocated "six couches, to be changed daily, like underwear." Liebner, who detested Holtz, suggested that the material of the napkin vary with

A man who is in the hospital to have his gangrene-infected leg amputated wakes up after the operation.

"How'm I doing?" he asks the doctor.

"Well," the doctor replies, **"I've got bad news and good news. The bad news is that we took off the wrong leg."**

"I can't believe it," says the patient. **"What's the good news?"**

"The other leg is getting better."

I called my doctor last week. I told him, ''Doc, I swallowed a bottle of sleeping pills.'' He told me to have a few drinks and get some rest.

—Rodney Dangerfield

the patient's complaint; Freud then recalled that he had had no success in treating the celebrated "Wolf Man" until he tried a scrap of terry cloth, to which the patient developed a massive transference. In a culminating speech at Weimar, Freud outlined his vision of the ideal solution: "Hygienic, disposable, inexpensive, and without any referential value whatsoever. I dream of a totally affect-less napkin that every analyst can afford."

Freud's experimental early napkins (many of which are still in private collections) show this drive toward simplicity and clarity—swatches of wool, gabardine, madras, burlap, and unbleached muslin, and, finally, a double layer of cheesecloth. He was making notes on the use of blotting paper when the Anschluss forced him to leave for London. Later that week in Vienna, the Nazis publicly burned most of his napkin file, including an irreplaceable sampler knitted by Lionel Walter, the Baron Rothschild.

The enormous current popularity of psychoanalysis in the United States is easily explained by the napkin historian. American technological know-how, plus the easy availability of materials, provided the answer Freud and his early disciples searched for but never found. In 1946, after extensive research at Mount Sinai Hospital, a team of pillow scientists at the Kimberly-Clark paper company test-marketed a prototype napkin in the analytic communities of Boston, New York, and Los Angeles. It was a double-ply, semi-absorbent, bleached-wood-fibre product, with a forty-per-cent rag content and an embossed edge. The response was overwhelming, and the course of psychoanalysis was forever altered. As Dr. Neimann Fek said, expressing the gratitude of his colleagues, "It took seventy years before we perfected the beard and the fee. Now, finally, the napkin. No one need ever be crazy again."

MARTIN MULL & ALLEN RUCKER
On the Couch

Jerry Butts, forty-three, had a problem. Since the age of sixteen, he had been plagued by a persistent nightmare that he couldn't shake. It was always the same: he is walking down the produce aisle at his local Safeway, stark naked. He knows people are laughing, but he doesn't know why. He keeps shopping as if nothing's wrong. A long-legged high school girl in gym shorts stops and asks about strawberries, but he's too tongue-tied to answer, so he snickers and leaves. He finally decides to make a mad rush for the parking lot, leaving his groceries behind, when suddenly a very fat woman blocks his way through the turnstile. She grabs him and starts to kiss and fondle him passionately. He's getting very aroused. People start gathering around, pointing at his privates and taking pictures. He's now stuck between the fat lady and the throng of shoppers. He starts to howl like a sick dog. Suddenly the fat lady turns into a chicken. He grabs her by the legs and runs out the door. The Safeway goes up in a fiery blaze, and Jerry wakes up in a cold sweat.

Jerry decided to seek professional help.

Doctor: Do you spell that with one or two Ts, Mr. Butts?
Jerry: One, I mean *two*, Dr. Steele, but what does that have to do with my dream?
Doctor: Just getting my records straight, Jerry, no cause for alarm.
Jerry: You know, I don't believe in this head-shrinking malarkey, Doc. I want you to know that right up front. I never have and I never will. It's too fuzzy around the edges. So don't try to provoke me and get me to say something sick about my mother, because I won't buy it. I don't know why I'm here, really. I just figured that after twenty-seven years of the same dream I should find some way to flush it out of my system, you know what I mean? I sure could never bring it up with my wife. She'd think it was about her weight problem.
Doctor: Your wife has a weight problem?
Jerry: No, she's just fat, I'm the one with the problem! [laughing] Just kidding. Listen, she's a wonderful mother and a great cook, and I wouldn't trade her for the world. Hey, I'm no prize, either. Let's just leave her out of this, okay?
Doctor: Sure, Jerry, if it's too painful to talk about . . .
Jerry: There you go again, putting words into my mouth. I didn't say anything about "painful"! Cecilia wasn't even around when I first had this godawful dream and anyway, she's no heave-o like the chicken-lady in the checkout line. You're grasping at straws, Doc, you're pitching horseshoes in the dark . . .

After twelve years of therapy my psychiatrist said something that brought tears to my eyes. He said, "No bablo ingles."
—Ronnie Shakes

"Lipshitz, go in for Kaplan."

Doctor: Jerry, psychoanalysis is an inexact science . . .

Jerry: You're telling me.

Doctor: Jerry, why are you sweating?

Jerry: Because I know what you're going to ask next.

Doctor: What do you suspect?

Jerry: Oh, something like . . . [mimicking Doctor] "Jerry, do you find your wife repulsive? Jerry, how often do you masturbate? Jerry, did your mother ever catch you? Did you like it?"

Doctor: Is that what you want to talk about, Jerry?

Jerry: Not on your life! That's none of your business. Your business is this cockamamy dream. Just work a little of your mumbo jumbo on that pesky heap of dung so I can get out of here in one piece!

Doctor: Okay, fine. Jerry, let's talk about chickens. Are you a pet lover? I mean, in the traditional sense? Have you ever owned a pet?

Jerry: Yes.

Doctor: A chicken?

Jerry: A dog.

Doctor: I see.

Jerry: You can't keep a chicken in the city.

Doctor: But you'd like to if you could. Is that what you're telling me?

Jerry: There you go again. I'm telling you I have a dog. That's all. Does that make me a psycho?

Doctor: Of course it doesn't. What's the dog's name?

"It was horrible," the man was telling his psychiatrist. "I was in Brazil on business, and I wired my wife that I'd be back a day early. I rushed home from the airport and found her in bed with my best friend. I don't get it. How could she do this to me?"

"Well," said the psychiatrist after a long pause, "maybe she didn't get your telegram!"

A grain salesman is driving to his next appointment when he looks out his car window and sees a three-legged chicken running parallel to his car. The car is going forty miles per hour, but somehow the chicken is keeping up. When the salesman speeds up to fifty, the chicken speeds up with him.

The amazed salesman starts going sixty, but there's the chicken, still beside him, and not even breathing hard. The salesman is about to speed up yet again when the chicken suddenly takes off and disappears in a cloud of dust.

The astonished salesman immediately slows down and pulls over to the side. He finds the farmer and says, "You won't believe what happened to me. I was doing sixty on this road and a three-legged chicken passed me like I was standing still!"

"Oh, yeah, I know all about it," says the farmer. "That chicken belongs to me. You see, there's three of us—myself, my wife, and little Davey, and whenever Louise serves chicken for dinner, we all want a drumstick. The only solution we could think of was to start raising three-legged chickens."

"That's remarkable," says the salesman. "How do they taste?"

"I don't really know," says the farmer. "We've never been able to catch one."

Jerry: I call her Chicken.

Doctor: I'm gonna write this down, Jerry. It might be a problem. Tell me your feelings about Chicken.

Jerry [agitated]: Now, that really ticks me off! To come here and pay you a hundred and fifty dollars and have you sit there and accuse me of having unnatural thoughts about my dog, now that's the last straw . . .

Doctor: Jerry, please, calm down, you misunderstood . . .

Jerry: The hell I misunderstood! You've been driving at this the whole time. First you make fun of my name, like everyone in high school did *every day,* then you pick on my wife for a while, making her out to be a worthless sack of potatoes, then you start in on my love of dogs. Next you'll probably go after the fact that I've never been in a fistfight and that once in Chicago a man pinched my wife on the butt and I just walked real fast the other way and that I'm stuck in a boring job at the post office and take orders from a black woman and will never be my own boss and see myself as a wimp and a jerk that will never get to Europe, never be able to afford a big-screen TV, and will always cut a wide berth around the produce section of any major supermarket. That's it, isn't it? That's how you have me pegged. Well, I'll tell you something, Herr Doctor, I may not be a superman like Sylvester Stallone or George Bush, but I'm no Charlie Manson, either. I can live without big-screen TV and fresh produce, and there's nothing wrong with me that a little talking-to-the-mirror can't handle, so get off my case, okay?

Doctor: Mr. Butts, I think you're right. I think you just cured yourself. Sure, we could dance around that butt-pinching incident for a while, but if that's as scary as it gets, you're not headed for the funny farm, I assure you. Next time you see that fat lady in the dream, give her a big hug back. Maybe the chicken will run away and you can finish your shopping.

Jerry: That's it? One session and I'm cured? I thought I'd be sitting here moaning and groaning for the rest of my life! A guy down at the office, Butch Jenkins, got drunk one night and told me he'd been seeing a shrink for nine fuckin' years and still can't get over the habit of sending naked pictures of his wife to *Hustler* magazine. Boy, he ought to come see you.

Doctor: Good idea. Be sure he brings the pictures.

Jerry: No problem. I've seen 'em, they're good. Listen, to change the subject, I *do* find my wife repulsive and . . .

Doctor: Sorry, time's up. Read my book.

FROM THE TOURNAMENT OF NEUROSES PARADE .

The "I Never Really Broke Away From My Parents" Float

The "In My Mind's Eye, I Will Always Be a Fat, Short, Frizzy-Haired, Glasses-and-Braces-Wearing Sixth Grader" Float

The "People Who Have Difficulty Forming Bonds of Intimacy with Other People" Float

The "I Only Want What Is Unattainable" Float

The "Hypochondria" Float

The "Fear of Chickens" Float

PROS AND CONS 115

MARSHALL BRICKMAN
The Kentish Sleep Journal

Sleep—along with its counterpart, being awake—accounts for much of the time spent by modern man during his life, and therefore merits serious attention by the trained observer. Certainly the most fascinating document to emerge from the burgeoning sleep-research field is the journal kept by Dr. Mordecai Kentish during a classic experiment in which he stayed awake for more than three hundred hours in order to study the effects of extensive sleep deprivation. Dr. Kentish, Winkle Professor of Clinical Psychology at Tony's College, Chicago, won the Nobel Prize in 1948 for his work in isolating and defining the common nap as "any rest episode up to twenty minutes' duration involving unconsciousness but not pajamas." He also pioneered the "Kentish Technique" of psychoanalysis, in which either the patient or the therapist gets to lie on the couch, depending on which of the two is sleepier. He is the author of the standard text "Sleep" and the widely known treatise on insomnia "How to Sleep," plus a third volume, "Where to Sleep," a thoughtful rating of motels found along the major interstate arteries, which includes an appendix listing inexpensive restaurants and the locations of important historical markers.

We would like to express our thanks to Mabley Kentish for releasing the Kentish papers for publication only months after her brother's experiments were so tragically interrupted, when he was carried off by a large bird. Selected portions of the Sleep Journal follow.

FIRST DAY (12 hours): Arrived at laboratory 9 P.M. Bucholtz [Kentish's devoted assistant, O. Bucholtz, a refugee who worked for Kentish for twelve years without remuneration of any kind, and with only one two-day vacation, which he spent walking around in the front yard] as usual leaves a mess—candy wrappers, a banana peel on the EEG, a half-filled container of coffee with a cigarette butt floating in it. Nevertheless, there can be no question of dismissing him; he is pathetically devoted to me, perhaps because of that time I let him watch me shave. The current record for sleeplessness is held by radio personality Galen Moon, the host of a telephone show, who remained awake for the entire two hundred hours required to take an irate call from a severe stutterer. (Moon, a noted insomniac, later revealed to me that even after his excruciating ordeal he could not fall asleep without first browsing through an article entitled "Cairo—Whither the New Agrarianism?," a soporific published every Sunday in the magazine section of the New York *Times*.) My intention is to exceed Moon's limit by at least one-third, utilizing no stimulants or artificial means whatsoever—nothing but the awesome powers of a disciplined intellect. At the end of each entry, as daily proof of my ability to sustain rational, sequential thought, I shall perform a simple test, by writing out the complete alphabet. Thus:

abcdefghijklmnopqrstuvwxyz

SECOND DAY (38 hours): Pulse, respiration, temperature, and blood pressure normal. A mild elation accompanied by great mental clarity. Chess with Bucholtz; a carefully laid trap of my own design (Ruy Lopez, with a slashing bishop attack) had the fool mated in seven moves. Intake: Breakfast—coffee and a scone with honey. Lunch—Bibb lettuce *rémoulade*. Dinner—butterfish and a praline. Physical coordination excellent; I jumped two feet straight up into the air without bending my knees—a difficult enough feat for a young man, and certainly remarkable for an advanced sedentary specimen such as myself. Wonderful feeling of crispness and efficiency. Three times eight is twenty-four. The cube root of eight is two. The capital of Chile is Santiago.

abcdefghijklmnopqrstuvwxyz
abcdefghijklmnopqrstuvwxyz
abcdefghijklmnopqrstuvwxyz

FIFTH DAY (109 hours): Sensation of mild granulation around the eyeballs, as if a small boy had flung pulverized antimony into my face. Pulse, temperature, respiration, blood pressure normal. (Annoying relative term, "normal." For whom?) In Bucholtz's case, temperature, pressure, respiration, and blood pressure can all be expressed by one integer in the low fifties. Chess with Bucholtz. Irresponsibly sacrificed my queen, both knights, both bishops, and all pawns within first thirteen moves; nevertheless managed to achieve stalemate by sending

Jung and Restless

Bucholtz on a brief errand, during which time I flushed his king down the toilet. The frontiers of the mind are limitless. The cube root of eight is *not* two; it is something else, possibly the color red.

abcdefghijklmnopqrstuvwxyz

SIXTH DAY (150 hours): No noticeable fatigue. Curious perceptual distortions, however. Everyday objects (i.e., my right hand, a chair) seem either too large or too small, but I cannot decide which. Chess with Bucholtz discontinued when I realized after twenty minutes that we had set up the pieces without the board and were playing directly on the table. Intake: Breakfast—coffee, scone. Dinner—butterfish and a slice of whole-wheat bread. Read article by Karsky in *International Journal of Orthopsychology,* on jealousy in moths. Difficult to follow, as the entire text apparently consists of the word "vibescu" repeated endlessly. These behaviorists will stoop to any cheap trick merely to publish. I am on to Karsky, which explains why he never speaks to me even though we have never met and he lives in Omsk.

abcdefgz

EIGHTH DAY (182 hours): Curious feeling of constriction in the frontal lobe, as if someone had forced a tiny cast-iron opera hat onto my head with a wooden mallet. Today, for the first time in our long association, Bucholtz made a witty remark. When I asked him if there were any telephone messages for me, he replied, "No, the phone hasn't rung all day." (!) He is unbearably funny; the juxtaposition of "all day"—i.e., the *entire day*—with the notion of the telephone *not ringing* was, I thought, a masterful stroke of ironic hyperbole, worthy of Goethe and especially remarkable in someone who still needs help dressing. When I finally caught my breath, I requested that he close the door, which he did in a similarly comical fashion, putting his hand on the knob and pushing the entire structure until it latched. Again I broke into gales of laughter (it was marvellous, really), which Bucholtz mocked (also amusingly) by looking at me directly *with both eyes!* He is quite a jolly fellow, this Bucholtz.

a b 3 defg hijklmnop p ppp

NINTH DAY (231 hours): Intake: Breakfast—cofscone. The fork is the one with the little points on it; the spoon, however, is round. That is how you can tell them apart. Temperature erutarepmet. Window open 3½ inches, chair oriented along N–S magnetic lines of force, thus enabling me to draw energy from the earth and maintain a healthy, full head of hair. All else normal, except for Bucholtz's plot to steal my face and sell it to the emperor. I have the persistent impression that a man named Al Bender possesses infinite knowledge, if we can only locate him and get him to talk. My brain remains miraculously alert. Some trouble, however, with the pancreas, which has been stealing catnaps. Thank God for the kidneys, which keep it awake with their constant bickering.

abz

> Scientists have found the gene for shyness. They would have found it years ago, but it was hiding behind a couple of other genes.
>
> —Jonathan Katz

NINTH DAY (234 hours): 4 A.M. Bucholtz asleep in the next room. The clock has just asked for a glass of water. Reasonable enough, but what is "water"? Increasing difficulty concentrating on simple tasks, such as snapping my luncheon peas across the room at Bucholtz. The dog outside has become a distraction, with its constant barking of "Iolanthe," but when I try to call the authorities, the phone bursts into flame. What would Lysenko say about this? And to whom would he say it? I understand "vibescu" now; Karsky is clearly a genius. Dear, dear Karsky! Misunderstood, ridiculed, mocked. And to think I almost mailed him a spider! I must go to him. I need paper to build a boat.

a bee cee dee eff gee aitch I jay

TWELFTH DAY (301 hours): Still no fatigue. Temperature 99°. Skies fair. Winds calm. Position 28°S by 188°W. The mate have eat of a tainted Gouda and muft be lafhed to the mizzen. Difpleasure on the foredeck, water maggoty. Three more given up to scurvey. May God help us in our tryalle.

At this point, the journal stops abruptly. Bucholtz, on awakening, reported finding his mentor rigid, his forehead against the light switch, his body making a hypotenuse between floor and wall. His eyes were open and unblinking, his pulse 180, his temperature 50°F. Removed to the hospital, Kentish was given a strong sedative and put to sleep for a week, after which he awoke refreshed and ate an enormous breakfast, including two paper cups. His notes, bearing extensive tooth marks, were recovered by O. Bucholtz and presented to Mabley Kentish, who will publish them this fall in popular edition, under the title "Copping Zs—Forty Winks to Oblivion."

BOB & RAY

Mr. Science

Ray: Now, as a public service paid for by the Philanthropic Council to Make Things Nicer, we invite you to spend another educational session with the idol of the nation's youngsters—Mr. Science. As we look in on the modern, well-equipped laboratory today, we see that little Johnny Schwab is just arriving to watch Mr. Science perform his latest fascinating experiment.

(Sound: Door slam)

Mr. Science: Oh, hello there, Jimmy. You're just in time to watch me perform my latest fascinating experiment.

Jimmy: Gee willikers, Mr. Science. I'm always fascinated by your fascinating experiments. Which one are you going to perform today?

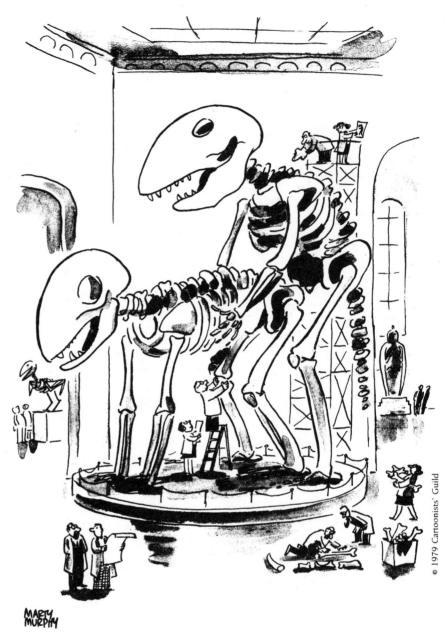

"You realize, Professor, that if this turns out to be some kind of hoax, we'll be the laughingstock of the whole archeology community."

Mr. Science: Well, Jimmy, today we're going to observe what happens when we boil water right here in the laboratory.

Jimmy: Great day in the morning, Mr. Science! . . . I don't understand what you're talking about.

Mr. Science: Well, it's really not as complicated as it sounds. You see, each chemical property has its own particular temperature point at which it changes from a liquid to a gas. And loosely defined, steam is the form of gaseous vapor that water is converted into when we heat it to 212 degrees.

Jimmy: Holy mackerel, Mr. Science. I don't understand that even worse than what you said the first time.

Einstein dies and goes to heaven. "I'm terribly sorry," says St. Peter, "but your suite isn't quite ready, so you'll have to spend a week in our temporary housing."

Arriving at the dorm, Einstein finds that he'll be sharing his room with four other men.

"Hello," he says to the first one. "I'm Albert Einstein."

"Glad to meet you," he replied. "By the way, my I.Q. is a hundred and eighty."

"Is that right?" says Einstein. "Then we'll be able to discuss quantum physics."

"And I," says the second man, "have an I.Q. of a hundred and fifty-nine."

"Splendid," says Einstein. "We can discuss the latest mathematical theories."

"As for me," says the third man, "my I.Q. is a hundred and twenty-five."

"Delighted to meet you," says Einstein. "We can discuss the current state of the arts."

"And you, sir," says Einstein, offering his hand to the fourth man, "I'm glad to meet you, too."

"I'm honored," says the fourth man. "But my I.Q. is only eighty-five."

"Oh, that's all right," says Einstein. "So tell me, where do you think interest rates are headed?"

Mr. Science: Well, don't worry about it, son. I'm sure it'll all become very clear to you after you've observed today's experiment. Now, in order to see what happens when we bring water to the boiling point, we must first prepare our laboratory equipment to heat it to 212 degrees.

Jimmy: Gosh-all hemlock, Mr. Science. What's that piece of laboratory equipment you're lighting with a match?

Mr. Science: This device is called a candle, Jimmy.

Jimmy: A candle! Holy suffering catfish. Wait'll I tell all the kids at school I've seen one of those.

Mr. Science: Now, just try to keep your enthusiasm under control, boy. We still haven't gotten to the most amazing part. Watch what happens when I hold this test tube filled with water over the lighted candle.

Jimmy: Golly Moses, Mr. Science! Nothing happened at all.

Mr. Science: Well, that's only because the water hasn't been heated quite long enough yet. Remember, I told you that all chemical properties are converted from liquid to vapor once their temperature rises sufficiently.

Jimmy: Great Jumping Jehoshaphat! The water's starting to get all bubbling on top. I guess doing that instead of turning into a vapor offers conclusive proof that water's not a chemical property. Right, Mr. Science?

Mr. Science: No. That's not quite correct, Jimmy. You see, those bubbles indicate that the water is starting to boil. And now, if you'll look closely, you can see steam beginning to rise from the test tube.

Jimmy: Oh, wowie-two-shoes! But that stuff sure looks an awful lot like the smoke that was rising from the candle. You wouldn't try to slip me the old rubber peach just because I'm a gullible child, would you, Mr. Science?

Mr. Science: Of course not, Jimmy. Notice how my hand gets wet when I pass it through the cloud of steam like this. And that means the vapor has converted itself back into water again.

Jimmy: Boy oh boy, your hand's sure wet, all right, Mr. Science. I feel as though one of nature's eternal secrets has just been unlocked before my very eyes.

Mr. Science: That's very cleverly phrased, Jimmy. And—

Jimmy: I'll bet this little bottle would get equally wet if I passed it through the cloud of steam.

Mr. Science: No. Don't do that, Jimmy. The contents of that bottle must never be exposed to heat! Keep it away from here, boy!

Jimmy: But I only want to see if the outside of the bottle will—

(*Sound: Explosion*)

Announcer: Mr. Science has been brought to you as a public service paid for by the Philanthropic Council to Make Things Nicer. Today's broadcast was the last in our current series.

DUCK'S BREATH MYSTERY THEATER

Ask Dr. Science

Why is the speed of light only 186,000 miles per second? Can't science do better than this?

Yes, you're right. It's a disgrace that light goes only a measly 186,000 miles per second, but physicists are working on the problem. There is already a prototype vehicle that goes 200,000 miles per second, but the headlights shine at only 186,000 miles per second. This is equivalent to driving down the freeway the wrong way with the headlights not only *out* but actually chasing you down the road. This is why so many scientists today no longer own a driver's license.

What would happen if the speed of light were only sixty miles per hour?

As we approach the speed of light, the aging process slows down. So, if the speed of light were sixty miles per hour, we would have even more people speeding, especially older people trying to stay young. As a matter of fact, physics would demand that we go faster than the speed of light. The safest thing is to drive at a steady sixty to keep time and the highway patrol off our necks. Airplanes would become obsolete in this slow light world, because you would be going so fast, relatively speaking, that you'd be back before you even left. This would make business trips unnecessary and lead to economic collapse. So, to answer your question, life, if the speed of light were sixty miles per hour, would be youthful, fast, and dark.

Why do objects become shorter and wider as they approach the speed of light?

There are two different kinds of light here, the light that fills our days and the light that fills our beers and diet sodas. The objects that become shorter and wider are those that consume too much light beer. The so-called "couch potato syndrome" could be more a side effect of gravity than of light, though the light emitted from a TV set seems to have an adverse effect on weight. TV light, or, as science calls it, "stupid light," seems to create an urge in couch potatoes to drink gallons of light beer. Why, we don't know. Stupid light contrasts with smart light, which is the intelligent radiation we get from the sun and Eveready batteries. When we approach the speed of smart light we don't get shorter and wider; we get dark, bump into things, and fall down. So, if you plan on breaking the light barrier, I advise you not to. Turn on the TV and crack a couple cold ones. You'll be fat, but you'll be safe.

DON NOVELLO

2282 N. Beachwood
Los Angeles,
California
September 10, 1976

Mars Team
Jet Propulsion Lab
4800 Oak Park Drive
Pasadena, California

Dear Mars Team, (Scientists, Engineers, Generals, etc.)

Congradulations on landing on Mars! Twice! (Viking I and Viking II.) And congrats on inventing that terrific arm you have for retrieving soil samples to see if life exists there. A SMALL SCOOP FOR A MACHINE, A GIANT SCOOP FOR MANKIND! You can use that—get it?

From what I understand, the main experiment to test if there is life on Mars consists of cooking the soil with intense heat and if *carbon* is burned off from it—that means there's some kind of life present.
That's where you're wrong! If carbon is burned off, that doesn't prove there's life on Mars! That proves there *was* life on Mars. You killed it!
I heard this fellow Carl Sagan say that life on Mars could be entirely different from life here. For instance, maybe they're real small. Maybe a whole country the size of the U.S. was in that scoop! Also maybe small dogs were present in that soil! How would we like it if they came down here and started scooping up people and dogs and testing us for carbon? We would be upset! And we would have a right to be upset!
What I think we should do is this:
Put a small microscope in the next Viking (Viking III you will probably call it) and take a good close look at that soil before you go burning it.

Also, I don't like this talk about there being a canyon on Mars that's three times larger than the Grand Canyon and saying "it makes the Grand Canyon look like a trench". A TRENCH?! Who said that? TREASON! The Grand Canyon will *always* be the #1 canyon and no lousy pictures from outer space are going to distort a national monument! The scenery in the U.S. is the best! Don't go confusing people talking about other places—especially if you can't even get there *if* you wanted to go.
Question: How much would it cost for gasoline if it was possible to drive to Mars at present prices? (53¢ per gallon—regular—self serve)

Carry On!

Lazlo Toth

Lazlo Toth

"I think I have a right to know. Who's Clara?"

BRUCE JAY FRIEDMAN

Lonely Guys

Who are the Lonely Guys?

They tend to be a little bald and look as if they have been badly shaken up in a bus accident. Jules Feiffer obviously had "Lonely Guy" stamped on his forehead in the cradle. Buck Henry. Guys like that. But it gets tricky. Woody Allen is doubtful. We're not talking shy here. That's another book. The Shy Guy's book. Warren Beatty gets you mixed up because of all his dating. He may be a secret Lonely Guy.

Why else would he have made *Shampoo*, which winds up with him on a hill, albeit a Beverly Hill, puzzling over the folly of the human condition? Jack Nicholson's too quirky. You might not want him on the team, but John Ehrlichman seems to be a Lonely Guy, especially when he is gathering literary materials down there in New Mexico. John Mitchell, too. A Conservative Lonely Guy.

Except for Truman, all presidents are Lonely Guys since they have to go off regularly and make decisions that affect the hearts and minds of all Americans for generations to come. They usually do that after lunch. One blooper, and that's it, for an entire generation to come. All of which makes for a tense Oval Office Lonely Guy. Was Nixon a Lonely Guy? Even at the crest of his powers, he ate a lot of Lonely Guy food. American cheese sandwiches and pale vanilla shakes. Until he started drinking those wines. Yet even his wines were Lonely Guy San Clemente wines.

Network heads are visionary Lonely Guys and so are the fellows in charge of FBI district branches. There are very few gay Lonely Guys unless you want to count some British ones who turn up at the seaside. It's possible there are entire gay couples that are Lonely Guys. Women can be Lonely Guys, too. Female stand-up comics, for example. Also women who are sensitive but are trapped inside lovely faces and bodies. Certain Wilhelmina models are in this pickle. She's not going to be throwing any eggs in the pan at four in the morning, but Jacqueline Onassis may be a Lonely Guy. On nights when she has been escorted to the ballet by the wrong Iranian. Kierkegaard was probably the first Modern Day Lonely Guy, although he may have disqualified himself when he came up with faith. (Lonely Guys know what the score is in this department.) Howard Hughes went over the line when he let those fingernails grow. Right fielders are Lonely Guys. So are free safeties, doormen and large dogs. Horses are Lonely Guys unless they are the spoiled favorites of girls named Wendy in Darien. All of Canada may be a Lonely Guy. "Boat People" thought they were Lonely Guys until they got settled in suburban homes in Sacramento. Married people are fond of saying that they are Lonely Guys, too. But this is like marching in solidarity for Choctaw rights, when you're not a Choctaw. No Polish directors are Lonely Guys since any time they like they can just reach out and grab a script girl and some caviar.

Lonely Guys lean against railings a lot and stare off in the distance with bunched-up jaw muscles. They had a bad time at summer camp and are afraid they are going to be sent back there, even at age forty. From the street, they peer in at cocktail lounges, through the potted palms, and decide the place is not for them. They take naps in the early evening and are delighted to wake up and find it's too late to go anywhere. A favorite activity of the Lonely Guy is to take a walk down by the river. Lonely Guys start to fill out forms with great enthusiasm, then quickly lose heart, right around the part that asks for their mother's maiden name.

SLIM WHITE MALE, 35, seeks attractive white female, 27. Must have tattoo (dogs, butterflies, okay; no rainbows, gnomes or battle scenes). Must own late-model foreign car with radial tires (and snows). Should be well tanned, blue eyed, blonde, (sunny yellow, not platinum or dishwater), and have own luggage. Must be T'ai Chi expert and familiar with multiple body-rub techniques. Must have own chili recipe (no celery). Must bathe, not shower. Must have working command of Latin (hear it, speak it, order and hail cabs in it). Must have own flesh-pulley equipment and collection of travelogues, intermission reels, and wrestling magazines (circa 1950–54, good to mint condition, bagged for clean and easy storage). Must possess own lifelike false face and iron-on refrigerator decals. Can be pensive but not moody. Must dig roller opera. Must possess lots (I mean it) of ketchup.

ALICE KAHN
Desperately Seeking . . . Anyone

Lillian and Esty, two elderly widows in a Florida adult community, are curious about the latest arrival in their building—a quiet, nice-looking gentleman who keeps to himself.

Esty says, "Lillian, you know I'm shy. Why don't you go over to him at the pool and find out a little about him? He looks so lonely."

Lillian agrees, and later that day, at the pool, she walks up to him and says, "Excuse me, mister. I hope I'm not prying, but my friend and I were wondering why you looked so lonely."

"Of course I'm lonely," he says, "I've spent the past twenty-five years in prison."

"You're kidding! What for?"

"For killing my third wife. I strangled her."

"What happened to your second wife?"

"I shot her."

"And, if I may ask, your first wife?"

"We had a fight and she fell off a building."

"Oh, my," says Lillian. Then, turning to her friend on the other side of the pool, she yells, "Yoo hoo, Esty, he's single!"

YOUNG WHITE URBAN MALE into radical politics but not from an ideological standpoint or an obnoxious activist approach, likes hiking in the woods on a rainy day but hates California (it's cold and damp) although unwilling to relocate. Not into spirituality or growth but believes there is a supreme intelligence that could be guiding the universe although isn't. Likes reading nineteenth-century French poets (in translation) and Anything by Larry McMurtry. Hates never having to say "I'm sorry." Into Amadeus, Miles, and Springsteen. An eclectic kinda guy. Can cook stir-fry or Weber dome barbecue only. Does own laundry but only with Ivory due to long-standing jock-itch situation. Seeks young woman (15 to 25) for afternoon of violin concerto in E, Fumé Blanc, and quiet talk about reducing nuclear risk.

YOUNG (DEPENDING ON YOUR DEFINITION) midsize city semiprofessional woman seeks one good man. Into aerobic meditation, the New Catholicism, veggie cuisine, and all-around whole-grain approach to life. I like dry, hot climates—the desert or the beach when the sun is blazing. Hate—absolutely despise—Larry McMurtry, Miles Davis, California wine, French poetry, jocks, political guilt trips. I don't want to meet with you, eat or sleep or bo-peep with you, proselytize you, cannibalize you, bring you down, or call in the clowns. All I really want to do, is baby be friends with you.

YOUNG BUT MATURING, LEARNING, reaching-out-and-touching-someone man interested in change. Wants a friend. A friend is all I've ever wanted. Really. Swear to supreme intelligence that ought to be guiding universe that friendship is the main thing I seek in a young, New Catholic woman. *Likes* woman who can stand her own ground. *Wants* a challenge. Wants a woman who knows what she likes and isn't afraid to say it. But no ballbusting feminist stereotypical left-wing nightmare women please.

OVER 30 (LET'S GET HONEST) attractive woman who likes to clean her house while exercising stone naked to Kenny Loggins music questions use of term *ballbuster*. Suggests undue amount of paranoia bordering on misogyny. Goes along with whole macho image conjured by mentioning Baudelaire and Bruce Springsteen. Into boots of Spanish leather. But warn you: Potential for these boots to do a Nancy Sinatra all over you.

RECEDING HAIRLINE BUT WHO'S to worry? Into *boots!* Are you kidding, I love boots. Boots is my life. Never mentioned Baudelaire by name. In fact, more of a Rimbaud kinda guy. Come to think of it, I like Cardinal Newman, Cesar Chavez, peace in El Salvador, and quiet walks in the woods in the rain but will consider the desert. Willing to relocate to the desert. Willing to try quiet walks in the rain in the desert. Driven wild by image of nude woman doing aerobic dusting. Come back, baby, I want to clean house with you.

EXERCISE TO HOLD LID on middle-age spread. Breasts starting to sag regardless of Joannie Greggins armlifts × 10. Hate the rain. Get severely depressed, worse than premenstrual, if it rains on my birthday. Please don't quote Elvis Presley lyrics. Reminds me of grammar school. Never picked for teams. Refused to give up candy for Lent. Got pimples. Unpopular. Created own bad rep in high school but for naught. Nobody tried to cop nothing. Still interested?

LONELY KINDA GUY DOESN'T care about grammar school or high school grief. Doesn't even care about high-priced spread (not too bad, is it?). Get out your boots. In the words of the immortal Pat Boone: April love can drip right off your fingers.

WIMPY WOMAN WONDERS WHAT all that talk about wanting strong woman was all about. What about boots bit? Would it matter to lonely kinda guy if wimpy kinda woman had actually lied about boots bit and, in fact, cleans house in dirty pink bunny slippers and chenille bathrobe?

AGING MAN WANTS to get laid.

YOUR SPACE OR MINE?

"I can't believe you're as lonely as you say, Mr. Minnick."

COLIN McENROE

How to Marry a Fanatic
(and Other Alternatives to Single Life)

I believe in turning negatives into positives, so when I read a few years ago that a single woman over forty stood a better chance of being killed by a terrorist than of finding a husband, I asked myself: How can these two troubled and problematic groups work *for* each other?

The answer was pretty darned obvious. Women of forty should just up and marry terrorists.

Stop and consider. Your basic terrorist is young, lonely, driven by impulses he scarcely understands. What he needs is a stable relationship with a woman who's been around the kiosk a couple of times. Give these guys a week or two of regular, well-balanced meals, bedtime at a reasonable hour, a William Hurt movie on the weekend. You'll marvel at the changes.

For the women, it's a chance to find a man with a demonstrated belief in commitment—a man who's not a wimp, a man who's interested in something more substantial than just a quick fling.

There are, however, a few key concerns to be factored in:

- Many terrorists do not feel comfortable in singles' bars. But more and more clubs are offering special events such as "Jihad Hours," "Jackal Night" and the ever-popular "Conga Line of Death." A woman interested in meeting a fanatic should attend these and be prepared to field such come-ons as "So, what satanic, sniveling, rapacious Western sign are you?" or "Do you debase yourself on these premises often, Western prostitute?"
- A cleverly worded personal ad, placed in a publication such as *Better Homes and Carbines,* may lure a shy terrorist out of hiding. To wit:

> **SWF, 40-ISH,** vivacious, tired of the bazaar scene, enjoys good books, long walks on burning sand, candlelight chanting, nasal ablutions. Seeks younger man for veiled thrills, wild-eyed dedication.

- A woman who winds up dating a terrorist should be prepared to assert herself. Many terrorists were mama's boys. They are accustomed to getting their ways and will often expect their dates to wait around while they and their friends plot the overthrow of capitalism long into the night.

  You will have to let Ahmed or Ian or Carlos know that *you* have a limited amount of recreational time and that a three-hour discussion of makeshift grenade launchers is not your idea of a sparkling night. (See my book *Men Who Hate Civilization and the Women Who Hijack Them.*)

CATHY *by Cathy Guisewite*

CATHY *by Cathy Guisewite*

- Let's say you get through all the awkward stages and decide you were meant for each other. The wedding itself may be the biggest hurdle you ever face.

  Do the planning yourself. The rap against terrorist weddings is there's never enough food, the band stinks (sometimes literally) and there's always some loopy out-of-town guest who fires his Uzi into the cake before it's cut (chew carefully).

  Just picking out a china pattern with a terrorist can be an ordeal.

  Jennifer G., thirty-two, a Manhattan interior designer and Morris dancer, recalls: "He said, 'Each plate must be showing a wondrous tableau from the Ayatollah's life, such as the flogging of a godless imperialist harlot, plus picture of the despot Reagan whose jaws are to be seen dripping with the blood of Allah's innocent people.' We settled on Royal Doulton, but I had to give in on towels. He insisted on sackcloth."

- If you marry a Libyan, keep your own name. That's the advice of Cleveland account executive and tumbler Mimi Qenoze, née Plotzwinkle, who suffered through the inconsistencies of modern transliteration. "The wedding announcement in the *Tribune* said Qujoutz and the *Plain Dealer* spelled it Ghamos. My checks read Kueqosca; the IRS does it Quatzna; and the yard guys call me Mrs. Kenosha."

The big question, though, seems to be: Is it worth it? Do they ever settle down?

You'll know the answer the first time the phone rings for him and it's:

"Anok, sacred comrade, today we strike fear into the engorged, dung-eating tick of Western imperialism."

"I cannot, my trusted friend. Things pile up. Today I am lashing the Scourge of Heaven against the unholy crabgrass, driving the devils of mildew from our exalted rec room and placing the righteous shoulder of belief to the removal of storm windows."

Then you will have found the husband inside your terrorist.

BRUCE FEIRSTEIN

Female Dating Styles Through the Ages

	17	25	35	48	66
Drinking alone	Diet Pepsi	Diet Pepsi	Diet Pepsi	Diet Pepsi	Pepsi
Drinking on a date	beer	black russian	Diet Pepsi	champagne	whiskey sour
What's the ideal age to get married?	28	28	28	28	28
Favorite drug	'ludes	coke and 'ludes	coke, 'ludes, and a corner office	really good coke, 'ludes, a corner office, and Valium	affection
Least believable lie	"He's just somebody I study with."	"He's just somebody I work with."	"He's only a friend."	"He's gay."	"How could you say that? He was my best friend's husband!"
Second least believable lie	"He's more than a quarterback."	"He's more than a health-club instructor."	"He's not a model, he's an actor."	"How can you say that? He's my friend's son!"	"Professional jai alai players happen to be very intelligent."
Favorite sport	losing her virginity	shopping	tennis	watching her friends' marriages break up	sex
Battle cry	"Let's go steady."	"I've got time."	"I'm running out of time."	"Gloria Steinem is still single."	"So is Kate Hepburn."
Most likely to have an affair with	her brother's best friend	her father's best friend	her husband's best friend	her son's best friend	pool boy at the cabana club
What she's really looking for	Mr. Right	Mr. Close	Mr. Distinct Possibility	Mr. Smith	pool boy at the cabana club
Stupidest line heard from a man	"You'd do it if you loved me."	"You'd do it if you liked me."	"It's better than sleeping alone."	"At this point who's counting?"	"Wake me if you change your mind."
Favorite complaint	"Men are crazy."	"Men are crazy."	"Men are crazy."	"Men are crazy."	"Men are crazy."
Sexual fantasy	Billy Idol	on a 747 with her boyfriend—or Don Johnson	her boyfriend *and* Don Johnson	Don Johnson, her best girlfriend, her boyfriend, and Robert Wagner	Buddy Ebsen
Typical statement	"My mother thinks we're getting too serious."	"My mother wants to know when we're getting married."	"My mother won't even discuss it."	"My daughter thinks we're getting too serious."	"My granddaughter wants to know when we're getting married."
Most frustrating line to hear from a man	"I don't dance."	"I always watch football on Sundays."	"I'm too old for rock 'n' roll concerts."	"I always do it this way."	"What?"
Worst reason for not having sex	"It'll wake my parents."	"It'll wake my roommate."	"It'll wake the neighbors."	"It'll wake the kids."	"You always fall asleep in the middle."
Dream date	a weekend in Manhattan	a weekend in Paris	a weekend in Rio	a weekend with somebody else	a weekend anywhere but Miami

Male Dating Styles Through the Ages

	17	25	35	48	66
Drink	beer	bourbon	vodka	double vodka	Maalox
Seduction line	"My parents are away for the weekend."	"My roommate is away for the weekend."	"My girlfriend is away for the weekend."	"My wife is away for the weekend."	"My second wife is dead."
Enticement	"Wanna see my new 'Vette?"	"Wanna see my new apartment?"	"Wanna see my new house?"	"Wanna see my new weekend house?"	"Wanna see my son's 'Vette?"
Complaint	"My parents don't understand me."	"My boss doesn't understand me."	"My wife doesn't understand me."	"My employees don't understand me."	"My kids don't understand me."
Favorite sport	sex	sex	sex	sex	sex
Drug	pot	coke	really good coke	power	coke, a limousine, the company jet
Definition of a successful date	"Tongue."	"Breakfast."	"She didn't set back my therapy."	"I didn't bump into her kids."	got home alive
Person he's most likely to have an affair with	his girlfriend's best friend	his girlfriend's roommate	his wife's best friend	his executive assistant	his second wife's best friend
Favorite fantasy	getting to third	airplane sex	*ménage à trois*	taking his company public	Swiss maid/Nazi love slave
House pet	roaches	stoned-out college roommate	Irish setter	children from his first marriage	Barbi Benton
Worst reason for not having sex	"My coach says not before a big game."	"Big presentation at the office."	"We did it last week."	"My back hurts."	"It reminds me of my last wife."
Least believable lie	"She's only 17!"	"She's only 17!"	"She's only 17!"	"She's only 17!"	"She's only 17!"
Reason they can't make a commitment	"Haven't lived enough."	"I'm waiting for my next raise."	"I'm waiting for my next promotion."	"I'm waiting for my next divorce."	"I still haven't lived enough."
Is it true that women fall faster but men fall harder?	"I'll never get over her."	"I'll never get over her."	"I'll never get over her."	"I'll never get over her."	"I think I'm finally over her."
What's the ideal age to get married?	25	35	48	66	17
Worse sexual cliché	"You can't leave me like this."	"But I *do* love you."	"But it's *not* just one night."	"But we do *like* each other."	"But I'm *happy* it was good for you. Now what about me?"
Ideal date	Triple Stephen King feature at a drive-in	"Split the check before we go back to my apartment."	"Just come over."	"Just come over and cook."	sex in the company jet on the way to Vegas to see Frank

It's been so long since I made love I can't even remember who gets tied up.   *—Joan Rivers*

JUDITH VIORST
Married Is Better

Married is better
Than sitting on a blanket in Nantucket
Where you get blotches and a red nose instead of
  adorable freckles and golden brown,
Hoping that someone with whom you would not
  be caught dead
From September to June
Will invite you to dinner.

And married is better
Than riding a double chair lift up at Stowe
On your way to an expert trail and you're a beginner,
Hoping the fellow for whom you are risking your life
Will invite you to dinner.
And one night, when you land at Kennedy,
And no one is there to meet you except your parents,
And you suddenly realize that you never saw the
    Parthenon
Because you were too busy looking around for a Greek
    god,
You also suddenly realize
Married is better.

And married is better
Than an affair with a marvelous man
Who would leave his wife immediately except that she
    would slash her wrists and the children would cry.
So instead you drink his Scotch in your living room and
    never meet his friends because they might become
    disillusioned or tell,

And when it's your birthday it's his evening with the
    in-laws,
And when it's his birthday he can't even bring home
    your present
(Because of the slashed wrists and the crying and all),
So even though you have his body and soul while his
    wife only has his laundry and the same name,
You somehow begin to suspect
Married is better.

And married is better
Than the subway plus a crosstown bus every morning,
And tuna on toasted cheese bread, no lettuce, at
    Schrafft's.
And a bachelor-girl apartment with burlap and foam
    rubber and a few droll touches like a samurai sword
    in the bathroom,
And going to the movies alone,
And worrying that one morning you'll wake up and
    discover you're an older woman,
And always projecting wholesome sexuality combined
    with independence, femininity, and tons of outside
    interests,
And never for a minute letting on
That deep in your heart you believe
Married is better.

My mother never breastfed me. She told me she liked me as a friend. —*Rodney Dangerfield*

MARK O'DONNELL
Marred Bliss

The front porch of Jane's family home. Jane arranges roses in a vase. Dink sits on the glider, reading the paper or just enjoying the evening. A typical midwestern scene. Jane is a pretty, prissy, inhibited young woman, wearing starched, modest clothes. Dink is a regular lug who's been talked into marriage but is willing to turn himself over to it.

Jane: Darkling?
Dink (looking up from his paper): What is it, dulling?
Jane: I thought we'd have ruses for the centerpieces. For us, and for all the guest tables. Ruses *are* traditional.
Dink: Ruses it is. *(He continues reading.)*
Jane (after a restless pause): Oh, honey, just *sink!*
Dink: What do you want me to sink about?
Jane: In less than forty-eight horrors, you and I will be moan and woof! *(Grins.)* Isn't it amassing?
Dink: It is amassing! *(He lowers his paper thoughtfully.)* So much has harpooned in just a few thief years!
Jane: It steams like only yesterday that you were the noise next door.
Dink: And you were that feckless-faced cod sitting up in the old ache tree!
Jane: And now we're encaged! I can hardly wait till we're marred!
Dink: Oh, hiney! *(He rises and makes to enfold her in his arms.)*
Jane: Now, now! I'm sure the tame will pass quickly till our hiney-moon! *(She eases out of his grasp.)* I'll go get you some of that nice saltpeter taffy that Smother brought back from A Frantic City.

(Jeery, a sexy, slouching sailor, appears at one corner of the stage.)

Jeery: Hello? . . . Any him at home? *(He carries a tiny bouquet.)*
Jane: Oh, my gash! It's Jeery, my old toyfriend!
Dink: Jeery! That bump! What's *he* brewing here?
Jane: Oh, dueling! Try to control your tamper! I'm sure he means no charm! Don't do anything you might regress!

(Jeery approaches.)

Jeery: Hollow!—Revised to see me?
Jane: Hollow, Jeery.
Dink: Hollow.

(Pause.)

Jeery: I'm completely beware that I'm out of police here. But *(looks to Jane)*—for old climb's sake, Jane, I brought you this little bunch of foul airs. A token of my excess steam. Lots of lack to you. And much lack to you, too, Dink.

Jane (*unsure*): Wail . . . (*She decides to accept the flowers.*) Spank you, Jeery.

Dink: Spank you very much.

Jeery: My shaft is at rancor in the harbor, and they gave me whore leave. I heard you were engorged, and I just wanted to slop by and pave my regrets.

Jane (*uncomfortably*): Well, blank you!

Dink: Blank you very much.

Jane (*uneasy with this standoff*): I think you two have already messed, haven't you?

Jeery: Oh, we've thrown each other for years!

Dink: We went to the same cruel . . . till Jeery dripped out to join the Nervy.

Jane: Of course, I remainder all that now! (*She is eager to lessen the awkwardness.*) Um—do you haunt to sit down?

Jeery: Well, only for a menace. (*They all sit down on the glider.*) I'm hooded over to Pain Street. There's a big trance at the Social Tub. I'll probably go and chick it out. (*There is an awkward silence as they sit on the crowded glider.*) Wail, wail, wail . . . So when do you two tie the net?

Jane: The day after temerity!

Jeery: That soon?

Dink (*curtly*): We've been enraged for over a year.

Jeery: Well, concatenations!

Dink: Rank you very much. (*Tense pause.*) . . . Jeery, it's getting awfully lout! You don't want to miss the trance!

(*From the other entrance comes Alas, a provocatively dressed woman with elaborate hair and a loose manner.*)

Alas: Hell's own? Hell's own?

Jane (*aside*): Oh, no! Is that who I slink it is? Why won't she let us align?

(*Alas advances.*)

Alas: Hell's own, every burden! Hell's own, Dink! . . .

Dink (*uncomfortable but heated*): Hell's own, Alas! . . . Fantasy seething you here!

Jane (*tartly*): I thought you'd be at the Social Tub trance, Alas. Aren't you on the degradation committee?

Alas (*offering a gift-wrapped bottle*): I may stoop by there later. I sinfully wanted to winch you both all the beast. Let icons be icons. Here's a battle of damn pain for you. I hype you enjoy it.

Jane (*suspicious*): How sweat of you. (*She takes the bottle and puts it aside.*) You know Jeery, don't you, Alas?

Alas: Yes, we mated years ago. How's the Nervy, Jeery?

Jeery: Great! I was born to be a soiler.

Hal and Sue are invited to a fancy Halloween party, and Sue rents costumes for both of them. She has been looking forward to it all week, but on the day of the party, Sue comes down with a flu and tells Hal to go alone.

Hal gets into his gorilla suit and drives off. After a nap, Sue wakes up feeling much better. Realizing that Hal hasn't even seen her costume, she decides it might be fun to show up at the party to see how her husband acts when she isn't around.

When Sue arrives, she spots Hal, who is dancing seductively with a series of attractive women. And when the gorilla notices Sue, who is dressed as Cleopatra, he immediately leaves his current partner to be with her. After some hot and heavy dancing, he suggests they go outside for a little walk. Sue agrees, and they soon find themselves making love in the woods. A little while later, Sue leaves the party and drives home, wondering what Hal will have to say about the evening.

Two hours later, Hal returns and finds Sue sitting up and reading in bed.

"How was it, dear?" she says.

"Oh, the same old stuff. You know I never have a good time when you're not around."

"Didn't you even dance?"

"No," he says. "In fact, I spent the entire evening playing cards in the den with two other guys. But the guy I loaned my costume to? He had a hell of a time."

(*There is another awkward silence as they regard her.*)

Dink (*to Alas*): Um—would you like to hit with us, Alas? Jane, you don't grind if Alas hits with us, do you?

Jane: Well, the glider's getting awfully clouded!

Alas: I'll just loin against the railing! (*She poses against the pillar seductively.*)

Dink: No, here, have my seed! (*He stands.*)

Jane: Dallying! (*She pulls him back into his seat.*) I think she'd rather remain stunning!

Dink (*getting agitated*): Jeery, you could awful her *your* seat! Don't they teach you manners in the harmed surfaces? (*Jeery bristles.*)

Jane (*to avoid a scene*): Look, qualm down! Maybe we should admit this is an awkward saturation! I have complete face in you, Dink, but I think it's in power taste for your old street-part to come around so soon before our welding!

Alas (*offended*): I can't bereave this! There's no reason to be subspecies, Jane!

Jane (*affronted*): No?

Alas: This is a good-wall visit, that's all! You're just high-stung!

Dink (*chiming in his objections*): And what about Jeery here! I don't luck having him luring at you!

Jeery (*contemptuously*): Oh, relapse, Dink! Afraid she'll realize her must-ache before the sorrow-money? (*to Alas:*) He's in debt, it's a mortgage of convenience!

Jane (*frightened by this sudden passion*): Toys, please! Clam yourself! (*Earnestly, to Dink:*) Dink, don't drought yourself this way! Where's the strong, stabled man I'm taking to the halter? You know I lug you, I'll always lug you. (*She puts her arms around him maternally.*) I want ours to be a beautiful cremation-trip. But it has to be based on *truss*. (*She hugs him even more suffocatingly, and not erotically.*) I want to be able to *truss* you.

Dink (*too independently to suit Jane*): All I did was offer Alas my seed. You act like I rammed off with her!

Jane (*feeling dressed down before company*): Well, maybe you'd rather ram off with her! She's been trying to reduce you since she got here!

Alas (*angry*): Don't spike like that to me! I bitter go.

Jane (*her insecurity making her hysterical*): Stew where you are! You're the claws of this! You *slot!*

Alas (*sneering at Jane*): What a little squirrel! I have nothing but potty for you!

(*The women suddenly slap each other; the men must intervene.*)

Jeery (*restraining Alas*): The whole tissue is ridiculous! Fighting over a man who's in doubt up to his ears!

Dink: At least I'm not diddled with funereal disease, you bellow-jellied bull-bottomed sin of the beach!

Jeery: You sod-damned cowbird!

(The men fight; now the women must intervene.)

    Alas: Stop it! Stop it!

(There is a momentary silence, as they all recover from their wounds.)

    Jane: Why are we having such trouble trying to communicate?
    Dink (taking the lead): Look, Alas . . . I heave nothing but harpy memories of our time together. I depreciate your good winces, but Jane and I are to be marred, and that's that. *(He looks to Jane to match his definitive renunciation.)*
    Jane (taking Jeery's hand briefly): And . . . Jeery . . . I leave you very much. You know that. But that's all winter under the fridge. *(She turns to Alas.)* Alas, I'm sorry I lost my torpor.
    Alas (with dignity): I understand. And I axe-up your apology. Anyway, I'm getting marred myself. To Henry Silverstone.
    Jane (impressed): The banker! But he's rather old for you, isn't he?
    Alas: Luckily, he's in very good wealth. *(A car horn honks from offstage.)* There's my chauffeured limbo now. I'd better get gilding. Conglomerations, and gall the best! . . . Goad bye!
    Dink (feeling bested): Bile!
    Jane (feeling outdone): Bile!

(Alas exits. Jeery now feels superfluous.)

    Jeery: Her own limbo! . . . Well, I guess I should leave you two lifeboats alone!
    Jane: Thanks for the foul airs, Jeery! Enjoy the trance!
    Jeery: Maybe I'll meet *my* future broad!
    Dink (as if to a buddy): That's the right platitude!
    Jeery: So long! Have a lot of skids!
    Dink: Bile!
    Jane: Bile! *(Jeery goes.)* He's a good spore, isn't he?
    Dink (reluctantly): I gas so.
    Jane (hugging him consolingly): But you're the uphill of my eye!
    Dink: Oh, hiney! *(He holds and tries to kiss her, but she resists him.)* Oh, come on! Ploys? Pretty ploys?

(She relents and gives him a peck and then quickly raises Alas's gift bottle between them.)

    Jane: Oh, look! A vintage battle of damn pain! Let's celibate! *(She pops it open and pours some of it into two empty lemonade glasses on the porch table. She raises her glass.)* Here, let's test each other! *(They toast.)* To *ice!*
    Dink: To *ass!*

(They drink.)

    Jane: Oh, galling! Our life together is going to be *blitz!*

(Blackout.)

IAN PRAISER & HOWARD GEWIRTZ

Take My Ex-Wife, Please

from TAXI

CAST

Alex Rieger	Judd Hirsch
Louie De Palma	Danny De Vito
Elaine Nardo	Marilu Henner
Tony Banta	Tony Danza
Jim Ignatowski	Christopher Lloyd
Latka Gravas	Andy Kaufman
Phyllis Rieger Consuelos	Louise Lasser
Jeff	J. Alan Thomas

SETS

Garage
La Belle Chateau Restaurant
Tool Room

Act One

Scene One

Fade in:
Interior garage—late afternoon
Elaine and Alex are at the table. Louie is in his cage. Latka is working on a cab. Tony enters, carrying a magazine under his arm and very excited.

Tony: Hey, guys, I got a date tonight you're not going to believe. Take a look at her picture. She's a model. *(Pointing to a page in the magazine)* The one in Calvin's.

They all express their approval. Louie comes over and grabs the magazine. Latka is close behind.

Louie: Let me get this straight, Banta. That girl with that rear has agreed to go out with you?
Tony: *(Grabbing the magazine back)* That's right, Louie.
Louie: And no money has changed hands?
Alex: Great looking woman.
Latka: She is a beauty, Tony.
Elaine: Yeah, a real knockout. Does she have a face?
Latka: Of course, she has a face. You think Tony would go out with her if she did not have a face?
Louie: I'd go out with her if she didn't have a head.
Tony: *(Pulling Alex aside)* Alex, can I talk to you alone for a

My hero!

Great tits.

Basis for a lasting relationship

second? See, there's a slight hitch. Cindy has a sister. They're very close, they like to do stuff together. She said she'd go out with me only if I'd find her sister a date, too. What do you say?

Alex: Look, Tony, I haven't had the best luck with blind dates. Ordinarily, when you set somebody up on a blind date, there's a reason—the reason being that they don't have a date—the reason for that being that nobody will go out with them—the reason for that being—

Tony: Cindy refers to her sister as the one with the body.

Alex: Okay, I'll help you out. But you owe me one.

Jim enters and saunters over to them.

Tony: Great. We're meeting at eight-thirty at this French place in the Village, La Belle Chateau.

Jim: French food. Sounds like a terrific evening.

Tony: It'll be a *great* evening, Jim.

Jim: Ah, the pâté foie, the sauce bernaise, the *mousse à chocolat. La cuisine Française est magnifique. C'est la plus bienne de la monde.*

Alex: Jim, you're speaking French.

Jim: (Surprised) *Moi? Parle Francais? C'est incroyable!*

Tony: Jim, knock it off.

Jim: Okey-doke. (Goes off singing à la Maurice Chevalier) "If the nightingale could sing like you . . ."

Louie: (Over the P.A.) Attention, attention, cabbies, I have a little ceremony to get out of the way here. Yesterday, Latka was road testing a cab when the engine caught on fire. He took his jacket and beat that fire out, risking life and limb to save the cab. Therefore, I am pleased to present Latka with the "Employee of the Month" Award. Latka, would you like to say a few words to the cabbies?

Latka: Thank you very much. (Over the P.A.; clears his throat) I am a dope.

Latka turns around, revealing many large burned-out holes in the jacket he is wearing over his overalls, and we:
Dissolve to:

Scene Two

Int. La Belle Chateau Restaurant—evening
It is a tasteful French restaurant in the Village: linen tablecloths, hurricane lamps, fresh flowers, and lazy susans on each table. There is a small bar along the wall. Phyllis Rieger Consuelos is seated in the waiting area, holding a glass of wine. The maitre d' goes over to her.

Maitre D': Madam, I can seat you now. Will you be dining, uh . . . are you . . . uh . . .

Phyllis: Alone. Is that what you are trying to say? Yes, I will be dining alone. Don't be afraid to say it. Here. Say it with me.

She takes his hands in hers to help him.

Maitre D'/Phyllis: Alone.

Phyllis: Good. We're both a little freer. No, no one is coming. I'm not waiting for anybody. We're all here.

Maitre D': Would you like a table in the corner?

Phyllis: I can't believe you're asking me that. *(Gratefully)* Please.

Maitre D': Very good. This way, madam.

Phyllis follows him to a table partially hidden by large plants. She averts her eyes from the other diners. She blows out the candle to make it darker and slides one of the potted plants a little closer to the table. Tony and Alex enter.

Tony: Hey, this is some fancy place.

Alex: It's been here for years. I used to bring dates here.

Tony: When?

Alex: When I didn't mind living the rest of the week on Wonder Bread. *(Looking at the chalkboard menu)* Well, one more week won't kill me.

Cindy Moratta enters. She doesn't see them yet.

Tony: Alex, there she is. Isn't she beautiful?

At this point, Sandy Moratta enters. She is Cindy's identical twin.

Alex, there she is again! Do you know what this means?

Alex: We struck twins.

Cindy spots the guys and she and her sister go up to them.

Cindy: Hi, Tony. I'd like you to meet my sister, Sandy.

Tony: Hi, Sandy. Cindy, Sandy, I want you to meet my friend, Alex.

Cindy: Hi!

Sandy: Hi!

Alex: Hi! Well, this is something, isn't it?

Cindy: It certainly is. *(To Sandy)* How are we going to tell them apart?

Sandy: Tony's wearing the loud tie.

The girls share a laugh.

Alex: That's cute.

Cindy: We do that on every first date. It breaks the ice.

Alex: I'm a sucker for women with a sense of humor.

Sandy: Oh-oh, we were eighteen before we came up with that one.

Jim enters and goes up to them.

Jim: Sorry, I'm late.

Tony: What do you mean, "late"? What are you doing here at all?

Jim: I decided to take you up on that invitation. Eight-thirty, La Belle Chateau. I can't wait to indulge in my passions. Good food, good friends, and . . . *(discovering the twins)* . . . good twins.

Alex: Jim, this is Sandy and Cindy Moratta.

Tony: *(Indicating Alex and himself)* Our dates.

Jim: *(To Cindy)* How do. *(To Sandy)* How's it going? *(Beat)* Egg split in the womb, huh?

Alex: Jim . . .

Jim: Oh yeah, right. *(To the twins)* I bet you get that all the time.

Tony: *(Sotto)* Alex, I got a big problem with this. *(Then)* Jim, I don't think you understand. You're not—

Jim: Say no more, Ton. I'm starting to realize what the problem is here.

Tony: Good.

Jim: There's nothing more uncomfortable than when people meet for the first time. The first hurdle is to find something we can all talk about. Now, I think we've all read the diaries of Anais Nin . . .

Cindy and Sandy look at each other, confused.

Alex: Would you girls excuse us for a moment? We've got something to straighten out.

Alex and Tony lead Jim to the corner near to where Phyllis is dining.

Tony: Jim, you made a mistake. Now, I understand that sometimes you get things mixed up, and it's really not your fault. So, it's okay, I'm not that mad at you.

Jim: Thanks, Tony. I appreciate that. Now, let's get back to the girls.

He starts off.

Alex: Tony, let me explain it to him.

Phyllis' table: She turns around and spots Alex. Her eyes widen with the realization of who it is. She turns quickly, so as not to be discovered.

Phyllis: Oh my God! *(Flagging down the maitre d'; sotto)* Waiter . . . waiter . . . *(no response)* Hey!

The maitre d' comes over.

Maitre D': Yes, madam?

Phyllis: May I have the check, please?

Maitre D': But why, madam? You haven't even ordered yet.

Phyllis: *(Calmly)* I want you to behave absolutely, perfectly calm. I want you to pretend that nothing is wrong.

Maitre D': What *is* wrong?

Phyllis: My ex-husband just walked in.

The maitre d' makes a genuine, panicked gasp.

Get a grip on yourself. Now, is there a side door or a meat locker I can hide in?

Phyllis cautiously looks back to take another peek. Alex spots her, and their eyes connect. She turns around quickly.

Alex: Oh my god! My ex-wife.

Jim: Really, Alex. Can we please stick to one topic?

Alex: I've got to go talk to her.

Alex walks off.

Tony: What about the girls? It's all going to fall apart.

Jim: Not to worry, Tony, I'm here now.

Tony and Jim go over to the girls. The maitre d' leads them to a table. Alex goes over to Phyllis. She has taken the plate that is under her butter dish and placed it in front of the chair next to hers. She messily dishes appetizers onto it from the lazy susan.

Alex: Phyllis?

She turns around, suddenly cool and collected.

Phyllis: Oh, hi, Alex.

Alex: That's all? "Hi, Alex?"

Phyllis: Hi, Alex, fix your collar.

Alex: That's more like it. Are you with somebody?

Phyllis: With somebody? (*Indicating the messy plate of appetizers*) Obviously, I'm with somebody.

Alex: Obviously you're with somebody sloppy. Well, I won't disturb you. Just wanted to say hello.

Phyllis: Alex . . . why don't you sit down?

"My best friend and my best friend's wife!!"

Wilson survives a shipwreck, along with Dennis, his fox terrier. After three days of floating on a life raft, they wash ashore on a deserted island.

Exploring the island, they soon come to a valley full of wild sheep. Wilson has never been attracted to animals, but he's so lonely and frightened that he finds himself looking longingly at one of the lambs. But as soon as he approaches her, Dennis starts yelping loudly until the animal runs away.

The next morning, consumed by thoughts of the lamb, Wilson gets up early and tiptoes back toward the valley. He soon finds the lamb, but once again, Dennis comes running over and scares her away.

Weeks pass. Wilson and Dennis are walking along the beach one morning when they stumble across a beautiful young woman lying on the sand. Wilson sees that she is unconscious, so he immediately begins to give her mouth-to-mouth resuscitation. She eventually comes to, and asks, "Where am I? What happened?"

"You must have survived a shipwreck," he replies. "You were unconscious, but I guess I reached you in time."

"I just don't know how to thank you," she says. Giving him a long, tender kiss, she looks in his eyes and says, "Please, let me express my appreciation. I'll do anything you want. Just tell me."

"Well," says Wilson, "actually, there *is* something. Would you mind looking after Dennis for a couple of hours?"

He does and feels uncomfortable.

Alex: Hey, you look terrific. You lost weight.
Phyllis: Thirty-five pounds.
Alex: How did you do it?
Phyllis: The grief diet. Your husband divorces you, then you cry and vomit for three months.
Alex: But look at those results. (*Off her look*) I'm sorry to hear about your divorce.
Phyllis: I don't want to talk about it, I'll survive. So, anyhow, here I am, back in New York reliving a few of the good times, circulating. Of course, it's not always this madcap.
Alex: Who are you with?

She indicates the maitre d'.

Phyllis: Him.

The maitre d' is seating another group at a table.

He's always so concerned that other people are having fun.
Alex: Phyllis, so you're dining alone. It's nothing to be ashamed of.
Phyllis: Really? What if I do it tomorrow night?
Alex: That's still perfectly all right.
Phyllis: How about the rest of the month?

Alex doesn't answer immediately. She takes his hands in hers.

Don't be afraid to say it with me. Pathetic.

Jim comes over to the table. His dignity is obviously wounded.

Jim: Alex, Tony has a message for you. Let me see if I remember it. Oh yeah, "Jim is embarrassing the hell out of me."
Alex: Tell him I'll be right back over there.
Jim: You tell him. I'm leaving.
Alex: Before you leave, Jim, I'd like you to meet my ex-wife, Phyllis.
Jim: Pleased to meet you, Phyllis. (*Beat*) Did you know that the finest goose liver pâté comes from geese whose feet are bound to the floor and force-fed through a meat grinder? (*Off her disgust*) It didn't go over big there, either.
Alex: Good night, Jim. I'll see you back at the garage.
Jim: Okey-doke. (*To Phyllis*) Nice meeting you.

Jim walks off.

Alex: My business manager.
Phyllis: Colorful character. I like him.

Alex turns to see Tony motioning him to come back to the table.

Alex: Phyllis, I'm being rude to my company.
Phyllis: Of course, Alex. Go back to them. I can see this is a big night for you.

Alex: This isn't a big night.

Phyllis: No? Then what is a big night? Beautiful triplets?

Alex: Nice seeing you again, Phyllis.

Phyllis: Wait, Alex, maybe we could get together some night. I'm staying at the Mayflower Hotel.

Alex: Yeah, sure, maybe. Take care, Phyllis.

He goes, then turns back.

Are you going to be okay?

Phyllis: Are you kidding? (*Starting to dish out some hors d'oeuvres*) Give me a little three-bean salad and I'm sitting on top of the world.

Alex rejoins Tony and the twins, but looks back in time to see Phyllis spoon the appetizers back into the lazy susan, put back the butter plate, and look very much alone as we:

Dissolve to:

Scene Three

Int. garage—next day
It is the beginning of the shift. Louie is in the cage. Tony is waiting for his turn on the pay phone. Latka enters.

Louie: Attention, cabbies. I have another little ceremony and the man of honor has just entered.

Latka covers his face with one hand and emphatically tries to wave Louie off with the other.

Now usually when a guy wins the "Employee of the Month" Award, he becomes a little complacent, but not Latka Gravas. Yesterday, while testing that same cab, lo and behold, another engine fire.

Latka even more emphatically waves Louie off.

And what did our Latka do? Lacking his trusty jacket, the man climbed into the engine compartment and stomped the fire out with his feet. So, in appreciation of his heroics, the Sunshine Cab Company is proud to present him with this tube of Unguentine. Latka, would you like to say something? Don't be embarrassed, eyebrows grow back.

Latka reluctantly goes up to the microphone. His eyebrows have been singed off. He takes his tube of Unguentine and speaks into the microphone.

Latka: (*Over the P.A.*) Many of you are probably asking yourselves just how dumb is this Latka Gravas? Well, let me tell you something. If the fire spreads into the carburetor and into the gas tank, the whole thing will blow up. What else could I have done?

Jeff: You could have run away.

Latka: (*Derisively*) Oh, run away? And then, I suppose . . . (*considers it*) Hm, run away.

Latka walks away pondering the wisdom of Jeff's words. Tony is on the pay phone.

Tony: (*Into phone*) Hello? Cindy? It's Tony . . . Yeah, I had a great time last night. Don't Alex and Sandy make a cute couple? . . . Well, maybe if she gave him another chance . . . Dour? . . . Cynical? . . . Depressing? . . . Morbid? Okay, so a guy cries a little bit at dinner—some women like that; they think it's sensitive. Look, Cindy, I don't know anybody else . . . I do? . . . (*Looks toward Jim*) Yeah, but she wouldn't be interested in . . . She is? . . . Yeah, I think he's between relationships . . . I'll see what I can do. Okay, bye.

She hangs up. Jim passes by.

Hey, Jim . . . Yo, Jim.
Jim: (*Indignant*) Are you addressing me, Tony?
Tony: Jim, I apologize about last night.
Jim: And you think that makes everything all right?
Tony: Doesn't it?
Jim: (*Embracing him*) Of course, it does, you lug.
Tony: Hey, Jim, I've got great news. Sandy Moratta wants to go out with you.

Jim just looks at him, puzzled.

You know, one of the beautiful girls last night.
Jim: Oh yeah, tell me more.
Tony: Well, she thought you were charming, interesting, and off-beat. And all the time I thought she found you disgusting.
Jim: So did I. Are we talking about the blonde?
Tony: Jim, they were both blond. They were identical twins.
Jim: Oh. The one with the blue eyes?
Tony: (*Giving up*) Yeah, that's the one, Jim. So, anyway, tonight I thought we'd all go see a movie, then maybe go over to Soho . . .
Jim: I don't think so, buddy. Send my regrets to the lady.
Tony: Jim, she's beautiful and she likes you. What more do you want?
Jim: Someone well-read.
Tony: Jim, she's beautiful and she likes you!
Jim: Tony, if you don't read, you don't care.
Tony: Jim, listen. If you don't go out with Sandy, Cindy won't go out with me.
Jim: Sorry, Tony, but the brain is like any other muscle. If you don't exercise it, it turns to mush.

Alex enters as Tony is pursuing Jim.

Tony: (*To Alex*) Why'd you have to become so dour last night?

Elaine has started down the stairs in time to have overheard Tony's remark.

Elaine: What does he mean, you were dour?
Alex: Elaine, would you mind if we don't talk about it? It's too depressing.

Elaine: What's too depressing?

Alex: What we're not talking about.

Jim: Hey, Alex. Your ex-wife seems like a nice lady. Does she read?

Elaine: Your ex-wife? Now you have to talk about it.

Alex: Okay. Jim got a little confused and showed up at the restaurant last night.

Elaine: Get to the ex-wife part.

Alex: Phyllis was there also . . . by herself. Her husband divorced her. Elaine, she looked so alone. She's never been alone before. She left home to marry me, then she left me to marry Carlo. I want to help her, but I don't know how. What happens when for the first time in your whole life, no one's there?

Elaine: You survive. That's what I did.

Alex: Elaine, you're strong and you have children to keep you company and love you. She doesn't have anyone to love her.

Elaine: So what do you do?

Alex: I've been asking myself that. I was once married to her. We did have a child together. There's a connection there, but what is it? I loved her once. She meant everything to me, I guess I meant everything to her. We had our whole lives planned together, we were going to die together . . . and I definitely don't want to get mixed up in all that again.

Elaine: Alex, do you want the advice of another ex-married person? You don't owe her anything. She didn't even invite you to your own daughter's wedding. She's going through a tough time now, but she has to get through it on her own.

Alex: You're right. If I go see her now, I'd just become an emotional crutch for her. There'd be phone calls at five in the morning, all-night vigils. This may sound selfish, but I swear, Elaine, I just can't handle Phyllis in my life again.

The telephone rings in the cage. Louie answers.

Louie: Rieger, it's Madam Ex.

As Alex crosses to the cage.

Alex: (To Elaine) This is really going to be hard for her, but it's got to be done. God, what a relief. (Into phone) Hello, Phyllis. (Gives Elaine a determined look) Uh-huh . . . uh-huh . . . uh-huh . . . no . . . no . . . absolutely not . . . no . . . Phyllis, no . . . Right. Goodbye.

He hangs up and crosses back to Elaine, looking upset.

Elaine: Alex, you did what you had to do.

Alex: Thank you, Elaine, and I guess I can keep telling myself that . . . on my date with her tonight.

And on Alex's fading look of determination, we:
Fade out.

END OF ACT ONE

THE OMEN

"None for me, thanks."

Act Two

Scene One

Fade in:

Int. La Belle Chateau Restaurant—evening

Phyllis is nursing a drink at a table. A well-dressed older couple is sitting nearby. Alex enters.

Alex: Phyllis, I'm sorry I'm late.

Phyllis: That's okay. Alex. I understand how it is for a man in your profession. When humanity hails a cab, someone has to answer.

Alex: That's a dig. I haven't even sat down yet.

Phyllis: Sorry. It's a reflex.

Alex sits down at the table.

Alex: Phyllis, I've done some thinking about you.

Phyllis: I've done some thinking about you, too. Alex, you're the only person I know who for the last eighteen years has done exactly what he wanted to do. I respect you for that. Good for you.

Alex: Why, Phyllis. That's the nicest thing I've ever heard you say.

Phyllis: (*Pointedly*) Alex, it's the nicest thing you've ever heard me say in public.

Alex: (*Getting the point*) Oh yeah.

They both laugh. Phyllis is starting to come on to him. She leans in farther and exposes her neck.

I should understand men better than I do, because I grew up with brothers. I wanted sisters—they're better for a girl. They teach you how to put on makeup, how to do your hair, give you dating tips. You know what brothers teach you? How to unhook a bra with your teeth.

—Carol Siskind

Phyllis: Recognize the scent?

Alex sniffs.

> *Alex:* Molinard de Molinard.
> *Phyllis:* That night in Brooklyn, it turned you into a racehorse.
> *Alex:* Phyllis!

Alex notices the older woman at the next table is leaning in to hear more.

> Look, let's talk about something else. How's Cathy?
> *Phyllis:* All right, Alex, I've lived with it, why shouldn't you? Our daughter has some problems. She's the only twenty-two-year-old who goes to the beauty parlor five times a week. She cries if her massage doesn't go well. You know what she does for amusement? She accuses the servants of stealing. But underneath it all, I think she's spoiled rotten. She's our monument.
> *Alex:* I can't believe it. She seems like the sweetest person on earth. What happened?
> *Phyllis:* You promise you won't take this wrong?
> *Alex:* Of course not.
> *Phyllis:* We feel it's completely your fault.
> *Alex:* Well, I realize I was around during the formative weeks . . .
> *Phyllis:* (Pleased) Alex, we're arguing. It's just like . . .
> *Alex:* (Wincing) . . . old times. Look, Phyllis, I think I should tell you why I came here tonight.
> *Phyllis:* I know why you came here tonight.

She blows him a little kiss.

> *Alex:* Phyllis, you obviously do not know why I came here tonight.
> *Phyllis:* Yes, I do.

The more he protests, the more playful she becomes.

> *Alex:* You do not.
> *Phyllis:* Yes, I do.
> *Alex:* All right, then tell me why I'm here.
> *Phyllis:* Well . . . (very suggestively) You know.
> *Alex:* That's what I figured, and that's where you're wrong. Phyllis, I'm here because you need a friend, and I'm offering my hand in friendship.
> *Phyllis:* You're right, Alex, I do need a friend, and I'm offering my lips in friendship. I'm offering my moist, red lips in friendship. I'm offering the works in friendship.

The woman at the next table "shhh's" her husband.

> *Alex:* Phyllis, please. You're trying to manipulate this into something that wouldn't be good for either of us.

Phyllis looks hurt.

KANGAROO JOKES

A kangaroo walks into a saloon and hops on a stool. He puts ten dollars on the bar and orders a vodka martini. The bartender serves the drink, then gives the kangaroo his change: two dollars. "Pardon me for staring," says the bartender, "but we don't see too many kangaroos in here." "Yeah," replies the kangaroo, "and at these prices you won't see too many more."

Above, a once-told tale. Competitors were asked to retell the anecdote in the style of a well-known individual.

LE JOKE KANGAROO—1965

"And there is another juicy story," Ina said, half closing her cracked-ice eyes, dipping lobster morsels into the silver lake of Gloria's Dom Perignon. "The kangaroo at the bar?" "Baba's current lover. Gives him ten dollars a day mad money. He can't afford it here but he must imitate us." "Poor Baba! Kangaroos aren't very good in bed." We watched him grudgingly hand the bartender his daily allowance. "If you complain about the price of eight-dollar drinks, you must be poor." "I wouldn't know." The candlelight was like melting butter.

—Truman Capote (Gerald Williams)

Once upon a midnight beery
Waiting for the owner, Cleary
To return and take me Weary
From the place and lock the door
In there came a hopping mammal
To the bar and lit a Camel
Then it ordered a martini
(Damnedest thing I ever saw)
"Vodka," it said, "Stolichnaya
Pile the ice a little higher
Less vermouth, I like it dryer
And some olives—*por favor.*"
Thinking fast to make a few
   bucks,
Back from ten I gave it two bucks,
Saying, "You're an odd one,
   Mister
Never seen your type before."
"At these prices? Nevermore."

—E. A. Poe (Mark Kabat)

Phyllis: Alex, why did you accept this date?
Alex: That's exactly what I've been trying to tell you—because I saw you sitting in this restaurant and you looked so alone.

Phyllis turns away from him and looks down at an escargot that she is extracting from a shell.

Phyllis, did I say something wrong?
Phyllis: No.

She takes the butter sauce, dips the escargot and lets it fly at Alex. It hits.

Oh, my goodness. Did I do that?
Alex: (*Wiping it off*) Well, it's tough to tell. It could have been anybody here.
Phyllis: I'm so embarrassed. It's like I couldn't control my hand. God, I don't know what to say.

She dips another escargot. This time Alex watches her like a hawk. When she's done, she leans over and pushes it up Alex's nose.

Alex: Phyllis, if you were up on your Emily Post, you'd know just how cheeky this is.
Phyllis: Did I do it again?
Alex: Yes, this time I'm fairly positive. You know, I'm getting the impulse to leave. Why are you doing this?
Phyllis: Who wouldn't after what you just said?
Alex: What did I just say?
Phyllis: You're here out of pity.
Alex: What? (*To older couple*) Look, you've been eavesdropping on everything. Did I say that?
Woman Diner: You said you felt sorry because she was alone. That's pity.
Alex: Phyllis, if that's the way you took it, I'm sorry, but you only interpret it that way because right now you're in a position where . . . where you're, um . . . where one might think that, um . . .

Phyllis starts crying.

Don't cry, please. Throw snails. This pâté looks promising. Toss that.

She just keeps crying.

Phyllis: Alex, please just leave me alone. Go away.
Alex: But, Phyllis, I can't leave you like this.
Phyllis: Alex, the more you say, the worse I feel.
Alex: But, Phyllis . . .
Phyllis: Please.
Alex: But . . .

Phyllis just glares at him so that he has no choice but to get up and, resigned, exit.

Dissolve to:

Scene Two

Int. garage—evening
Louie is in the cage. Jim is by the coffee machine. Sandy enters and goes up to Louie.

> *Sandy:* Excuse me, I'm looking for a friend.
> *Louie:* You found one, honey.
> *Sandy:* Oh, there he is. *(Calling)* Jim!
> *Louie:* *(To himself, following Sandy)* Jim? Jim?

She goes up to Jim.

> *Sandy:* Hi, Jim. How come you haven't returned any of my calls?
> *Jim:* Fair question. Who are you?
> *Sandy:* Sandy Moratta. My sister and I went out with you and Tony the other night and I'd really like to see you again.
> *Jim:* Oh yeah. Well, I thought about it, Sandy, and I just don't think we're intellectually compatible.
> *Louie:* Iggy, Iggy, Ig . . .

Louie gestures for Jim to come to him.

> *Jim:* *(To Sandy)* Excuse me. I think I'm being paged.

Jim goes to Louie.

> *Louie:* Lean in closer.

Jim does. Louie slaps him on top of the head with a rolled-up newspaper.

MORE KANGAROO JOKES

A kangaroo walks into a saloon and hops on a stool. He puts ten dollars on the bar and orders a vodka martini. The bartender serves the drink, then gives the kangaroo his change: two dollars. "Pardon me for staring," says the bartender, "but we don't see too many kangaroos in here." "Yeah," replies the kangaroo, "and at these prices you won't see too many more."
—Milton Berle (Philip Milstein)

Tank you veddy much. There is kangaroo, from zoo, and he hop into a bar to buy a drink. He put ten dollars on the bar. Where does he get the ten dollars? He is kangaroo! Tank you veddy much.
—Andy Kaufman (Robert Eich)

Ingmar Bergman presents
The Joke.
The action takes place in a bar or any spiritual wasteland. The bartender is underlining a borrowed copy of Hegel when a kangaroo places a fifty-kroner note on the bar.
Kangaroo: An Akvavit martini, please. (The bartender nods and fixed the drink.)
Bartender: Here we are. And your change. (He hands him a ten-kroner note.) Frankly, we don't see your type in these parts.
Kangaroo: Indeed. You have much to learn about economics!
(There is much laughter as the other patrons exchange private jokes at the expense of the bartender.)
—(Larry Laiken)

Jim: What is it, boss?
Louie: I did that for every man who's ever drawn a breath. The fact that that girl wants you is an inexplicable freak of nature. It's like a two-headed snake. You understand what I'm saying, Iggy?
Jim: Nope. Not a clue.

Jim goes back to Sandy. Louie follows.

Sandy, let me ask you a question. When was the last time you read a book?

Louie hits himself on the forehead.

Sandy: Do magazines count?

Jim shakes his head.

I'd like to read more, but I've been so busy working out to stay in shape.
Louie: (*Extremely frustrated*) Time well spent, Iggy?
Jim: Sandy, if you come to my apartment, I think I can promise you one of the most meaningful experiences of your life.
Louie: (*Hopeful*) Huh?

Jim starts to lead Sandy out of the garage.

Jim: I just happen to have Durant's "History of Civilization." Volume Five will make you silly.
Sandy: Ooh.
Jim: (*Chuckling*) Those crazy Huguenots.

Jim and Sandy exit.

Louie: (*Calling after them*) That's it, Romeo. Huguenots will get her hot. Jerk! Jerk! Why don't you go all the way—read her the Crusades.

Louie exits. Elaine and Alex enter and go to the table.

Elaine: Alex, don't feel so bad.
Alex: Elaine, you were right; you were right; you were right. I shouldn't have gone to see her. Now, she's even more messed up than before.
Elaine: But it's not your fault.
Alex: Yes it is. The attraction has always been there, I should have known what was going to happen and I should have never let it. Why didn't I just leave it be?
Elaine: Alex, she'll be all right. Nobody can blame you for what you tried to do.

Elaine places her hand on Alex's. A very sullen and depressed Phyllis enters the garage, unnoticed, and sees them.

Phyllis: (*Quietly*) Alex?

He looks up and sees her. Immediately he breaks from Elaine.

Alex: Phyllis!
Phyllis: No, please. I'm not really here. Don't pay any attention.

Phyllis takes Alex and Elaine's hands and puts them back where they were.

(Longingly to Elaine) How is it? Warm? Strong?

Elaine gets up.

Elaine: I'm going to let you two work this out privately.

Elaine exits.

Phyllis: There's nothing to work out. Alex, I want to apologize for throwing food. I thought about it, and I may have been a little childish. You tried to be kind to me and I appreciate it, and I just came to tell you that and to say I'm going away.

Alex: Where are you going?

Phyllis: To Miami. I have a grandmother there.

Alex: Your grandmother is still alive?

Phyllis: No. *(She takes Alex's hands)* Goodbye, Alex.

She starts to exit.

Alex: Phyllis . . .

He suddenly notices that all eyes are riveted on them.

(To others) Do you mind?

They do. In fact, several indignantly nod their heads.

Let's go someplace where we can talk.

Alex takes her by the hand and leads her quickly into the toolroom.

Cut to:

Scene Three

Int. toolroom—continuous

Alex and Phyllis enter and close the door behind them.

Alex: Phyllis, I'm not sure where to start.

Phyllis: You can start by saying you want to take me back.

Alex: No, Phyllis . . .

She starts to exit. Alex stops her.

Why does it have to be all or nothing? The divorce lasted longer than the marriage, so we must be doing something right. Phyllis, just hear me out and then you never have to see me again. Here it is. No matter what you think of me, I'll always love you. And, yes, Phyllis, I do feel a little sorry for you now, but you're in a situation where someone who does care about you would feel sorry for you. Phyllis, will you allow me to feel sorry for you?

Phyllis: Okay.

She starts to leave.

I'll tell you something, Alex. I'll always love you, too. And you know something else? I felt sorry for you, too, for a lot of years. After all, your wife and child ran out on you and you're stuck in a nowhere job.

Alex: Feel better?

MORE KANGAROO JOKES

STEWED KANGAROO

1 six-foot kangaroo
15 bunches carrots (diced)
6 fifths imported vodka
Seasoning
2 rabbits (optional)

Cut the kangaroo into 2-inch squares and add the diced carrots. Pour vodka over meat and carrots. Season and cook at 425 degrees for 8 days. Serves 150. If more are expected, add rabbits, but only as needed, as one does not like to find a hare in the stew.
—Julia Child (Cassie Tully)

3:00 5 *Mr. Roo*—Comedy (BW) Roo talks Wilbur into taking him to a bar, gets upset over prices. Wilbur: Alan Young.
—(Brian Plante)

One look at the titular marsupial in Disney's pernicious *The Last Kangaroo* and you know he is a mutant. Even less talented is Dean Jones as the inquisitive innkeeper . . .
—John Simon (Robert Gindo)

Phyllis: A little.

Alex: Well, you want to know something else, Phyllis, that you can really feel sorry for me about?

Phyllis: Yes, please.

Alex: In the past eighteen years, I haven't had a relationship as good as the one we had.

Phyllis: Awww, Alex. Really?

She looks at him with genuine sympathy.

Alex: Phyllis, can we be friends? We were married but we were never friends. Can't we just try being friends? Maybe we'd be good at that.

Phyllis: (Experimenting) My friend, Alex. My buddy, Alex. My old chum, Alex . . . who fathered my child. Did I ever thank you for that, pal? (Beginning to sob) Alex, what am I going to do?

Alex puts his arms around her and she cries on his shoulder.

Alex: You're going to cry because you're hurt, then sooner or later, it's going to stop hurting, because almost all things do. And, Phyllis, you're going to be all right . . . You're going to be all right. And, whenever you need me, I'll be there for you.

Phyllis: You really mean that?

Alex: Yes.

Phyllis: Where will you be?

Alex: At home or at work.

Phyllis: Well, which one?

Alex: Well, it depends on when you call.

Phyllis: You don't mean it, do you?

Alex: Yeah, I mean it.

Phyllis: Then give me your address. I want an address.

Alex: Phyllis, friends trust each other. Let's make a deal. You don't go to Miami, and I'll give you my address and never move without telling you. Deal?

He offers her his hand to shake.

Phyllis: Deal.

They shake hands, which turns into a hug, and we . . .
Fade out.

END OF ACT TWO

Tag

Fade in:
Int. garage—day
Louie is in his cage. The night shift cabbies are present. Latka runs in, throws the door shut behind him, puts his fingers in his ears, shuts his eyes, we hear a huge explosion, and we . . .
Fade out.

THE END

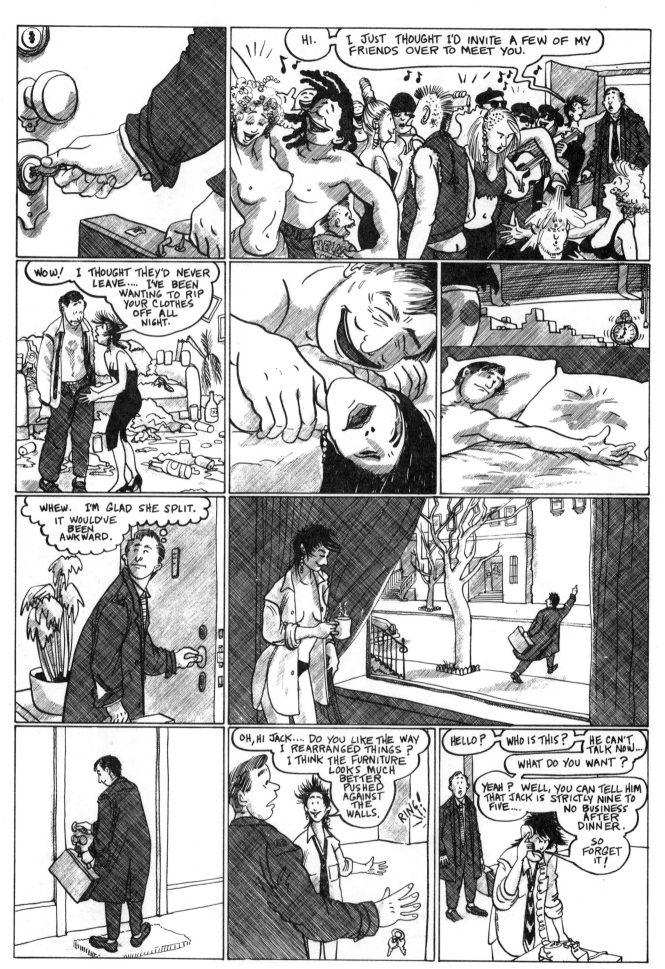

WOODY ALLEN & MARSHALL BRICKMAN

Annie and Alvy

From ANNIE HALL

The darkened auditorium is filled with college students applauding and cheering, excited, as Alvy stands on spotlighted stage holding the microphone.

Alvy (*Gesturing*): W-where am I? I-I keep . . . I have to reorient myself. This is the University of Wisconsin, right? So I'm always . . . I'm tense and . . . uh, when I'm playin' a col— I've a very bad history with colleges. You know, I went to New York University and, uh, tsch, I was thrown out of NYU my freshman year . . . for cheating on my metaphysics final. You know, I looked within the soul of the boy sitting next to me—(*The audience laughs; they're with him*)—and when I was thrown out, my mother, who's an emotionally high-strung woman, locked herself in the bathroom and took an overdose of mah-jongg tiles. (*More applause and laughter*) And, uh, tsch, I was depressed. I was . . . in analysis, I-I, uh, was suicidal; as a matter of fact, uh, I would have killed myself but I was in analysis with a strict Freudian and if you kill yourself . . . they make you pay for the sessions you miss.

Interior. Backstage of theater.
Students mill around Alvy handing him pens and paper for autographs. Annie is next to him, talking over the chattering fans.

Annie: Alvy, you were . . . Alvy, you were just great. I'm not kidding. It was— You were so neat.
Alvy: C-c-coll—College audiences are so wonderful.
Annie: Yeah. Yeah. And you know something? I think that I'm starting to get more of your references, too.
Alvy: Are yuh?
Annie: Yeah.
Alvy: Well, the twelve o'clock show is completely different than the nine.
Young Woman (*Interrupting*): May I have your autograph?
Annie (*Overlapping above speech*): Oh.
Alvy (*To Annie, while autographing*): You're so sure about it.
Annie: Oh, I'm really, uh, looking forward to tomorrow. I mean, you know, I think that it'll be really nice to meet Mother and Father.

They start moving toward the exit, a girl snapping a picture of Alvy with a flash camera as they walk through the crowd.

Alvy: Yeah, I know, they'll hate me immediately. (*To one of his fans*) Thank you.
Annie: No, I don't think so. No, I don't think they're gonna hate you at all. On the contrary, I think—
Alvy: Yeah.

Annie: It's Easter. You know, we'll have a nice dinner, we'll sit down and eat. I think they're gonna really like you.

Exterior. Annie's parents' home—day.

The camera shows a neat two-story house surrounded by a well-manicured green lawn, then cuts to:

Interior. Dining room.

Alvy and the Halls are eating Easter dinner. The sun is pouring through a big picture window, shining on a large, elegantly laid out table. Alvy sits, at one end, rubbing his nose and chewing, the Halls flanking him on either side: Mr. and Mrs. Hall, Grammy, and Annie's brother, Duane.

Mom Hall (Holding her wine glass): It's a nice ham this year, Mom.

Grammy Hall takes a sip of her wine and nods.

Annie (Smiling at Duane): Oh, yeah. Grammy always does such a good job.

Dad Hall (Chewing): A great sauce.

Alvy: It is. (*Smacking his lips*) It's dynamite ham.

Grammy Hall stares down the table at Alvy; a look of utter dislike. Alvy tries not to notice.

Mom Hall (To Dad Hall, smoothing her hair): We went over to the swap meet. Annie, Gram and I. Got some nice picture frames.

Annie: We really had a good time.

Grammy continues to stare at Alvy; he is now dressed in the long black coat and hat of the Orthodox Jew, complete with mustache and beard.

Mom Hall (Lighting a cigarette and turning to Alvy): Ann tells us that you've been seeing a psychiatrist for fifteen years.

Alvy (Setting down his glass and coughing): Yes. I'm making excellent progress. Pretty soon when I lie down on his couch, I won't have to wear the lobster bib.

Mom Hall reacts by sipping from her glass and frowning. Grammy continues to stare.

Dad Hall: Duane and I went out to the boat basin.

Duane: We were caulkin' holes all day.

Dad Hall: Yeah. (*Laughing*) Randolph Hunt was drunk, as usual.

Mom Hall: Oh, that Randolph Hunt. You remember Randy Hunt, Annie. He was in the choir with you.

Annie: Oh, yes, yes.

Alvy, leaning his elbow on the table, looks out toward the camera.

Alvy (To the audience): I can't believe this family. (*Making chewing sounds*) Annie's mother. She's really beautiful. And they're talkin' swap meets and boat basins, and the old lady at the end of the table (*Pointing to Grammy*) is a classic Jew hater. And, uh, they, they really look American, you know, very healthy and . . . like they never get sick or anything. Nothing like my family. You know, the two are like oil and water.

The screen splits in half: on the right is Alvy's family—his mother, father, aunt and uncle—busily eating at the crowded kitchen table. They eat quickly and interrupt one another loudly. On the left the Halls in their dining room. Both dialogues overlap, juxtaposed.

> *Alvy's Father:* Aw, let 'im drop dead! Who needs his business?!
> *Alvy's Mother:* His wife has diabetes!
> *Alvy's Father:* Di-diabetes? Is that any excuse? Diabetes?
> *Alvy's Uncle:* The man is fifty years old and doesn't have a substantial job.
> *Alvy's Aunt (Putting more meat on her husband's plate):* Is that a reason to steal from his father?
> *Alvy's Uncle:* Whatta you talkin' about? You don't know what you're talking about.
> *Alvy's Aunt:* Yes, I know what I'm talking about.
> *Alvy's Mother (Interrupting):* George, defend him!
> *Alvy's Uncle (Over Alvy's father's muttering):* No Moskowitz he had a coronary.
> *Alvy's Aunt:* You don't say.
> *Mom Hall:* Stupid Thelma Poindexter . . . to the Veterans Hospital.
> *Dad Hall:* My God, he's the new president of the El Regis. Let me tell you, the man is somethin' else.
> *Mom Hall:* That's Jack's wife. We used to make that outta raisins—
> *Annie:* Oh, yes, that's right. Did you see the new play?
> *Mom Hall:* Oh, you remember her, Annie.
> *Annie:* Yes, I do.

The two families start talking back and forth to one another. The screen is still split.

> *Mom Hall:* How do you plan to spend the holidays, Mrs. Singer?
> *Alvy's Mother:* We fast.
> *Dad Hall:* Fast?
> *Alvy's Father:* Yeah, no food. You know, we have to atone for our sins.
> *Mom Hall:* What sins? I don't understand.
> *Alvy's Father:* Tell you the truth, neither do we.

Cut to:
Interior. Duane's bedroom—night.
Duane, sitting on his bed, sees Alvy walking past the open door.

> *Duane:* Alvy.
> *Alvy (Walking in):* Oh, hi, Duane, how's it goin'?
> *Duane:* This is my room.
> *Alvy (Looking around):* Oh, yeah? (*He clears his throat*) Terrific.
> *Duane:* Can I confess something?

Alvy sighs and sits down, leaning his arm on Duane's dresser. Duane's face is highlighted by a single lamp.

Duane: I tell you this because, as an artist, I think you'll understand. Sometimes when I'm driving . . . on the road at night . . . I see two headlights coming toward me. Fast. I have this sudden impulse to turn the wheel quickly, head-on into the oncoming car. I can anticipate the explosion. The sound of shattering glass. The . . . flames rising out of the flowing gasoline.

Alvy (Reacting and clearing his throat): Right. Tsch, well I have to—I have to go now, Duane, because I-I'm due back on the planet earth.

He slowly gets up and moves toward the door.

Cut to:

Interior. Kitchen.

Alvy is at the sink washing dishes as the screen cuts to the scene of last month's argument. Annie's voice is heard.

Annie (Offscreen): I'm home!

Alvy (Turning): Oh, yeah? How'd it go?

Annie (Comes into the kitchen and puts down a bag of groceries on the kitchen table): Oh, it was . . . (Laughing) really weird. But she's a very nice woman.

Alvy: Yeah?

Annie: And I didn't have to lie down on the couch. Alvy, she had me sitting up. So I told her about—about the-the family and about my feelings toward men and about my relationship with my brother.

Alvy: M'm.

Annie: And then she mentioned penis envy . . . Did you know about that?

Alvy: Me? I'm—I'm one of the few males who suffers from that, so, so . . . you know.

Annie: M'hm.

Alvy: G-go, on, I'm interested.

Annie: Well, she said that I was very guilty about my impulses toward marriage, and-and children.

Alvy: M'hm.

Annie: And then I remembered when I was a kid how I accidentally saw my parents making love.

Alvy: Tsch. Rea— All this happened in the first hour?

Annie: M'hm.

Alvy: That's amazing. I-I-I . . . I've been goin' for fifteen years, I—you know, I don't got . . . nothing like that in—

Annie: Oh, I told her my dream and then I cried.

Alvy: You cried? I've never once cried. Fantastic . . .

Annie (Taking groceries from the bag): Yeah.

Alvy: I whine. I-I-I sit and I whine.

Annie: In-in . . . Alvy, in my dream Frank Sinatra is holding his pillow across my face and I can't breathe.

Alvy: Sinatra?

After his annual checkup, Bob is shocked to learn that he has somehow contracted a rare disease and has only twelve hours to live.

Arriving home in utter despair, he tells his wife the terrible news and begins to cry. Overcome with grief, Helen hugs him tight and says, "Honey, I'm going to give you a night you'll never forget!"

Whereupon they go to bed early and make passionate love with an ardor they haven't felt in years.

When they're done, Bob turns to his wife and says, "Honey, that was *wonderful,* the best we've ever had. Can we do it again?"

This time it's even more passionate. Later, as Helen is about to doze off, Bob gives her a nudge and says, "Honey, come on. How about one more time?"

"That's easy for *you* to say. *You* don't have to get up in the morning."

Annie: Yeah, and he's strangling me . . .

Alvy: Yeah?

Annie: . . . and I keep, you know, it's—

Alvy (Taking a bottle of juice and some celery from the bag): Well, well, sure . . . because he's a singer and you're a singer, you know, so it's perfect. So you're trying to suffocate yourself. It-it makes perfect sense. Uh, uh, that's a perfect analytic . . . kind of insight.

Annie (Pointing her finger at Alvy): She said, your name was Alvy Singer.

Alvy (Turning to Annie): Whatta you mean? Me?

Annie: Yeah, yeah, yeah, you. Because in the dream . . . I break Sinatra's glasses.

Alvy (Putting his hand to his mouth): Sinatra had gl— You never said Sinatra had glasses. So whatta you saying that I-I'm suffocating you?

Annie (Turning, a jar in her hand): Oh, and God, Alvy, I did . . . this really terrible thing to him. Because then when he sang it was in this real high-pitched voice.

Alvy (Thinking): Tsch, what'd the doctor say?

Annie (Putting away some groceries): Well, she said that I should probably come five times a week. And you know something? I don't think I mind analysis at all. The only question is, Will it change my wife?

Alvy: Will it change your wife?

Annie: Will it change my life?

Alvy: Yeah, but you said, "Will it change my wife!"

Annie: No, I didn't. *(Laughing)* I said, "Will it change my life," Alvy.

Alvy: You said, "Will it change . . . " Wife. Will it change . . .

Annie (Yelling out, angry): Life. I said, "life."

Alvy turns toward the camera.

Alvy (To the audience): She said, "Will it change my wife." You heard that because you were there so I'm not crazy.

Annie: And, Alvy . . . and then I told her about how I didn't think you'd ever really take me seriously, because you don't think that I'm smart enough.

She walks out of the room.

Alvy (To Annie's back, gesturing): Why do you always bring that up? Because I encourage you to take adult-education courses? I think it's a wonderful thing. You meet wonderful, interesting professors.

Cut to:
Exterior. Street.
Annie stands at the open door of a cab, Alvy next to her gesturing as people and cars move by.

Alvy: Adult education is such junk! The professors are so phony. How can you do it?

Annie: I don't care what you say about David, he's a perfectly fine teacher!

Alvy (Interrupting): David! David! I can't believe this!

Annie: And what are you doing following me around for, anyway?

Alvy: I'm following you and David, if you—

Annie (Interrupting): I just think we oughta call this relationship quits!

Annie gets into the cab; Alvy leans over and closes the door.

Alvy: That's fine. That's fine. That's great! *(He turns toward the camera as the cab drives away)* Well, I don't know what I did wrong. *(Gesturing)* I mean, I can't believe this. Somewhere she cooled off to me! *(He walks up to an older woman walking down the street carrying groceries)* Is it—is it something that I did?

Woman on the Street: Never something you do. That's how people are. Love fades.

She moves on down the street.

Alvy (Scratching his head): Love fades. God, that's a depressing thought. I-I-I-I have to ask you a question. *(He stops another passer-by, a man)* Don't go any further. Now, with your wife in bed, d-d-does she need some kind o' artificial stimulation like-like marijuana?

Man on the Street: We use a large vibrating egg.

He walks on.

Alvy (Continuing to walk): Large vibrating egg. Well, I ask a psychopath, I get that kind of an answer. Jesus, I-I, uh, here . . . *(He moves up the sidewalk to a young trendy-looking couple, arms wrapped around each other)* You-you look like a really happy couple. Uh, uh . . . are you?

Young Woman: Yeah.

Alvy: Yeah! So . . . so h-h-how do you account for it?

Young Woman: Uh, I'm very shallow and empty and I have no ideas and nothing interesting to say.

Young Man: And I'm exactly the same way.

Alvy: I see. Well, that's very interesting. So you've managed to work out something, huh?

Young Man: Right.

Young Woman: Yeah.

Alvy: Oh, well, thanks very much for talking to me.

He continues to walk past some other passers-by and moves into the street. A mounted policeman comes by and stops near him. Alvy looks at the horse, as if to speak.

Alvy's Voice-Over: You know, even as a kid I always went for the wrong women. I think that's my problem. When my mother took me to see Snow White, everyone fell in love with Snow White. I immediately fell for the Wicked Queen.

The scene dissolves into a sequence from the animated Snow White *and the*

Seven Dwarfs. *The Wicked Queen, resembling Annie, sits in the palace before her mirror. Alvy, as a cartoon figure, sits beside her, arms crossed in front of him.*

Wicked Queen: We never have any fun anymore.
Cartoon Figure Alvy: How can you say that?
Wicked Queen: Why not? You're always leaning on me to improve myself.
Cartoon Figure Alvy: You're just upset. You must be getting your period.
Wicked Queen: I don't get a period! I'm a cartoon character. Can't I be upset once in a while?

Rob, as a cartoon figure, enters and sits down on the other side of the Wicked Queen.

Cartoon Figure Rob: Max, will you forget about Annie? I know lots of women you can date.
Cartoon Figure Alvy: I don't wanna go out with any other women.
Cartoon Figure Rob: Max, have I got a girl for you. You are going to love her. She's a reporter—

The cartoon figures of Alvy and Rob walk past the Wicked Queen; the screen dissolves into the interior of a concert hall. Rob's voice carries over from the cartoon scene as the screen shows Alvy with the female reporter. It's very crowded, noisy; policemen and reporters are everywhere. Alvy stands with his hands in his pockets, watching the commotion.

Cartoon Figure Rob's Voice-Over: —for *Rolling Stone*.
Female Reporter: I think there are more people here to see the Maharishi than there were to see the Dylan concert. I covered the Dylan concert . . . which gave me chills. Especially when he sang "She takes just like a woman. And she makes love just like a woman Yes, she does And she aches just like a woman But she breaks just like a little girl." *(They move toward the aisles as a guard holds up his hands to stop them)* Up to that I guess the most charismatic event I covered was Mick's Birthday when the Stones played Madison Square Garden.
Alvy (Laughing): Man, that's great. That's just great.
Reporter: You catch Dylan?
Alvy (Coughing): Me? No, no. I-I couldn't make it that ni— My-my raccoon had hepatitis.
Reporter: You have a raccoon?
Alvy (Gesturing): Tsch, a few.
Reporter: The only word for this is trans-plendid. It's trans-plendid.
Alvy: I can think of another word.
Reporter: He's God! I mean, this man is God! He's got millions of followers who would crawl all the way across the world just to touch the hem of his garment.
Alvy: Really? It must be a tremendous hem.
Reporter: I'm a Rosicrucian myself.

The miracle is that men and women get together at all. Men do not understand us. I hear from one guy I don't think I'm seeing anymore, he calls me out of the blue, then he says, "It's only been two weeks." I'm thinking: two weeks? Do you know what that is in girl years?
—Carol Siskind

Alvy: Are you?

Reporter: Yeah.

Alvy: I can't get with any religion that advertises in *Popular Mechanics.* Look—(*The Maharishi, a small, chunky man, walks out of the men's room, huge bodyguards flanking him while policemen hold back the crowds*)—there's God coming outta the men's room.

Reporter: It's unbelievably trans-plendid! I was at the Stones concert in Altamount when they killed that guy, remember?

Alvy: Yeah, were yuh? I was—I was at an Alice Cooper thing where six people were rushed to the hospital with bad vibes.

Interior. Alvy's Bedroom—Night.

The reporter is sitting up in bed, lighted cigarette in her hand. Alvy, lying next to her, rubs his eyes and puts on his eyeglasses.

Reporter (*Looking down at herself*): I hope you don't mind that I took so long to finish.

Alvy (*Sighing*): Oh, no, no, don't be . . . tsch . . . don't be silly. You know, (*Yawning*) I'm startin' t'—I'm startin' to get some feeling back in my jaw now.

Reporter: Oh, sex with you is really a Kafkaesque experience.

Alvy: Oh, tsch, thank you. H'm.

Reporter: I mean that as a compliment.

Alvy (*Making sounds*): I think—I think there's too much burden placed on the orgasm, you know, to make up for empty areas in life.

Reporter: Who said that?

Alvy (*Rubbing his chin and shoulder*): Uh, oh, I don't know. It might have been Leopold and Loeb. (*The telephone rings. Alvy picks it up, rising up slightly from the bed, concerned, as he talks*) Hello . . . Oh, hi . . . Uh, no, what—what's the matter? What-what-what . . . You sound terrible . . . No, what— Sure I— Whatta yuh—what kind of an emergency? . . . No, well stay there. Stay there, I'll come over right now. I'll come over right now. Just stay there, I'll come right over.

He hangs up. The reporter sits in bed still, taking in the situation.

Interior. Annie's apartment. Hallway.

Annie, looking slightly distraught, goes to open the door to Alvy's knock.

Alvy: What's— It's me, open up.

Annie (*Opening the door*): Oh.

Alvy: Are you okay? What's the matter? (*They look at each other, Annie sighing*) Are you all right? What—

Annie: There's a spider in the bathroom.

Alvy (*Reacting*): What?

Annie: There's a big black spider in the bathroom.

Alvy: That's what you got me here for at three o'clock in the morning, 'cause there's a spider in the bathroom?

Annie: My God, I mean you know how I am about insects—

Alvy (*Interrupting, sighing*): Oooh.

Explaining why the keys of his piano were so yellow, Victor Borge insisted that it was not because the piano was old, but because "the elephant smoked too much."

Annie: I can't sleep with a live thing crawling around in the bathroom.

Alvy: Kill it! For Go— What's wrong with you? Don't you have a can of Raid in the house?

Annie (Shaking her head): No.

Alvy, disgusted, starts waving his hands and starts to move into the living room.

Alvy (Sighing): I told you a thousand times you should always keep, uh, a lotta insect spray. You never know who's gonna crawl over.

Annie (Following him): I know, I know, and a first-aid kit and a fire extinguisher.

Alvy: Jesus. All right, gimme a magazine. I— 'cause I'm a little tired. *(While Annie goes off to find him a magazine, Alvy, still talking, glances around the apartment. He notices a small book on a cabinet and picks it up.)* You know, you, you joke with me—about me, you make fun of me, but I'm prepared for anything. An emergency, a tidal wave, an earthquake. Hey, what is this? What? Did you go to a rock concert?

Annie: Yeah.

Alvy: Oh, yeah, really? Really? How-how'd you like it? Was it— was it, I mean, did it . . . was it heavy? Did it achieve total heavy-ocity? Or was it, uh . . .

Annie: It was just great!

Alvy (Thumbing through the book): Oh, humdinger. When— Well, I got a wonderful idea. Why don'tcha get the guy who took you to the rock concert, we'll call him and he can come over and kill the spider. You know, it's a—

He tosses the book down on the cabinet.

Annie: I called you; you wanna help me . . . or not? H'h? Here.

She hands him a magazine.

Alvy (Looking down at the magazine): What is this? What are you— Since when do you read the *National Review?* What are you turning into?

Annie (Turning to a nearby chair for some gum in her pocketbook): Well, I like to try to get all points of view.

Alvy: It's wonderful. Then why don'tcha get William F. Buckley to kill the spider?

Annie (Spinning around to face him): Alvy, you're a little hostile, you know that? Not only that, you look thin and tired.

She puts a piece of gum in her mouth.

Alvy: Well, I was in be— It's three o'clock in the morning. You, uh, you got me outta bed, I ran over here, I couldn't get a taxi cab. You said it was an emergency, and I didn't ge— I ran up the stairs. Bel— I was a lot more attractive when the evening began. Look, uh, tell— Whatta you— Are you going with a right-wing rock-and-roll star? Is that possible?

Annie (Sitting down on a chair arm and looking up at Alvy): Would you like a glass of chocolate milk?

Alvy: Hey, what am I—your son? Whatta you mean? I-I came over t'—

Annie (Touching his chest with her hand): I got the good chocolate, Alvy.

Alvy: Yeah, where is the spider?

Annie: It really is lovely. It's in the bathroom.

Alvy: Is he in the bathroom?

Annie (Rising from chair): Hey, don't squish it, and after it's dead, flush it down the toilet, okay? And flush it a couple o' times.

Alvy (Moving down the hallway to the bathroom): Darling, darling, I've been killing spiders since I was thirty, okay?

Annie (Upset, hands on her neck): Oh. what?

Alvy (Coming back into the living room): Very big spider.

Annie: Yeah?

Alvy: Two . . . Yeah. Lotta, lotta trouble. There's two of 'em.

Alvy starts walking down the hall again, Annie following.

Annie: Two?

Alvy (Opening a closet door): Yep. I didn't think it was that big, but it's a major spider. You got a broom or something with a—

Annie: Oh, I-I left it at your house.

Alvy (Overlapping): —snow shovel or anything or something.

Annie (Overlapping): I think I left it there, I'm sorry.

Reaching up into the closet, Alvy takes out a covered tennis racquet.

Alvy (Holding the racquet): Okay, let me have this.

Annie: Well, what are you doing . . . what are you doing with—

Alvy: Honey, there's a spider in your bathroom the size of a Buick.

He walks into the bathroom, Annie looking after him.

Annie: Well, okay. Oooh.

Alvy stands in the middle of the bathroom, tennis racquet in one hand, rolled magazine in the other. He looks over at the shelf above the sink and picks up a small container. He holds it out, shouting offscreen to Annie.

Alvy: Hey, what is this? You got black soap?

Annie (Offscreen): It's for my complexion.

Alvy: Whatta—whatta yuh joining a minstrel show? Geez. (*Alvy turns and starts swapping the racquet over the shelf, knocking down articles and breaking glass*) Don't worry! (*He continues to swat the racquet all over the bathroom. He finally moves out of the room, hands close to his body. He walks into the other room, where Annie is sitting in a corner of her bed leaning against the wall*) I did it! I killed them both. What-what's the matter? Whatta you—(*Annie is sobbing, her hand over her face*)—whatta you sad about? You— What'd you want me to do? Capture 'em and rehabilitate 'em?

A man and a woman meet in a bar.

"Your place or mine?" she says.

"Hey, if it's going to be a hassle, forget it."

WHAT WE TALK ABOUT WHEN WE'RE FALLING IN LOVE

BY LYNN BARRY ©1988 edited by JAY KENNEDY

29% • WE CANNOT BELIEVE HOW PERFECT WE ARE FOR EACH OTHER.

WE BOTH LOVE TO DANCE.

THE WHITE ALBUM CHANGED BOTH OF OUR LIVES.

WE'RE BOTH ALLERGIC TO BEESTINGS.

WE BOTH FEAR THE DENTIST.

WE BOTH LOVE LEFTOVER CHINESE FOOD.

WE BOTH USE PLASTIC GARBAGE BAGS.

14% • WE HAVE NEVER FELT THIS WAY ABOUT ANYONE IN OUR ENTIRE LIVES.

I THOUGHT I FELT SURE BEFORE, BUT NOW I'M SURE I'M SURE.

SAME WITH ME.

11% THE COMPULSIVE RETELLING OF THE MIRACULOUS STORY OF OUR COMING TOGETHER AS ORDAINED BY THE HAND OF FATE.

WAIT! YOU LEFT OUT THE DOG PART!

OH YEAH! HOW WE BOTH SAID "NICE DOG" AT THE EXACT SAME TIME!

THAT'S WHEN I KNEW.

SAME HERE.

9% MUTUAL CREATION OF A MYTHIC DREAM OF IDEAL FUTURE TOGETHER WITH NO FORESEEABLE PROBLEMS.

O.K., SO WE'LL GET A PLACE IN L.A., A PLACE IN NEW YORK, WE'LL BOTH QUIT OUR JOBS, WRITE A SCREEN PLAY, AND THEN WE'LL TRAVEL.

7% DESCRIPTIVE OUTPOURINGS ABOUT PAST MATES WHO NEVER UNDERSTOOD US.

SHE ACCUSED ME OF BEING WITHHOLDING.
HE WAS WITHHOLDING.
SHE WAS OVERBEARING.
HE SAID I WAS OVERBEARING.

6% BITTER SOLILOQUIES ABOUT PARENTS WHO NEVER UNDERSTOOD US.

I MEAN, MY MOM CALLED OLD YELLER "JUST A MOVIE," YOU KNOW?

OH MY GOD.

HOLD ME.

6% MELANCHOLY MONOLOGUES ABOUT NEVER HAVING BEEN UNDERSTOOD BY ANYONE ELSE.

I'VE ALWAYS FELT, WELL, "DIFFERENT" YOU KNOW?

SAME HERE.

5% RANDOM CHILDHOOD MEMORIES AND EXPLANATION OF SCARS.

I FELL OFF A TEETER-TOTTER ONCE.

5% WHO CARES IF I'M NEGLECTING ALL RESPONSIBILITY, THIS IS MORE IMPORTANT.

SO, FIRE ME.

2% • WHAT TIME IS IT?

2% • WE NEED TO EAT.

2% • WE NEED TO SLEEP.

2% • DO YOU HAVE ANY SHAMPOO AND CAN I USE YOUR TOOTHBRUSH?

.001% WHAT COULD POSSIBLY GO WRONG?

I JUST NEED A LITTLE TIME ALONE, THAT'S ALL.

WHAT FOR?

MARGE PIERCY
The Answer to All Problems

We aren't available, we can't talk to you
right now, but you can talk to us, we say,
but think of the astonishment if machines
suddenly spoke truth: What do you want?

You'd best have a damned good reason for bothering
me, intruding on my silence. If you're bored,
read a good book. Masturbate on your own time.
Call weather or your mother or a talk show.

If you're a creditor, I've just been cremated.
If you're my ex, I'm fucking a perfect body
in Acapulco. Hi, I'm too shy to answer.
I'm scared of obscene calls. I'm paranoid.

I'm sharing a bottle of wine and a loaf of bread
with my lover, our flesh smokes with desire,
our lips brush, our clothes uncoil hissing,
and you have a problem? Try prayer.

Hi obtuse one, it may be eleven on the West Coast
but it's two a.m. here and as you listen
a pitch too high for you to hear is giving
you herpes and melting your elastic and velcro.

Hi, this is the machine. My person is standing
two feet away to see if you're worth the effort.
Hi. If you hang up without leaving a message
your teeth will loosen overnight. I hate drones.

Hi, can my machine call your machine
and make an appointment? Can my machine
mate with yours and breed Walkmans?
Hi, my humans have been murdered and cannot come.

THIS IS HAROLD NORDLEY SPEAKING... I'M NOT IN RIGHT NOW BUT IF YOU'D CARE TO LEAVE A MESSAGE...OOPS! HERE I COME NOW...

© 1982 M. Stevens

Your karma ran over my dogma.   —Anon.

PART THREE

I WOULDN'T WANT
TO PAINT IT

© 1990 by S. Gross

S.GROSS

STEVEN WRIGHT
The Other Side of the Ice

It's a small world, but I wouldn't want to paint it.

I used to be a narrator for a bad mime.

I have a microwave fireplace. You can lie down in front of the fire for an evening in eight minutes.

When I was a baby I kept a diary. Recently I was rereading it. It said: Day One: Still tired from the move. Day Two: Everybody talks to me like I'm an idiot.

I remember turning from one year old to two years old. I was real upset, because I figured in one year my age doubled. If this keeps up, by the time I'm six I'll be ninety.

For my birthday I got a humidifier and a dehumidifier. Put 'em in the same room and let 'em fight it out. Then I filled my humidifier with wax; now my room's all shiny.

A friend of mine named Dennis, his parents are midgets. But he's not a midget. He's a midget dwarf. He's the guy who poses for trophies.

About four years ago—no, it was yesterday—I went to the hardware store and bought some used paint. It was in the shape of a house. I also bought some batteries, but they weren't included. So I had to buy them again.

When I go to Spain I'm flying Air Bizarre. It's a good airline, you buy a combination one way-round trip ticket. You leave any Monday, they bring you back the previous Friday. That way you still have the weekend.

I'm going to court next week, I've been selected for jury duty. It's kind of an insane case. Six thousand ants dressed up as rice and robbed a Chinese restaurant.
I don't think they did it. I know a few of them and they wouldn't do anything like that.

I lost a buttonhole. Where am I going to get a buttonhole?

Years ago I worked in a natural organic health food store in Seattle, Washington. One day a man walked in and said, "If I melt dry ice, can I swim without getting wet?"

I said, "I don't know, let me ask Tony."

Two days later I was fired for eating cotton candy and drinking straight Bosco on the job. So I figured I'd leave the area because I had no ties there anyway except for this girl I was seeing. We had conflicting attitudes. I really wasn't into meditation; she really wasn't into being alive.

I told her I knew when I was going to die because my birth certificate has an expiration date on it.

I decided to leave and go to California, so I packed up my Salvador Dalí print of two blindfolded dental hygienists trying to make a circle on an Etch-A-Sketch. And I headed for the highway and began hitching. Within three minutes I got picked up by one of those huge trailer trucks carrying twenty brand-new cars. I climbed up the side of the cab and I opened the door and the guy said, "I don't have much room in here, why don't you get in one of the cars in the back." So I did. He was really into picking up people because he picked up nineteen more. We all had our own car! Then he went ninety miles an hour and we all got speeding tickets.

I have a telescope on the peephole on my door, so I can see who's at the door for two hundred miles. "Who is it? Who is it gonna be when you get here?"

I like to skate on the other side of the ice.

Last night I was in a bar, and I walked up to this beautiful woman, and I said, "Do you live around here often?"
She said, "You're wearing two different color socks."
I said, "Yes, but to me they're the same, cause I go by thickness."
And she said, "How do you feel?"
And I said, "Well, you know, when you're sitting on a chair and you lean back so you're just on two legs, and you lean too far and you almost fall over, and you catch yourself? I feel like that all the time."

I finally went to the eye doctor, I got contacts, but I only need them when I read so I got flip-ups. I keep them on my desk right next to my typewriter. I have the oldest typewriter in the world. It types in pencil.

I got up the other day and everything in my apartment had been stolen and replaced with an exact replica.

I was walking down the street and I saw a man who had wooden legs and real feet.

I got up this morning, couldn't find my socks, so I called information. I said, "Hello, information?"
She said, "Yes?"
I said, "I can't find my socks."
She said, "They're behind the couch."

One time right in the middle of a job interview I took out a book and I started reading. He said, "What the hell are you doing?"

I said, "Just let me ask you one question. If you were in a vehicle and you were traveling at the speed of light, and then you turned your lights on, would they do anything?"

He said, "I don't know."

I said, "Forget it, then, I don't want to work for you."

A while ago I was in Las Vegas, I was at the roulette table having a furious argument over what I considered an odd number.

I got on an elevator and this older guy got on with me. I was over near the buttons. I pushed number four, I said, "Where are you going?"

He said, "Phoenix." So I pushed Phoenix.

Door opened, two tumbleweeds blew on. We stepped off, we were in downtown Phoenix. I said, "You're the kind of guy I'd really like to hang around with."

I have a large seashell collection which I keep scattered on beaches all over the world. Maybe you've seen it.

For a while I lived in Vermont with a guy named Winnie. We lived in a house that ran on static electricity. If we wanted to cook something, we had to take a sweater off real quick.

The ice-cream truck in my neighborhood plays "Helter Skelter."

The man who lives above me designs synthetic hair balls for ceramic cats. The woman who lives beside me tried to rob a department store with a pricing gun. She walked in and said, "Give me all the money in the vault, or I'll mark down everything in the store."

One night I couldn't sleep so I got up. I got hungry so I went down to this store I know that's open twenty-four hours. When I got down there, there was a guy outside locking it up, he said, "Sorry, we're closed."

I said, "What do you mean, you're closed? The signs says, 'Open 24 hours.'"

He said, "Not in a *row*."

Last night I had a dream that all the babies prevented by the pill showed up. They were mad.

I was once walking through the forest alone, and a tree fell right in front of me, and I didn't hear it.

I had a postcard from my best friend George. It was a satellite picture of the entire earth, and on the back he wrote, "Wish you were here."

STEPHANIE BRUSH

Life: A Warning

THE BIG FIVE POPULAR FEARS OF OUR TIME

In a recent survey, 1,000 Americans were asked to name the fear that torments them the most. They're listed here in no particular order-of-fearsomeness, but most everyone has a personal favorite on this list.

1. Fear of Gradual Hysteria

Gradual hysteria is what happens when you feel your life is completely out of control.

Many of us attempt to exert control by redecorating our homes, for example. We move a picture and find that there is a rectangular spot on the wall where the picture used to be. Then we move the TV stand and find that there are four identical indentations in the rug. Then we move the TV stand back and find that there are now eight identical indentations in the rug. Then someone starts drilling into the pavement outside the window, and the phone rings exactly once, and stops, and we run to answer it, and hear only a metallic click and start to scream, very quietly. We feel that God is talking to us. "Just try it," He is saying. "Just try and make something out of your life."

Gradual hysteria happens in this way to just about everybody. It is usually triggered by loud noises, helplessness, and cumulative stress, and yes, it has the power to destroy everything in its path. But you'd rather have that happening to you than to someone else, wouldn't you?

2. Fear of People Who Have Had Too Much Assertiveness Training

There was a movement back in the seventies in which thousands of ineffectual nebbishes decided that they were not standing firm where it counted in life and they went out and shelled out $300 at adult-education classes around the country, so that they could Learn to Say No! To Get Their Needs Met! To Not Take a Lot of BS from the Guy at the Auto Body Shop!

They walk among us now, and the threat they pose is inestimable.

Have they become, in fact, "assertive" people? Let's be serious. Assertiveness comes from being *born* knowing you're going to get the goods in life, whatever they may be. You don't have to take *courses* in this stuff, okay? And the reason an assertiveness-trained nebbish is a dangerous commodity is that he suspects he is still a nebbish but he's not sure whether it shows or not. *It shows*, all right?

He starts to breathe heavily at the cleaners' because he's just found a spot on his jacket that wasn't there before, and now he is trying to remember his "lines" for the big confrontation to come.

Sometimes, Assertiveness-Trained Nebbishes get the heady feeling of "being honest" and "owning their feelings"—and they do embarrassing things like embrace you and say, "I hate your rug, but the honesty of this moment feels beautiful."

Whatever we do, it is essential for us to impress on our friends that we liked them better when they were obsequious, waffling little toadies. At least then we knew what we were dealing with. At least life had some kind of structure.

There is some work being done to "de-program" these people, sort of like former members of cults. But it is too soon to tell whether this technique is going to have any effect.

3. Insomnia: Fear of Consciousness

"Consciousness" is a state of awareness of all the realities of life. If we had to live in a state of total awareness all the time, if we had to dwell on realities like crime and war and what happens to the members of "Menudo" after they turn fifteen, then we should all surely become mad and highly depressed.

So sleep was invented to spare us from total consciousness. But the more we can't sleep, the more conscious—and therefore *anxious*—we become. The same scientists who have clocked things like REM cycles and muscle-activity cycles have also clocked pre-sleep anxiety cycles.

- Cycle I usually involves WORK ANXIETY: Did I remember to turn off my office light? Does my boss like me? Would my boss recognize me if he saw me in a small crowd?

- Cycle II involves CURRENT-EVENTS ANXIETY: Is there plutonium in my drinking water? Will the world be safe for my children? With street crime in the state it's in, would it be all right if I asked my dog to walk himself at night?

- Cycle III occurs when the mind drifts off to a netherworld of half-formed dreads and sinister potentialities. What if my family got sick and died? What if they were tied to a stake in the Amazon rain forest and eaten by termites? What if I were on a quiz show and had to know the Gross National Product of Burma?

Some of these fears, unfortunately, have more than a little merit (although for what it's worth, the GNP of Burma is 657,000 Bwenzii a year, and there are no termites in the Amazon rain forest. Then again, there's nothing to stop them from being flown in.).

It is estimated that over 45 percent of the population suffers from insomnia on any given night; which means that on any given night YOU ARE ALONE WITH 150 MILLION OTHER AMERICANS. So when you think about it, it would make sense if you were given these people's phone numbers, so you'd at least have someone to talk to. (And yet, paradoxically, if you called them, they would scream into the receiver, "What are you, *crazy?* It's *three o'clock in the morning!*" And they would call the police.)

4. Fear of Amnesia

There are really three varieties of amnesia we need to talk about here:

"Random" amnesia strikes about 5 million Americans a year, including an undisclosed number of dental patients who "forget" to floss between meals, and a number of hotel guests who "forget" to return the towels, stationery, and light fixtures to the rooms where they found them. Also every year, twelve or thirteen natives of Florence, Oregon, fall victim to *group* amnesia and awaken and imagine themselves to be natives of Florence, Italy. They immediately start painting frescoes all over the sides of municipal buildings, and each year the frescoes have to be sandblasted off, at the expense of thousands to the taxpayers, since no one in Oregon is known to have any artistic talent.

By far the most virulent form of amnesia is SOAPSTAR amnesia, which occurs relentlessly in daytime television. Hardly a day goes by when someone on one of the major networks is not suffering from a complete memory loss—*"What do you mean 'Nicki Matuszak?' I've never heard of a 'Nicki Matuszak' in my life! I'm a beekeeper! Stay away from me!"*

These poor doomed sufferers are destined to wander around strange towns in brunette wigs and unattractive clothing, marry people they have never met before, and ignore the pleas of their husbands and wives on television ("Nicki! It's me, Stefano! I never meant to shoot you in the brain! Please come home!").

Naturally, if we watch a lot of daytime TV, we are afraid that this fate could befall us (although we secretly wonder how TV amnesiacs can use their American Express cards for months at a time, pay the finance charge, and still not have a clue to their identity).

NOW YOU'VE GOT THE VIEW ALL OUT OF ORDER.

PIRARO · © CHRONICLE FEATURES 1988.

5. Fear of Major Brain-Loss

Many people are afraid of appearing helpless, foolish, and "brainless." For example, of being in serious car crashes and becoming "vegetables." (Although if you get incinerated in a *plane* crash, you get to become a "mineral," which is probably much, much worse.)

A far greater threat than this, however, is that of having a song you really hate running through your head that you just can't get rid of. It certainly happens more frequently. NO ONE EVER HAS A SONG THEY *LIKE* RUNNING THROUGH THEIR HEAD. Large numbers of college graduates still hear "Yummy, Yummy, Yummy," by the Ohio Express, and some people have gone nearly insane with a continual rendition of "Hey! You! Get Offa My Cloud!" as performed by the Ray Conniff Singers.

Add to the dangers of brain-loss the persistent lure of religious cults, lurking tantalizingly with "all the answers" around every corner. Beyond even the Hare Krishnas and the Unification Church lies the "Pepsi Generation," a dangerous cult headed by singer LIONEL RICHIE. Instead of working regular hours and contributing to the Gross National Product, the Pepsi Generation spends hours taking dancing lessons and having their teeth professionally polished. They venerate organized volleyball and drive dune buggies to all their major appointments. Fortunately, they are closely watched and monitored by a number of federal agencies.

A BIG CONCERN

As terrible as the fear of existence is, the fear of nonexistence is even worse. Maybe if we only knew what happened to us after we died, it would all be easier.

One speculation is that we go to the Land of the Umbrellas. You've probably seen them at the end of every rainstorm. Lying in the gutter, crumpled, skeletal, inside-out, bereft of personal history. Who did these umbrellas belong to? Where are they going? What use are they now?

Others say that after death we go to the land of the M&M's—the place where the M&M's go after they fall behind the cushions on the sofa. Or some say it's the land of the Other Shoe. (Ever drive along the road and see one shoe lying on the pavement, and wonder how it got there? You never see *both shoes;* the other shoe has gone to join the umbrellas and the M&M's.)

In the end it is probably foolish to speculate about such matters. In ancient times the biggest fear was that you would have a terrible life and be reincarnated, and the next life would be even worse. Nowadays, life is Hollywood, and if your life's been bad, you don't have to worry about there being a sequel. Not if Part I didn't make any money.

Life is a 3-D movie without the glasses. —*Ronnie Shakes*

JANE WAGNER *as performed by Lily Tomlin*

Time and Space

They asked me once my thoughts on infinity and I told
  'em
with all I had to think about, infinity was not on my list
of things to think about. It could be time on an ego trip,
for all I know. After all, when you're pressed for time,
infinity may as well
not be there.
They said, to them, infinity is
time-released time.

Frankly, infinity doesn't affect
me personally one way or the other.

You think too long about infinity, you could go
stark raving mad.
But I don't ever want to sound negative about going
  crazy.
I don't want to overromanticize it either, but frankly,
goin' crazy was the *best* thing ever happened to me.
I don't say it's for everybody;
some people couldn't cope.

But for me it came at a time when nothing else seemed
  to be
working. I got the kind of madness Socrates talked about,
"A divine release of the soul from the yoke of
custom and convention." I refuse to be intimidated by
reality anymore.
After all, what is reality anyway? Nothin' but a
collective hunch. My space chums think reality was
  once a
primitive method of
crowd control that got out of hand.
In my view, it's absurdity dressed up
in a three-piece business suit.

I made some studies, and
reality is the leading cause of stress amongst those in
touch with it. I can take it in small doses, but as a lifestyle
I found it too confining.
It was just too needful;
it expected me to be there for it *all* the time, and with all
I have to do—
I had to let something go.

Now, since I put reality on a back burner, my days are
jam-packed and fun-filled. Like some days, I go hang out
around Seventh Avenue; I love to do this old joke:
I wait for some music-loving tourist from one of the
  hotels
on Central Park to go up and ask someone,
"How do I get to Carnegie Hall?"
Then I run up and yell,
"Practice!"
The expression on people's faces is priceless. I never
could've done stuff like that when I was in my *right*
  mind.
I'd be worried people would think I was *crazy*.
When I think of the fun I missed,
I try not to be bitter.

See, the human mind is kind of like . . .

a piñata. When it breaks open,
there's a lot of surprises inside. Once you get the piñata
perspective, you see that losing your mind
can be a peak experience.

I was not always a bag lady, you know.
I used to be a designer and creative consultant. For big
companies!
Who do you think thought up the color scheme
for Howard Johnson's?
At the time, nobody was using
orange and aqua
in the same room together.
With fried clams.

Laugh tracks:
I gave TV sitcoms the idea for canned laughter.
I got the idea, one day I heard voices
and no one was there.

Who do you think had the idea to package panty hose
in a plastic goose egg?

WOODY ALLEN
The Kugelmass Episode

Kugelmass, a professor of humanities at City College, was unhappily married for the second time. Daphne Kugelmass was an oaf. He also had two dull sons by his first wife, Flo, and was up to his neck in alimony and child support.

"Did I know it would turn out so badly?" Kugelmass whined to his analyst one day. "Daphne had promise. Who suspected she'd let herself go and swell up like a beach ball? Plus she had a few bucks, which is not in itself a healthy reason to marry a person, but it doesn't hurt, with the kind of operating nut I have. You see my point?"

Kugelmass was bald and as hairy as a bear, but he had soul.

"I need to meet a new woman," he went on. "I need to have an affair. I may not look the part, but I'm a man who needs romance. I need softness, I need flirtation. I'm not getting younger, so before it's too late I want to make love in Venice, trade quips at '21,' and exchange coy glances over red wine and candlelight. You see what I'm saying?"

Dr. Mandel shifted in his chair and said, "An affair will solve nothing. You're so unrealistic. Your problems run much deeper."

"And also this affair must be discreet," Kugelmass continued. "I can't afford a second divorce. Daphne would really sock it to me."

"Mr. Kugelmass—"

"But it can't be anyone at City College, because Daphne also works there. Not that anyone on the faculty at C.C.N.Y. is any great shakes, but some of those co-eds . . . "

"Mr. Kugelmass—"

"Help me. I had a dream last night. I was skipping through a meadow holding a picnic basket and the basket was marked 'Options.' And then I saw there was a hole in the basket."

"Mr. Kugelmass, the worst thing you could do is act out. You must simply express your feelings here, and together we'll analyze them. You have been in treatment long enough to know there is no overnight cure. After all, I'm an analyst, not a magician."

"Then perhaps what I need is a magician," Kugelmass said, rising from his chair. And with that he terminated his therapy.

A couple of weeks later, while Kugelmass and Daphne were moping around in their apartment one night like two pieces of old furniture, the phone rang.

"I'll get it," Kugelmass said. "Hello."

"Kugelmass?" a voice said. "Kugelmass, this is Persky."

"Who?"

"Persky. Or should I say The Great Persky?"

"Pardon me?"

"I hear you're looking all over town for a magician to bring a little exotica into your life? Yes or no?"

"Sh-h-h," Kugelmass whispered. "Don't hang up. Where are you calling from, Persky?"

Early the following afternoon, Kugelmass climbed three flights of stairs in a broken-down apartment house in the Bushwick section of Brooklyn. Peering through the darkness of the hall, he found the door he was looking for and pressed the bell. I'm going to regret this, he thought to himself.

Seconds later, he was greeted by a short, thin, waxy-looking man.

"*You're* Persky the Great?" Kugelmass said.

"The Great Persky. You want a tea?"

"No, I want romance. I want music. I want love and beauty."

"But not tea, eh? Amazing. O.K., sit down."

Persky went to the back room, and Kugelmass heard the sounds of boxes and furniture being moved around. Persky reappeared, pushing before him a large object on squeaky roller-skate wheels. He removed some old silk handkerchiefs that were lying on its top and blew away a bit of dust. It was a cheap-looking Chinese cabinet, badly lacquered.

"Persky," Kugelmass said, "what's your scam?"

"Pay attention," Persky said. "This is some beautiful effect. I developed it for a Knights of Pythias date last year, but the booking fell through. Get into the cabinet."

"Why, so you can stick it full of swords or something?"

"You see any swords?"

Kugelmass made a face and, grunting, climbed into the cabinet. He couldn't help noticing a couple of ugly rhinestones glued onto the raw plywood just in front of his face. "If this is a joke," he said.

"Some joke. Now, here's the point. If I throw any novel into this cabinet with you, shut the doors, and tap it three times, you will find yourself projected into that book."

Kugelmass made a grimace of disbelief.

"It's the *emess*," Persky said. "My hand to God. Not just a novel, either. A short story, a play, a poem. You can meet any of the women created by the world's best writers. Whoever you dreamed of. You could carry on all you like with a real winner. Then when you've had enough you give a yell, and I'll see you're back here in a split second."

"Persky, are you some kind of outpatient?"

"I'm telling you it's on the level," Persky said.

Kugelmass remained skeptical. "What are you telling me—that this cheesy homemade box can take me on a ride like you're describing?"

"For a double sawbuck."

Kugelmass reached for his wallet. "I'll believe this when I see it," he said.

Persky tucked the bills in his pants pocket and turned toward his bookcase. "So who do you want to meet? Sister Carrie? Hester Prynne? Ophelia? Maybe someone by Saul Bellow? Hey, what about Temple Drake? Although for a man your age she'd be a workout."

"French. I want to have an affair with a French lover."

"Nana?"

"I don't want to have to pay for it."

"What about Natasha in *War and Peace?*"

"I said French. I know! What about Emma Bovary? That sounds to me perfect."

"You got it, Kugelmass. Give me a holler when you've had enough." Persky tossed in a paperback copy of Flaubert's novel.

"You sure this is safe?" Kugelmass asked as Persky began shutting the cabinet doors.

"Safe. Is anything safe in this crazy world?" Persky rapped three times on the cabinet and then flung open the doors.

Kugelmass was gone. At the same moment, he appeared in the bedroom of Charles and Emma Bovary's house at Yonville. Before him was a beautiful woman, standing alone with her back turned to him as she folded some linen. I can't believe this, thought Kugelmass, staring at the doctor's ravishing wife. This is uncanny. I'm here. It's her.

Emma turned in surprise. "Goodness, you startled me," she said. "Who are you?" She spoke in the same fine English translation as the paperback.

It's simply devastating, he thought. Then, realizing that it was he whom she had addressed, he said, "Excuse me. I'm Sidney Kugelmass. I'm from City College. A professor of humanities. C.C.N.Y.? Uptown. I— oh, boy!"

Emma Bovary smiled flirtatiously and said, "Would you like a drink? A glass of wine, perhaps?"

She is beautiful, Kugelmass thought. What a contrast with the troglodyte who shared his bed! He felt a sudden impulse to take this vision into his arms and tell her she was the kind of woman he had dreamed of all his life.

"Yes, some wine," he said hoarsely. "White. No, red. No, white. Make it white."

"Charles is out for the day," Emma said, her voice full of playful implication.

After the wine, they went for a stroll in the lovely French countryside. "I've always dreamed that some mysterious stranger would appear and rescue me from the monotony of this crass rural existence," Emma said, clasping his hand. They passed a small church. "I love what you have on," she murmured. "I've never seen anything like it around here. It's so . . . so modern."

"It's called a leisure suit," he said romantically. "It was marked down." Suddenly he kissed her. For the next hour they reclined under a tree and whispered together and told each other deeply meaningful things with their eyes. Then Kugelmass sat up. He had just remembered he had to meet Daphne at Bloomingdale's. "I must go," he told her. "But don't worry, I'll be back."

"I hope so," Emma said.

He embraced her passionately, and the two walked back to the house. He held Emma's face cupped in his palms, kissed her again, and yelled, "O.K., Persky! I got to be at Bloomingdale's by three-thirty."

There was an audible pop, and Kugelmass was back in Brooklyn.

"So? Did I lie?" Persky asked triumphantly.

"Look, Persky, I'm right now late to meet the ball and chain at Lexington Avenue, but when can I go again? Tomorrow?"

"My pleasure. Just bring a twenty. And don't mention this to anybody."

"Yeah. I'm going to call Rupert Murdoch."

Kugelmass hailed a cab and sped off to the city. His heart danced on point. I am in love, he thought, I am the possessor of a wonderful secret. What he didn't realize was that at this very moment students in various classrooms across the country were saying to their teachers, "Who is this character on page 100? A bald Jew is kissing Madame Bovary?" A teacher in Sioux Falls, South Dakota, sighed and thought, Jesus, these kids, with their pot and acid. What goes through their minds!

Daphne Kugelmass was in the bathroom-accessories department at Bloomingdale's when Kugelmass arrived breathlessly. "Where've you been?" she snapped. "It's four-thirty."

"I got held up in traffic," Kugelmass said.

Kugelmass visited Persky the next day, and in a few minutes was again passed magically to Yonville. Emma couldn't hide her excitement at seeing him. The two spent hours together, laughing and talking about their different backgrounds. Before Kugelmass left, they made love. "My God, I'm doing it with Madame Bovary!" Kugelmass whispered to himself. "Me, who failed freshman English."

As the months passed, Kugelmass saw Persky many times and developed a close and passionate relationship with Emma Bovary. "Make sure and always get me into the book before page 120," Kugelmass said to the magician one day. "I always have to meet her before she hooks up with this Rodolphe character."

"Why?" Persky asked. "You can't beat his time?"

"Beat his time. He's landed gentry. Those guys have nothing better to do than flirt and ride horses. To me, he's one of those faces you see in the pages of *Women's Wear Daily*. With the Helmut Berger hairdo. But to her he's hot stuff."

"And her husband suspects nothing?"

"He's out of his depth. He's a lacklustre little paramedic who's thrown in his lot with a jitterbug. He's ready to go to sleep by ten, and she's putting on her dancing shoes. Oh, well . . . See you later."

And once again Kugelmass entered the cabinet and passed instantly to the Bovary estate at Yonville. "How you doing, cupcake?" he said to Emma.

"Oh, Kugelmass," Emma sighed. "What I have to put up with. Last night at dinner, Mr. Personality dropped off to sleep in the middle of the dessert course. I'm pouring my heart out about Maxim's and the ballet, and out of the blue I hear snoring."

"It's O.K., darling. I'm here now," Kugelmass said, embracing her. I've earned this, he thought, smelling Emma's French perfume and

---

Two old friends make a pact that the first one to die will do everything possible to make contact with the other. The following summer, Mel dies of a heart attack, leaving Dave lonely and depressed. A month after the funeral, Dave picks up the phone, and it's Mel—just as he promised.

"Mel, old pal, it's great to hear from you. Boy, I really miss you. Tell me, what do you do all day?"

"Dave, you're not going to believe it. In the morning, I get up for a big breakfast, and then I screw. After that I go out and lie around in the sun, and screw some more. Then it's time for lunch. Then, in the afternoon, a nap and then more screwing until dinner. Then one last screw before I go to sleep."

"Mel, that's *remarkable*. I had no idea heaven would be like that."

"Who's in Heaven? I'm a bull in Wisconsin!"

burying his nose in her hair. I've suffered enough. I've paid enough analysts. I've searched till I'm weary. She's young and nubile, and I'm here a few pages after Leon and just before Rodolphe. By showing up during the correct chapters, I've got the situation knocked.

Emma, to be sure, was just as happy as Kugelmass. She had been starved for excitement, and his tales of Broadway night life, of fast cars and Hollywood and TV stars, enthralled the young French beauty.

"Tell me again about O.J. Simpson," she implored that evening, as she and Kugelmass strolled past Abbé Bournisien's church.

"What can I say? The man is great. He sets all kinds of rushing records. Such moves. They can't touch him."

"And the Academy Awards?" Emma said wistfully. "I'd give anything to win one."

"First you've got to be nominated."

"I know. You explained it. But I'm convinced I can act. Of course, I'd want to take a class or two. With Strasberg maybe. Then, if I had the right agent—"

"We'll see, we'll see. I'll speak to Persky."

That night, safely returned to Persky's flat, Kugelmass brought up the idea of having Emma visit him in the big city.

"Let me think about it," Persky said. "Maybe I could work it. Stranger things have happened." Of course, neither of them could think of one.

"Where the hell do you go all the time?" Daphne Kugelmass barked at her husband as he returned home late that evening. "You got a chippie stashed somewhere?"

"Yeah, sure, I'm just the type," Kugelmass said wearily. "I was with Leonard Popkin. We were discussing Socialist agriculture in Poland. You know Popkin. He's a freak on the subject."

"Well, you've been very odd lately," Daphne said. "Distant. Just don't forget about my father's birthday. On Saturday?"

"Oh, sure, sure," Kugelmass said, heading for the bathroom.

"My whole family will be there. We can see the twins. And Cousin Hamish? You should be more polite to Cousin Hamish—he likes you."

"Right, the twins," Kugelmass said, closing the bathroom door and shutting out the sound of his wife's voice. He leaned against it and took a deep breath. In a few hours, he told himself, he would be back in Yonville again, back with his beloved. And this time, if all went well, he would bring Emma back with him.

At three-fifteen the following afternoon, Persky worked his wizardry again. Kugelmass appeared before Emma, smiling and eager. The two spent a few hours at Yonville with Binet and then remounted the Bovary carriage. Following Persky's instructions, they held each other tightly, closed their eyes, and counted to ten. When they opened them, the carriage was just drawing up at the side door of the Plaza Hotel, where Kugelmass had optimistically reserved a suite earlier in the day.

"I love it! It's everything I dreamed it would be," Emma said as she swirled joyously around the bedroom, surveying the city from their window. "There's F.A.O. Schwarz. And there's Central Park, and the Sherry is which one? Oh, there—I see. It's too divine."

On the bed there were boxes from Halston and Saint Laurent. Emma unwrapped a package and held up a pair of black velvet pants against her perfect body.

"The slacks suit is by Ralph Lauren," Kugelmass said. "You'll look like a million bucks in it. Come on, sugar, give us a kiss."

"I've never been so happy!" Emma squealed as she stood before the mirror. "Let's go out on the town. I want to see *Chorus Line* and the Guggenheim and this Jack Nicholson character you always talk about. Are any of his flicks showing?"

"I cannot get my mind around this," a Stanford professor said. "First a strange character named Kugelmass, and now she's gone from the book. Well, I guess the mark of a classic is that you can reread it a thousand times and always find something new."

© 1990 by Thomas W. Cheney

The lovers passed a blissful weekend. Kugelmass had told Daphne he would be away at a symposium in Boston and would return Monday. Savoring each moment, he and Emma went to the movies, had dinner in Chinatown, passed two hours at a discothèque, and went to bed with a TV movie. They slept till noon on Sunday, visited SoHo, and ogled celebrities at Elaine's. They had caviar and champagne in their suite on Sunday night and talked until dawn. That morning, in the cab taking them to Persky's apartment, Kugelmass thought, It was hectic, but worth it. I can't bring her here too often, but now and then it will be a charming contrast with Yonville.

At Persky's, Emma climbed into the cabinet, arranged her new boxes of clothes neatly around her, and kissed Kugelmass fondly. "My place next time," she said with a wink. Persky rapped three times on the cabinet. Nothing happened.

"Hmm," Persky said, scratching his head. He rapped again, but still no magic. "Something must be wrong," he mumbled.

"Persky, you're joking!" Kugelmass cried. "How can it not work?"

"Relax, relax. Are you still in the box, Emma?"

"Yes."

Persky rapped again—harder this time.

"I'm still here, Persky."

"I know, darling. Sit tight."

"Persky, we *have* to get her back," Kugelmass whispered. "I'm a married man, and I have a class in three hours. I'm not prepared for anything more than a cautious affair at this point."

"I can't understand it," Persky muttered. "It's such a reliable little trick."

But he could do nothing. "It's going to take a little while," he said to Kugelmass. "I'm going to have to strip it down. I'll call you later."

Kugelmass bundled Emma into a cab and took her back to the Plaza. He barely made it to his class on time. He was on the phone all day, to Persky and to his mistress. The magician told him it might be several days before he got to the bottom of the trouble.

"How was the symposium?" Daphne asked him that night.

"Fine, fine," he said, lighting the filter end of a cigarette.

"What's wrong? You're as tense as a cat."

"Me? Ha, that's a laugh. I'm as calm as a summer night. I'm just going to take a walk." He eased out the door, hailed a cab, and flew to the Plaza.

"This is no good," Emma said. "Charles will miss me."

"Bear with me, sugar," Kugelmass said. He was pale and sweaty. He kissed her again, raced to the elevators, yelled at Persky over a pay phone in the Plaza lobby, and just made it home before midnight.

"According to Popkin, barley prices in Kraków have not been this stable since 1971," he said to Daphne, and smiled wanly as he climbed into bed.

The whole week went by like that.

On Friday night, Kugelmass told Daphne there was another symposium he had to catch, this one in Syracuse. He hurried back to the Plaza, but the second weekend there was nothing like the first. "Get me back into the novel or marry me," Emma told Kugelmass. "Meanwhile, I want to get a job or go to class, because watching TV all day is the pits."

"Fine. We can use the money," Kugelmass said. "You consume twice your weight in room service."

"I met an Off Broadway producer in Central Park yesterday, and he said I might be right for a project he's doing," Emma said.

"Who is this clown?" Kugelmass asked.

"He's not a clown. He's sensitive and kind and cute. His name's Jeff Something-or-Other, and he's up for a Tony."

Later that afternoon, Kugelmass showed up at Persky's drunk.

"Relax," Persky told him. "You'll get a coronary."

"Relax. The man says relax. I've got a fictional character stashed in a hotel room, and I think my wife is having me tailed by a private shamus."

"O.K., O.K. We know there's a problem." Persky crawled under the cabinet and started banging on something with a large wrench.

"I'm like a wild animal," Kugelmass went on. "I'm sneaking around town, and Emma and I have had it up to here with each other. Not to mention a hotel tab that reads like the defense budget."

"So what should I do? This is the world of magic," Persky said. "It's all nuance."

"Nuance, my foot. I'm pouring Dom Pérignon and black eggs into this little mouse, plus her wardrobe, plus she's enrolled at the Neighborhood Playhouse and suddenly needs professional photos. Also, Persky, Professor Fivish Kopkind, who teaches Comp Lit and who has always been jealous of me, has identified me as the sporadically appearing character in the Flaubert book. He's threatened to go to Daphne. I see ruin and alimony; jail. For adultery with Madame Bovary, my wife will reduce me to beggary."

"What do you want me to say? I'm working on it night and day. As far as your personal anxiety goes, that I can't help you with. I'm a magician, not an analyst."

By Sunday afternoon, Emma had locked herself in the bathroom and refused to respond to Kugelmass's entreaties. Kugelmass stared out the window at the Wollman Rink and contemplated suicide. Too bad this is a low floor, he thought, or I'd do it right now. Maybe if I ran away to Europe and started life over . . . Maybe I could sell the *International Herald Tribune*, like those young girls used to.

The phone rang. Kugelmass lifted it to his ear mechanically.

"Bring her over," Persky said. "I think I got the bugs out of it."

Kugelmass's heart leaped. "You're serious?" he said. "You got it licked?"

"It was something in the transmission. Go figure."

"Persky, you're a genius. We'll be there in a minute. Less than a minute."

Again the lovers hurried to the magician's apartment, and again Emma Bovary climbed into the cabinet with her boxes. This time there was no kiss. Persky shut the doors, took a deep breath, and tapped the box three times. There was the reassuring popping noise, and when Persky peered inside, the box was empty. Madame Bovary was back in her novel. Kugelmass heaved a great sigh of relief and pumped the magician's hand.

"It's over," he said. "I learned my lesson. I'll never cheat again, I swear it." He pumped Persky's hand again and made a mental note to send him a necktie.

Three weeks later, at the end of a beautiful spring afternoon, Persky answered his doorbell. It was Kugelmass, with a sheepish expression on his face.

"O.K., Kugelmass," the magician said. "Where to this time?"

"It's just this once," Kugelmass said. "The weather is so lovely, and I'm not getting any younger. Listen, you've read *Portnoy's Complaint?* Remember The Monkey?"

"The price is now twenty-five dollars, because the cost of living is up, but I'll start you off with one freebie, due to all the trouble I caused you."

"You're good people," Kugelmass said, combing his few remaining hairs as he climbed into the cabinet again. "This'll work all right?"

"I hope. But I haven't tried it much since all that unpleasantness."

"Sex and romance," Kugelmass said from inside the box. "What we go through for a pretty face."

Persky tossed in a copy of *Portnoy's Complaint* and rapped three times on the box. This time, instead of a popping noise there was a dull explosion, followed by a series of crackling noises and a shower of sparks. Persky leaped back, was seized by a heart attack, and dropped dead. The cabinet burst into flames, and eventually the entire house burned down.

Kugelmass, unaware of this catastrophe, had his own problems. He had not been thrust into *Portnoy's Complaint*, or into any other novel, for that matter. He had been projected into an old textbook, *Remedial Spanish,* and was running for his life over a barren, rocky terrain as the word *tener* ("to have")—a large and hairy irregular verb—raced after him on its spindly legs.

I must warn you that underneath these clothes I'm wearing boxer shorts and I know how to use them.

—*Robert Orben*

RONNIE SHAKES
My Shrink Sends Me Hate Mail

My girlfriend didn't just fake orgasms. She lip-synched them to recordings.

After we made love she was crying. I said, "Tears of joy?" She said, "Yes. I'm so glad it's over!"

Sometimes the unexpected does happen. Once, this exquisite woman fell for me. After we made love, she gave me a check for a hundred dollars. I said, "Honey, I don't get paid for sex." She said, "This is hush money."

The Pope is very predictable. I saw a headline once, POPE DENOUNCES FALKLAND WAR. No kidding. I'd like to see a headline, POPE LOSES CHURCH IN POKER GAME. VATICAN MOVED TO ATLANTIC CITY.

One question on hospital admittance forms really gets me. "Sex: Male or Female?" Do I want to be in a hospital where they can't tell the difference?

I'm not well liked. My shrink sends me hate mail.

Where there's a will there's a dead person.

As a teenager I just wanted to fit in, just be one of the boys. It was tough. I went to an all black school. I went so far as to have them print my negative in the yearbook. I think it was the black teeth that gave me away.

Roaches, oh, do I have roaches. Some of them have tusks. Finally, I got an exterminator. He was a weird guy, a little unorthodox, but highly recommended. The first time he came over, I asked him, "Well, how do you kill them? Spray? Powder? Traps?"
He says, "No, crucifixion. We're going to make examples out of these roaches."
So I got out the toothpicks. He must have set up twenty-five, thirty thousand miniature crucifixes all over the apartment with roaches taped to them. That night the termites came out and cut them down.

I was an ugly baby. On my birth certificate there was a listing for Probable Cause.

FRANCIS LEVY

The Unspeakables
Tonight's Episode: The Al Camus Story

Walter Winchell (voiceover): Despite the passage of strict Prohibition laws, illegal manufacturers of meaningless terms continued to flourish and operate. . . .

The offices of Ludwig Wittgenstein and the Unspeakables in Cambridge, England. The sound of typewriters pecking. Wittgenstein studies a blank sheet of paper. Bert Russell looks puzzled by something as he walks over to Wittgenstein's desk.

Russell: I've been working on this mind/body thing, but I haven't come up with any leads.

Wittgenstein: Have you talked with that Arendt girl?

Russell: Claims she knows nothing about it. I've got an idea she's formulating something, though.

Wittgenstein: I'd put a tail on her.

Russell: One of my men's staking out the New School right now.

Winchell (V.O.): Paris in the '30's was fast becoming a hotbed for the manufacture and distribution of inflated ideas. An influx of self-proclaimed thinkers was reaching epidemic proportions. One of the most dangerous was the notorious Al Camus. In his eagerness to foist unverifiable opinions on an unsuspecting public, Camus had established a clandestine network of mom-and-pop operations. Ludwig Wittgenstein and the Unspeakables were called in when local authorities could no longer cope with the problem.

Ludwig Wittgenstein's Paris hotel room. Name tags are attached to all objects. The chair is labeled "chair," the sofa, "sofa," etc. On a wall is the motto: "There are no innuendos." Wittgenstein is awakened from his sleep by the ring of the phone. He flips on the light and picks up the receiver. The label "man" is attached to his forehead.

A. J. Ayer, another of Wittgenstein's Unspeakables, is standing in a phone booth on the Boulevard Saint Germain. Several Frenchmen in berets sit in the nearby cafe Aux Deux Magots, a well-known hangout for the loquacious, and eye him suspiciously.

Ayer: You'd better get over here as fast as possible, Ludwig!

Wittgenstein: What's up?

Ayer: I'd describe it, if it were possible. You know what I mean?

Wittgenstein: I don't, but okay.

A Left Bank speakeasy, the "I 'n' Thou," run by the infamous Marty Buber. Words like "freedom," "fate," and "mankind" flow freely. Erich Fromm, a young student who works nights as a waiter, carries an ice bucket to Susanne K. Langer. The bucket contains a copy of Henri Bergson's Time and Free Will.

Langer: I won't say existence precedes essence.
Fromm: We can quibble later. Al needs words.

Ludwig Wittgenstein and his Unspeakables burst through the doors of the "I 'n' Thou." There are screams and cries of "I've lost my place" as philosophical treatises fall to the floor.

Wittgenstein: All right, lay down your nouns.

In the back room of the "I 'n' Thou," Al Camus is fingering a copy of Spinoza, unaware of the clamor outside. Jack Sartre and his sidekick Simone face him across a small candlelit table.

Sartre: We'll give your people *Being and Nothingness* however they want it, installments, paperback, Book-of-the-Month Club. You name it.

Camus: That's officially generous of you, Jack. That's enough words to keeps a speakeasy like the "I 'n' Thou" going for a year. . . . What's the price?

Sartre looks to Simone, who looks back at him and nods.

Sartre: (Nervously) You got to give up your relativism.
Camus: With you it's always choices, choices, choices.
Simone: If you're ever going to have a successful relationship with Others, you're going to have to overcome your fears of commitment.

When a tree falls in the forest and no one is around.

(Fromm breaks in on Camus and his cronies.)

Fromm: (Breathlessly) It's Wittgenstein!
Camus: Let's beat it.
Sartre: I'm willing to stand up to him for the sake of principle.
Simone: I wish you'd think of somebody else instead of everybody else for once.
Winchell (V.O.): In the fall of 1932 Ludwig Wittgenstein returned to Cambridge empty-handed. Al Camus, Jack Sartre, and his sidekick Simone had successfully eluded the Unspeakables again. . . .

Wittgenstein is sitting at his desk. The label "failure" hangs from his forehead. Russell rubs his eyes wearily as he reports in.

Russell: There's been another outbreak of abstract thinking.
Wittgenstein: I had a hunch something like this was coming down the pike.
Russell: It's worse than we expected. There are already several schools of thought.
Wittgenstein: Anything new on that fellow with the beard—the one who was hung up on infant sex?
Russell: He's turning into one of the biggest suppliers of the speakeasies.
Wittgenstein: Listen, Bert. I'm going to go sharpen my pencil. In the meanwhile I want a 24-hour surveillance on his sentences.
Russell: We'll try our best, Ludwig. But they're pretty hard to follow.

GEORGE CARLIN

A Place for Your Stuff

Hi! How are ya? You got your stuff with you? I'll bet you do. Guys got stuff in their pockets; ladies got stuff in their purses. Of course, some ladies have pockets, and some guys have purses. They're just different ways of carrying your stuff.

Then there's the stuff you left in your car. You got stuff in the trunk. Lotta different stuff! Spare tire, jack, tools, an old blanket, an extra pair of sneakers. You know, just in case you wind up barefoot on the highway some night.

Then you got *other* stuff in your car, in the glove box. Stuff you want to get to in a hurry: maps, sunglasses, .357 magnum. You know, just in case you wind up barefoot on the highway some night.

Then there's all that stuff on the floor of your car. It's called *garbage!*

So stuff is important. You gotta take care of your stuff. You gotta have a *place* for your stuff. Everybody's gotta have a place for his stuff. That's what life is all about, tryin' to find a place for your stuff! That's all your house is. Your house is nothin' but a place to keep your stuff. If you didn't have so much stuff, you wouldn't need a house. You could just walk around all the time.

So that's all your house is. It's just a pile of stuff with a cover on it. You can see that when you're taking off in an airplane. You look down and see all the little piles of stuff. Everybody's got his own little pile of stuff. And they lock it up. That's right! When you leave your house you gotta lock it up. Wouldn't want somebody to come by and *take* some of your stuff. 'Cause they always take the wrong stuff. They always take the *good* stuff. They don't bother with that crap you're saving: *National Geographics,* commemorative plates, your prized collection of Central American underwear. Ain't nobody interested in your kid's fourth-grade arithmetic papers. They just want the *good* stuff. The shiny stuff. The electronic stuff.

So really, your house is nothing more than a place to keep your stuff while you go out and get—*more stuff!!* 'Cause that's what this country is all about—tryin' to get more stuff. Even stuff you don't want and stuff you don't need. Stuff that's poorly made and overpriced. Even stuff you can't afford! You gotta keep on gettin' more stuff. Otherwise your neighbor might wind up with more stuff than you. Can't let *that* happen.

So you keep getting more and more stuff and putting it in different places. In the attic, in the basement, in the garage. And if you're young and still single, you might even have some stuff you left at your parents' house. Baseball cards, comic books. Actually, your parents threw that shit out years ago.

So basically, by this time you got a house full of stuff. And even though you might like your house, sooner or later you gotta move. You gotta get a *bigger* house. Why? *Too much stuff!* You gotta move all your stuff. Or maybe you gotta put some of your stuff in storage. Storage. Imagine that! There's a whole industry based on keeping an eye on other people's stuff.

Or maybe you could *sell* some of your stuff. Have a yard sale, or a garage sale. There are some people who drive around all weekend just looking for garage sales. They don't have enough problems with their own stuff, they wanna buy *other* people's stuff.

Or you could take your extra stuff to the swap meet, or the flea market, or the rummage sale or the auction. There's a lotta ways to get rid of your stuff. You can even *give* your stuff away. The Salvation Army and Goodwill will actually come to your house and pick up your stuff. And then they give it to people who don't *have* much stuff. It's part of the redistribution of stuff.

Enough about *your* stuff. Let's talk about other people's stuff. Have you ever noticed that when you go to somebody else's house, you never quite feel a hundred percent at home? You know why? There's no room for your stuff! Somebody else's stuff is all over the place. And what cheesy stuff it is!

(Picks up something and looks at it) "Jesus. Where'd they get *this* stuff? Pier One?"

And you know how sometimes you're visiting someone, and unexpectedly you have to stay overnight? It gets real late, and you decide to stay over? So they put you in a bedroom they don't use too often . . . because their grandmother died in it eleven years ago! And they haven't moved any of her stuff? Not even the vaporizer?

Or whatever room they put you in, there's usually a dresser or a night stand and there's never any room on it for your stuff. Somebody *else's* shit is on the dresser! Have you noticed that their stuff is *shit*, and your shit is *stuff*? You say, "Get this shit off of here and let me put my stuff down!"

"Crap" is also a form of stuff. Crap is the stuff that belongs to the person you just stopped living with.

(Holding phone receiver) "When are you gonna come over here and pick up the rest of your crap?"

Now, let's talk about travelling with your stuff. Sometimes you go on vacation and you gotta take some of your stuff with you. Mostly stuff to wear. But which stuff should you take? Can't take *all* your stuff. Just the stuff you really like, the stuff that fits you well that month. When you go on vacation, you've actually gotta bring a smaller, *second version* of your stuff.

Let's say you're going to Honolulu for two weeks. You gotta take two big suitcases full of your stuff, and you check that stuff into the luggage compartment. Plus you also got your carry-on stuff, *and* the stuff you bought in the airport, *and* the stuff you're gonna steal from the airline: silverware, soap, blanket, salt and pepper shakers. Too bad these headsets don't work at home.

So you're set to go. You got stuff in the overhead rack, stuff under the seat in front of you, stuff in the seat pocket, and stuff in your lap. And you fly to Honolulu, claim your stuff—if the airline didn't lose it— and go to your hotel. And the first thing you do in any hotel room is put away your stuff. There's lot of places in a hotel room to put away your stuff.

(Frenetic and half-crazed) "I'll put some stuff here, put some stuff in there. Hey, don't put your stuff in there. That's *my* place! You put your stuff over there, I'll put my stuff over here. Hey, here's another place! Put some stuff in here. And here's *another* place! You know what? We got more places than we got stuff! We're gonna have to go out and buy . . . *more stuff!!*"

Finally you put away all your stuff, but you don't quite feel at ease yet because you know you're a long way from home. But you sense that you *must* be okay because you do have some of your stuff with you. And so you relax in Honolulu on that basis. That's when your

friend from Maui calls and says, "Hey, why don't you come over to Maui for the weekend and spend a couple of nights over here?"

Oh no! Now whad'ya bring? Can't bring all *this* stuff. You're gonna have to bring an even smaller version of your stuff. Just enough stuff for a weekend on Maui. The *third version* of your stuff.

And as you're flying over to Maui, you realize that you're really spread out now. You've got stuff all over the world! You've got stuff at home, stuff in the garage, stuff at your parents' house . . . maybe! Stuff in storage, stuff in Honolulu, and stuff on the plane. Supply lines are getting longer and harder to maintain!

But finally you get over to your friends' place on Maui, and they give you a little room to sleep in, and there's a little night stand. Not much room for your stuff, but it's okay because you don't have much stuff now. You've got your autographed 8 by 10 photo of Kurt Waldheim, a large can of gorgonzola-flavored Cheez Whiz, a small, unopened packet of brown confetti, a relief map of Botsuanaland, and a family-size jar of peppermint-flavored crud. And you know that even though you're a long way from home, you must be okay because you *do* have some peppermint-flavored crud. And so you begin to relax on Maui on that basis. That's when your friend says, "Hey, I think tonight

I WOULDN'T WANT TO PAINT IT   195

we'll go over to the other side of the island, visit my sister, and maybe spend the night over there."

Oh no! *Now* whad'ya bring? Right! You gotta bring an even *smaller* version of your stuff. The *fourth version* of your stuff. Just the stuff you know you're gonna need: money, keys, comb, wallet, lighter, hankie, pen, cigarettes, contraceptives, Vaseline, whips, chains, whistles, dildoes, and a book. Just the stuff you *hope* you're gonna need.

By the way, if you go to the beach while you're there, you gotta figure out the *fifth version* of your stuff: cigarettes and wallet. You can always borrow someone's suntan lotion. And maybe, while you're lying on the beach, you decide to go over to the refreshment stand and get a hot dog. Right! The sixth and most important version: your wallet. It's got the only stuff you really can't do without.

By this time you're pretty fed up with your stuff and all the problems it creates. So finally, about a week later, you get back home and you clean out the closets, the attic, the basement, the garage, the storage locker and every other place you've got some stuff, and you get it all down to manageable proportions. Just the right amount of stuff to lead a simple and uncomplicated life.

That's when the phone rings, and it's a lawyer. Your rich aunt has died and left you all *her* stuff. Oh no! Now whad'ya do? You do the only thing you can do. You tell the lawyer to stuff it.

JACK HANDEY
Deep Thoughts

Dad always thought laughter was the best medicine, which I guess is why several of us died of tuberculosis.

Maybe in order to understand mankind, we have to look at the word itself: "Mankind." Basically, it's made up of two separate words—"mank" and "ind." What do these words mean? It's a mystery, and that's why so is mankind.

I hope if dogs ever take over the world, and they choose a king, they don't just go by size, because I bet there are some Chihuahuas with some good ideas.

Contrary to what most people would say, the most dangerous animal in the world is not the lion or the tiger or even the elephant. It's a shark riding on an elephant's back, just trampling and eating everything they see.

The memories of my family outings are still a source of strength to me. I remember we'd all pile into the car—I forget what kind it was—and drive and drive. I'm not sure where we'd go, but I think there were some trees there. The smell of something was strong in the air as we played whatever sport we played. I remember a bigger, older guy that we called "Dad." We'd eat some stuff, or not, and then I think we went home.

I guess some things never leave you.

It takes a big man to cry, but it takes a bigger man to laugh at that man.

If I lived back in the Wild West Days, instead of carrying a six-gun in my holster, I'd carry a soldering iron. That way, if some smart-aleck cowboy said something like, "Hey, look. He's carrying a soldering iron!" and started laughing, I could just say, "That's right, it's a soldering iron. The soldering iron of justice."

Then everyone would get real quiet and ashamed, because they made fun of the soldering iron of justice, and I could probably hit them up for a free drink.

I guess we were all guilty, in a way. We all shot him, we all skinned him, and we all got a complimentary bumper sticker that said, "I Helped Skin Bob."

I bet the main reason the police keep people away from a plane crash is they don't want anybody walking in and lying down in the crash stuff, then, when somebody comes up, act like they just woke up and go, "What was *that?!*"

The face of a child can say it all, especially the mouth part of the face.

Ambition is like a frog sitting on a Venus flytrap. The flytrap can bite and bite, but it won't bother the frog because it only has little tiny plant teeth. But some other stuff could happen and it could be like ambition.

I'd rather be rich than stupid.

If you were a poor Indian with no weapons, and a bunch of conquistadors came up to you and asked where the gold was, I don't think it would be a good idea to say, "I swallowed it. So sue me."

If you define cowardice as running away at the first sign of danger, screaming and tripping and begging for mercy, then yes, Mr. Brave Man, I guess I'm a coward.

I bet what happened was they discovered fire and invented the wheel on the same day. Then, that night, they burned the wheel.

Like so many others of his generation, Todd had been raised to believe he was invulnerable to dynamite. Todd had some growing up to do, and also some blowing up.

I bet one legend that keeps recurring throughout history, in every culture, is the story of Popeye.

When you go in for a job interview, I think a good thing to ask is if they ever press charges.

To me, boxing is like a ballet, except there's no music, no choreography, and the dancers hit each other.

What is it that makes a complete stranger dive into an icy river to try to save a solid-gold baby? Maybe we'll never know.

We tend to scoff at the beliefs of the ancients. But we can't scoff at them personally, to their faces, and this is what annoys me.

Probably the earliest flyswatters were nothing more than some sort of striking surface attached to the end of a long stick.

If you're like me, you probably blame a lot of things on rubber bands. If there's bad news in the newspaper, you blame it on the rubber band which kept it rolled up. Or if you get your bank statement, and there's less money in your account than you thought you had, you blame it on the rubber band that holds the statement and the checks together.
Why do we do that?

I think someone should have had the decency to tell me the luncheon was free. To make someone run out with potato salad in his hand, pretending like he's throwing up, is not what I call hospitality.

Nowadays, the hottest comic strip in the country is Gary Larson's bizarre single-panel, "The Far Side." Far Side books are at the top of the bestseller lists and gift shops are filled with Far Side cards, mugs, posters and other stuff. With a big cash bonanza like this, it won't be long before other cartoonists jump on the bandwagon and start using Larson's approach as well. Speaking of jumping on the bandwagon, here's what we think it will be like…

When Other Comic Strips Start Using The "FAR SIDE" Formula

ARTIST: BOB CLARKE   WRITER: CHARLIE KADAU

THE BLOOM COUNTY SIDE

"No, Frank! The seals! Just the seals!"

THE GARFIELD SIDE

"Okay, here it comes, here it comes…Oh, what a joy! This is one Thanksgiving Day Parade that dogs will be talking about for years to come."

THE BEETLE SIDE

"Jenkins, I've done it! I've perfected a fool-proof star wars defense system! All my calculations are right in here, you must see them!"

THE CATHY SIDE

It was right after the soup and just before the main course that Cathy decided she would never, under any circumstances, ever go on another blind date again. Never.

THE SPIDERMAN SIDE

"It must have fallen down during the night and...Hey! Lookee what's underneath it!"

THE B.C. SIDE

"It's agreed then: you call it in the air...winners get to lounge around in trees all day eating bananas and losers have to develop civilization and live in hot, crowded cities."

THE FAMILY CIRCUS SIDE

"Well, I thought this was the spot where we left daddy...I remember we buried him in the sand about an hour ago right here next to a 'No Littering' sign."

THE HAGAR SIDE

"Hagar, there's someone here who wants to speak to you about your helmet, and he doesn't look happy."

THE MENACE SIDE

Dennis was about to discover he had finally pushed Mr. Wilson's patience just a little too far.

THE PEANUTS SIDE

Inside Snoopy's den

"Evolution's been good to you, Sid."

MERRILL MARKOE

What the Dogs Have Taught Me

Recently I had occasion to spend entirely too much time all by myself in a rather isolated Connecticut suburb. Seemingly endless days were turning into seemingly endless nights. And slowly but surely I found myself becoming the victim of boredom. Until it occurred to me that I was simply living wrong. I was ill-prepared for the peacefulness of my environment. I realized that all I had to do to achieve real daily contentment, was to study more closely the two perfectly acclimated creatures who shared my days with me.

> **"I'm so upset, I had to shoot my dog."**
> **"Was he mad?"**
> **"He wasn't happy."**

DAILY ROUTINE

1. The day is divided into two important sections: Meal Time. And Everything else.
2. Anytime that is not meal time is potentially nap time. The best time to take a nap is when someone comes into your house through a window.
3. The most relaxing position for napping is on your side with all

four limbs parallel. The best location for a nap is of course the dead center of the street out in front of your house.

MEAL TIME

1. Because there does not seem to be anything around to eat certainly does not mean there is nothing to eat. It goes without saying that you should carefully check the lower third of everyplace for edibles. And don't discount things which are mouth-size because you cannot identify them. These things can, and should, be considered as gum.

2. The act of staring at the underside of a table or a chair often sets in motion a series of events that eventually results in food.

3. Once you have received your meal, submerge your head into it as you would a shower. And never ever look up again until all of the contents are gone. Be sure to stay with what appears to be an empty dish long after it has been emptied. There may be a still uneaten subatomic particle that you have overlooked.

4. When it comes to seeking beverages, remember that location and packaging mean nothing. There are absolutely no exceptions to this rule.

PERSONAL SECURITY

1. The greatest undiscussed threat to suburban life as we know it is squirrels. No matter what you must do, just be sure there are none in your yard.

2. At the first hint of any irregular noise, run from room to room yelling loudly. If someone comes into the house, run over to them

An international law firm is advertising for a paralegal who can type, answer the phone, take dictation, and speak more than one language.

To their surprise, the first applicant is a black and white Scotch terrier. They are even more astonished to find that the dog can type 125 words a minute, has an excellent telephone voice, and knows shorthand.

The personnel manager is flabbergasted. "You're really an extraordinary dog," she says. "But what about the foreign language requirement?"

"Meow," replies the dog.

A man with a dog walks into a bar. "Get out," says the bartender. "You can't bring that dog in here."

"Wait a minute," says the man. "This is no regular dog. He can *talk*."

"Sure he can," says the bartender. "Listen, if that dog can talk, I'll give you a hundred bucks."

The man puts the dog on a stool, and says, "Okay, sport, what's on top of a house?"

"Roof!"

"Right. And what's on the outside of a tree?"

"Bark!"

"Good. Now let's try something harder. Can you name a surrealist French sculptor?"

"Arp!"

"Excellent. And who would you say was the greatest baseball player of all time?"

"Ruth!"

The bartender is furious. "Listen pal," he says, "you better take that dog out of here before I punch both of you."

As soon as they're on the street, the dog turns to the man and asks, "Do you think I should have said 'DiMaggio'?"

whether you know them or not. Then kiss them and throw yourself at them so violently that they either fall over or else you are forced away physically.

RECREATION AND LEISURE

1. One of the most enjoyable activities you will participate in is any form of activity that involves a ball. There are two important and equally amusing sets of rules that you will want to know.
   A. THE COMMON FORM, which involves receiving a thrown ball and returning it with great speed to the thrower.
   B. THE PREFERRED FORM, in which you receive the thrown ball and take it to a secluded spot and try to eat it.
   C. An additional form of amusement that will occur from time to time involves the chance to ride somewhere in a motor vehicle. Remember that when you see a car door open, you must try to get in. Once you are inside a car, your only goal is to get out.

ETIQUETTE

1. There are only two important facial expressions to master. Complete Overwhelming Unbridled Joy, and Nothing at All.
2. The most practical way to get dry is to shake violently near a clothed person. A second effective method is to stand on a light-colored fabric.
3. In the event of a trip to the doctor, always be on your guard. If you are vaccinated, always remember to urinate on the physician. (In fact, it is just good practice to try to urinate as much as possible. I am not sure why this is. It just is.)
4. If you really want something from someone, stare at them very intently. As a second tactic, it is proper to grovel shamelessly.

Since I have taken to sleeping under my bed, I have found a peace and tranquility that I used to think was the private reserve of ascetics. Yes, there's a good life to be had. And that's what the dogs have taught me.

JERRY SEINFELD
No Pockets

A dog will stay stupid. That's why we love them so much. The entire time we know them, they're idiots. Think of your dog. Every time you come home, he thinks it's *amazing*.

He has no idea how you accomplish this every day. You walk in the door, the joy of this experience overwhelms him. He looks at you, *he's back, it's that guy, that same guy.* He can't believe it. Everything is amazing to your dog. *Another can of food? I don't believe it!*

"Why don't you hang out the window like other dogs?"

A dog walks into a Western Union office to send a telegram. When the clerk hands him a form, the dog takes a pen in his teeth and slowly writes, "Bow wow wow, bow wow wow, bow wow."

The clerk reads it, counts the words, and says, "Are you aware, that there are only eight words here, and that you can send ten words for the same price? Perhaps you'd like to add another 'bow wow'?"

"I *could,*" said the dog, "but don't you think that would sound just a little ridiculous?"

Dogs want to be people. That's what their lives are about. They don't like being dogs. They're with people all the time, they want to graduate. My dog would sit there all day, he would watch me walk by, he would think to himself, *I could do that! He's not that good!*

That's why the greatest, most exciting moment in the life of a dog is the front seat of the car. You and him in the front seat. It's the only place where your head and his head are on the exact same level. He sits up there, he thinks, *this is more like it. You and me together, this is the way it should be.*

You know what cracks me up? He looks out the front. That makes me laugh, because he's a dog. What's he looking at? *What are you going to make, a right or a left? I don't even know where I am.*

They have a hard time. They stand up, they sit down, they can't handle the turns either way. No matter which way you turn, he's not ready.

They don't know what to do. And then comes the great moment of frustration. You stop someplace and get something to eat. This kills him. You get a hamburger, this blows his mind. Instant food whenever you want it? You know what this means to him? You ever see the look on his face? He looks over at you. *How'd you get that? Are they giving it to everybody now? You think I could get one? I can't get one.* They can't get anything.

Dogs have no money. Isn't that amazing? They're broke their entire lives. But they get through. You know why dogs have no money? No pockets.

Dogs come when they're called; cats take a message and get back to you.   —*Mary Bly*

ED BLUESTONE
illustrated by M. K. BROWN

The Day the Animals Discovered Death

I WOULDN'T WANT TO PAINT IT

PETER ELBLING
Interview with a Dolphin

Dr. John C. Lilly was the first human to communicate with a dolphin and thus became a cause célèbre of the '80s. Playboy magazine immediately assigned him to do an interview for their March 1985 issue. The results were somewhat disappointing.

Playboy: How did you like the halibut?
Dolphin: It was a little salty. I like mackerel better.
Playboy: Aha, aha.
Dolphin: And you can only take a bite or two at a time because they tend to come apart in your throat.
Playboy: Aha, aha.
Dolphin: It's much better to swallow them whole. Quite frankly, if I've got my eyes closed and something just pops in, I'm hard-pressed to tell what it is. You know?
Playboy: Aha, aha.
Dolphin: There are exceptions.
Playboy: Like what?
Dolphin: Well, a shark . . . or a whale . . . I mean, you can tell them right away because they won't fit in your mouth. I'll tell you a funny story if you like.
Playboy: Sure.
Dolphin: Well, a couple of friends of mine and I were just swimming around one afternoon down Malaga way. D'you know where Malaga is?
Playboy: Aha, aha.
Dolphin: Great eats. Anyway, we're just lazing around when someone, I don't remember who . . . it was probably Harry . . . no, it wasn't, it was Burt . . . anyway, doesn't matter, anyway, he says why don't we close our eyes, you know, just for a joke, and see who can catch the most. No, wait a moment, it had to be Harry 'cause Burt just got caught in that tuna net. Yeah, it was definitely Harry. . . .
Playboy: Aha, aha.
Dolphin: Anyway, getting back to the story . . . whoever it was, and it probably was Harry, so let's say it *was* Harry, just for argument's sake . . . Harry says, let's just close our eyes . . .
Playboy: Aha, aha.
Dolphin: . . . and see what pops into our mouths.
Playboy: Aha, aha.
Dolphin: We're all lying sort of dead-looking with our eyes closed. Get the picture?
Playboy: Aha, aha.
Dolphin: Good. Whenever one of us swallows something, we shout out, "Hey," to let the other fellows know . . . and we're going

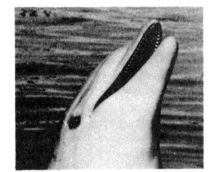

"You know where Malaga is?"

"S'funny . . . just gone right out of my head. . . . Hmmmm. . . ."

"Seaweed? Why would I want to talk about seaweed?"

along . . . and there's a "hey" and another "hey" when suddenly I hear a "glump." Not a big "glump," but a "glump," see. So I say to myself, now, wait a minute! Wait a minute! Someone's not playing fair. I mean if we agreed to go "hey," why mess up a good thing with a "glump"? I thought . . . I know, they're jealous because I'm winning. I mean, I've got a big mouth, bigger than Burt's or Harry's, and just before the "glump" I'd probably done about three "heys" to every one of theirs, right? So I opened my eyes, just to see what was going on. And what do you think I saw?

Playboy: Aha, aha.

Dolphin: I said, what do you think I saw?

Playboy: Oh, I don't know. I really don't know.

Dolphin: Go on! Just one quick guess.

Playboy: I'm sorry, but I can't even imagine . . . What was it?

Dolphin: S'funny . . . just gone right out of my head. . . . Hmmmm . . .

Playboy: What?

Dolphin: Wow . . . isn't that strange . . . right on the tip . . . and then . . . nothing. Don't worry about it . . . it'll come back to me . . . isn't that strange . . . I was just talking about . . .

Playboy: How you and your friends . . .

Dolphin: Oh, forget it! Doesn't matter. It'll come back when I'm not thinking about it. Does that ever happen to you? Does to me. Sometimes I'll be thinking about one thing and something completely different will pop right into my head. For instance, I can be talking about, oh, let's say . . . er . . . er . . . I can be talking about . . . anything . . . you name it . . . go on, name something.

ELEPHANT JOKES

How can you tell if there are elephants under your bed?

You can touch the ceiling with your nose.

What's the difference between an elephant and a jar of peanut butter?

The elephant doesn't stick to the roof of your mouth.

How do you get down from an elephant?

You don't get down from an elephant, you get down from a goose.

What has big ears, weighs two thousand pounds, and has two trunks?

An elephant going on vacation.

How can you tell when an elephant is getting ready to charge?

He takes out his Visa card.

What did the elephant say to Mikhail Gorbachev?

Nothing. Elephants don't speak Russian.

Why did the elephants quit their job at the factory?

They got tired of working for peanuts.

What is gray and powdery?

Instant elephant.

What weighs four thousand pounds and sings?

Harry Elefonte.

What's gray and stamps out jungle fires?

Smokey the Elephant.

Why do elephants have wrinkled ankles?

They lace their sneakers too tightly.

Playboy: Oil spills . . .

Dolphin: No, I don't talk about them much . . . name something else.

Playboy: Seaweed.

Dolphin: Seaweed? Why would I want to talk about seaweed?

Playboy: Well, you said name . . .

Dolphin: Forget it . . . let's say I was talking about . . . er . . . I'll think of something. . . .

Playboy: Sure . . .

Dolphin: Sharx . . . right! Let's say I was talking about sharx . . . all of a sudden a cod pops into my mind.

Playboy: Aha, aha.

Dolphin: I'll tell you a funny story. I was swimming along one day, on my way down to Mexico.

Playboy: Aha, aha.

Dolphin: Yeah, terrific eats down in Mexico . . . haddox as big as . . . well, er . . . big haddox . . . anyway . . . where was I?

Playboy: On your way down to . . .

Dolphin: Mexico . . . right, right, right, right, I remember. Anyway, I'm swimming along minding my own business, you know, taking it easy. . . . Anyway . . . all of a sudden this big cod swims right out in front of me from behind a rock, and misses me by about an inch. No wait, half an inch, half an inch. And then he just swims away. Not an "Excuse me" or a "I beg your pardon." Nothing! Just plain nothing. No sense of direction, cods . . . just stop whenever they want. No signals. Nothing.

The livestock would gather every morning, hoping for one of Farmer Dan's popular "airplane" rides.

EVOLUTION'S BEEN GOOD TO YOU, SID   213

TONY HENDRA & SEAN KELLY

The Book of Creation

CHAPTER 1

I N the beginning God created Dates.
² And the date *was* Monday, July 4, 4004 B.C.

³ And God said, Let there be light; and there was light. And *when* there was Light, God saw the Date, *that* it was Monday, and he *got* down to work; for verily, he had a Big Job *to do.*

⁴ And God made pottery shards and Silurian mollusks and pre-Cambrian limestone strata; and flints and Jurassic Mastodon tusks and Picanthropus erectus skulls and Cretaceous placentals made he; and those cave paintings at Lasceaux. And that was *that,* for the first Work Day.

⁵ And God saw that he had made many wondrous things, *but* that he had not wherein to put *it* all. And God said, Let the heavens be divided from the earth; and *let* us bury all of these Things which we have made in the earth; *but* not too deep.

⁶ And God buried all the Things which he had made, and that was *that.*

⁷ And the morning and the evening *and* the overtime were Tuesday.

⁸ And God said, Let there be wa-ter; and let the dry *land* appear; and that was *that.*

⁹ And God called the dry *land* Real Estate; and the water called he *the* Sea. And in the land and beneath *it* put he crude *oil,* grades one through six; and *natural* gas put he thereunder, and prehistoric carboniferous forests yielding anthracite and other ligneous matter; and all these called he Resources; and *he* made them Abundant.

¹⁰ And likewise all that was *in* the Sea, even unto two hundred miles from the dry *land,* called he resources; all that was therein, *like* manganese nodules, for instance.

¹¹ And the morning unto the evening *had been* an long day; *which* he called Wednesday.

¹² And God said, Let the earth bring forth abundantly every moving creature I *can* think of, with or without back bones, with or without wings or feet, or fins or claws, vestigial limbs and all, right *now;* and let each *one* be of a separate species. For lo, I can make *whatsoever* I like, *whensoever* I like.

¹³ And the earth brought forth abundantly *all* creatures, great and small, with and without backbones, with and without wings and feet and fins and claws, vestigial limbs and all, *from* bugs *to* brontosauruses.

¹⁴ But God blessed them all, saying, Be fruitful and multiply and *Evolve Not.*

¹⁵ And God looked upon the species he had made, and saw that the earth was exceedingly crowded, and he said *unto* them, Let each species compete for what it needeth; for Healthy Competition is My Law. And the species competeth amongst themselves, the cattle and the creeping things, the dogs and the dinosaurs; and some madeth it and some didn't; and the dogs ate the dinosaurs and God was pleased.

¹⁶ And God took the bones from the dinosaurs, and caused them to appear *mighty* old; and cast he them about the land and the sea. And he took every tiny *creature* that had not madeth it, and caused *them* to become fossils; and cast he them about *likewise.*

¹⁷ And just to put matters beyond the valley of the shadow of a *doubt* God created carbon dating. And *this* is the origin of species.

¹⁸ And in the Evening of the day which *was* Thursday, God saw that

he had put in *another* good day's work.

19 And God said, Let us make man in our image, after our likeness, *which is* tall and well-formed and pale of hue: and let us *also* make monkeys, which resembleth us not in any wise, *but* are short and ill-formed and hairy. And God added, Let man *have* dominion over the monkeys and the fowl of the air and every species, endangered or otherwise.

20 So God created Man in His *own* image; tall and well-formed and pale of hue created He him, and nothing at all like the monkeys.

21 And God said, Behold I have given you every herb bearing seed, which is upon the face of the earth. But ye shalt not smoketh it, *lest* it giveth *you* ideas.

22 And to every beast of the earth and every fowl of the air I have given also every green herb, and to them it shall be for *meat*. But they shall be *for you*. And the Lord God your Host suggesteth that the flesh of cattle goeth well with that of the fin and the claw; thus shall Surf be wedded unto Turf.

23 And God saw everything he had made, and he saw that it was very good; and God said, It *just* goes to show Me what the private sector can accomplish. With a lot of fool regulations this could have taken *billions of years*.

24 And on the evening of the fifth day, *which had been* the roughest day yet, God said, Thank me it's Friday. And God made the weekend.

CHAPTER 2

THUS the heavens and the earth were finished, and *all* in five days, and all less than six thousand years *ago;* and if thou believest it not, in a sling *shalt* thou find thy hindermost quarters.

2 Likewise God took the dust of the ground, and the slime of the Sea and the scum of the earth and formed Man therefrom; and *breathed* the breath of life right in his face. And he *became* Free to Choose.

3 And God made an Marketplace eastward of Eden, in which the man was free *to* play. And this *was* the Free Play of the Marketplace.

4 And out of the ground made the LORD God *to grow* four trees: the Tree of Life, and the Liberty Tree, and the Pursuit of Happiness Tree, and the Tree of the Knowledge of Sex.

5 And the LORD God commanded the man, saying, This *is* my Law, which is called the Law of Supply and Demand. Investeth thou in the trees of Life, Liberty, and the Pursuit of Happiness, and thou shalt make for thyself an *fortune*. For *what* fruit thou eatest not, that thou mayest sell, and with the seeds thereof expand *thy* operations.

6 But of the fruit of the tree of the Knowledge of Sex, thou mayest not eat; nor mayest thou invest therein, nor profit thereby nor expand *its* operations; for that is a mighty waste of seed.

7 And the man was exceeding glad. But he asked the LORD God: Who then *shall* labor in this Marketplace? For am I not management, *being* tall and well-formed and pale of hue?

8 And the LORD God said unto himself, Verily, this kid hath the potential which is Executive.

9 And out of the ground the LORD God formed every beast of the field and every fowl of the air, and brought them unto Adam to labor for him. And they labored for peanuts.

10 Then Adam was again exceeding glad. But he spake once more unto the LORD God, saying, Lo, I am free to play in the Marketplace of the LORD, and have cheap labor in plenty; but to whom shall I sell my surplus fruit and realize a fortune thereby?

11 And the LORD God said unto himself, Verily, this is an Live One.

12 And he caused a deep sleep to fall upon Adam and he took from him one of his ribs, which was an spare rib.

13 And the spare rib which the LORD God had taken from the man, made he woman. And he brought her unto the man, saying:

14 This is Woman and she shall purchase your fruit, to eat it; and ye shall realize a fortune thereby. For Man produceth and Woman consumeth, wherefore she shall be called the Consumer.

15 And they were both decently clad, the Man and the Woman, from the neck even unto the ankles, so they were not ashamed.

CHAPTER 3

Now the snake in the grass was *more* permissive than any beast of the field which the LORD God *had* made. And he said *unto* the woman, Why hast thou accepted this lowly and submissive *role?* For art thou not human, *even* as the man is human?

2 And the woman said unto the snake in the grass, the LORD God hath ordained that I am placed under the man, and must do whatsoever he telleth me to do; for is *he* not the Man?

3 But the snake in the grass laughed an cunning laugh, and said unto the woman, Is it not right and just that thou shouldst fulfill thy *potential?* For art thou not comely in thy flesh, even as the man is comely in his flesh?

4 And the woman said, Nay, I know not, for hath not the LORD God clad us decently, from the neck even unto the ankles; and forbidden that we eat of the Tree of the Knowledge of Sex?

5 But the snake in the grass said unto the woman, whispering even into her very ear, saying, Whatsoever feeleth good, do thou *it;* and believeth thou me, it feeleth *good.*

6 And when the woman saw the fruit of the Tree of the Knowledge of Sex, that it was firm and plump and juicy, she plucked thereof, and sank her teeth *therein,* and gave also to her husband, *and* he likewise sank his teeth *therein.*

7 And the eyes of *both* of them were opened, and they saw that they were not naked.

8 And the woman loosened *then* Adam's uppermost garment, and he likewise loosened hers; and she loosened his nethermost garment, and the man *then* loosened her nethermost garment; until they were out of their garments both, and *likewise* of their minds.

9 And, lo!, they did dance *upon* the grass of the ground, and they did rock backward, and roll forward continually;

10 And as they did rock and roll, the serpent that *was* cunning did play upon a stringéd *instrument* of music, and did smite his tail upon the ground in an hypnotic rhythm; and he did sing *in a voice* that was like unto four voices: She loveth you, yea, yea, yea.

[11] And they did both twist and shout, and fall into an frenzy, both the man *and* the woman, and lay *themselves* upon the ground, and commit there abominations.

[12] And when they *were* spent from their abominations, they did take the herb bearing seed, and did *roll* it and smoke it; and lo! it gaveth them ideas, even as the LORD God *had* said; and they were like *to commit* new abominations.

[13] Now the LORD God was walking in the garden in the cool of the day, with his dog; and as Adam and his wife were *beginning* these new abominations, the LORD God did stub the toe of his *foot* upon their hindermost quarters.

[14] And the LORD God *waxed* wroth, and said unto Adam, Wherefore art thou naked? And what is *that* thou smokest? And why art thou not at thy *work?* For have I not said that it is the man's part to produce, and the part of the woman to consume whatsoever he produceth?

[15] And Adam and his wife did look *upon* one another, and did giggle.

[16] Whereupon the LORD God waxed exceeding wroth, and he said, Hast thou eaten of the tree, whereof I commanded *thee* that thou *shouldst* not eat?

[17] And the man said, The woman *whom* you gavest to be *with me* made me do it.

[18] And the LORD God said unto the woman, What is *this* that thou hast done? And the woman said, The snake in the grass made me do it.

[19] And the snake in the grass said, The devil made *me* do it.

[20] And the LORD God said unto the snake in the grass, Thou art an permissive *beast;* wherefore art thou cursed to crawl upon thy belly, and be *made into* belts and boots and handbags hereafter.

[21] Unto the woman He said, Since thou hast harkened unto the snake in the grass which is broad-of-mind and permissive; henceforth let it be thy lot to be confused and *scattered* in thy brains, and to be plagued by demons who shall tempt thee to become that which thou canst not be: such as an warrior, or an extinguisher of fires, or an operator of heavy machinery.

[22] And since thou hast put aside the decent clothing wherein I clad thee, here after no garment *shall* satisfy thee, and thou shalt be overcome by longings to change thy raiment *every* spring and fall.

[23] And above all this, since thou hast desired to taste of the fruit of the Tree of the Knowledge of Sex, now let thy *very* body be a curse unto thee. From generation unto generation, men *shalt* whistle and hoot after thee *as* thou passest; yea, and women also.

[24] And unto Adam he said, Woe unto thee who hast harkened not to the voice of the LORD thy God, but rather to her who is *thy* inferior; for thou wast free to choose. Now shalt thou be banished from the Marketplace and the Free Play thereof; *neither* shalt thou pluck the fruit from the Trees of Life and Liberty and the Pursuit of Happiness.

[25] In the sweat of thy face *shalt* thou earn thy bread, and bankruptcy shall be *thy* lot; and upon thy back, as a burden *unto* thee, thou shalt bear Big Government; for thou hast sinned.

[26] And the LORD God said unto the man, Behold, thy knowledge of sex shall be as a curse upon thee and thy generations; and thy loins shall be a trial unto thee.

[27] For whensoever thou goest into a public place, *then* shall thy member rise *up;* when thou sitteth to eat and drink among thy fellows, likewise shall it rise *up;* yea, even when thou standeth before the people to preach unto *them* in *my* name, shall it rise *up,* and be a scandal unto thee, and make an unseemly lump *in* thy garments; yet when thou goest into thy wife shall thy member wither, and rise *up* not.

[28] And then the LORD God was silent, and waxed sad, and made as if to leave them *there.* But he turned, and spoke softly *unto* Adam and his wife Eve, saying, Knowest thou *something?* Mine *only* hope is this: That someday, ye have children who do *unto* you the way ye have done *unto* Me.

I fear that one day I'll meet God, he'll sneeze, and I won't know what to say. —*Ronnie Shakes*

MEL BROOKS & CARL REINER

Two Thousand Year Old Man

Sir, what did you do for a living?

Well, many years ago, thousands of years ago, there was no heavy industry.

We know that.

The most things that we manufactured or that we ever made was . . . we would take a piece of wood, see, and rub and rub it and clean it and look at it and hit earth with it and hit a tree with it.

For what purpose?

Just to keep busy. There was nothing to do. There was absolutely nothing to do. We had no jobs, don't you see?

What other jobs were there? There must have been something else besides hitting a tree with a piece of stick?

Hitting a tree with a piece of stick was already a good job. I mean, you couldn't *get* that job! Mainly sitting and looking in the sky was a big job. And another job was watching each other. That was light work, looking at each other. . . .

Sir, did you ever have any formal job as we know it today?

Yeah, well, I was a manufacturer. I was an owner.

What kind of factory did you have?

I used to make the Star of David. The Jewish stars. I was one of the first makers of that.

Oh, yes, the little thing you wear.

As soon as religion came in, I was one of the first in that. I figured this was a good thing.

How did you make them, did you have tools?

Well, we didn't have lathes. I employed six men, see, each with a point. And they used to run together in the middle of the factory and in their great speeds they would fuse the thing.

Thus making the Star.

Yes. We would make two a day, because of the man accidents. You have six men running at high speeds with points, you, you—you have plenty of accidents.

I see. You never thought of going into anything else?

No. I had an offer once. A fellow came to me—Simon.

What did Simon ask you to do?

He said, "We have a new thing, a new item, a winner, it looks like a winning item that's gonna be a big seller. It's called a cross." I looked at it and I turned it over and I looked at all sides of it and I said, "It's simple. It's too simple." I didn't know then it was *eloquent*. I didn't know it would be such a hit.

You turned him down?

And I said, "I'm sorry, but I'm too busy." See, I could have fired four men—two men run together, *bang!*, we got a cross. I would have saved . . . I woulda had over a hundred dollars today if I'd went into crosses.

The Cardinal was addressing a meeting of local priests. "I've got good news and bad news," he said. The good news is that God called me last night, and basically, everything is all right. The bad news is that she called from Salt Lake City."

CLOSE, BUT NO CIGAR!

© 1986 by B. Kliban

MARTIN COHEN & SHELDON SHACKET

The Profit by Kehlog Albran

Frank Perdue is granted a private audience with the Pope. "Your holiness," he says, "I've heard that the Church has suffered some financial reversals, so I'm here with a proposal that can benefit both of us. I'm prepared to donate a hundred million dollars to the Church, provided you make one small change in the Lord's Prayer. Where it says, 'Give us this day our daily bread?' Well, I'd like you to consider changing just the end of that line to: 'Give us this day our daily chicken.' "

The Pope is taken aback. "That's a most unusual request," he says, "but it's certainly a substantial kindness that you're offering the Church. Let me discuss your offer with the College of Cardinals, and I'll be back in touch with you in a few days."

As soon as Perdue leaves, the Pope convenes an emergency meeting of the Cardinals. "Boys," he says, "I think we're going to have to review the Wonder Bread account."

What of Facial Hair, the nubile lad asked.

The Master replied:

As maturity encroaches upon adolescence, as the child becomes the man (or ugly woman) he (or she) begins to grow first the downy fuzz and, subsequently, the rich, wiry outcropping that has come to be called Beard.

It is no small coincidence that a great scribe or teller of tales is called by the similar word Bard.

Many an otherwise canny person has fallen upon troubled times by confusing these words.

For it is true that a Bard can have a Beard, but a Beard cannot have a Bard.

One can shave a Beard, and, for that matter, one can shave a Bard.

But having shaved a Beard, it no longer exists.

Whereas having shaved a Bard you continue to have a Bard.

A Beardless Bard.

Then an old woman said,
Speak to us of Black Magic, Master.
He then replied:

As a youth I passed an old Orphanite travelling toward Carthage.

He was a sorcerer who practiced Falinentography, and had mastered arts as black as carbon.

To prove his skill he changed a tree frog into an apricot, a feather into a pineapple, and a butterfly into a ham.

Did that satisfy your doubts? the woman asked.

No, not really, but we had a grand breakfast, the Master recalled. . . .

A maker of lenses asked,
What of Glass, Master?
He then answered:
Glass is one of Earth's miracles, like fire and water.
It is a solid object, so real, yet so transparent, it defies the senses.
It is wondrous, though made of the most common materials, sand and lime.

Yet if one element is changed in quantity or substance, you have not Glass.

If you subtract the sand and use common earth, you have not Glass.

If you subtract the lime and replace it with lemon, you have not Glass.

If you subtracted the sand and added sugar, you would have not Glass.

What would you then have, Master, the man asked.

Lemonade, the Master replied.

A priest asked,

What is Fate, Master?

And he answered:

It is that which gives a beast of burden its reason for existence.

It is that which men in former times had to bear upon their backs.

It is that which has caused nations to build by-ways from City to City upon which carts and coaches pass, and alongside which inns have come to be built to stave off Hunger, Thirst and Weariness.

It is that which has caused great fleets of ships to ply the Seven Seas wherever the wind blows.

And that is Fate? said the priest.

Fate . . . I thought you said Freight, responded the Master.

That's all right, said the priest.

I wanted to know what Freight was too. . . .

And a scholar asked, Should a man drink wine, ales, and liquors to excess?

He then said:

He who drinks too much wine will feel the price of that ecstasy the next morning.

For exotic liquors must be taken in moderation or all will pay the penalty of misuse.

Man is the only creature to have the ability to create intoxicants.

No other animal has the taste for spirits.

Nature allows no other animal to taste of that pleasure, because nature depends upon all other animals to remain stable and predictable.

Man is the only animal that is allowed the dubious privilege of overindulgence.

Have you ever seen another animal drunk and falling down in the street, sobbing, stinking, and acting totally insane?

No, I haven't, Master, replied the scholar.

Then you haven't met my horse, the Master stated.

Then a nervous man said,

Speak to us of Patience.

And he said:

I know of a man who was so impatient that he tried to make love to a virgin while shoeing his horse.

Was not the virgin embarrassed, Master? the man asked.

Not as much as I—er—the man, the Master recalled.

Christ died for our sins. Dare we make his martyrdom meaningless by not committing them?

—*Jules Feiffer*

The Vatican Rag

Words and Music by Tom Lehrer

First you get—down   on your knees,— Fid-dle with—your ro-sa-ries,—
So get down—up - on your knees,— Fid-dle with—your ro-sa-ries,—

Bow your head with great re-spect,— and gen-u-flect, gen-u-flect, gen-u-flect!
Bow your head with great re-spect,— and gen-u-flect, gen-u-flect, gen-u-flect!

Do what-ev - er steps you want— if You have cleared them with the Pon-tiff,
Make a cross—on your ab-do-men, When in Rome— do like a Ro-man,

DETERIORATA

GO PLACIDLY AMID THE NOISE AND WASTE AND remember what comfort there may be in owning a piece thereof. Avoid quiet & passive persons unless you are in need of sleep. Rotate your tires. Speak glowingly of those greater than yourself & heed well their advice, even though they be turkeys; know what to kiss & when. Consider that two wrongs never make a right but that three do. Wherever possible, put people on hold. Be comforted that in the face of all aridity & disillusionment & despite the changing fortunes of time, there is always a big future in computer maintenance. Remember the Pueblo. Strive at all times to bend, fold, spindle, & mutilate. Know yourself; if you need help, call the FBI. Exercise caution in your daily affairs, especially with those persons closest to you—that lemon on your left, for instance. Be assured that a walk through the ocean of most souls would scarcely get your feet wet. Fall not in love therefore; it will stick to your face. Gracefully surrender the things of youth, birds, clean air, tuna, Taiwan; & let not the sands of time get in your lunch. Hire people with hooks. For a good time, call 555-4311; ask for Ken. Take heart amid the deepening gloom that your dog is finally getting enough cheese; & reflect that whatever misfortune may be your lot, it could only be worse in Milwaukee. You are a fluke of the universe; you have no right to be here, & whether you can hear it or not, the universe is laughing behind your back. Therefore make peace with your God whatever you conceive Him to be—Hairy Thunderer or Cosmic Muffin. With all its hopes, dreams, promises, & urban renewal, the world continues to deteriorate. Give up.

Tony Hendra

WOODY ALLEN

Examining Psychic Phenomena

And then there was the Society of Dyslexic Theologians. They argued constantly about the existence of Dog.

There is no question that there is an unseen world. The problem is, how far is it from midtown and how late is it open? Unexplainable events occur constantly. One man will see spirits. Another will hear voices. A third will wake up and find himself running in the Preakness. How many of us have not at one time or another felt an ice-cold hand on the back of our neck while we were home alone? (Not me, thank God, but some have.) What is behind these experiences? Or in front of them, for that matter? Is it true that some men can foresee the future or communicate with ghosts? And after death is it still possible to take showers?

Fortunately, these questions about psychic phenomena are answered in a soon to be published book, *Boo!*, by Dr. Osgood Mulford Twelge, the noted para-psychologist and professor of ectoplasm at Columbia University. Dr. Twelge has assembled a remarkable history of supernatural incidents that covers the whole range of psychic phenomena, from thought transference to the bizarre experience of two brothers on opposite parts of the globe, one of whom took a bath while the other suddenly got clean. What follows is but a sampling of Dr. Twelge's most celebrated cases, with his comments.

APPARITIONS

On March 16, 1882, Mr. J. C. Dubbs awoke in the middle of the night and saw his brother Amos, who had been dead for fourteen years, sitting at the foot of his bed flicking chickens. Dubbs asked his brother what he was doing there, and his brother said not to worry, he was dead and was only in town for the weekend. Dubbs asked his brother

"Somehow I thought the whole thing would be a lot classier."

what it was like in "the other world," and his brother said it was not unlike Cleveland. He said he had returned to give Dubbs a message, which was that a dark-blue suit and Argyle socks are a big mistake.

At that point, Dubbs's servant girl entered and saw Dubbs talking to "a shapeless, milky haze," which she said reminded her of Amos Dubbs but was a little better-looking. Finally, the ghost asked Dubbs to join him in an aria from *Faust,* which the two sang with great fervor. As dawn rose, the ghost walked through the wall, and Dubbs, trying to follow, broke his nose.

This appears to be a classic case of the apparition phenomenon, and if Dubbs is to be believed, the ghost returned again and caused Mrs. Dubbs to rise out of a chair and hover over the dinner table for twenty minutes until she dropped into some gravy. It is interesting to note that spirits have a tendency to be mischievous, which A. F. Childe, the British mystic, attributes to a marked feeling of inferiority they have over being dead. "Apparitions" are often associated with individuals who have suffered an unusual demise. Amos Dubbs, for instance, had died under mysterious circumstances when a farmer accidentally planted him along with some turnips.

SPIRIT DEPARTURE

Mr. Albert Sykes reports the following experience: "I was sitting having biscuits with some friends when I felt my spirit leave my body and go make a telephone call. For some reason, it called the Moscowitz Fiber Glass Company. My spirit then returned to my body and sat for another twenty minutes or so, hoping nobody would suggest charades. When the conversation turned to mutual funds, it left again and began wandering around the city. I am convinced that it visited the Statue of Liberty and then saw the stage show at Radio City Music Hall. Following that, it went to Benny's Steak House and ran up a tab of sixty-eight dollars. My spirit then decided to return to my body, but it was impossible to get a cab. Finally, it walked up Fifth Avenue and rejoined me just in time to catch the late news. I could tell that it was reentering my body, because I felt a sudden chill, and a voice said, 'I'm back. You want to pass me those raisins?'

"This phenomenon has happened to me several times since. Once, my spirit went to Miami for a weekend, and once it was arrested for trying to leave Macy's without paying for a tie. The fourth time, it was actually my body that left my spirit, although all it did was get a rubdown and come right back."

Spirit departure was very common around 1910, when many "spirits" were reported wandering aimlessly around India searching for the American Consulate. The phenomenon is quite similar to transubstantiation, the process whereby a person will suddenly dematerialize and rematerialize somewhere else in the world. This is not a bad way to travel, although there is usually a half-hour wait for luggage. The most astonishing case of transubstantiation was that of Sir Arthur Nurney, who vanished with an audible *pop* while he was taking a bath and suddenly appeared in the string section of the Vienna Symphony Orchestra. He stayed on as the first violinist for twenty-seven years, although he could only play "Three Blind Mice," and vanished abruptly one day during Mozart's Jupiter Symphony, turning up in bed with Winston Churchill.

PRECOGNITION

Mr. Fenton Allentuck describes the following precognitive dream: "I went to sleep at midnight and dreamed that I was playing whist with a

---

A traveling preacher finds himself caught in a tremendous rainstorm. Within a few hours, the motel he's staying in is flooded. As the water rises, the preacher climbs to the roof and starts praying.

Just then, a coast guard rescue party floats by in a rowboat. "Let's go, mister, into the boat."

"I'll stay here," says the preacher. "The Lord will save me."

An hour later, a second boat reaches the motel. "Sir, you better get in. The water is still rising."

"No thanks," says the preacher. "The Lord is my salvation."

Toward evening, the motel is almost completely under water, and the preacher is clinging to the satellite dish on the roof.

"Hey buddy, get in the boat! This is your last chance."

"I'm all right," says the preacher, looking toward heaven. "I *know* the Lord will provide."

As the boat departs, the satellite dish is hit by lightning, and the preacher is killed.

When he arrives at the Pearly Gates, he is furious. "What happened?" he shouts. "I thought the Lord would provide!"

Within seconds, a thunderous reply is heard: "Gimme a break, pal. I sent three boats!"

plate of chives. Suddenly the dream shifted, and I saw my grandfather about to be run over by a truck in the middle of the street, where he was waltzing with a clothing dummy. I tried to scream, but when I opened my mouth the only sound that came out was chimes, and my grandfather was run over.

"I awoke in a sweat and ran to my grandfather's house and asked him if he had plans to go waltzing with a clothing dummy. He said of course not, although he had contemplated posing as a shepherd to fool his enemies. Relieved, I walked home, but learned later that the old man had slipped on a chicken-salad sandwich and fallen off the Chrysler Building."

Precognitive dreams are too common to be dismissed as pure coincidence. Here a man dreams of a relative's death, and it occurs. Not everyone is so lucky. J. Martinez, of Kennebunkport, Maine, dreamed he won the Irish Sweepstakes. When he awoke, his bed had floated out to sea.

TRANCES

Sir Hugh Swiggles, the skeptic, reports an interesting séance experience:

We attended the home of Madame Reynaud, the noted medium, where we were all told to sit around the table and join hands. Mr. Weeks couldn't stop giggling, and Madame Reynaud smashed him on the head with a Ouija board. The lights were turned out, and Madame Reynaud attempted to contact Mrs. Marple's husband, who had died at the opera when his beard caught fire. The following is an exact transcript:

Mrs. Marple: What do you see?
Medium: I see a man with blue eyes and a pinwheel hat.
Mrs. Marple: That's my husband!
Medium: His name is . . . Robert. No . . . Richard . . .
Mrs. Marple: Quincy.
Medium: Quincy! Yes, that's it!
Mrs. Marple: What else about him?
Medium: He is bald but usually keeps some leaves on his head so nobody will notice.
Mrs. Marple: Yes! Exactly!
Medium: For some reason, he has an object . . . a loin of pork.
Mrs. Marple: My anniversary present to him! Can you make him speak?
Medium: Speak, spirit. Speak.
Quincy: Claire, this is Quincy.
Mrs. Marple: Oh, Quincy! Quincy!
Quincy: How long do you keep the chicken in when you're trying to broil it?
Mrs. Marple: That voice! It's him!

The time has come for St. Peter's annual three-week vacation, and Jesus volunteers to fill in for him at the Pearly Gates. "It's no big deal," St. Peter explains. "Sit at the registration desk, and ask each person a little about his or her life. Then send them on to housekeeping to pick up their wings."

On the third day, Jesus looks up to see a bewildered old man standing in front of him.

"I'm a simple carpenter," says the man. "And once I had a son. He was born in a very special way, and was unlike anyone else in this world. He went through a great transformation even though he had holes in his hands and feet. He was taken from me a long time ago, but his spirit lives on forever. All over the world people tell his story."

By this time, Jesus is standing with his arms outstretched. There are tears in his eyes, and he embraces the old man.

"Father," he cries out. "It's been so long!"

The old man squints, stares for a moment, and says, "Pinocchio?"

© 1990 by Leigh Rubin

Medium: Everybody concentrate.

Mrs. Marple: Quincy, are they treating you okay?

Quincy: Not bad, except it takes four days to get your cleaning back.

Mrs. Marple: Quincy, do you miss me?

Quincy: Huh? Oh, er, sure. Sure, kid. I got to be going. . . .

Medium: I'm losing it. He's fading. . . .

I found this séance to pass the most stringent tests of credulity, with the minor exception of a phonograph, which was found under Madame Reynaud's dress.

There is no doubt that certain events recorded at séances are genuine. Who does not recall the famous incident at Sybil Seretsky's, when her goldfish sang "I Got Rhythm"—a favorite tune of her recently deceased nephew? But contacting the dead is at best difficult, since most deceased are reluctant to speak up, and those that do seem to hem and haw before getting to the point. The author has actually seen a table rise, and Dr. Joshua Fleagle, of Harvard, attended a séance in which a table not only rose but excused itself and went upstairs to sleep.

CLAIRVOYANCE

One of the most astounding cases of clairvoyance is that of the noted Greek psychic, Achille Londos. Londos realized he had "unusual powers" by the age of ten, when he could lie in bed and, by concentrating, make his father's false teeth jump out of his mouth. After a neighbor's husband had been missing for three weeks, Londos told them to look in the stove, where the man was found knitting. Londos could concentrate on a person's face and force the image to come out on a roll of ordinary Kodak film, although he could never seem to get anybody to smile.

In 1964, he was called in to aid police in capturing the Düsseldorf Strangler, a fiend who always left a baked Alaska on the chests of his victims. Merely by sniffing a handkerchief, Londos led police to Siegfried Lenz, handyman at a school for deaf turkeys, who said he was the strangler and could he please have his handkerchief back.

Londos is just one of many people with psychic powers. C. N. Jerome, the psychic, of Newport, Rhode Island, claims he can guess any card being thought of by a squirrel.

PROGNOSTICATION

Finally, we come to Aristonidis, the sixteenth-century count whose predictions continue to dazzle and perplex even the most skeptical. Typical examples are:

"Two nations will go to war, but only one will win."

(Experts feel this probably refers to the Russo-Japanese War of 1904–5—an astounding feat of prognostication, considering the fact that it was made in 1540.)

"A man in Istanbul will have his hat blocked, and it will be ruined."

(In 1860, Abu Hamid, Ottoman warrior, sent his cap out to be cleaned, and it came back with spots.)

"I see a great person, who one day will invent for mankind a garment to be worn over his trousers for protection while cooking. It will be called an 'abron' or 'aprone.' "

(Aristonidis meant the apron, of course.)

"A leader will emerge in France. He will be very short and will cause great calamity."

(This is a reference either to Napoleon or to Marcel Lumet, an eighteenth-century midget who instigated a plot to rub béarnaise sauce on Voltaire.)

"In the New World, there will be a place named California, and a man named Joseph Cotten will become famous."

(No explanation necessary.)

Lord Byron arrives in Heaven, and finds his old friend Shelley waiting at the gate.

"Percy, I can't believe it. You died two years ago. Why aren't you inside?"

"St. Peter says he's already got too many poets," says Shelley. "So I've been waiting here for you. Maybe together, we can convince him to let us in."

When St. Peter appears, he greets Byron by name. "You two have both been naughty," he says, "and I've already told your friend here that we're pretty full. We've only got room for one of you, so I'm asking you each to write a verse for me about one of my favorite places—Timbuktu. I'll be back in an hour to see what you've come up with."

When St. Peter returns, Shelley proudly recites his poem:

With feet upon the burning sand
I gazed upon the promised land
And in the far-off distant view
The paradise of Timbuktu.

"Very nice," says St. Peter. And then, turning to Byron, he says, "Your turn, sir."

With a wink to his friend, Byron begins:

Tim and I a-hunting went
And spied three maidens in a tent
As they were three, and we were two,
I bucked one, and Timbuktu.

Student Bloopers compiled by
ANDERS HENRIKSSON

Life Reeked with Joy

History, as we know, is always bias, because human beings have to be studied by other human beings, not by independent observers of another species.

During the Middle Ages, everbody was middle aged. Church and state were co-operatic. Middle Evil society was made up of monks, lords, and surfs. It is unfortunate that we do not have a medivel European laid out on a table before us, ready for dissection. After a revival of infantile commerce slowly creeped into Europe, merchants appeared. Some were sitters and some were drifters. They roamed from town to town exposing themselves and organized big fairies in the countryside. Mideval people were violent. Murder during this period was nothing. Everybody killed someone. England fought numerously for land in France and ended up wining and losing. The Crusades were a series of military expaditions made by Christians seeking to free the holy land (the "Home Town" of Christ) from the Islams.

In the 1400 hundreds most Englishmen were perpendicular. A class of yeowls arose. Finally, Europe caught the Black Death. The bubonic plague is a social disease in the sense that it can be transmitted by intercourse and other etceteras. It was spread from port to port by inflected rats. Victims of the Black Death grew boobs on their necks. The plague also helped the emergance of the English language as the national language of England, France and Italy.

The Middle Ages slimpared to a halt. The renasence bolted in from the blue. Life reeked with joy. Italy became robust, and more individuals felt the value of their human being. Italy, of course, was much closer to the rest of the world, thanks to northern Europe. Man was determined to civilise himself and his brothers, even if heads had to roll! It became sheik to be educated. Art was on a more associated level. Europe was full of incredible churches with great art bulging out their doors. Renaissance merchants were beautiful and almost lifelike.

The Reformnation happened when German nobles resented the idea that tithes were going to Papal France or the Pope thus enriching Catholic coiffures. Traditions had become oppressive so they too were crushed in the wake of man's quest for ressurection above the not-just-social beast he had become. An angry Martin Luther nailed 95 theocrats to a church door. Theologically, Luthar was into reorientation mutation. Calvinism was the most convenient religion since the days of the ancients. Anabaptist services tended to be migratory. The Popes, of course, were usually Catholic. Monks went right on seeing themselves as worms. The last Jesuit priest died in the 19th century.

After the refirmation were wars both foreign and infernal. If the

Spanish could gain the Netherlands they would have a stronghold throughout northern Europe which would include their posetions in Italy, Burgangy, central Europe and India thus serrounding France. The German Emperor's lower passage was blocked by the French for years and years.

Louis XIV became King of the Sun. He gave the people food and artillery. If he didn't like someone, he sent them to the gallows to row for the rest of their lives. Vauban was the royal minister of flirtation. In Russia the 17th century was known as the time of the bounding of the serfs. Russian nobles wore clothes only to humour Peter the Great. Peter filled his government with accidental people and built a new capital near the European boarder. Orthodox priests became government antennae.

The enlightenment was a reasonable time. Voltare wrote a book called *Candy* that got him into trouble with Frederick the Great. Philosophers were unknown yet, and the fundamental stake was one of religious toleration slightly confused with defeatism. France was in a very serious state. Taxation was a great drain on the state budget. The French revolution was accomplished before it happened. The revolution evolved through monarchial, republican and tolarian phases until it catapulted into Napolean. Napoleon was ill with bladder problems and was very tense and unrestrained.

History, a record of things left behind by past generations, started in 1815. Throughout the comparatively radical years 1815–1870 the western European continent was undergoing a Rampant period of economic modification. Industrialization was precipitating in England. Problems were so complexicated that in Paris, out of a city population of one million people, two million able bodies were on the loose.

Great Brittian, the USA and other European countrys had demicratic leanings. The middle class was tired and needed a rest. The old order could see the lid holding down new ideas beginning to shake. Among the goals of the chartists were universal suferage and an anal parliment. Voting was to be done by ballad.

A new time zone of national unification roared over the horizon. Founder of the new Italy was Cavour, an intelligent Sardine from the north. Nationalism aided Italy because nationalism is the growth of an army. We can see that nationalism succeeded for Itally because of France's big army. Napoleon III–IV mounted the French thrown. One thinks of Napoleon III as a live extension of the late, but great, Napoleon. Here too was the new Germany: loud, bold, vulgar and full of reality.

Culture fomented from Europe's tip to its top. Richard Strauss, who was violent but methodical like his wife made him, plunged into vicious and perverse plays. Dramatized were adventures in seduction and abortion. Music reeked with reality. Wagner was master of music, and people did not forget his contribution. When he died they labeled his seat "historical." Other countries had their own artists. France had Chekhov.

World War I broke out around 1912–1914. Germany was on one

side of France and Russia was on the other. At war people get killed, and then they aren't people any more, but friends. Peace was proclaimed at Versigh, which was attended by George Loid, Primal Minister of England. President Wilson arrived with 14 pointers. In 1937 Lenin revolted Russia. Communism raged among the peasants, and the civil war "team colours" were red and white.

Germany was displaced after WWI. This gave rise to Hitler. Germany was morbidly overexcited and unbalanced. Berlin became the decadent capital, where all forms of sexual deprivations were practised. A huge anti-semantic movement arose. Attractive slogans like "death to all Jews" were used by governmental groups. Hitler remilitarized the Rineland over a squirmish between Germany and France. The appeasers were blinded by the great red of the Soviets. Moosealini rested his foundations on eight million bayonets and invaded Hi Lee Salasy. Germany invaded Poland, France invaded Belgium, and Russia invaded everybody. War screeched to an end when a nukuleer explosion was dropped on Heroshima. A whole generation had been wiped out in two world wars, and their forlorne families were left to pick up the peaces.

According to Fromm, individuation began historically in medieval times. This was a period of small childhood. There is increasing experience as adolescence experiences its life development. The last stage is us.

DAVE BARRY

The Civil War: A Nation Pokes Itself in the Eyeball

The seeds of the Civil War were sown in the late eighteenth century when Eli Whitney invented the "cotton gin," a machine capable of turning cotton into gin many times faster than it could be done by hand. This created a great demand for cotton-field workers, whom the South originally attempted to recruit by placing "help wanted" advertisements in the newspaper:

ATTENTION SELF-STARTERS!
Are you that special "can-do" kind of guy or gal who's looking for a chance to work extremely hard under horrible conditions for your entire life without getting paid and being severely beaten whenever we feel like it, plus we get to keep your children? To find out more about this exciting career opportunity, Contact: The South.

Oddly enough, this advertisement failed to produce any applicants, and so the South decided to go with slavery. Many people argued that slavery was inhuman and cruel and should be abolished, but the slave owners argued that it wasn't so bad, and that in fact the slaves actually were *happy,* the evidence for this being that they sometimes rattled their chains in a rhythmic fashion.

By the mid-nineteenth century, slavery was the topic of heated debate among just about everybody in the country except of course the actual slaves, most of whom were busy either working or fleeing through swamps. The crisis deepened in 1850, when President Zachary Taylor died of cholera. Taylor's death led to the presidency of a man whose name has since become synonymous, in American history, with the term "Millard Fillmore": Millard Fillmore.

HIGHLIGHTS OF THE FILLMORE ADMINISTRATION

1. The Earth did not crash into the Sun.

After Fillmore came Franklin Pierce and James Buchanan, who as far as we can tell were both president at the same time. This time-saving measure paved the way for the election of Abraham Lincoln, who was popular with the voters because he possessed an extremely rustic set of origins.

THE ORIGINS OF ABRAHAM LINCOLN

Lincoln's family was poor. He was born in a log cabin. And when we say "a log cabin," we are talking about a cabin that consisted entirely of *one single log.* That is how poor Lincoln's family was. When it rained, everybody had to lie down under the log, the result being that Lincoln grew up to be very long and narrow, which turned out to be the ideal physique for splitting rails. Young Abe would get out there with his ax, and he'd split hundreds of rails at a time, and people would come from miles around. "Dammit, Lincoln," they'd say, "those rails cost good money!" But in the end they forgave young Abe, because he had the ax.

He was also known for his honesty. In one famous historical anecdote, Lincoln was tending store, and a customer accidentally left his change on the counter, and young Abe picked it up and walked fourteen miles with it, only to glance down and realize that his face was on the penny. This anecdote gave Lincoln the nickname that was to serve him so well in politics—"Old Ironsides"—and it earned him an invitation to appear as a contestant on *The Lincoln-Douglas Debates,* the most popular show of the era. Lincoln was able to get to the bonus round, where he correctly answered the question "How much is four score plus seven?," thus winning the Samsonite luggage *and* the presidency of the United States.

This resulted in yet another famous historical anecdote. When Lincoln assumed the presidency, he was clean-shaven, but one day he got a letter from a little girl suggesting that he grow a beard. So he did, and he thought it looked pretty good, so he decided to keep it. A short while later, he got another letter from the little girl, this time suggesting that he wear mascara and rouge and maybe a simple string of pearls. Fortunately, just then the Civil War broke out.

THE CIVIL WAR

This was pretty depressing. Brother fought against brother, unless he had no male siblings, in which case he fought against his sister. Sometimes he would even take a shot at his cousin. Sooner or later, this resulted in a horrendous amount of devastation, particularly in the South, where things got so bad that Clark Gable, in what is probably the most famous scene from the entire Civil War, turned to Vivien Leigh, and said: "Frankly, my dear, I don't think we're in Kansas anymore." This epitomized the feeling of despair that was widespread in the Confederacy as the war ended, and it left a vast reservoir of bitterness toward the North. But as the old saying goes, "Time heals all wounds," and in the more than 120 years that have passed since the Civil War ended, most of this bitterness gradually gave way to subdued loathing, which is where we stand today.

RECONSTRUCTION

After the Civil War came Reconstruction, a period during which the South was transformed, through a series of congressional acts, from a totally segregated region where blacks had no rights into a totally segregated region where blacks were supposed to have rights but did not. Much of this progress occurred during the administration of President Ulysses S. Grant, who in 1868 defeated a person named Horatio Seymour in a race where both candidates had the backing of the Let's Elect Presidents with Comical First Names party, whose members practically wet their pants with joy in 1876 over the election of Rutherford B. Hayes, who went on to die—you can look this up—in a place called Fremont, Ohio. Clearly the troubled nation had nowhere to go except up.

An American manufacturer is showing his machine factory to a potential customer from Albania. At noon, when the lunch whistle blows, two thousand men and women immediately stop work and leave the building.

"Your workers, they're escaping!" cries the visitor. "You've got to stop them."

"Don't worry, they'll be back," says the American. And indeed, at exactly one o'clock the whistle blows again, and all the workers return from their break.

When the tour is over, the manufacturer turns to his guest and says, "Well, now, which of these machines would you like to order?"

"Forget the machines," says the visitor. "How much do you want for that whistle?"

DON'T LAUGH, YOU'RE NEXT!

© 1983 by Skip Morrow

DAVE BARRY
Major Nonhumorous Events Occur

While the United States was struggling to get out of the Depression, the nations of Europe were struggling to overcome the horror and devastation and death of World War I so they could go ahead and have World War II. By the 1930s everybody was just about ready, so Germany, showing the kind of spunky "can-do" spirit that has made it so popular over the years, started invading various surrounding nations. Fortunately these were for the most part *small* nations, but Germany's actions nevertheless alarmed Britain and France, which decided to strike back via the bold and clever strategy of signing agreements with Adolf Hitler. Their thinking was: If you can't trust an insane racist paranoid spittle-emitting criminal dictator, whom can you trust?

Shockingly, this strategy did not prove to be effective. In 1939 Germany invaded Poland in retaliation for Poland's flagrant and provocative decision to be right next door. Britain and France then declared war against Germany, which immediately invaded France and managed to conquer it after an epic battle lasting, by some accounts, as long as thirty-five minutes, with the crushing blow coming near the end when Germany's ally, Italy, sent in its much-feared troops, who penetrated nearly two hundred feet into southern France before their truck broke down.

At this point things looked pretty bleak for the Allied, or "good" side. The last bastion of goodness was Great Britain, a feisty, plucky little island in the North Atlantic led by Prime Minister Winston Churchill, who had won the respect and loyalty of the British people for his ability to come up with clever insults at dinner parties. For example, there was the famous one where this woman says to him, "Lord Churchill, you're drunk!" And he replies, "Madam, I may be drunk, but BLEAAARRRGGGHHH" all over her evening gown. Churchill used this gift of eloquence to rally his countrymen when Britain was down to a three-day supply of pluck and a German invasion appeared imminent. "We shall fight them on the beaches," he said. "We shall fight them in the streets, and in the alleys, and in those things where it's like a dead end, only there's like a circle at the end, you know? Cul somethings."

Thus inspired, the British persevered, but by 1941 it was clear that they could not hold out long without military support from the United States. At the time Americans were strongly opposed to becoming directly involved, but that was to change drastically on the fateful December morning of October 8, when the Japanese, implementing a complex, long-term, and ultimately successful strategy to dominate the

U.S. consumer-electronics market, attacked Pearl Harbor. And so it was time to have

WORLD WAR II

The best evidence we have of what World War II was like comes from about 300 million movies made during this era, many of them featuring Ronald Reagan. From these we learn that the war was fought by small groups of men, called "units," with each unit consisting of:

- One Italian person
- One Jewish person
- One Southern person
- One Tough but Caring Sergeant, and of course
- One African-American.

These men often fought together through an entire double feature, during which they would learn, despite their differing backgrounds, how to trickle syrup from the corners of their mouths to indicate that they had been wounded. In the actual war, of course, real blood was used. In fact, the actual war was extremely depressing, which is why we're going to follow our usual procedure here and skip directly to

The Turning Point

The turning point of the war came when the Allies were able to break the code being used by the Axis high command. The way this happened was, a young British intelligence officer was looking at some captured Nazi documents, and suddenly it hit him. "Hey!" he said. "This is written in *German!*" From that moment on, it was only a matter of time before June 1944, which was when the schedule called for the Normandy Invasion. The Germans knew it was coming, but they didn't know where; thus it was that when, on the morning of October 8, thousands of ships disgorged tens of thousands of troops on the beaches of Normandy, the Germans felt pretty stupid. "So *that's* why they were calling it the 'Normandy Invasion'!" they said. Stunned by this blow, the Germans began a slow, bloody retreat before the forces of General George C. Scott, and within months the Americans had liberated France, whose people continue until this day to show their gratitude to American visitors by looking at us as though we are total Piltdown men when we try to order food.

The Final Stages of the War

America entered the final stages of the war under the leadership of Roosevelt's successor, Harry S Truman, a feisty, plucky little island in the North Atlantic, who . . . No, excuse us, we mean: a feisty, plucky native of Missouri (the "Sho' Nuff" State) who grew up so poor that his family could not afford to put a period after his middle initial, yet who went on to become a failed haberdasher. It was Truman who made the difficult decision to drop the first atomic bomb on the Japanese city of Hiroshima, the rationale being that only such a devastating, horrendous display of destructive power would convince Japan that it had to surrender. Truman also made the decision to drop the second atomic bomb on Nagasaki, the rationale being that, hey, we had another bomb.

MARTIN MULL & ALLEN RUCKER
Am I White?

The search for personal identity is as old as man, and maybe older. Most of us begin this search when we are eighteen, eighteen and a half, or nineteen, sitting around in a college dorm or army barracks, chatting with friends. But many of us, in the hubbub of daily life, never get around to such introspection, and when we die no one knows where to bury us or what to say at the funeral. If that's a potential problem for you, read on.

The following questionnaire was developed after years of intense research at the Institute for White Studies (IFWS), Zanesville, Ohio, under a grant from the J. C. Penney Company, Expand-A-Belt Division. It is intended for the private use of our readers and cannot be used or reproduced on job or home loan applications, résumés, civil service entrance exams, or census reports without the express written consent of the Institute. Furthermore, no question or answer should be construed to reflect directly on the effectiveness or durability of the Expand-A-Belt line of fine fashions.

This test should be administered only under optimum conditions. These include:

1. A quiet room, preferably a licensed Christian Science Reading Room. Or a study room at your local library if you don't believe that bunk about not going to a doctor when you're sick, as if a shot of penicillin spells the difference between Heaven and the Hot Place.
2. A No. 2 lead pencil, well sharpened. Mongol makes a good one. (Please initial all erasures.)
3. If you need a radio to help you think, keep it tuned to mild, middle-of-the-road music, no lyrics.
4. Upon completion, write at the bottom of your exam: "I have neither given nor received help on this paper." Sign your name, date it, and send, along with $106 (cash or money order—no checks, please), to:

Tell Me If I'm White or Not

THE INSTITUTE FOR WHITE STUDIES

Miracle Whip Square

Zanesville, Ohio 60605

You may now begin. You have fifteen minutes. Keep your own time.

1. Do you wear Expand-A-Belt trousers?
   _____ Always.
   _____ Only at home.
   _____ Wish I could.
   _____ Not available in my area.

2. Can you slam-dunk a basketball?
   _____ Yes.
   _____ No.
   _____ Could touch the rim in high school.

3. How many ways does Wonder bread help build strong bodies?
   _____ Eight.
   _____ More than eight.
   _____ At least eight.

4. How many neckties do you own? (Men only)
   _____One.
   _____One hundred.
   _____Several hundred.

5. When a sultry, raven-haired Latin temptress in a low-cut sequined gown slinks up to you at the bar and asks for a light, you . . . (Men only)
   _____Tell her she shouldn't smoke.
   _____Shake hands and give her your business card.
   _____Shout "Hoy-oh!" loudly, like Ed McMahon on *The Tonight Show*.

6. A great hamburger does not contain which of the following:
   _____Lipton's onion soup mix.
   _____Mayonnaise, and tons of it.
   _____Artificial grill marks.
   _____Jewish pickles.

7. The first thing you notice about another's home is:
   _____How it smells.
   _____Its resale value.

8. You are traveling to Europe on an expensive cruise ship. At seven in the morning there is a knock on your stateroom door and a man with a thick accent you can't pinpoint announces what sounds like breakfast. You . . .
   _____Make an attempt to learn his language.
   _____Insist that he learn yours.
   _____Tip him lavishly and bow, praying to God that it's the custom and he's really a waiter and not a terrorist.

9. A game of Scrabble becomes unbearable when:
   _____Your opponent won't stop talking about the storm-window business.
   _____Everybody leaves the room when it's your turn.
   _____There's no more Cheetos.
   _____Your Italian neighbor gets a triple on the word "goombahz" (with a "z").

10. The beauty of Expand-A-Belt trousers is:
    _____You don't need a belt.
    _____They stay up anyway.
    _____They are a perfect gift idea.
    _____They go great with the Expand-A-Jacket.

It was early Friday afternoon, and Mr. Henderson announced that he was going home early for the weekend. His employees were sure that the boss was going to play golf and wouldn't be calling in, so within ten minutes, all of them left, too.

But when Joe, the shipping clerk, came home, he found Mr. Henderson in bed with his wife. He quietly left the house and went to a movie.

The next Friday, Mr. Henderson again announced that he was going home early. This time, too, the employees started leaving, too—all except Joe.

"What's the matter, Joe?" somebody asked. "You can leave. The boss won't be coming back."

"I know," he replied, "but last week I left early and I almost got caught!"

11. Your teenage daughter announces that she is a born-again Christian. There's a long silence, and then you:
_____ Jokingly ask what it cost, because the first time she was born set you back $600 and change.
_____ Tell her she's adopted.
_____ Go over your will with an eraser.
_____ Act like you didn't understand and say "Gesundheit."

12. How often do you check your breath?
_____ Upon reading this.
_____ When others wince.
_____ Once a year.

Take a breather. If these questions are tough for you, you probably aren't White and can go home now. Good night. If you're still not sure, keep working.

13. The world's most nearly perfect food is:
_____ Processed cheese.
_____ Stinky French cheese.
_____ Stinky German cheese.
_____ Donuts.

14. It's two days before Christmas. Your mail carrier, a non-White, announces that he's been fired from the post office, effective today, and that his wife is expecting triplets. He's provided excellent mail service for fourteen years, so you:
_____ Give him a lecture on birth control.
_____ Complain about all the junk mail you get.
_____ Tell him to wait while you go in the house and send your wife out with a check for one dollar.

15. A condominium is:
_____ Less than a home.
_____ A perfect home for your mother-in-law.
_____ Something that leaves a ring in your son's wallet.

16. You are waiting in your boss's car as he ducks into a 7-11 store for some Tums. The glove compartment inexplicably opens and out pops a large white bed sheet with two eyeholes and a hood. You:
_____ Ask if he's been sleeping in his car.
_____ Put it on as a joke and go into the 7-11 after him, yelling "Woogie, woogie, woogie!"
_____ Write a TV movie about your discovery.

17. You just bought a new car and that evening, you must hand it over to a Third World parking valet at your favorite restaurant. You:

_____ Ride with him as he parks it.

_____ Drive home and walk back to the restaurant.

_____ Empty the glove compartment into the trunk and give him only the ignition key.

_____ Eat at Denny's.

18. Upon hearing the oft-used phrase "Man's Best Friend," you immediately think of:

_____ Brut.

_____ A five iron.

_____ Bob Guccione.

_____ Expand-A-Belt trousers.

You're through. Push your paper away and take another breather. Better yet, stand up and stretch. It can't hurt. If it does hurt, sit down. No reason to kill yourself. It's just a harmless questionnaire, not an insurance physical.

If you are like any of the hundreds of people who have completed this exam, you are excited and confused. How did I do? Where do I stand? What's my score? Did I win?

First of all, the test was divided into four major areas. One, misleading or "trick" questions. Two, questions of no import whatsoever. Three, "gimmes," or questions only an idiot could get wrong. And four, questions required under a pre-existing contract with the fine folks at Expand-A-Belt fashions.

For example, question number 6, the one about hamburgers, was a dead giveaway. If you included "Jewish pickles" on your ideal burger, then give this book to a Methodist and go see *Yentl*. You'll learn a lot more about yourself than you will here. Suffice it to say that Barbra Streisand plays a young boy. That's all we're going to say. We don't want to spoil it for you.

Question number 7, however, was a trick question. If the first thing you notice about another's home is "how it smells," you were right. If the first thing you notice is "its resale value," you were also right. No matter what you answered, you were right, and well on your way to being White. Congratulations.

Free speech is the right to shout "theater" in a crowded fire. —*Abbie Hoffman*

LIGHT BULB JOKES

How many morons does it take to screw in a light bulb?

Ten. One to hold the bulb, nine to rotate the ladder.

How many New Yorkers does it take to screw in a light bulb?

None of your damn business.

How many New Jersey-ites does it take to screw in a light bulb?

Three. One to change the bulb, one to be a witness, and the third to shoot the witness.

How many Californians does it take to screw in a light bulb?

Four. One to screw in the bulb and three to share the experience.

How many Oregonians does it take to screw in a light bulb?

Six. One to screw in the bulb, and five more to chase off the Californians who have come up to share the experience.

How many WASPS does it take to screw in a light bulb?

Two. One to mix the drinks and one to call the electrician.

How many Christian Scientists does it take to screw in a light bulb?

One. To sit and pray for the old bulb to go back on.

How many Jews does it take to screw in a light bulb?

Three. One to call the cleaning woman and two to feel guilty about calling the cleaning woman.

How many Jewish-American Princesses does it take to screw in a light bulb?

Two. One to pour the Tab, and one to call Daddy.

How many Jewish mothers does it take to screw in a light bulb?

None. No, it's okay, I'll sit in the dark.

How many Zen Masters does it take to screw in a light bulb?

Two. One to screw in the bulb and one not to screw in the bulb.

How many medical students does it take to screw in a light bulb?

Five. One to screw in the bulb and four to yank the ladder out from under him.

How many graduate students does it take to screw in a light bulb?

One—but it takes him nine years.

How many auto mechanics does it take to screw in a light bulb?

Two. One to screw in the wrong-sized bulb and one to replace the burned-out socket.

How many feminists does it take to screw in a light bulb?

That's not funny!

How many college girls does it take to screw in a light bulb?

That's *women*, and that's not funny either.

How many nuclear engineers does it take to screw in a light bulb?

Seven. One to install the new bulb, and six to figure out what to do with the old one for the next ten thousand years.

How many Teamsters does it take to screw in a light bulb?

Fifteen. You got a problem with that?

How many psychiatrists does it take to screw in a light bulb?

Only one, but the bulb really has to want to change.

How many Marxists does it take to screw in a light bulb?

None. The old light bulb contains the seeds of its own revolution.

How many straight San Franciscans does it take to screw in a light bulb?

Both of them.

How many surrealists does it take to screw in a light bulb?

Two. One to hold the giraffe, and the other to fill the bathtub with brightly colored bicycles.

How many lawyers does it take to screw in a light bulb?

How many can you afford?

How many Senators does it take to screw in a light bulb?

Just one. He holds the bulb and the universe revolves around him.

PHILIP ROTH
Good Morning

In 1950, just seventeen, and Newark two and a half months behind me (well, not exactly "behind": in the mornings I awake in the dormitory baffled by the unfamiliar blanket in my hand, and the disappearance of one of "my" windows; oppressed and distraught for minutes on end by this unanticipated transformation given my bedroom by my mother)—I perform the most openly defiant act of my life: instead of going home for my first college vacation, I travel by train to Iowa, to spend Thanksgiving with The Pumpkin and her parents. Till September I had never been farther west than Lake Hopatcong in New Jersey—now I am off to Ioway! And with a blondie! Of the Christian religion! Who is more stunned by this desertion, my family or me? What daring! Or was I no more daring than a sleepwalker?

The white clapboard house in which The Pumpkin had grown up might have been the Taj Mahal for the emotions it released in me. Balboa, maybe, knows what I felt upon first glimpsing the swing tied up to the ceiling of the front porch. *She was raised in this house. The girl who has let me undo her brassiere and dry-hump her at the dormitory door, grew up in this white house. Behind those* goyische *curtains! Look, shutters!*

"Daddy, Mother," says The Pumpkin, when we disembark at the Davenport train station, "this is the weekend guest, this is the friend from school whom I wrote you about—"

I am something called "a weekend guest"? I am something called "a friend from school"? What tongue is she speaking? I am "the *bonditt,*" "the *vantz,*" I am the insurance man's son. I am Warshaw's ambassador! "How do you do, Alex?" To which of course I reply, "Thank you." Whatever anybody says to me during my first twenty-four hours in Iowa, I answer, "Thank you." Even to inanimate objects. I walk into a chair, promptly I say to it, "Excuse me, thank you." I drop my napkin on the floor, lean down, flushing, to pick it up, "Thank you," I hear myself saying to the napkin—or is it the floor I'm addressing? Would my mother be proud of her little gentleman! Polite even to the furniture!

Then there's an expression in English, "Good morning," or so I have been told; the phrase has never been of any particular use to me. Why should it have been? At breakfast at home I am in fact known to the other boarders as "Mr. Sourball," and "The Crab." But suddenly, here in Iowa, in imitation of the local inhabitants, I am transformed into a veritable geyser of good mornings. That's all anybody around that place knows how to say—they feel the sunshine on their faces, and it just sets off some sort of chemical reaction: Good *morning! Good* morning! Good *morning!* sung to half a dozen different tunes! Next they all start asking each other if they had "a good night's sleep." And asking

Berkowitz is having a drink at his hotel when he spots a beautiful young woman at the other end of the bar. "Bartender," he says, "give that lady whatever she likes, and put it on my tab."

When the drink is delivered, the woman gives Berkowitz a warm smile. A moment later he's at her side. "That was very kind of you," she says. "Won't you sit down?"

After a few minutes of small talk, she says, "Let me be honest with you. You're a very nice man, but I don't think you realize that I'm a professional. I'd be delighted to go upstairs with you for a hundred dollars. If that's not what you had in mind, I certainly understand, and I'll say good-bye now, no hard feelings."

"I'm surprised," says Berkowitz. "But you're a beautiful lady, and I like you, too. I've never done something like this before, but sure, let's go upstairs."

When they get to Berkowitz's room, he says, "I was wondering. There's something about you that makes me think you might be Jewish."

"Well, I am," she replies a little defensively. "Why do you ask?"

"Well, I'm Jewish, too," says Berkowitz. "And since we're both Jewish, I was hoping you would give me a discount."

"Dammit," she replies, "I was afraid this would happen. Okay, twenty percent off. But I want you to know, at these prices I'm not making any profit!"

me! Did I have a good night's sleep? I don't really know, I have to think—the question comes as something of a surprise.

Did I Have A Good Night's Sleep? Why, yes! I think I did! Hey—did you? "Like a log," replies Mr. Campbell. And for the first time in my life I experience the full force of a simile. This man, who is a real estate broker and an alderman of the Davenport town council, says that he slept like a log, and I actually *see* a log. *I* get it! Motionless, heavy, *like a log!* "Good *morning*," he says, and now it occurs to me that the word "morning," as he uses it, refers specifically to the hours between eight A.M. and twelve noon. I'd never thought of it that way before. He wants the hours between eight and twelve to be *good*, which is to say, enjoyable, pleasurable, beneficial! We are all of us wishing each other four hours of pleasure and accomplishment. Why, that's terrific! Hey, that's very nice! Good morning! And the same applies to "Good afternoon"! And "Good evening"! And "Good night"! My God! The English language is *a form of communication!* Conversation isn't just cross-fire where you shoot and get shot at! Where you've got to duck for your life and aim to kill! Words aren't only bombs and bullets—no, they're little gifts, containing *meanings!*

Wait, I'm not finished—as if the experience of being on the inside rather than the outside of these *goyische* curtains isn't overwhelming enough, as if the incredible experience of my wishing hour upon hour of pleasure to a houseful of *goyim* isn't sufficient source for bewilderment, there is, to compound the ecstasy of disorientation, the name of the street upon which the Campbell house stands, the street where *my* girl friend grew up! skipped! skated! hop-scotched! sledded! all the while I dreamed of her existence some fifteen hundred miles away, in what they tell me is the same country. The street name? Not Xanadu, no, better even than that, oh, more preposterous by far: *Elm.* Elm! It is, you see, as though I have walked right through the orange celluloid station band of our old Zenith, directly into "One Man's Family." Elm. Where trees grow—which must be elms!

To be truthful, I must admit that I am not able to draw such a conclusion first thing upon alighting from the Campbell car on Wednesday night: after all, it has taken me seventeen years to recognize an oak, and even there I am lost without the acorns. What I see first in a landscape isn't the flora, believe me—it's the fauna, the human opposition, who is screwing and who is getting screwed. Greenery I leave to the birds and the bees, they have their worries, I have mine. At home who knows the name of what grows from the pavement at the front of our house? It's a tree—and that's it. The kind is of no consequence, who cares what kind, just as long as it doesn't fall down on your head. In the autumn (or is it the spring? Do you know this stuff? I'm pretty sure it's not the winter) there drop from its branches long crescent-shaped pods containing hard little pellets. Okay. Here's a scientific fact about our tree, comes by way of my mother, Sophie Linnaeus: If you shoot those pellets through a straw, you can take somebody's eye out and make him blind for life. (SO NEVER DO IT! NOT EVEN IN JEST! AND IF ANYBODY DOES IT TO YOU, YOU

TELL ME INSTANTLY!) And this, more or less, is the sort of botanical knowledge I am equipped with, until that Sunday afternoon when we are leaving the Campbell house for the train station, and I have my Archimedean experience: Elm Street . . . . . then . . . . . elm *trees!* How simple! I mean, you don't *need* 158 points of I.Q., you don't *have* to be a genius to make sense of this world. It's really all so very simple!

A memorable weekend in my lifetime, equivalent in human history, I would say, to mankind's passage through the entire Stone Age. Every time Mr. Campbell called his wife "Mary," my body temperature shot into the hundreds. There I was, eating off dishes that had been touched by the hands of a woman named *Mary.* (Is there a clue here as to why I so resisted calling The Monkey by her name, except to chastise her? No?) Please, I pray on the train heading west, let there be no pictures of Jesus Christ in the Campbell house. Let me get through this weekend without having to see his pathetic *punim*—or deal with anyone wearing a cross! When the aunts and uncles come for the Thanksgiving dinner, please, let there be no anti-Semite among them! Because if someone starts in with "the pushy Jews," or says "kike" or "jewed him down"— Well, I'll jew them down all right, I'll jew their fucking teeth down their throat! No, no violence (as if I even had it in me), let *them* be violent, that's *their* way. No, I'll rise from my seat—and *(vuh den?)* make a speech! I will shame and humiliate them in their bigoted hearts! Quote the Declaration of Independence over their candied yams! Who the fuck are they, I'll ask, to think they own Thanksgiving!

Then at the railroad station her father says, "How do you do, young man?" and I of course answer, "Thank you." Why is *he* acting so nice? Because he has been forewarned (which I don't know whether to take as an insult or a blessing), or because he doesn't know yet? Shall I say it then, before we even get into the car? Yes, I must! I can't go on living a lie! "Well, it sure is nice being here in Davenport, Mr. and Mrs. Campbell, what with my being Jewish and all." Not quite ringing enough perhaps. "Well, as a friend of Kay's, Mr. and Mrs. Campbell, and a Jew, I do want to thank you for inviting me—" Stop pussyfooting! What then? Talk Yiddish? *How?* I've got twenty-five words to my name—half of them dirty, and the rest mispronounced! Shit, just shut up and get in the car. "Thank you, thank you," I say, picking up my own bag, and we all head for the station wagon.

Kay and I climb into the back seat, *with the dog.* Kay's dog! To whom she talks as though he's human! Wow, she really *is* a *goy.* What a stupid thing, to talk to a dog—except Kay isn't stupid! In fact, I think she's smarter really than I am. And yet talks to a dog? "As far as dogs are concerned, Mr. and Mrs. Campbell, we Jews by and large—" Oh, forget it. Not necessary. You are ignoring anyway (or trying awfully hard to) that eloquent appendage called your nose. Not to mention the Afro-Jewish hairpiece. Of course they know. Sorry, but there's no escaping destiny, *bubi,* a man's cartilage is his fate. *But I don't want to escape!* Well, that's nice too—because you can't. *Oh, but yes I can—if I should want to!* But you said you don't want to. *But if I did!*

As soon as I enter the house I begin (on the sly, and somewhat to my own surprise) to sniff: what will the odor be like? Mashed potatoes? An old lady's dress? Fresh cement? I sniff and I sniff, trying to catch the scent. There! is *that* it, is that Christianity I smell or just the dog? Everything I see, taste, touch, I think, "*Goyish!*" My first morning I squeeze half an inch of Pepsodent down the drain rather than put my brush where Kay's mother or father may have touched the bristles with which they cleanse their own *goyische* molars. True! The soap on the sink is bubbly with foam from somebody's hands. Whose? *Mary's?* Should I just take hold of it and begin to wash, or should I maybe run a little water over it first, just to be safe. But safe from *what?* Schmuck, maybe you want to get a piece of soap to wash the soap with! I tiptoe to the toilet, I peer over into the bowl: "Well, there it is, boy, a real *goyische* toilet bowl. The genuine article. Where your girl friend's father drops his gentile turds. What do you think, huh? Pretty impressive." Obsessed? Spellbound!

Next I have to decide whether or not to line the seat. It isn't a matter of hygiene, I'm sure the place is clean, spotless in its own particular antiseptic *goy* way: the question is, what if it's warm yet from a Campbell behind—from her mother! *Mary!* Mother also of Jesus Christ! If only for the sake of my family, maybe I should put a little paper around the rim; it doesn't cost anything, and who will ever know?

I will! *I* will! So down I go—and it *is* warm! Yi, seventeen years old and I am rubbing asses with the enemy!

JACKIE MASON

The Difference Between Jews and Gentiles

You don't know one Jew anywhere who can do anything with his hands. It's because of this simple fact: that Jews were raised never to do anything with their hands and to this day they can't do nothing. That's right—if a Jewish car breaks down, it's all over. There's nothing they can do.

Watch a gentile car break down. Did you ever see the difference? If a gentile car breaks down, in two seconds they're under the car, on top of the car. . . . It becomes an airplane and he flies away.

A Jewish car breaks down and you always hear the same things:
"It stopped."
And the wife always says, "It's your fault."

And the husband says, "I know what it is. It's in the hood."

She says, "Where's the hood?"

He says, "I don't remember."

Takes a Jew three hours to open a hood and when he finally opens it up: "Wow, is it busy here!"

Then he makes a move and she says, "Watch out, you'll hurt yourself!"

If you doubt the truth of this, go to any gentile home and you'll see the truth of it. A gentile home is a completely different environment than a Jewish home. A gentile home is a workshop and a Jewish home is a museum. Go in any gentile home, they hit you with hammers, nails, screwdrivers, banging. . . . The whole house is a workshop. They take you right to the basement. They're fixing and banging and clanging. They fix everything. They build it, rebuild it. . . . The toilet was once a chair. The living room was once a kitchen. The ping-pong table was once a furnace. The second floor was once a chimney. The whole wall was once in Philadelphia. . . .

Every Jew who gets married knows he's going to spend the rest of his life going from one Chinese restaurant to another. They make a deal with a Chinaman before the wedding that this'll be it.

Did you ever notice that Chinese people never eat in a Jewish restaurant? For five thousand years every Jew is eating in a Chinese restaurant. Did you ever see one Chinaman in a Jewish restaurant? The sonsofbitches. I never met a Chinaman who said to me, "I'm looking for a piece of gefilte fish."

When gentiles leave a theater they all do the same thing. They say, "Have a drink? How about you? Have a drink?"

And every Jew will be saying the same thing too: "Did you eat yet?"

That's a simple fact. Gentiles never finish drinking, Jews never finish eating. What do you think Jews talk about for breakfast? Where to eat lunch. That's all they talk about.

At lunch: "Where should we have dinner?"

Dinner: "Where should we have coffee?"

"But we had coffee."

"But we didn't have cake yet."

"Let's go for a walk."

"We walked already, but we didn't have cake yet."

Four o'clock in the morning: "Let's have sex."

"We had sex, but we didn't have cake yet."

Gentiles know nothing about food. It's not their field. They know nothing about it, and they'll eat anything you serve them. To them it's not an emotional problem. It's not a major issue. No matter what it is, it's better than nothing and they eat it.

Ever see a gentile order breakfast? They only know one thing:

"Give me ham and eggs. That's good enough."

During the winter of 1926, Thelma Goldstein from Chicago treated herself to her first real vacation in Florida. Being unfamiliar with the area, she wandered into a restricted hotel in North Miami.

"Excuse me," she said to the manager. "My name is Mrs. Goldstein, and I'd like a small room for two weeks."

"I'm awfully sorry," he replied, "but all our rooms are occupied."

Just as he said that, a man came down and checked out.

"What luck," said Mrs. Goldstein. "Now there's a room."

"Not so fast, madam. I'm afraid that this hotel is restricted. No Jews allowed."

"Jewish? Who's Jewish? I happen to be a Catholic."

"I find that hard to believe. Let me ask you, who was the son of God?"

"Jesus, son of Mary."

"Where was he born?"

"In a stable."

"And why was he born in a stable?"

"Because a schmuck like you wouldn't let a Jew rent a room in his hotel."

Ever hear a Jew order breakfast? Every Jew orders breakfast like this:

"Listen, I want it once over light on this egg, and on the other egg I want under the quarter. This'll be under a half and this'll be under a minute. I'd like a slight two-minute egg on this side. I want the bacon, but not on the same plate. I want the potatoes on a third plate, and this on a fourth plate. . . . I want the coffee not to the top . . . closer to two-thirds . . . not less than a half. . . . I want the bread toasted . . . not very toasted . . . slightly toasted . . . not exactly toasted . . . but I want it brown . . . not very brown . . . it should *look* brown. . . ."

You have to be a lunatic not to think that Jews eat more than gentiles. Of course they eat more. Every coffee shop owner knows it. Why do you think, if you go into any gentile neighborhood, anywhere in the world, and you order a piece of cake it comes out one-tenth the size of the piece in a Jewish coffee shop? Did you ever go into a coffee shop in a real gentile neighborhood? Go to Wyoming and order a piece of cake. Did you ever see how small a piece of cake comes out? To a Jew it would be a *cookie*.

DOONESBURY   *Duke Gives a Speech by Garry Trudeau*

REAL PEOPLE   249

PAUL SIMMS
Drugs of the Future

The government deregulated mood-altering and recreational drugs in 1994. Within months the Nader Group had prepared a consumers' guide to today's most popular drugs.

Ecstacy Lite:

A milder version of Ecstacy that induces a milder, less embarrassing level of euphoria.

TYPICAL TESTIMONIAL: "I suddenly had this contented feeling. Like I'd just been told I had a really good credit rating."

POTENTIAL SIDE EFFECTS: User may experience a very mild depression, equivalent to the sense of loss one feels upon losing a favorite comb.

Heroinette:

All the side effects of heroin, with none of the mental slowdown.

TYPICAL TESTIMONIAL: "Five minutes after shooting up, I was drooling, nodding, and absentmindedly scratching my arms and legs. Later, I vomited. But I was completely lucid and conscious, so I could enjoy every single second of it."

POTENTIAL SIDE EFFECTS: Loss of friends.

Direct Access:

An electrode is connected to the neurons in your brain's "pleasure center." An unobtrusive flesh-colored wire runs out of your ear and is connected to a big red button. Each time you push the button, a mild electrical pulse provides a psychoelectrical stimulus directly to a very special part of your brain.

TYPICAL TESTIMONIAL: "Like having a five-hour orgasm, with none of the laundry problems."

POTENTIAL SIDE EFFECTS: May make some users ejaculate out of their tear ducts.

Anticrack:

The perfect antidote to a good hit of crack.

TYPICAL TESTIMONIAL: "I'm a crack connoisseur. I can tell good crack from bad crack, and I use both extensively. Anticrack did just as it promised. It took me down to a relaxed, contemplative state, whereby I could calmly and rationally decide to take some more crack. Crack,

> **Here's a little warning sign if you have a cocaine problem. First of all, if you come home to your house, you have no furniture, and your cat's going, "I'm out of here, prick," WARNING.**
>
> **Number 2, if you have this dream and you have cocaine in your sleep and you can't fall asleep, and you have cocaine in your sleep and you can't fall asleep, and you wake up and you're doing cocaine, bingo.**
>
> **Number 3. If on your tax form it says fifty thousand dollars for snacks, MAYDAY.**
>
> —Robin Williams

cheney

© 1990 by Thomas W. Cheney

anticrack, crack, anticrack—I went back and forth like this for quite a while, trying to find an even point. Suddenly a month had passed and I found myself in Milwaukee."

POTENTIAL SIDE EFFECTS: None when used correctly.

Even-Odd:

Ingesting this pill ensures a fifty-fifty chance that you will die within the next fifteen minutes. Quite a thrill—makes you make the most of the next fifteen minutes. A gambler's delight.

TYPICAL TESTIMONIAL: "My whole life passed before my eyes. I swore to myself that if I survived I would spend the rest of my life helping others. I did, and I've dedicated my life to turning other people on to this wonderful drug. At least half of them have reported spiritual awakenings similar to mine."

POTENTIAL SIDE EFFECTS: 50 percent chance of death.

Cash-on-Hand:

You pay a predetermined amount of cash. The dealer then takes you to a secluded location and opens a briefcase full of up to two thousand dollars—in genuine 1980s-style cash money! You are permitted to look at the cash for thirty seconds, or until you faint from excitement. Your cash payment is then added to the dealer's briefcase, making your next Cash-on-Hand high even more profound.

TYPICAL TESTIMONIAL: "The second time was even better: seeing my own cash money in there with all that other cash money was just too much. I had to get more cash money so that I could see it again."

POTENTIAL SIDE EFFECTS: May cause irreversible wistfulness and nostalgia for the late 1980s.

Drugs. I can take them or leave them. But they're much more effective when I take them.
—Ronnie Shakes

A. WHITNEY BROWN
The Big Picture in Words, Explained

IN THE BEGINNING WAS THE WORD.

This is what it says in the Bible, which means, "The Book." Although, with just one Word it probably wasn't much of a book at the time.

Things were very succinct back then. When a man gave his word, he was out. But people got along, because they were wise, and a word, to the wise, is sufficient.

In any case, as it turned out, there was one guy who couldn't get a Word in edgewise. He spoke softly. But, just by coincidence, he also carried a big stick and this led to the discovery that action speaks louder than words. After that, talk was cheap.

Very soon a picture was worth a thousand words, and the price has been going up ever since. A picture of a sunflower by Van Gogh, for example, recently sold for 42 million pictures of George Washington, even though the actual sunflower was probably not worth as much as the actual George Washington.

The Big Picture is worth more than a thousand big words, because big words often have double meanings, which makes them only worth half as much. At least that's what I think, but I wouldn't take my word for it.

But what is the Big Picture? To explain that, I'd like to go back twenty years, to the final months of the decade that has come to be known as the Sixties. I was a shiftless teenage derelict, hitchhiking from dead concert to dead concert, trying to see through my hair.

I wasn't concerned with geopolitical events, international affairs, cultural anomalies, or hygiene. I had set off to find myself, but most of the time I was so stoned I was lucky if I could find my shoes.

But I wasn't alone. I was part of an entire generation in search of meaning. It was a generation so starved for understanding we were able to read significance into Donovan lyrics. We didn't have a clue as to what was going on.

In fact, we greeted each other with the very question: "What's going on, man? What's happening?"

We didn't say, "Nice to see you," or "How have you been?" like people with a non-crumbling value system. We wanted to know what was happening.

"What's happening, bro?" But nobody knew. It was the question of the decade.

"What it is." That's the best answer you could get. What the hell kind of answer is that?

By the end of the decade I was beginning to think the question was purely rhetorical. It was a long ten years. Time really seemed to drag after Kennedy died. Not only that, but everything suddenly seemed less important. It was a time when even patriotism seemed foolish.

> **I worked some gigs in the Deep South. To be frank, I found these people anything but deep. Alabama, you talk about Darwin's waiting room. There are guys in Alabama who are their own fathers.**
>
> —Dennis Miller

I still asked what I could do for my country once in a while, but it didn't sound the same as when Kennedy asked it. The way it came out was, "Hey, man, what can I do?"

My problem was I lacked a comprehensive world view. Slowly, I arose from my lethargy and began to compile one. I started by reading the newspapers. Unfortunately, the press only deals in current events. Wars, coups, scandals, disasters, crimes; I could go on and on, but there's no use beating a dead horse. (I mean aside from the pure joy of it.)

All these actual facts do nothing but obscure the perspective. Besides, there's always the chance they might have left out some crucial story.

The news of the world troubled me. I had heard of the world but I hadn't realized so much was going on in it. It worried me. Nevertheless, I began to feel intelligent. I made a mental note to share this feeling with my friends, but I found it hard to make any when I did.

True insight doesn't come from traipsing the overused path of reason and logic. No, my friends, it must be drawn instinctively, cold and pure, from those ever flowing fountains of ignorance and prejudice within us all.

Gradually, the turmoil of current events began to arrange itself into a mighty mosaic of cause and effect. A larger human conflict loomed behind it all; ignorance versus bliss.

I found a map of the world and began to study geography. I was astounded by the number and variety of continents on the earth. I learned six by name, and began to feel worldly.

Alienation made me identify with foreigners, and I fell in with a group of them. As an American, I was amazed by how smart they were. I accepted them as equals, greatly underestimating them. I tried to see the world as they did, and succeeded in seeing it as I thought they saw it. Finally, they got drunk and robbed me. It was then I realized something few of my countrymen do: there are glaring differences among non-Americans.

Knowing that, the world becomes an interesting place.

RANDY COHEN

When He Reemerges

A QUIZ

You've got a terrible cold. Riding home on the bus, you feel a sneeze coming on. As you reach for a Kleenex, you notice that sitting across from you is Richard M. Nixon, the only American president ever to resign from office. Do you still cover your mouth?

At a dinner party you're startled to find him on your right. He says "Pass the Triscuits, please." What do you do? Remember: the entree will be veal with a wonderful Sauternes sauce. Seated to your left is supermodel Elle MacPherson; Mel Gibson is across from you. They both find you wildly appealing. Stay or go?

He appears on "Sesame Street" to teach kids conflict resolution. He suggests: if you disagree with a playmate, get tough; threaten to set him on fire. Would you continue to watch "Live From Lincoln Center" on that same station?

You fall wildly in love and foresee a future of unalloyed bliss. Walter Cronkite, the most trusted man in America, comes out of retirement to do a single broadcast, exposing your fiancé as Richard Nixon. Having undergone reconstructive surgery at a secret government installation, he's thoroughly transformed, inside and out. These procedures cost billions of tax dollars that otherwise would have gone to rebuild our nation's crumbling infrastructure. Do you call the caterers and cancel the wedding?

A contestant on TV's "$25,000 Pyramid," you find yourself paired with the saurian former president. Do you give him good clues? Perhaps you deliver a stirring denunciation to host Dick Clark and stalk off the set? Suppose all the prize money goes to the Heart Fund? What if the Republican party's elder statesman took you aside during the first commercial and personally apologized for the Christmas bombing of Hanoi? You've convinced he's really sorry. Dick Clark presents the first category, "Things dropped out of a B-52." What do you say to President Nixon?

HEY, KIDS, TRY THESE AT HOME

Pretend you're the ghost of Roy Cohn. (Ask your mom for an old bed sheet. Talk in a scary voice.) Invite Mr. Nixon for dinner at 21 and dancing at Regine's. Reminisce about the good old days with Joe McCarthy. Sneer at the stupidity of your critics—what a bunch of jerks!

In a singsong voice chant something presidential as you jump rope. Think of rhymes for Operation Phoenix. Go Double Dutch: try rhyming executive privilege, protective reaction, Greek colonels.

Build a Play-Doh model of Cambodia. Drop cans of peas (ugh!) and beets (yuck!) and Spaghettios (yum!) all over it. Drop a canned ham on Phnom Penh. Then pretend your dog is on a Senate oversight committee; deny everything.

Use your crayons to draw a jail with Jimmy Hoffa inside. Now draw one without Jimmy Hoffa inside.

With flour and water and strips of ripped-up newspaper, build a model of President Nixon and of his national security adviser, Henry Kissinger. Have your new dolls make sophisticated chit-chat about silly things Daniel Ellsberg said on the telephone when he didn't think they were listening. Pretend your Nixon and Kissinger dolls are kneeling in prayer. What do you suppose they're praying for?

One winter day, President Nixon was looking out the window of the Lincoln Bedroom when he noticed some writing in the snow. Looking more closely, he saw that somebody had apparently etched in urine the words "Nixon must go."

Furious, the President summoned the FBI and demanded that they immediately find out who was responsible for this outrage.

The following day, the President received a call from the FBI. "Sir, we have good news and bad news. The good news is that we have tested the urine and ascertained its origin. It came from former Vice President Agnew."

"Oh no," said the President. "What's the bad news?"

"I hate to tell you this," said the agent, "but it was Pat's handwriting."

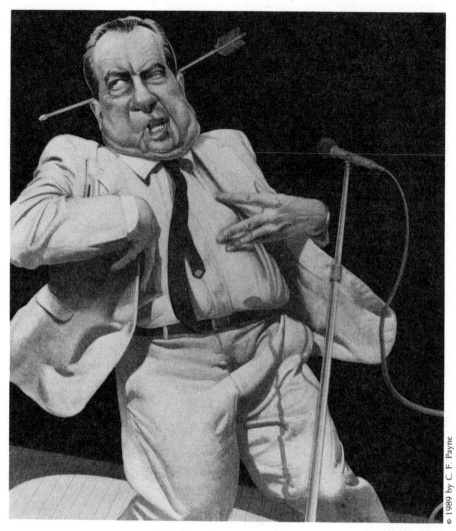

"Well, pardon-n-n me!"

ASK NIPPER AND CHIPPER, THE CARTOON MORALIST BEAVERS

Nipper (voice of Cyndi Lauper) says, "Don't be a prig. You don't have to share a guy's politics to share a beer." (Nipper is the worldly one.) "Everybody makes mistakes. I'll bet there's plenty of stuff in your past you're not so proud of. Wait, there's the doorbell. It's Dick! Come into my lodge, pal. And look who he's brought—Attila! He scourged the known world. But hey, let bygones be bygones. Let's not dwell on the past. And look who else is here—enteric parasites. They've laid waste millions. What could they do? Bacteria got to swim, viruses got to fly. Besides, being nice to R.N. creates a lot of jobs."

Chipper (voice of Danny DeVito) says, "Oh, right—if it happened five minutes ago, it doesn't count." (Chipper is up to here with indignation.) "Hound that evil monster to the grave! And then throw stones at his statue!"

SOME HANDY PHRASES TO CLIP AND CARRY

For our noble cause, I would accept hors d'oeuvres from the Devil himself.

I'm just here to research this novel I'm writing. A few years from now. I keep a diary. When I remember to write in it.

It's easy to sit on your backside and criticize, but it's darn hard to topple Chile's elected government and dispose of Salvador Allende.

What do you call that jelly stuff? You use it to burn people to bits? It's like Saran Wrap?

It's those dirty rotten Jews from New York who are behind it.

WHEN HE REEMERGES

Turn off the lights. Be very quiet. Hope he thinks there's nobody home.

Stand at closed window and mime: We've all got the measles. (Hint: Sounds like "easels"; move your arms like an artist painting at his easel. It also sounds like "weasels"; kill a chicken and drink its blood.)

Say "We're just on our way out. Care to join us? We're going to blow up the neighbors' garage. We don't like their cat."

"I'm sorry; you can't come in. You were bad."

LARRY GELBART
The Scandal Continues

Herewith two excerpts from Mastergate. *In the first scene Secretary of State Bishop is badgered by Senator Knight; in the second, Maj. Manley Battle, a war hero, is coddled by Senator Bunting.*

Knight: Mr. Secretary, some six months to half a year ago you were questioned by the subcommittee of this committee. Do you recall your appearance at that particular time?

Bishop: I believe I looked pretty much as I do now.

Knight: Do you remember our discussing the Mastergate situation at that particular frame in time?

Bishop: Senator, we discussed a great many subjects, as I may or may not recall. If you could possibly reload your question, sir?

Knight: You testified then that you were categorically opposed to

A prominent biogeneticist is conducting advanced research on the similarities between primates and humans. After a decade of preparation, he is now ready for his most daring experiment to date: the mating of a human with a gorilla.

Having spent years searching for the proper gorilla, he finally selects a supple simian from the San Diego Zoo. Finding the human partner, however, will be more difficult. First, he designs an extensive and detailed forty-page questionnaire. Next, he places a classified ad in the *New York Review of Books*: "Wanted: Single White male, between 25 and 27 years of age, with a Master's degree, non-smoker, who loves Mozart, animals and long walks on the beach, to impregnate a female gorilla. Stipend: $300."

To his delight, the researcher receives over two hundred letters, and promptly sends a copy of the questionnaire to each of the respondents. Over 90 percent of the questionnaires are returned, but only one applicant fulfills all the requirements.

An interview is arranged, and the applicant arrives to meet with the researcher. They talk for three hours, and the researcher finally says, "I'm thrilled to have found you. You're exactly the man I've been looking for. Are you free to begin on Monday?"

"Just a minute," says the young man. "You've asked me a lot of questions, but before we go any further, I have a few requirements of my own. First, there'll be no kissing on the lips. Second, any offspring from this union must be raised in my own faith. And, finally, could you give me a couple of weeks to scrape up the three hundred bucks?"

---

the entire Mastergate idea, and yet, subsequently and prior, and all the times in between, you did all that you could to make the plan succeed. Wouldn't you say that that was sending out a somewhat scrambled signal, sir?

Bishop: Not at all. Since everyone knew I was against the plan, I assumed everyone would know that I was against whatever it was I was doing.

Knight: Forgive me, sir, but how could you hope to convince anyone that you were opposed to something you were so busy supporting?

Bishop: By resigning as often as I could—without actually damaging my effectiveness on the job.

Knight: The job of implementing policies you had no particular faith in?

Bishop: The Secretary of State doesn't spend his time just attending state funerals and going to poison gas conferences. It's not all fun and games, you know.

Knight: It didn't trouble you, all the carrying on that was going on?

Bishop: Senator, at the very onslaught to all this, I issued a strict appeal that I was to remain completely uninformed as much as possible about this whole operation, so that I could maintain a perfectly honest front about what was going on behind my back.

Knight: And just how did you put your ignorance into action?

Bishop: I was content to let the Director of Central Intelligence, Mr. Slaughter, make whatever arrangements were being made with the person with whom he was making them with.

Knight: And with whom would that person have been?

Bishop: Vice President Burden. (*This news causes quite a stir.*) Before you jump to any conclusions, I hasten to add that the Vice President personally assured me that even though he approved of these arrangements, he can prove he knew nothing about them, since he was in the room at the time they were made.

Knight: Would you say that the Vice President was there in the capacity of acting for the President?

Bishop: The President needs no help with his acting, sir.

Knight: Would it be your opinion that the President knew that the Vice President knew?

Bishop: Knew what?

Knight: Everything that he didn't know.

Bishop: No one else was in a position not to know as much as the President didn't.

Bunting: I wonder if I might ask you to use the map we have here for the purpose of your using it, Major. If I could just ask my niece and nephew to roll it out, please?

Battle: Yes, sir. (*Two of the pages roll out the map. Battle walks up to it and picks up a wooden pointer, as the flashbulbs begin popping. After a bit of discreet posing:*) San Elvador lies just right of center here in Central

Vance and Willie, retired insurance executives, decide to drive cross-country. After seven long days on the road, they finally arrive in California. Exhausted, they take rooms in the first hotel they find, where both men soon fall into a deep sleep.

At breakfast the next morning, Vance says to Willie: ''I had the most amazing dream last night. There I was in Disneyland, with my best friend from childhood, each of us with thirty dollars in our pockets that our mothers gave us. And the most amazing thing of all was that there were no lines. We went on all the rides and ate as much candy as we wanted. I had the time of my life.''

''That's great,'' says Willie. ''I also had a wonderful dream last night. No sooner had I gone to bed when I heard a knock on the door. I opened it, and there was Marilyn Monroe in a white sundress. I was beat, but this was the opportunity of a lifetime, so I asked her to come in. We made love, and it was fabulous. And boy, was I ready to sleep after *that*.''

''What a wonderful dream,'' says Vance.

''Wait, it's not over. After Marilyn left, I had just put my head down when there was another knock on the door. I dragged myself out of bed, and there was Sophia Loren in a bathrobe. Without a word, she slinked in, dropped the robe, and as exhausted as I was, I dragged myself into bed and it was absolutely incredible.''

Vance laughs. ''*Then* you went to sleep?''

America. It has a democratic form of government that has been run by its army for the past forty years. It is passionately anti-Communist, with a vigorous opposition press, a strong, vocal church and free elections that are promised regularly. But most geopolitically significant, there is San Elvador's unmistakable proximity-ship to its immediate neighbor to the far left, Ambigua.

Bunting: Ambigua is totalitarily Lenin-Marxist in your opinion, Major?

Battle: It's as Red as the ace of hearts, sir. The whole nine yardski.

Bunting: And completely controlled by Moscow?

Battle: Does the Pope ride an encyclical? (*Crowd laughs.*) Not that I mean to make light of the Communist menace. Or the Catholics, either.

Bunting: Major, I'm sure that this committee, as well as the country for which we stand, would be most appreciative for you to share some of your daylight with us on that sad and benighted land.

Battle: Yes, sir. The Republic of Ambigua, or La Republica de Ambigua, is yet another betrayed revolution in which a legitimate set of high ideals were once cruelly twisted and cynically Sovietized. The United States has had a long period of the most intimate relations with the Ambiguan government, the last eighteen of Ambigua's presidents being West Point graduates. But a coup occurred and the reins of power changed hands three years ago when the former President of Ambigua, General Delinqua, and the country's Prime Minister, Mrs. Delinqua, were in New York on an emergency shopping trip, at which point the government was taken over by Dr. Overtega, a former podiatrist, and his band of foot soldiers. Within days, Ambigua became a Red Sea. Overnight, a landing strip was built to accommodate the most advanced Soviet bombers: planes so fast a Russian pilot could have a burrito in Ambigua and wash it down with a bowl of borscht in Lenin's tomb. Soviet adviseniks armed the Elvadorians with vast quantities of automatic Baryshnikovs, ground-to-air rockets and heat-seeking machetes. But most provocatively, and least acceptably, they dug underground nucular missile silos below *our* underground nucular missile silos so that we were in danger of being the first military force in history to ever be attacked simultaneously from behind *and* from below.

''I wanted to,'' says Willie, ''but there was a third knock on the door.''

''Let me guess. Dolly Parton in a towel?''

''Close. It was Raquel Welch, wearing a negligee.''

''And you did it *again?*''

''Believe me, I wanted to, but I just couldn't. Too tired. She was so disappointed.''

''So you closed the door on Raquel Welch? Some friend you are! Why didn't you call *me?*''

''I did! But your mother said you went to Disneyland.''

"First of all, I don't like your sign."

S. GROSS

FRAN LEBOWITZ
My Day

12:35 P.M.—The phone rings. I am not amused. This is not my favorite way to wake up. My favorite way to wake up is to have a certain French movie star whisper to me softly at two-thirty in the afternoon that if I want to get to Sweden in time to pick up my Nobel Prize for Literature I had better ring for breakfast. This occurs rather less often than one might wish.

Today is a perfect example, for my caller is an agent from Los Angeles who informs me that I don't know him. True, and not without reason. He is audibly tan. He is interested in my work. His interest has led him to the conclusion that it would be a good idea for me to write a movie comedy. I would, of course, have total artistic freedom, for evidently comic writers have taken over the movie business. I look around my apartment (a feat readily accomplished by simply glancing up) and remark that Dino DeLaurentiis would be surprised to hear that. He chuckles tanly and suggests that we talk. I suggest that we *are* talking. He, however, means *there* and at my own expense. I reply that the only way I could get to Los Angeles at my own expense is if I were to go by postcard. He chuckles again and suggests that we talk. I agree to talk just as soon as I have won the Nobel Prize—for outstanding achievement in physics.

Sister Maria lives in a very strict convent where the nuns are allowed to say only two words every ten years. After ten years, she goes to see the Mother Superior.

"Bed hard," she says.

Another ten years go by, and again Sister Maria meets with the Mother Superior. This time she says, "Food bad."

Another ten years go by, and it's time for the third meeting. By now Sister Maria is so unhappy that she blurts out the words, "I quit."

"No wonder," comes the reply. "You've been here thirty years and all you've done is bitch, bitch, bitch."

The eminent acting teacher was telling his students about the worst actress he had ever seen. She couldn't find work until she married a rich producer who included her in all of his shows.

One of his plays was the stage adaptation of *The Diary of Anne Frank,* where her portrayal of Anne was so wretched that when the Gestapo came to take her away, the few people who were left in the audience stood up as one and shouted, "She's in the attic!"

12:55 P.M.—I try to get back to sleep. Although sleeping is an area in which I have manifested an almost Algeresque grit and persistence, I fail to attain my goal.

1:20 P.M.—I go downstairs to get the mail. I get back into bed. Nine press releases, four screening notices, two bills, an invitation to a party in honor of a celebrated heroin addict, a final disconnect notice from New York Telephone, and three hate letters from *Mademoiselle* readers demanding to know just what it is that makes me think that I have the right to regard houseplants—*green, living* things—with such marked distaste. I call the phone company and try to make a deal, as actual payment is not a possibility. Would they like to go to a screening? Would they care to attend a party for a heroin addict? Are they interested in knowing just what it is that makes me think that I have the right to regard houseplants with such marked distaste? It seems they would not. They would like $148.10. I agree that this is, indeed, an understandable preference, but caution them against the bloodless quality of a life devoted to the blind pursuit of money. We are unable to reach a settlement. I pull up the covers and the phone rings. I spend the next few hours fending off editors, chatting amiably, and plotting revenge. I read. I smoke. The clock, unfortunately, catches my eye.

3:40 P.M.—I consider getting out of bed. I reject the notion as being unduly vigorous. I read and smoke a bit more.

4:15 P.M.—I get up feeling curiously unrefreshed. I open the refrigerator. I decide against the half a lemon and jar of Gulden's mustard and on the spur of the moment choose instead to have breakfast out. I guess that's just the kind of girl I am—whimsical.

5:10 P.M.—I return to my apartment laden with magazines and spend the remainder of the afternoon reading articles by writers who, regrettably, met their deadlines.

6:55 P.M.—A romantic interlude. The object of my affections arrives bearing a houseplant.

9:30 P.M.—I go to dinner with a group of people that includes two fashion models, a fashion photographer, a fashion photographer's representative, and an art director. I occupy myself almost entirely with the art director—drawn to him largely because he knows the most words.

2:05 A.M.—I enter my apartment and prepare to work. In deference to the slight chill I don two sweaters and an extra pair of socks. I pour myself a club soda and move the lamp next to the desk. I reread several old issues of *Rona Barrett's Hollywood* and a fair piece of *The Letters of Oscar Wilde*. I pick up my pen and stare at the paper. I light a cigarette. I stare at the paper. I write, "My Day: An Introduction of Sorts." Good. Lean yet cadenced. I consider my day. I become unaccountably depressed. I doodle in the margin. I jot down an idea I have for an all-black version of a Shakespearean comedy to be called *As You Likes It*. I look longingly at my sofa, not unmindful of the fact that it converts cleverly into a bed. I light a cigarette. I stare at the paper.

4:50 A.M.—The sofa wins. Another victory for furniture.

DAVE BARRY
Into the Round File

I like to cheer myself by pretending that my mail actually screams when I throw it into the wastebasket:

Dear **MR. BARRY:**

You have almost certainly won a trillion dollars. We're dead serious, **MR. BARRY.** We're a gigantic publishing company and we just woke up this morning and we said, "By God, let's send one trillion dollars to **MR. BARRY,** no strings attached." That's just the kind of gigantic publishing company we are. And frankly, **MR. BARRY,** you are under no obligation whatsoever to take a six-week trial subscription to a new magazine called *Photographs of Homes That Are Much Nicer Than Yours,* because all we really want to do, **MR. BARRY,** is send you one trillion

AIEEEEEEEEEEEEE

Dear Resident of the 15,924th District:

This is the first of an interminable series of newsletters I'll be sending you at your expense so that you'll have photographs of your representative in Washington representing you by eating breakfast with the President. I recently had an opportunity to exchange views with the President during an informal working orientation breakfast for the 742 new congresspersons, and the President and I agreed that one of the most important issues facing the nation, including the 15,924th district, is mineral resources on the ocean floor. I am pleased to report that I have been appointed to the influential Manganese Subcommittee of the House Special Select Committee on Grayish-White Metallic Elements, and I'm planning a fact-finding trip to

AIEEEEEEEEEEEEE

Dear Friend:

Every day, all over the world, innocent children with large, soulful eyes are getting terrible diseases. Also, countless furry little endangered species are being dismembered by industrialists wielding chain saws. This is all your fault. So we want you to send some money to

AIEEEEEEEEEEEEE

Dear Electric Customer:

Due to inflation, we have been forced to apply for a rate— No, wait, forget that. We can't use inflation anymore. Uh, let's see— Oh yeah. Due to the fact that our new Harbor Vista nuclear generating plant, if we ever get it finished, may have some piping problems that would cause it to emit a deadly cloud of radioactive gas the size of Canada, we

> **A well-dressed old man is sitting on the curb, crying. A younger man is walking by, and seeing the fellow in tears, he says, "Sir, what's wrong? Can I help you?"**
>
> **"I shouldn't complain," he says. "You see, I've got three grown children from my first wife, may she rest in peace. And they all come to visit me. And my new wife—she's thirty-two, gorgeous, and a lawyer to boot."**
>
> **"That's wonderful, but why are you crying?"**
>
> **"It's terrible," he says. "I forgot where I live."**

have been forced to apply for a rate increase so we'll be able to afford a really top-notch lawyer with his own jet and everything. We realize that, since we just got a rate increase last week, this may seem

AIEEEEEEEEEEEEE

Dear Mr. Barry:

In a recent column, you stated that Abraham Lincoln ran the hundred-yard dash in 8.4 seconds, and that ice fishermen have the same average IQ scores as mailboxes. As an avid ice fisherman, and chairman of the History Department at Myron B. Thalmus Junior College, I would like to know where you get your

AIEEEEEEEEEEEEE

Dear **MR. BARRY:**

Really! We mean it! One trillion dol

AIEEEEEEEEEEEEE

Dear Mr. Barry:

Unless you're the kind of worthless scum that sat idly by while those thugs beat up that woman in New York some years back, you probably have been giving a lot of thought to your family's financial security. No doubt you have said to yourself countless times, "Sure, I'd love to invest $10,000 or more in Liquidated Option Debenture Fiduciary Instruments of Trust, but I don't know where to mail a certified or cashier's check." Well, your worries are over, because

AIEEEEEEEEEEEEE

Dear Brother Barry:

As you are no doubt aware, the Reverend Bud Albumen didn't develop one of the fastest-growing evangelical organizations in south central Kentucky just by accident. He developed it by building really top-notch studio facilities. But these facilities cost money, which is why the Lord told the Reverend Albumen to tell you to send in a Love Offering of $13.50 per member of your household, or a special rate of $6.75, which is a 50 percent discount, for children under ten. Just as soon as the Reverend Albumen receives your Love Offering, he will ask the Lord not to bring disease and suffering and mudslides to your home, but remember, he can't do this until he receives your

NO! NOT THE SCISSORS! PLEASE DON'T AAARRRGGGH

An old woman goes into a park and sits down next to an elderly man.

"Guess how old I am," he says.

"I don't want to," she replies.

"Please?"

"Well, if you really want me to, you'll have to take off all your clothes."

The man is surprised to hear this, but he complies with her request.

"Good," she says. "Now jump up and down."

He does this, too.

"Fine," she says, "now pretend you're flying. Excellent. You can stop now. Watching you, I would guess that you're about a month away from your eighty-seventh birthday."

"That's absolutely amazing," he replies. "You're exactly right. But how—?"

"It wasn't hard," she replies. "You told me yesterday."

BILL FRANZEN
37 Years

> **You know when you're getting old, there are certain signs. I walked past a cemetery and two guys ran after me with shovels.**
> —Rodney Dangerfield

"This is never very easy," Dr. Tudor said. "But it showed up, plain as day, after your physical. It's going to be quite a shock—you, a healthy young man of thirty-seven and all—but it's my job to level with you. Believe me, now's when I wish I was testing seat belts or something. Because you have exactly thirty-seven years left to live."

I'd had a feeling it wasn't going to be good news, but . . . cut down in thirty-seven more years . . . it was almost too much. My mind went numb, and I searched Dr. Tudor's face for some small ray of hope. But all he said was "Go ahead and scream if you want. I wouldn't blame you."

Scream? I couldn't even make my mouth say bye-bye. I just wandered out of Dr. Tudor's office, and—maybe ten minutes later, maybe two hours later—found myself wading barefoot through the reflecting pool in front of the library. Nickels, dimes, even pennies felt good under my feet and between my toes. I tried to feel which presidents were on them. Then some guy, all silver buttons, shouted at me to get out, but he needn't have wasted his energy: I'd decided to get out anyway, before I got any sadder. See, I loved the feeling of being barefoot. But how many more times would I be able to squeeze going barefoot into the final thirty-seven years of my life?

I had more hard questions for myself during the long drive home. Like why hadn't I ever slept in a lighthouse before? And how come my

© 1978 by B. Kliban

264 **I WOULDN'T WANT TO PAINT IT**

years of collecting metal cigar tubes seemed so foolish now? And why hadn't I just gone ahead and tramped something like "Bring Me the Head of Ronald McDonald" into the snow on the hill next to the exit ramp, instead of only *thinking* about doing it? Or pulled up the carpeting in the living room to see what's been causing the little lump that's in the middle every day and in front of the fireplace every night? And why hadn't I ever bothered to get HIYA put on my rear license plate? Just who did I think I was kidding with the way I'd been "living"?

Well, when I finally walked in the door that evening, I didn't say a word about my visit to Dr. Tudor. Can you imagine—"Hey, honey! Kids! Take a good look at me during 'Entertainment Tonight' and dinner because in thirty-seven years . . ." No way. I was crazy about my wife, Valinda, our daughter, Jenny, and Liza, the little neighbor girl who was around so much she was all ours except for the paperwork. And I didn't think that *they* should have to carry around any of this new weight inside me. But, you know, I guess I misjudged just how heavy that weight really was. Because after I'd lied to them, told them things were awfully slow now in the pool-table-sales game and that I'd be home barefoot a lot over the next year, that heaviness dragged me right down to the basement bar. I never even bothered to flick on the beer sign down there. Just stretched out on one of the pool tables in the dark, drinking whiskey straight out of a bottle through a flexible straw to try to dissolve the lead bowling ball buried deep in my stomach. Yeah, and at first that was good medicine. But then later, after two straight weeks of the police bringing me home just as it was getting light, and with my memory so loused up that, no, I honestly *didn't* remember sleeping in the shallow end of the penguin pool or in the tulips growing along the floral clock's big hand . . . well, that just had to be rough on my Valinda, and on my Jenny, and on our neighbors' little Liza.

So if I didn't want to keep hurting them or go handing in my room key thirty-seven years early on an already tight schedule, I had to clean up my act while there was still time. First I turned the caps on all the liquor bottles in the house just as tight as they'd go. Then I rounded up Valinda and Jenny and Liza, herded them into the laundry room, and told them the truth.

Geez, I'd underestimated them! They were so strong they just stood or sat on the machines and watched me while I cried. And right away some of the heaviness of that weight that was lodged in my gut lifted. We'd always been close, but now, it seemed to me, we drew even closer. Those three gals of mine became my pillars of strength, and when they really couldn't be home with me, they'd leave notes like "Honey—Margo still wants to try cutting and frosting my hair. Back soon," or "Daddy—Me and Liza are walking to the mall to buy rabbits. See you in time for dinner. Love, Jenny."

Boy, just tell a guy he's got only thirty-seven years left on the planet and, once he's finished going a few rounds with the whiskey bottle, watch him scramble for meaning. Watch him turn off "Mary Tyler

MORE LIGHT BULB JOKES

How many anti-abortionists does it take to screw in a light bulb?

Six. One to screw in the bulb, and five to testify that it was lit from the moment they began screwing.

How many country singers does it take to change a light bulb?

Four. One to screw it in and three to write about the old one.

How many bureaucrats does it take to change a light bulb?

One to spot the burned-out bulb, his supervisor to authorize a requisition, a requisition typist, three clerks to file requisition copies, a mail clerk to deliver the requisition to the purchasing department, a purchasing agent to order the bulb, a clerk to forward the purchasing order, a receiving clerk to receive the bulb . . .

Moore" reruns he's seen three times and, instead, get outside and enjoy life, maybe drive to the bank, maybe take the long way. Watch him gradually cut his sleep time from eight hours to, say, seven and a quarter. Then see him decide there'll be no more reading Stephen King's *Cujo* and then going to the movie *Cujo* two months later. See him start picking one or the other—no more of this "both" stuff.

What Dr. Tudor probably doesn't know is that he's actually done me a favor. Sure, I "got through" those first thirty-seven years, but now I'm going to start making every day of the next thirty-seven really count. You want to know something else? Back when I was living like some immortal fool, my life was never very exciting. But now—heck, I get a big charge out of just taking a key down to the hardware store and watching them make a duplicate. *I might not even need it.* But the sight of all those different-colored keys hanging on their hooks, and . . . ummmm . . . the manly smell of ground metal—those are experiences you can't go on having forever. Because that's another thing: I used to *smell*, right? But now, thanks to Dr. Tudor, my senses are turned up so crazy high, I'm *smell-ING*. And where I used to *see*, now I'm *see-ING*. For instance, for thirty-seven years a pink pocket comb lying on the sidewalk was just a pink pocket comb lying on the sidewalk. But now—*now*—it's suddenly a five-inch-long bubble-gum-colored pink pocket comb with twenty-three thick teeth and thirty-three thin ones and BOBBIE'S HAIR SHACK in gold stamped on the spine and UNBREAKABLE in raised pink letters next to it, lying on the sidewalk near a newsstand, three feet away from a ripped-off cover of *Bear Archery Digest*. See what I mean? Sure, I may have only thirty-seven years left until I sign off, but at least we're talking, I think, about thirty-seven years of some kind of heightened reality. And someday, soon, I might even do some parachuting off observation decks.

Tip O'Neill has been going to Marcello the barber for thirty-four years.

"What's new, my friend?" says the barber.

"I'm very excited," says Tip. "Next week I'm going to Italy."

"That's nice," says the barber. "How are you getting there?"

"On Alitalia Airlines," says Tip.

"Alitalia? That's terrible. It's the worst airline in the world. Where will you be staying?"

"At the Hilton, in Rome."

"No, not the Hilton. That's a terrible hotel! And what are you going to do over there?"

"Among other things, I've got a private audience with the Pope."

"Private? Ha! You'll see. When you go to see the Pope, there'll be a thousand people there with you."

Two weeks later, Tip comes back.

"So, how was your trip?" says the barber.

"Well, Marcello, it was magnificent. The service on Alitalia was terrific. The Hilton in Rome was immaculate. And when I saw the Pope, it was just the two of us."

"Really? What did the Pope say?"

"Well, when I leaned over to kiss his ring, he looked down at me and said, 'Tip, where did you get that lousy haircut?'"

THIS SECTION CLOSED

© 1990 by S. Gross

S. GROSS

PART FOUR

MATTERS OF TASTE

COLIN McENROE
The Lost Ann Landers Letters

And the 3d biggest lie is . . .

Dear Readers:

A while back, I was asked to print the three biggest lies in the world. I was able to come up with only two: "I'm from the government and I'm here to help you," and "The check is in the mail."

I asked my readers if they could supply the third biggest lie. Thousands rose to the occasion. The mail was simply wonderful. Here's a sampling:

From Lebanon, Pa.: It's a good thing you came in today. We have only two more in stock.

Wilmington, Del.: Sorry, dear, not tonight. I have a headache.

Sparta, Wis.: I promise to pay you back out of my next paycheck.

Woodbridge, N.J.: Five pounds is nothing on a person with your height.

Harrisburg, Pa.: But officer, I only had two beers.

Hammond, Ind.: You made it yourself? I never would have guessed.

Baltimore: Of course I will respect you in the morning.

Eau Claire, Wis.: It's delicious, but I can't eat another bite.

Dear Ann Landers:

A few years ago, you published an inspirational poem, and it touched me so that I clipped it out and carried it around in my wallet until it became all wore out and frayed and yellow, and eventually I picked up some kinda infection from it so that nobody would shake hands with me for about four and a half years, not to mention the smell. Boy, it was a good poem though. Anyway, recently my wallet fell into a nuclear breeder reactor, but I fished it out so as not to lose the poem, but it was pretty much illegible by then and some of the *e*'s had a tendency to leap off the page and scurry around the room, and anyway, "Dan" (my second marriage, his first) says we can't afford reading glasses for me, even though I notice nothing is too good for those exotic pigeons (their third marriage) he keeps on the roof. Anyway, I took the clipping of the poem to this research lab in Dubuque where they have been analyzing the Shroud of Murray, an ancient fabric which, it is believed, St. Peter was planning to use for new slipcovers. Even the institute scientists' (their first marriage) most advanced carbon treatments, however, were not able to bring out the poem and the only word they were able to reconstruct was "earwax," which I don't remember from the first time around. Any chance you could reprint the poem? Boy, I have half a mind to go up there with some Ginsu cutlery and turn those pigeons into moussaka. What do you think the deal is with "Dan" and those pigeons anyway? And what kind of jerk goes around with quotation marks hanging over his name? I am,

Pooped in Paducah

Dear Ann Landers:

Say a word or two on behalf of us wives of [government nostril inspectors/licensed sausage casing repairmen/wet blasters]. We have

Charlotte, N.C.: Your hair looks just fine.

Philadelphia: It's nothing to worry about—just a cold sore.

La Palma, Calif.: I've finished my homework. Now can I read Ann Landers?

Mechanicsburg, Pa.: It's a terrific high and I swear you won't get hooked.

Dallas: The river never gets high enough to flood this property.

Manassas, Va.: The delivery is on the truck.

Tacoma, Wash.: Go ahead and tell me. I promise I won't get mad.

Billings, Mont.: You have nothing to worry about, honey. I've had a vasectomy.

Philadelphia: The three biggest

had to endure the old stereotype that our husbands are [dirtballs/reptiles/ingenious wax replicas]. I was out to lunch the other day with some [girlfriends/Roman Catholic cardinals/Zulu warriors] and one of them made a cheap and heartless joke about my husband's [breath/DNA/nose bag]. My husband works hard for a dollar, and he is real close to getting one. Also, it is not my fault he married me. How about it, Ann?

Prickly in Prescott

Dear Ann Landers:

I am a young, attractive, pleasant man who has a nice job and is perfectly normal in every way, except that there is some kind of lemur growing right out of my stomach and I am engaged to marry a 174-year-old woman from a dwarf star and I can't fall asleep at night until a dump truck has dumped at least 380 pounds of loose feldspar—the chunks being no smaller than one and a half inches per facet—onto my prone body. So settle an argument between me and my invisible condor Jim Ed: in Australian-rules football, how many wattles must there be before a murmansk is called? Is it different in the Olympics?

Normal (Perfectly) in Bobo, N.M.

Dear Ann Landers:

I'm not one to pry, and I'm not one to tell other people how to raise their children, and I'm not one to go where I'm not wanted, and I'm not one to show up at weddings of people I don't know and hurl frozen turkey giblets at the bridal party, and I'm not one to paint faces on coconuts and arrange them around the living room and turn on loud music and scream "Party down!" at them.

But I do all these things anyway. What do you make of it?

Not One to Ask

lies: I did it. I didn't do it. I can't remember.

Chicago: This car is like brand new. It was owned by two retired schoolteachers who never went anywhere.

Boston: The doctor will call you right back.

Montreal: So glad you dropped by. I wasn't doing a thing.

US Stars and Stripes: You don't look a day over 40.

Washington, D.C.: Dad, I need to move out of the dorm into an apartment of my own so I can have some peace and quiet when I study.

Windsor, Ont.: It's a very small spot. Nobody will notice.

Cleveland: The baby is just beautiful!

New York: The new ownership won't affect you. The company will remain the same.

Holiday, Fla.: I gave at the office.

Lansing, Mich.: You can tell me. I won't breathe a word to a soul.

Huntsville, Ala.: The puppy won't be any trouble, Mom. I promise I'll take care of it myself.

Minneapolis: I'm a social drinker and I can quit anytime I want to.

Barrington, Ill.: Put the map away. I know exactly how to get there.

Troy, Mich.: You don't need it in writing. You have my personal guarantee.

Greenwich, Conn.: Sorry the work isn't ready. The computer broke down.

Mexico City: I'll do it in a minute.

Elkhart, Ind.: The reason I'm so late is we ran out of gas.

Scarsdale, N.Y.: Our children never caused us a minute's trouble.

Detroit: This is a very safe building. No way will you ever be burglarized.

Glendale, Calif.: Having a great time. Wish you were here.

Ann Landers

MAKEUP RULES I MADE UP—DON'T BREAK THEM!

With so many different kinds of cosmetics and so many different types of coloring, shading, and toning that can be achieved by using them, there simply is no one correct makeup method. What's right for moi may not be right for you (for example, you probably use a little less ear-liner). However, what is *wrong* for moi is definitely wrong for you, too. Consult my Ten Tone Commandments. If you avoid these makeup sins, chances are your appearance will be heavenly.

I	NEVER USE YELLOW LIPSTICK
II	NEVER PUT ANYTHING ON YOUR FACE THAT COMES IN A CAN
III	NEVER PURCHASE BEAUTY PRODUCTS IN HARDWARE STORES
IV	NEVER COLOR YOUR TEETH
V	NEVER PUT FLOWERS IN YOUR NOSE
VI	NEVER PUT ANYTHING BLUE ON YOUR CHEEKS
VII	NEVER USE ANYTHING THAT STINKS, STINGS, OR STAINS
VIII	NEVER USE ANYTHING THAT MAKES YOU CRY, SNEEZE, LOOK OLD, OR TURN RED AND BUMPY
IX	NEVER BRAID YOUR EYELASHES
X	NEVER POWDER YOUR TONGUE

GUESTPITALITY

Dear ———,

I could see how happy you were to have me at your dinner, and I just wanted to write to tell you that I enjoyed myself very much. The hors d'oeuvres were on the whole excellent, with the exception of the sour cream dip which was a little tasteless. Dinner was delicious! The hollandaise sauce was particularly good. One little thing I would really look out for in the future, though, is overcooking the broccoli—it was ever so slightly mushy.

I thought your choice of guests was for the most part very well made. I must say, however, that I wonder about Dr. ———, who took a rather offhand observation I made about comets being filled with marmalade in entirely the wrong way. He may be deranged.

Your toast was so touching. I know you can't thank me enough for attending your party, but it was sweet of you to try!

Yours,
Miss Piggy

MANNERS FOR TODAY

How do you do?

How nice of you to take time out of your busy day to read this article!

By any chance, do you have a doily in your home?

Have you curtsied today?

Do you have a clean cloth hankie in your pocket or purse?

If you've answered "Yes" to any of these questions, I'm not at all surprised, for many people like you, people of taste and quality, are returning to graciousness.

All over this big, proud land, people are beating their roach clips into sugar tongs, wearing gowns to work, and insisting on salad forks.

One cannot help but applaud this trend—for the fresh charm it brings to our lives and for the chance it gives us to wear our old suits.

But many people today are seeking guidelines: "What do I do with the doily in my home?" "Did I curtsy at the right time?" "Is a hankie like a napkin?"

And so I have set typewriter to paper to write a few signposts, so that the road of return to graciousness might be made all the clearer.

I hope most sincerely that you will take pleasure in reading them.

MEETING AND GREETING

Thank heavens for the myriads of tidy, dark-suited Japanese businessmen in America!

For they have reintroduced us to the charming custom of bowing when we meet, a practice that is becoming daily more commonplace in our cosmopolises.

Bows are of two types: formal and informal. A click of the heels adds a lively Prussian flourish to the formal bow.

A man's bow is his response to a woman's curtsy. There is nothing so easy for any woman to acquire as a delightful curtsy: an inclined head, a gently bent knee, a demurely lifted hem, all conspire to say, "Why, *there* you are! How very good it is to see you."

However, an error women frequently make in curtsying is to lift their dresses over their heads. This is to be avoided.

Bows and curtsies should only be executed the first or second time you meet someone within an hour; after that merely look away or smile. Continuous bowing and curtsying are silly.

When a man meets a woman on the street, he should bow, doff his hat with his right hand, and remove any smoking material from his mouth. If he carries a Malacca walking stick, it should be placed over his left arm.

There is no vulgarity greater than for a man to stand talking to a woman with his hat on and smoking material in his mouth.

A gentleman should rise when a lady enters the room. The exceptions to this rule are in a restaurant (where he should only rise for a woman coming to his table) and in a theater. Men are advised to check their laps for drinks and food platters before they rise.

Recent years have also seen a revival of the gracious Continental custom of hand kissing in our country.

When a woman is introduced to a man she extends her right hand, palm downward, to be kissed. The man bows and presses his lips lightly against her fingers. *Under no circumstances* should the man seize upon this gesture as an opportunity to place his tongue between the woman's fingers, lick her arm, nibble on her nails, or try to suck off her rings. Unfortunately, there are those men who see the extended hand as an invitation to the escalation of osculation. They continue up the arm to points north. Don't do it! (The same precautions are to be followed when kissing a pope's or a bishop's hand.) Needless to say, this custom obliges the woman to keep her right hand and fingernails spotlessly clean and lightly perfumed.

A final note to men: if the woman's hand is extended palm *upward*, it should not be kissed. Instead, she should be tipped, usually figured at 15 percent of the bill.

A SIDE NOTE ON TIPPING

As a rule you should tip as often, as much, and as many people as possible. *Anyone* who performs a service for you expects to be tipped, including police officers, firemen, and railroad-train engineers.

SOME FRANK TALK ABOUT FEMALE IMPERSONATORS AND HOMOSEXUALS

There is so much confusion in sexual identity these days, it is hard to know how to behave toward whom.

For instance, how is one to regard the large giggly gangs of female impersonators, or transvestites, that have become a commonplace sight on the streets of our major cities?

Many shopkeepers close their doors to these "outlaw women," who, like frolicsome, raffish bands of cosmetized otters, lay waste to lingerie, accessory, and beauty departments with their pranks and petty thievery. Yet withal they are, by choice, though not technically, *women*, and as such must be accorded all the rights and privileges attendant thereto.

We also see today a lot of people jumping on the homosexual bandwagon. Every day more and more men are having their ears pierced and putting their house keys on their belts. But male homosexuals are *men*. They should be treated as such. Do not pander to them in conversation by trying to bring the topic around to drapery fabrics, hair styling, or sailors. Do not offer to light a "gay"'s cigarette or open a car door for him. If you are a "straight" man and try to kiss a homosexual's hand, there is the chance that it will be misinterpreted as a "come-on" and could lead to trouble—or marriage! These days, who knows?

The same goes for female homosexuals, or "lesbos"—they are men and should be treated like "one of the guys." Try to make them feel at ease by talking to them about subjects you know they'll be interested in, like hockey, big rigs, and power tools.

EATIQUETTE

Eating with friends or family should not be considered merely "putting on the feedbag" or a "pig-out." It is, rather, a solemn, time-honored social ritual, and with the withering away of organized religion, barn raisings, and public executions, one of the very few we have left.

Indeed, our dinner tables are the Dikes of Decency. We must sandbag them with "please" and buttress them with place cards.

And so I offer my...

GUIDE TO GUSTATORY GRACIOUSNESS

1. Never show chewed food to others. Nothing could be less interesting to a truly refined diner.

2. Napkins are not hankies. Do not blow your nose in a napkin. (I was once dining in a seafood restaurant in Boston when a young woman did this. It was revolting. I'm not going to name names, she knows who she is.)

3. Sit erect. Sitting "sidesaddle," turning the chair backward, putting your feet or shoes on the table show bad breeding.

4. Offer compliments to your host or hostess on the preparation, taste, and texture of the food. A good host or hostess *never* tries to elicit compliments from the guests by saying, "This food tastes awful, doesn't it?" This is the so-called "reverse psychology" so popular today. Yet it is nothing more than patently transparent begging for compliments.

5. Never eat soft or runny foods such as butter, puddings, poultry stuffings, and soup with your fingers. The exception is at a luau

THE ONLY KIND OF ELBOWS ALLOWED ON THE TABLE

where poi is served.

6. Fried chicken may be picked up and eaten with the fingers outdoors, but not indoors. A garage is considered outdoors.

7. If conversation lags, it is perfectly permissible to perform table tricks or create food sculpture, landscaping, and architecture for the amusement of the guests. Magically scratching a dime out from under an overturned tumbler, building a log cabin of asparagus, or artfully crafting someone's portrait in rémoulade and catsup can add just the perfect grace note to a formal dinner.

TABLE SETTING AND TABLE SEATING

Of course, you'll want to use your prettiest tablecloth, be it a lacy heirloom from Granny or an easy-care vinyl floral. Whichever you choose, take care that it blends most harmoniously with your flatware and dinner service.

Remember to check carefully between the tines of the forks for old food particles that may have lodged there. This is the athlete's foot of utensils. Compared to it, water spots on glassware are peccadilloes.

Napkins? Of course! For the personal touch use paper napery and monogram each guest's napkin with a ballpoint pen.

A centerpiece provides an attractive focal point for the table as well as a convenient "blind" for the shy guest to hide behind. It is

also an effective way to state the "theme" of the dinner.

TV has become so much a part of family life today that it has become correct to bring the set to the dinner table. With its brightly colored moving images, this little chatterbox makes an attractive and entertaining dinner companion. Ringed about with radish rosettes and Greek olives, it also makes an attractive centerpiece which can do double duty as a food warmer, cozying a basket of buns or a creamy casserole. Why, some old tube sets may even get hot enough for you to put a fondue on top!

How about wine? When served with dinner, wine should never be drunk from the bottle. Food particles in the mouth flow back into the bottle, clouding the wine and leaving it unsightly. The thoughtful host or hostess *always* provides glasses or cups. The best wines do not have screw caps.

In seating your guests the liveliest conversational group will be formed by following the boy-girl/boy-girl arrangement. Couples who clown around too much with each other should be broken up.

A NOTE ABOUT FAST-FOOD DINING

Following today's trend toward greater convenience and less cooking, more and more families and singles are converting their stoves into storage space and decorative planters and eating at fast-food outlets. The food there is hearty and basic and should be eaten as swiftly and as spotlessly as it is prepared. The many containers the food is served in should be thoughtfully disposed of in the receptacles provided. Unfortunately, in many of our larger cities these outlets are patronized by drug dealers, prostitutes, and outpatients from mental institutions who are the worst types of litterbugs.

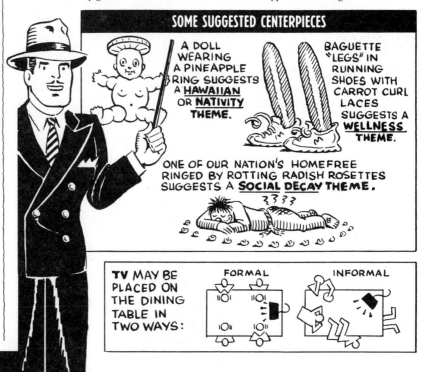

SOME SUGGESTED CENTERPIECES

A DOLL WEARING A PINEAPPLE RING SUGGESTS A HAWAIIAN OR NATIVITY THEME.

BAGUETTE "LEGS" IN RUNNING SHOES WITH CARROT CURL LACES SUGGESTS A WELLNESS THEME.

ONE OF OUR NATION'S HOMEFREE RINGED BY ROTTING RADISH ROSETTES SUGGESTS A SOCIAL DECAY THEME.

TV MAY BE PLACED ON THE DINING TABLE IN TWO WAYS:

FORMAL

INFORMAL

CONVERSATION—
TOPICAL FISHING

In the streamlined world of today, men no longer retire to the library after dinner for cigars, brandy, and conversation. Instead, the guests, male and female alike, adjourn to the living room to abide in an atmosphere of candy eating, light chitchat, and witty and urbane conversation before their coats are returned.

A good way to begin conversation is to "go fishing" for topics. Select a conversational topic the way a fisherman selects a lure, and cast it before the "fish" to whom you are trying to talk. For instance, your tackle box might look like this:

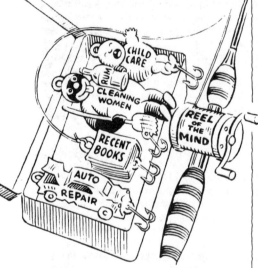

Cast a lure by saying, "Are you fond of sports?" and keep trying till the fish rises to the bait.

By all means do not use the worms of malicious prattle and gossip.

Traditionally it has been suggested that one should also avoid the subjects of politics, religion, and details of operations. This is good advice and should be adhered to. However, a recent trend suggests some new candidates for the old list of taboo topics. That trend has been toward the discussion of bed and bathroom behavior. A concomitant trend has been the telling of couch-time stories (the description of one's psychoanalysis or

psychotherapy). These subjects are purely personal and have no place in the conversational equipage of a truly cultivated man or woman. They should be kept behind closed doors and out of our tackle boxes!

PARTY GAMES
CAN BE FUN

An alternative to conversation is the game. The host or hostess should not attempt to force or coerce guests into playing games.

They should only be played by general consensus of the guests. If you agree to play and find yourself paired off with someone you hate, set your feelings aside and by the end of the game you'll probably like the guest much better.

At party games, expensive prizes are usually offered. If you win, accept the prize with glee but don't be a "show-off" or gloat over your good fortune. By the same token, if you win a booby prize, don't sulk, throw a tantrum, or leave the party abruptly.

KNOWING WHEN TO SAY
"GOODBYE"

Guests and hosts may sit facing each other for hours, not knowing how to say, "The party's over" for fear of affront.

Extreme sensitivity is called for here.

The guests must be watchful for the host's stifled yawn, brushing of teeth, or sudden change into pajamas.

The host should be aware of guests' sitting with their eyes closed, drooling on themselves, suddenly pitching forward, or slumping in their chairs.

The host or hostess should not attempt to encourage guests to leave by turning out the lights, asking them to take out the garbage, or bringing their coats into the room and suggesting that "we try to guess whose coat is whose."

When it becomes apparent that the party is indeed over, it is enough for one person to say, "Well, tomorrow's a working day. . . ." or "Wow, look at the time! I can't believe it's ten-thirty already!" Then everyone will get up and move smoothly toward the door.

At the door the guests thank the host and hostess for a wonderful evening. Everyone says "Goodbye." They never say "Au revoir" or "Arrivederci" unless they have been speaking French or Italian. Everyone bows and curtsies. It makes an utterly charming and cultivated scene.

If, by chance, the guests walk into a closet, the host will want to be sure that all the correct things are hung there, so now let's look at . . .

TODAY'S MAN—
IVY NOT JIVEY,
DRESSY NOT MESSY

The trend is emphatically toward greater formality in men's garments. Men are everywhere putting off their alike-as-biscuits-in-a-pan dungarees and are putting on conservative, fully cut cheviot and worsted trousers, usually in shades of charcoal, dark blue, and brown, in sixteen- and twenty-two-ounce weights.

This is good. Let us encourage it. But we must deplore those trousers that are without cuffs. Cuffless trousers, along with covered buttons, are regarded by the best tailors as strictly "Carnaby Street."

Today's man also has suits in his wardrobe. That is, trousers and jackets that match, or "go together," being made of the same material.

Suits to be avoided are those with short sleeves, gussets, flounces, and dust ruffles. Jacket sleeves, while similar in appearance to trouser legs, should *never* have cuffs.

The way a suit fits is very important. A man should always buy a suit that is *his size*. A suit that is either too large or too small looks funny.

HOW TO BUY A SUIT

IF YOU CANNOT SEE YOUR HAND, THE SUIT IS PROBABLY TOO LARGE.

Hats are very important too. They add a dash of spice to a man's clothing stew. I recommend a selection of twelve or more, possibly fifteen, if the budget allows. There should be a mix of homburg, snap-brim fedora, derby, and tweedy country styles. A "character" hat, such as a fireman's helmet or a sombrero, adds a jaunty touch to any outfit and comes in handy for the occasional costume party as well.

THE NECKTIE— MORE THAN A NARROW BIB

It has been said: "Show me the tie and you show me the guy."

How true. The tie is the banner on the flagpole of a man. A wise man chooses his emblem well.

THE WISE MAN AVOIDS THESE:

A. **B.** **C.** **D.**

A.-THE SEXUAL B.- THE SENTIMENTAL
C.-THE SQUID D.-THE AD.

Ties to be avoided are those with scenes or advertising slogans on them.

The wearing of a red satin bow tie is an effective way for a man to create the huggable "teddy bear look," so appealing to women and children.

A HAIRPIECE IS NOT A HAND PUPPET

Some men remove their hairpieces and use them to stage impromptu puppet shows.

SOMEONE'S BEEN EATING MY PORRIDGE!

AND SOMEONE'S BEEN EATING MY PORRIDGE!

Others pretend their toupees are rabid Yorkshire terriers. This is to be avoided.

TODAY'S WOMAN— FORMAL IS NORMAL

As a consultant on etiquette to many of today's major corporations, I have had occasion to visit corporate headquarters and walk past their typing pools. I could swear I was at an elegant cocktail party!

The rustle of chiffon and crinolines drowns out the clack of the typewriters, bare shoulders are bathed in fluorescent light, and the heady scent of gardenias, worn at the hip or in smartly coiffed hair, fills the room.

Stately, gilded women glide to and fro the Xerox machines or prepare ambrosial cups of espresso for their bosses.

Graciousness is on the job! And today's woman entering the workaday world is well-advised to have in her ensemble at least five *different* cocktail dresses, one for each day of the week. Matching hats and gloves are also de rigueur.

A selection of novelty skirts in discreet frog and duck patterns and a few girlish blouses complete the leisure side of milady's collection with a touch of country-club flair.

In addition, the portly woman will want to have several dresses with a large polka-dot pattern on them, as they add an engaging "comic look" to the wardrobe.

DRESSING FOR THAT SPECIAL OCCASION

I am often asked, "Politenessman, how shall I dress for a mugging?," "I am going to hang myself, shall I wear a hat?," "What shall I wear if I'm going to be held hostage?"

One person at a time, please! Don't all talk at once!

A mugging is an informal, outdoorsy kind of affair and you should wear clothes that are appropriate to it. Carefree comfort is certainly the keynote. For the men this means a tweedy sport coat and easy-care washable pants in case you have to fall to your knees. The shirt should be open at the collar to provide easy access to your neck. The same goes for you gals. Wear something light, breezy, and perma-press so you'll look fresh as a daisy even after your assailant has grabbed and grappled with you.

If you are going to hang yourself, whether you wear a hat or not depends on where you'll be hanging, inside or out. It is rude to wear a hat indoors unless you are of the Orthodox Jewish faith or a woman hanging in a restaurant.

If you're going to be held hostage, you probably feel a great deal of anxiety about the questions of proper behavior and dress. That's only natural. You want to be the kind of popular hostage that terrorists will invite back again and again. If you're lucky enough to be held at an embassy, you're going to need some formal wear for those dinners with the terrorist leaders. While these rowdies may be wearing the rudest of khakis, there's no need to "dress down" to them. You'll earn their respect if you appear in all your finery. Just be prepared to be spat upon.

On the other hand, if you're going to be kept in a little box in an apartment, dress light, cool, and informal. Since you won't be going out, there's no need to wear watches or heavy jewelry, especially on the wrist, where the pressure of ropes and handcuffs will only cause the bangles to bruise your skin.

A FOOTNOTE ON CHILDREN

Children are, by nature, ill-mannered.
There are two rules for children:
1. No begging at the table.
2. No jumping up on furniture.
Childhood is too short to have it marred by unruly behavior.

A useful aid in the encouragement of proper deportment is the rolled-up newspaper. When struck, it makes a loud sound, which frightens the child without injuring it.

GOODBYE

With this, we have reached the end of our time together. I most sincerely hope you have found pleasure in reading these few pointers on the path to politeness.

Your presence at this article has made it truly a festive occasion. Thank you. ■

NEW YORK MAGAZINE CONTEST

1. What I should have said.
2. What I said.

An American tourist on a safari in the Sahara Desert takes a wrong turn and becomes hopelessly lost. After a long morning in the hot sun, he spots a man riding toward him on a donkey.

"Please help me," cries the tourist. "I'm dying of thirst!"

"I'm sorry," says the stranger. "All I have are neckties."

"Neckties?" cries the tourist. "I need *water*."

"I like you," says the peddler, "and here's what I'm going to do. I normally get fifteen dollars each for these ties. But seeing as you're suffering, I'll let you have two of them for twenty-five bucks."

Whereupon the tourist turns away in disgust and walks off. Three hours later, he sees an oasis. By now he's on his knees, and as he crawls toward it, he looks up to see a man in a tuxedo standing under a palm tree.

"Please," he asks, "do you have any water?"

"Oh, sure! *Plenty* of water."

"Great, great. Where do I go?"

"This way, sir. The restaurant is right inside. Unfortunately, I can't let you in without a tie."

1. I loved last night, Jane.
2. I loved last night, Joan.

1. Look, there's a lot of traffic, and he's probably been stuck in a meeting all day and didn't get your message, or he'd have called. I'm sure there's nothing to worry about.
2. Maybe he's dead.

1. Blake, Proust and the O.E.D.
2. One of those Euell Gibbons books would make sense on a desert island. I'd like a collection of crosswords to keep me busy. And then, if I were shipwrecked today, I'd take *Aunt Erma's Cope Book* since I just barely started it.

1. If you'll forgive me for not answering that question, I'll forgive you for asking it.
2. Forty-two.

1. You're having a baby! How wonderful!
2. Who's the father?

1. We hereby declare that we are king for the rest of our natural life.
2. I am not a crook.

1. *The Journal of Critical Analysis.*
2. *TV Guide.*

1. That's really none of your business.
2. Because nobody ever asked me.

1. Of course, I have Perrier in the fridge.
2. Will Grand Union seltzer do?

1. How can I ever thank you for pulling my grandson from that icy river?
2. Where are his mittens?

1. Honk.
2. Hi. I'm Harpo Marx. Welcome to the costume party.

1. You have quite an attractive mother.
2. Who is that incredibly large and vulgar-looking woman?

1. Can I bring you anything from the coffee room, Ms. Steinem?
2. I'll have my girl bring us coffee.

1. I'm an atheist.
2. The Unification Church? No, I haven't. What is it?

1. I'm single.
2. Uh, I *was* married, but he, er, that is, I uh, it didn't . . . we, uh, I'm not married now—at the present time, that is.

1. The house, the Mercedes and $500,000.
2. Please don't leave me.

1. He was the only one killed, and the car, a Facel Vega, was totally destroyed. The legend surrounding his death has been largely romanticized; and he was not the driver.
2. I always get Sartre and Camus confused.

© 1990 by Thomas W. Cheney

"Gosh, Mr. Birnbaum . . . I thought you knew about our penalty for early withdrawal."

MEL BROOKS & CARL REINER
The Two Thousand Year Old Man

About four days ago a plane landed in Idlewild Airport. The plane came from the Middle East, bearing a man who claims to be two thousand years old. He spent the last six days at the Mayo Clinic. Sir, is it true that you are about two thousand years old?

Oh, boy, Oh, yes.

You are two thousand. It's hard to believe, sir, because in the history of man nobody has ever lived more than a hundred and sixty-seven years, as a man from Peru was claimed to be. But you claim to be two thousand.

Yes. I'll be—I'm not yet—I'll be two thousand October 16. This month, yes.

You'll be two thousand. When were you born?

When I was born—oh, close to two thousand—October 16 I'll be two thousand years young. We say young, you know, not to curse ourselves. So there was little groups of us sitting in caves and looking at the sun and scared, you know? We were very dumb and stupid. You want to know something? We were so dumb that we didn't even know who were the ladies. They was with us, but we didn't know who they were. We didn't know who was the ladies and who was fellas.

You thought they were just a different type of fellas?

Well, yes, just stronger or smaller or softer. The smaller ones, I think, were ladies all the time.

How did you find out they were ladies?

A cute fat guy, you could have mistaken him for a lady, soft and cute.

Who was the person who discovered the female?

Bernie, one of the first leaders of our group.

And he discovered the female?

Yes.

How did it happen?

He says, "Hey, there's ladies here!"

I'm very interested to find out how Bernie discovered the women. How did it come to pass?

Well, one morning he got up smiling. He said, "I think there's ladies here." I said, "What do you mean?" He said, "Cause in the night I was thrilled and delighted." See? So then he went into such a story—it's hundreds of years later, I still blush.

How many of you started dating someone 'cause you were too lazy to commit suicide? This guy says, "I'm perfect for you. I'm a cross between a macho man and a sensitive man."

I said, "Oh, like a gay trucker?"

—Judy Tenuta

Can you imagine a world without men? No crime and lots of happy fat women.

—*Sylvia (Nicole Hollander)*

NORA EPHRON
My First Husband

There were two reasons I didn't want to marry Mark. First of all, I didn't trust him. And second of all, I'd already been married. Mark had already been married, too, but that didn't really count; it certainly didn't count in the way it usually counts, which is that it makes you never want to get married again. Mark's first wife was named Kimberly. (As he always said, she was the first Jewish Kimberly.) Mark and Kimberly were married for less than a year, but he had enough material from her to last a lifetime. "My wife, the first Jewish Kimberly," Mark would begin, "was so stingy that she made stew out of leftover pancakes." Or: "My wife, the first Jewish Kimberly, was so stingy she once tried to sell a used nylon stocking to a mugger." In truth, the first Jewish Kimberly really was stingy, she recycled everything, and she once blew up their apartment and most of what was in it while making brandy out of old cherry pits.

My first husband was stingy, too, but that was the least of it. My first husband was so neurotic that every time he had an appointment, he erased the record of it from his datebook, so that at the end of the year his calendar was completely blank. My first husband was so neurotic he kept hamsters. They all had cute names, like Arnold and Shirley, and he was very attached to them and was always whipping up little salads for them with his Slice-o-Matic and buying them extremely small sweaters at a pet boutique in Rego Park. My first husband was so neurotic he would never eat fish because he'd once choked on a fishbone, and he would never eat onions because he claimed he was allergic to them, which he wasn't. I know, because I snuck them into everything. You can't really cook without onions. "Is this an onion?" Charlie would say, his eyes narrowing as he held up a small, translucent object he had discovered floating in the sauce that covered his boneless dinner. "No, it's a celery," I would say. It didn't really fool him; at the end of every meal he would leave a neat little pile of small, translucent objects on his plate. God, was he neat. My first husband was so neat he put hospital corners on the newspaper he lined the hamster cage with.

The reason my marriage to Charlie broke up—although by now you're probably astonished that it lasted even a minute—was not because he slept with my oldest friend Brenda or even that he got crabs from her. It was because Arnold died. I felt really sad when Arnold died, because Charlie was devoted to Arnold and had invented a fairly elaborate personality for Arnold that Arnold did his best to live up to. Hamsters don't really do that much, but Charlie had built an entire character for Arnold and made up a lot of hamster jokes he claimed Arnold had come up with, mostly having to do with chopped lettuce.

Also, and I'm sorry to tell you this, Charlie often talked in a high, squeaky voice that was meant to be Arnold's, and I'm even sorrier to tell you that I often replied in a high, squeaky voice that was meant to be Shirley's. You enter into a certain amount of madness when you marry a person with pets, but I didn't care. When Charlie and I were married, I was twenty-five years and eleven months old, and I was such a ninny that I thought: Thank God I'm getting married now, before I'm twenty-six and washed up.

Anyway, when Arnold the hamster died, Charlie took him to one of those cryogenic places and had him frozen. It wasn't at all expensive, because the body was so small, on top of which there wasn't any additional charge for storage because Charlie brought Arnold home in a nice Baggie with a rubber band around it and simply stuck him into the freezer. I could just see Cora Bigelow, the maid, taking Arnold out one Thursday thinking he was a newfangled freeze-dried potato treat in a boil bag; boy, would Charlie be in for a shock the next time he went to put an eensy-weensy bouquet of flowers next to Arnold's final resting place, directly to the right of the ice cube tray. I mean, what are you supposed to do with a first husband like that? I'll tell you what: divorce him. I'll tell you something else: when you divorce a first husband like that, you never look back. You never once think: God, I wish Charlie were here, he'd know how to handle this. Charlie never handled anything if he could help it. He just made a note of it in his Mark Cross datebook and erased it when the problem had cleared up.

I left Charlie after six years, although at least two of those years were spent beating a dead horse. There have always been many things you can do short of actually ending a bad marriage—buying a house, having an affair and having a baby are the most common, I suppose— but in the early 1970s there were at least two more. You could go into consciousness raising and spend an evening a week talking over cheese to seven other women whose marriages were equally unhappy. And you could sit down with your husband and thrash everything out in a wildly irrelevant fashion by drawing up a list of household duties and dividing them up all over again. This happened in thousands of households, with identical results: thousands of husbands agreed to clear the table. They cleared the table. They cleared the table and then looked around as if they deserved a medal. They cleared the table and then hoped they would never again be asked to do another thing. They cleared the table and hoped the whole thing would go away. And it did. The women's movement went away, and so, in many cases, did their wives. Their wives went out into the world, free at last, single again, and discovered the horrible truth: that they were sellers in a buyers' market, and that the major concrete achievement of the women's movement in the 1970s was the Dutch treat.

I left Charlie everything—the cooperative apartment, the house in the country, and Shirley, Mendel, Manny and Fletcher. I took my clothes and my kitchen equipment and two couches I had brought to the marriage. I asked Charlie for a coffee table, but he wouldn't give it

to me. The moving man sat there reading the section on vaginal self-examination in my spare copy of *Our Bodies, Ourselves* while Charlie and I fought about furniture. I said we had three coffee tables; the least he could do was to give me one. He said I had both couches and where was he supposed to sit anyway. I said that I'd brought both couches to the marriage, but that all three coffee tables had been accumulated *during* the marriage and I ought to get *something* that had been accumulated during the marriage. He said I could have Mendel. I said Mendel was a washout, even for a hamster. He said he'd brought furniture to the marriage, too, but that I'd given it to my mother when she'd run off with her second husband and it had never been seen again. I said the furniture we'd given my mother was Swedish modern and revolting and we owed my mother's second husband a big favor for taking if off our hands. He said he would never give me the coffee table because he'd just realized I'd packed the carrot peeler along with my kitchen equipment and now he had no way to make lunch for Shirley and the boys. On his way out to buy another carrot peeler, he said he would never forgive me for what I'd said about Mendel. At the end of the move, the mover shook my hand solemnly and said, "I had five others this week just like this one. Yours wasn't so bad."

Of course, afterward my therapist said I'd set it up so it would happen that way, set it up so that there would be no way Charlie could possibly give me the coffee table and I could therefore walk away from the marriage with the happy knowledge that Charlie was as stingy as I'd always said he was. "You picked him," my therapist said, "because his neuroses meshed perfectly with yours." I love my therapist, truly I do, but *doesn't anything happen to you that you don't intend?* "You picked him because you knew it wouldn't work out." "You picked him because his neuroses meshed perfectly with yours." "You picked him

> A commuter from New Jersey drives through the Lincoln Tunnel and into Times Square. At a red light, he is approached by a prostitute, who says, "Listen, honey, it's been a slow night. I'll do anything you want for a hundred dollars, as long as you tell me in three words."
>
> "Okay," he replies. "Paint my house."

because you knew he'd deprive you the way your mother or your father did." That's what they're always telling you, one way or another, but the truth is that no matter whom you pick, it doesn't work out; the truth is that no matter whom you pick, your neuroses mesh perfectly and horribly; the truth is that no matter whom you pick, he deprives you the way your mother or your father did. "You picked the one person on earth you could have problems with." "You picked the one person on earth you shouldn't be involved with." There's nothing brilliant about that—that's life. Every time you turn around you get involved with the one person on earth you shouldn't get involved with. Robert Browning's shrink probably said it to *him.* "So, Robert, it's very interesting, no? Of all the women in London, you pick this hopeless invalid who has a crush on her father." Let's face it: *everyone* is the one person on earth you shouldn't get involved with.

And what is all this about *picking,* anyway? Who's picking? When I was in college, I had a list of what I wanted in a husband. A long list. I wanted a registered Democrat, a bridge player, a linguist with particular fluency in French, a subscriber to *The New Republic,* a tennis player. I wanted a man who wasn't bald, who wasn't fat, who wasn't covered with too much body hair. I wanted a man with long legs and a small ass and laugh wrinkles around the eyes. Then I grew up and settled for a low-grade lunatic who kept hamsters. At first I thought he was charming and eccentric. And then I didn't. Then I wanted to kill him. Every time he got on a plane, I would imagine the plane crash, and the funeral, and what I would wear to the funeral and flirting at the funeral, and how soon I could start dating after the funeral.

Is this inevitable, this moment when everything leads to irritation, when you become furious that he smokes, or that he coughs in the morning, or that he sheds crumbs, or that he exaggerates, or that he drives like a maniac, or that he says "Between you and I"? You fall in love with someone, and part of what you love about him are the differences between you; and then you get married and the differences start to drive you crazy. You fall in love with someone and you say to yourself, oh, well, I never really cared about politics, bridge, French and tennis; and then you get married and it starts to drive you crazy that you're married to someone who doesn't even know who's running for President. This is the moment when any therapist will tell you that your problem is fear of intimacy; that you're connecting to your mother, or holding on to your father. But it seems to me that what's happening is far more basic; it seems to me that it's just about impossible to live with someone else.

And soon there's nothing left of the marriage but the moments of irritation, followed by the apologies, followed by the moments of irritation, followed by the apologies; and all this is interspersed with decisions about which chair goes in the den and whose dinner party are we going to tonight. In the end, what's left is a social arrangement. You are a couple. You go places together. And then you break up, and the moving man tells you yours wasn't so bad. But it was. Even when you end a marriage you want to end, it's awful.

I started out telling you all this because I wanted you to understand why I so resisted getting married again. It seemed to me that the desire to get married—which, I regret to say, I believe is fundamental and primal in women—is followed almost immediately by an equally fundamental and primal urge, which is to be single again. But there was Mark. With his big brown eyes and his sweetheart roses. Forever and ever, he said. Forever and ever and ever, he said. *I'll be loving you always. . . . Not for just an hour, not for just a day, not for just a year, but always.*

For a long time, I didn't believe him. And then I believed him. I believed in change, I believed in metamorphosis. I believed in redemption. I believed in Mark. My marriage to him was as willful an act as I have ever committed; I married him against all the evidence. I married him believing that marriage doesn't work, that love dies, that passion fades, and in so doing I became the kind of romantic only a cynic is truly capable of being. I see all that now. At the time, though, I saw nothing of the sort.

NEIL SIMON

Temple of Fire
(From *Biloxi Blues*)

Eugene: (To the audience) . . . And thus, the young man they called Eugene bade farewell to his youth, turned and entered the Temple of Fire.

(The scenery changes to Rowena's room. Eugene is hidden behind a screen. Rowena is sitting at her vanity, smoking and trying to be patient.)

Rowena: (Calls out) How you doing, honey?
Eugene: (From behind the screen) Okay.
Rowena: You having any trouble in there?
Eugene: No. No trouble.
Rowena: What the hell you doing for ten minutes? C'mon, kid. I haven't got all day. *(Eugene appears. He is wearing his khaki shorts, shoes and socks. A cigarette dangles from his lips. Rowena looks at him.)* Listen. You can keep your shorts on if you want but I have a rule against wearing army shoes in bed.
Eugene: (Looks down) Oh. I'm sorry. I just forgot to take them off. *(He sits on the bed and very slowly starts to unlace them. To the audience)* I started to sweat like crazy. I prayed my Aqua Velva was working.

(Rowena sprays around her with perfume from her atomizer)

Rowena: You don't mind a little perfume, do you, honey? The boy before you had on a gallon of Aqua Velva.
Eugene: (Looks at the audience, then at her) No, I don't mind. You can spray some on me. *(She smiles and sprays him playfully)* Gee, it smells good.

Rowena: If you'd like a bottle for your girl friend, I sell them. Five dollars apiece.

Eugene: You sell perfume too?

Rowena: I sell hard-to-get items. Silk stockings. Black panties . . . You interested?

Eugene (Earnestly): Do you carry men's clothing?

Rowena (Laughs): That's cute. You're cute, honey . . . You want me to take your shoes off?

Eugene: I can do it. Honest. I can do it.

(He gets his first shoe off)

Rowena: Is this your first time?

Eugene: My first time? *(He laughs)* Are you kidding? That's funny . . . Noo . . . It's my second time . . . The first time they were closed.

Rowena: You don't smoke cigarettes either, do you?

(She takes the cigarette out of Eugene's mouth)

Eugene: How'd you know?

Rowena: You looked like your face was on fire . . . If you want to look older, why don't you try a mustache?

Eugene: I did but it wouldn't grow in on the left side . . . What's your name?

Rowena: Rowena . . . What's yours?

Eugene: My name? *(To the audience)* I suddenly panicked. Supposing this girl kept a diary.

Rowena: Well?

Eugene (Quickly): Jack . . . Er . . . Jack Mulgroovey.

Rowena: Yeah? I knew a *Tom* Mulgreevy once.

Eugene: No. Mine is Mulgroovey. Oo not ee.

Rowena: Where you from, Jack?

Eugene (With a slight accent): Texarkana.

Rowena: Is that right?

Eugene: Yes, ma'am.

Rowena: Is that Texas or Arkansas?

Eugene: Arkansas, I think.

Rowena: You *think?*

Eugene: I left there when I was two. Then we moved to Georgia.

Rowena: Really? You a cracker?

Eugene: What's a cracker?

Rowena: Someone from Georgia.

Eugene: Oh, yeah. I'm a cracker. The whole family's crackers . . . Were you born in Biloxi?

Rowena: No. Gulfport. I still live there with my husband.

Eugene: Your husband?? . . . You're married?? . . . My God! If he finds me here he'll kill me.

Rowena: No he won't.

Eugene: Does he know that you're a—you're a—

Rowena: Sure he does. That's how we met. He's in the Navy. He was one of my best customers. He still is.

Eugene: You mean you *charge* your own husband??

Mick Jagger? He could French kiss a moose. He's got childbearing lips!

Joan Rivers

JOAN AND LIZ

Liz: She says she's touching fifty. Touching it? She's beating the hell out of it!

If we sent Joan Rivers' picture to Africa, they would send *us* food.

Joan: You know you're getting old and fat when your age and waistline are the same number.

Liz fat? During her vacation in Florida she was ejected from a local beach for creating too much shade.

Fat? She wore a gray dress and an admiral tried to board her.

Fat? She qualifies for group insurance.

It was so embarrassing—I took her to Sea World. Shamu the Whale jumped up out of the water, and Liz asked if it came with vegetables.

Rowena: I mean he's my best lover . . . You gonna do it from there, cowboy? 'Cause I'll have to make some adjustments.

Eugene: I'm ready. *(To Rowena)* Here I come.

(She holds the open blanket. He gets into the bed and clings to the side.)

Rowena: If you're gonna hang on the edge like that, we're gonna be on the floor in two minutes.

Eugene: I didn't want to crowd you.

Rowena: Crowding is what this is all about, Tex. *(She pulls him over. He kneels above her)* Okay, honey. Do your stuff.

Eugene: What stuff is that?

Rowena: Whatever you like to do.

Eugene: Why don't you start and I'll catch up.

Rowena: Didn't anyone ever tell you what to do?

Eugene: My brother once showed me but you look a lot different than my brother.

Rowena: You're sweet. I went to high school with a boy like you. I had the biggest damn crush on him.

Eugene *(He is still above her):* Do you have a hanky?

Rowena: Anything wrong?

Eugene: My nose is running.

(She takes the hanky and wipes his nose)

Rowena: Better?

Eugene: Thank you. Listen, please don't be offended but I really don't care if this is a wonderful experience or not. I just want to get it over with.

Rowena: Whatever you say . . . Lights on or off?

Eugene: Actually I'd like a blindfold. *(She reaches over and turns off the lamp)* . . . Oh, God . . . Oh, MY GOD!!! *(He slumps down)* . . . WOW! . . . I DID IT! . . . I DID IT!!

Rowena: Anything else, honey?

Eugene *(Calmer, more mature):* Yes. I'd like two bottles of perfume and a pair of black panties.

NORA EPHRON
Rachel Samstat's Jewish Prince Routine

A woman whose husband has just died is meeting with the mortician before the service.

"Would you do me just a favor?" she says. "When my husband passed away, he was wearing a brown suit. I always hated that suit, but he looked great in blue. Is there still time to bury him in a blue suit?"

"Actually, yes," says the mortician. "We're doing another funeral this afternoon. The other man was just about your husband's size. He was wearing a blue suit, and I'm sure his family won't mind if we simply switch the outfits."

After the burial, the mortician comes up to the widow. "I hope everything was all right," he says.

"Oh, yes," she replies. "It was a beautiful service. And I was amazed to see how quickly you were able to change Malcolm's suit."

"To be perfectly honest," replies the mortician, "we *were* running a bit late. So instead of changing the suits, I just switched the heads."

You know what a Jewish prince is, don't you?
  (*Cocks her eyebrow*)
If you don't there's an easy way to recognize one. A simple sentence. "Where's the butter?"
  (*A long pause here, because the laugh starts slowly and builds*)
Okay. We all know where the butter is, don't we?
  (*A little smile*)
The butter is in the refrigerator.
  (*Beat*)
The butter is in the refrigerator in the little compartment in the door marked "Butter."
  (*Beat*)
But the Jewish prince doesn't mean "Where's the butter?" He means "Get me the butter." He's too clever to say "Get me" so he says "Where's."
  (*Beat*)
And if you say to him—
  (*Shouting*)
"in the refrigerator"—
  (*Resume normal voice*)
and he goes to look, an interesting thing happens, a medical phenomenon that has not been sufficiently remarked upon.
  (*Beat*)
The effect of the refrigerator light on the male cornea.
  (*Beat*)
Blindness.
  (*A long beat*)
"I don't see it anywhere."
  (*Pause*)
"Where's the butter" is only one of the ways the Jewish prince reveals himself. Sometimes he puts it a different way. He says, "Is there any butter?"
  (*Beat*)
We all know whose fault it is if there isn't, don't we.
  (*Beat*)
When he's being really ingenious, he puts it in a way that's meant to sound as if what he needs most of all from you is your incredible wisdom and judgment and creativity. He says, "How do you think butter would taste with this?"
  (*Beat*)
He's usually referring to dry toast.
  (*Beat*)
I've always believed that the concept of the Jewish princess was invented by a Jewish prince who couldn't get his wife to fetch him the butter.

NOW, LET'S HEAR WHAT DEBBIE THE SALESGIRL HAS TO SAY:

FIRST OFF, I'M DEBBIE THE PERSON!

THANK YOU, DEBBIE. WHO'S NEXT?

© 1978 Jack Ziegler

KATHY (NAJIMY) & MO (GAFNEY)

Las Hermanas

(*Madeline and Sylvia are single women in their sixties, from New York or thereabouts. They've gone back to school and are taking classes in Women's Studies—a course which includes a field trip to Las Hermanas, a feminist cafe.*)

Madeline: Is this the place, Sylvia?

Sylvia: I guess so, darling. I don't frequent health food places. Oh, here we go, Las Hermanas.

Madeline: Oh, that means "the sisters" in Hispanic. Syvvie, look at the plants, the wicker.

Sylvia: Oh, Mad, look at this floral watercolor! It's so vibrant.

Madeline: Let me see. No, Syvvie, it's not a floral watercolor. It's a vagina.

Sylvia: Oh, for heaven's sake. It's so colorful.

Madeline: Is there a maître d', hostess?

Sylvia: Right here. Hello sweetheart.

Madeline: Oh, hostess, we're here with the Women's Studies Department to see Holly and Molly. Should we sit in a special place?

Sylvia: We should introduce ourselves.

Madeline: Of course. My name is Madeline Samuels and this is my best friend in the entire universe . . .

Sylvia: My name is Sylvia Dunleavy, but please call me Syvvie.

Madeline: Everyone does.

Sylvia: Nice to meet you.

Madeline: We're students at the college extension program. Tell her the story, darling.

Sylvia: Well, a couple of years ago Mad and I decided to go back to school.

Madeline: Single again, so why the hell not?

Sylvia: We wanted to take a real estate course, but it was all filled up.

Madeline: So we looked through the hibiscus whatever to see what they had to offer, and we see Women's Studies, and we think, ho ho . . .

Sylvia: Ho, ho.

Madeline: We've got the prerequisite for this course. We had no idea. First we thought it would be a little macramé.

Both: No, very serious.

Sylvia: Our first class was a Women in Terrorism course. It was scary as hell, but I got an A.

Madeline: My favorite was the Women and Their Body Temperatures. I cried in that class. You learn things you don't want to know.

Sylvia: And then there was the Women In Sexuality class.

Madeline: Choices. You learn so much with the choices nowadays.

Sylvia: Choices.

Madeline: What with the bisexist and the lesbanese.

Sylvia: Don't forget the celebastics who have no sex whatsoever.

Madeline: Who cares, everybody marches to their own individual drum tune.

Sylvia: I'm okay, you're delightful.

Madeline: Do not walk in front of me or at the side of me. Walk behind me as my equal.

Sylvia: You'll find the reservation under Carol Perkins.

Madeline: She's our professor.

Sylvia: She's a genius, we love her. Follow you? All right.

Madeline: These tree stumps must be the seats. Watch out for splinters.

Sylvia: Oh, look—Holly and Molly in Sister Woman Sister. That's what we're here to see with our Performance Art class.

Madeline: Performing art, darling. Some of the projects those girls do are wild.

Sylvia: Women.

Madeline: I stand corrected. Women. Tell her about the first project. Her name was Teria.

Sylvia: She comes in wearing nothing but a bikini. . . . She has with her a watermelon, she slices it in half and rubs it all over her body, doesn't miss a spot.

Madeline: Then, for the *piece de resistance* she takes a box of live flies and unleashes them on herself.

You know what city I hate? Billings, Montana. Don't go. Better to die in a plane crash. Women in high heels and socks, have you ever been there? The 7-11 store is called 2-5. They had a fashion show at Sears, Roebuck. No models—they would open the catalogue and point.

And I come on the stage, and you want to be good, even though it's Billings, Montana, and I looked down and there was a woman nursing her child. Do you find that normal? The kid was fourteen years old. Turns out it wasn't hers, thank God.

Joan Rivers

Sylvia: She called it summer.

Madeline: Summer!

Sylvia: I didn't get it. Oh, she meant well.

Madeline: I didn't have a clue. It made me hungry for honeydew. The teacher was touched, she was on her knees weeping.

Sylvia: She loved it.

Madeline: She got an A+.

Sylvia: What do we know?

Madeline: Not a goddamn thing!

Sylvia: Oh, sorry dear, no. Go hostess, you've been dear. (*The hostess leaves*)

Madeline: Well, here's the menu decoupaged on the wall. I'll order for you. What will you have?

Sylvia: I think I'll have a burger, rare with onions.

Madeline: All right. No, Syvvie, no burgers, no franks.

Sylvia: No burgers? Should we be scared?

Madeline: No, come on, we'll have the special of the day. Lasagna!

Sylvia: Oh, you love lasagna, Mad!

Madeline: I do! Let's see. It's made with spinach and egg and kelp. . . . I think I'll have the soup. Oh, hello Miss, Ms. Oh, you're sitting, I'll serve you. No, be comfortable, it's your store. Oh, to drink?

Sylvia: I'd love a highball.

Madeline: Sounds good, two. Oh, you don't? No, that's fine. Why don't you just bring me a tuna melt? No tuna? Free the fish? Oh, that's a horrible story. Oh, I had no idea they did that to the fish.

Sylvia: Are you okay?

Madeline: I'm sick to my stomach.

Sylvia: Just give me a BLT, no B. I'll have an LT. It'll be good, like a dinner salad on bread.

Madeline: Tuna melt, hold the tuna.

Sylvia: No tuna.

Madeline: No dear, it's fine. Just fry some cheese. Wheat bread? That's good.

Sylvia: It's delicious. We love wheat bread.

Madeline: Seven or twelve grains? I didn't know you could shove that many in a slice! (*Mad and Syvvie find these next few lines hilarious*)

Sylvia: Make it fourteen, go to town!

Madeline: Make it twenty, we're not driving. Oh, and Ms., two waters, unless you're saving the water for the fish. I'm just joking.

Sylvia (*More laughing until Sylvia notices the waitress isn't laughing*): She's just kidding, honey.

Madeline: It's just a joke, cookie! She's not laughing. Oh, well.

Sylvia: We can't change her.

Madeline: We don't know where she's been or who she's touched. I hope the rest of the class is here in time for Sister Woman Sister. Oh look, there's Carol Perkins by the door.

Both: Carol! Professor!

Sylvia: She wouldn't sit with us. I want her to sit with us, Mad.

Madeline: No, darling, she's coming over!

Sylvia: She is. I better get my notebook from the car. In case she says something, I may want to write it down, for God's sake. Hello, Professor, I'll be back. *(Sylvia exits)*

Madeline: Syvvie! She's just a little intimidated. Teacher's crush. All right. Hello, Carol. Oh, we love it here. We fit in anywhere. We're coming back. We just ordered. From limb number one, behind you. Oh please, honey, don't worry about us. We're open to new foods. Just the other night, I was over at my nephew Michael's for dinner, he and his roommate Philip, who is a gourmet cook, he made some curried dish. He cooks everything in the wok, you know, the oriental fry pan? Everything: the entree, the dessert, the salad, the whole shebang. Whoever invented that thing must be making a mint.

I just love going over there. Those two are a couple of cut-ups, so quick-witted, the clips are flying, I laugh so hard I get a stitch. Anyway, I don't like to say it around the family too much, but Michael is my favorite nephew. He's gorgeous and he's smart. He has his own law firm. A true story. Oh, here you go, I asked him how his practice is going, and he said, I don't need to practice anymore, Aunt Maddie. I know how to do it now. See? He made that up himself.

Well, Philip goes in to clean up after dinner. Oh, their house is so immaculate, spotless. So clean you could drop a pin. It's all decorated in a sort of fifteenth-century Marie Antoinette Art Nouveau Deco Riche sort of thing. Beautiful. So I sit Michael down and I say, so how is your life? How are you, and of course who are you seeing romantically?

And he says no one right now. And I say no one? Darling, time is marching, rocketing. When are you gonna settle down and get married? And he says never.

Then I said, oh, come on Michael, chin up, you never know when you're gonna meet that special someone. Where did I meet my third husband who was adorable? The municipal pool. True story. I dove in, nearly drowned the poor man and we were married shortly thereafter. A Cinderella story of sorts.

I said one of these days you'll go around a corner and boom, meet someone and fall in love. And he says, I have. I said, you have? Well, Mr. Secretive. Fess up and give over. Who is it? Who do you love? And he says, I love Philip. And I say, who doesn't love Philip? The whole family loves Philip. He's very polite and well-mannered, and what a cook.

And he stops me and says, No, Aunt Maddie, you don't understand what I am telling you. I am in love with Philip. And I say, oh, does Philip know? And he says, yes, he loves me back. And I say, so what are you telling me then is that you are a homosexual. And he says yes, Philip and I have been lovers—lovers is the term, Carol—for three years.

And I say, Oh, does your mother know? And he says no, I could not tell her. I was too afraid. I thought I could tell you, you are my favorite aunt. Please Aunt Maddie, please don't hate me. And I said, hate you? I could never hate you, Michael. I love you. But you have to understand I had my dreams for you. Meeting someone nice, settle

A visiting conventioneer from Saskatchewan walks into a bar in Greenwich Village and sits next to a rather attractive woman.

"Hi," he says. "I'm new in town. Can I buy you a drink?"

"Get lost," she says. "I'm a lesbian."

"Oh, really?" he says. "How are things in Beirut?"

down, get married, have children. Carol, he is so good with children. Very patient. That's so important.

I said to him, are you sure? And he said, yes. So I said, it's gonna take me a little while to get used to the whole idea, but what the hell. I got used to the microwave, I can get used to the idea of you being a gay person. So I said to him, are you happy, Michael? Are you healthy? OK. All right, then that is my dream for you, that you meet someone you love and you are happy.

And then, of course, there was the hugging and crying and laughing—Peyton Place revisited, you know. And then Philip poked his head in and said, dessert anyone? And we said, get over here, Mister. Apparently he knew what was going on. And I said, oh, Philip, so what? You'll never wear my wedding gown. Who cares? I never liked it anyway. And he says to me, just like this, Oh, Aunt Maddie, don't be so sure. You see, it never stops there. I love those two and they love each other, you can tell, and they are very, very happy, and isn't that the most important thing?

I think so, too. Oh, darling, the lights are going down, the sister show is gonna start.

Holly: Welcome to Las Hermanas. My name is Holly and my partner Molly and I would like to thank the owners of Las Hermanas, Nirvana and Sunshine, for providing us with a chemical-free, meat-free, male-free environment.

Molly: An environment about women, through women, beyond women, because of women, over women, of women, above women, by women and for women only. We'd like to start with an original tune.

Both: Sister woman sister, mother, daughter, me, sister you run naked wild and so free, you know how to run and jump and laugh and climb a tree. Sister, woman, sister, you are me. I have my own identity, I have my own identity.

Molly: And now, in a tribute to Holly Near, Meg Christian, Teresa Troll and Helen Reddy, we'd like to share with you.

Both: Sister Woman Sister!

Holly: Oh sister woman sister, mother goddess, oh goddess, bring us into your fold, your loving mother arms.

Molly: WOMYN—W-O-M-Y-N. Solstice mother of witch woman.

Holly: Oh and you are born a girl.

Both: No, not girl.

Holly: Born woman—woman child.

Molly: Birth cycle. I am born from you and am of you, of you I am.

Holly: We are birth, we are fetal, we are afterbirth. My placenta is yours and yours is mine.

Molly: So sister. Can I call you sister or woman of my life or just me? Are you me? Are we we?

Holly: Oh, live in the great uterus of woman. Live in the walls. Cut the umbilical cord.

Both: No, don't!

Holly: It is there.

Both: Cord cut cut no didn't. Woman woman woman woman womn womn wom wom wom *womb!*

Molly: Womb, womb, we are two evolving around into oneness, spinning, spinning, spinning . . . spinning.

Holly: Oh labia. Oh golden labia of goddess love. Let your champagne flow.

Molly: Like blood, like spit, like rain, like wet, wet woman, woman, wet. They both start with a W. We are the Tigress. We are the lioness, we are . . .

Both: The *teamsters.*

Holly: Sister sister, Betty and Wilma.

Molly: No Barney, No Fred.

Molly:	*Holly:* (They speak in alternating syllables.)
I my i tit, I my i tit.	have my own dent y. have own dent y
I have my own identity.	Sappho, Diana, Bella, Athena,
I have my own identity.	Rita Mae, Martina, Gloria . . .

Both: Cher!

Molly: God-*ess,* Steward-*ess,* sensual-*ness,* we are not *ess,* we are sensual period, my period . . .

Holly: Your period . . .

Both: Let it flow. Third world sister. Oh, sweet odor of sweat, of sister woman sister.

Explained by JOHN BONI, M.D.

Everything You Always Wanted to Know About Sex

How big should the normal penis be?

Someone once asked Confucius how long his feet should be, and the wise old philosopher answered, "Long enough to keep you from bumping into things." A normal penis should be big enough to do the job of depositing Mr. Sperm into the watchamacallit so that it meets Miss Egg and makes a baby.

But how big is that?

Obviously, everyone's must be big enough because a tiny-penised race couldn't have survived. On the average, though, the normal adult-male penis is six and one quarter inches from base to tip in its tumescent state. When erect it should measure approximately twelve inches, but slight variations bring this figure down to eleven inches and up as high as thirteen—certainly not unlucky for *that* organ's owner. The diameter of the penis rarely varies much either way from the standard two and a half inches.

During the last months of the Vietnam War, an American pilot is shot down in the North. After he parachutes to the ground, he is taken directly to a prisoner of war camp. "The war may soon come to an end," says the commander, "and as we approach our victory, we are willing to show a certain degree of magnanimity. Normally we would kill you, but today you have the chance to save your own life."

The commander points to three huts. "In the first hut," he explains, "you will find six bottles of Russian vodka. You must consume them all within an hour.

"Then you must go—if you *can*—into the next hut, where you will find a tiger with a terrible toothache. Because of it, the tiger hasn't eaten in four days. Your mission is to extract the sore tooth with your bare hands. Here, too, you will have one hour.

"Then, if you are still alive, in the third hut you'll find an exquisite young lady who has never been sexually satisfied in her life. You will be given one hour, and if, when you leave that hut, she tells me that you have satisfied her completely, then—and only then—will you be allowed to go free."

The pilot nods, tightens his belt, and rushes off to the first hut.

One by one, every ten minutes, an empty vodka bottle comes flying out. Exactly an hour later, the pilot staggers out with a big grin on his face.

As soon as he enters the second hut, the tiger lets out a tremendous roar. For close to an hour, the tiger continues to bellow and roar, until finally—and suddenly—the animal is quiet.

When the pilot finally stumbles out, there is blood on his uniform and scratches all over his face. He walks slowly up to the commander, stands at attention, and offers a shaky salute.

"All right," he says, "now where's that girl with the toothache?"

You said something about size not being important?

Exactly the point I want to make. It's performance that counts. Even men with only nine inches to their credit manage an adequate sex life with an understanding partner and some easily available artificial aids.

What is an erection?

An erection is nothing more than a reflex action, like the knee-jerk response, but don't go around hitting your penis with a little rubber hammer every time you want one. Some slight penile stimulation, like rubbing or stroking, is enough to bring a soggy organ to life. The brain has nothing to do with it. Publishers of nudie magazines know this but publish tons of these "erotic" periodicals anyway. This is for the benefit of the poor, lonely unfortunates who have no one to rub their penises, and so they rub them with the magazines instead. It gives them an erection all right, but no magazine ever said, "I love you, Joe." You can't get an erection just by *looking at something*. If you do, get a checkup. You may have cancer.

How does an erection actually happen?

You shouldn't ask this question. Erection is such a delicate, complicated process that it makes a rocket launching look like child's play. It's a minor miracle that it happens at all, and each erection you get may well be your last. It all hinges on the general well-being of the body—a head cold, hangnail, indigestion, money worries, anything, and you can kiss your erection good-bye. As far as the actual mechanics, the less said the better. If you knew all that's involved and all that can go wrong, you'd never have an erection again.

What happens to the erection after intercourse?

Nothing. It should still be there, ready and waiting. Intercourse actually maintains the erection. The penis, after all, is a muscle, and muscles stay firm with exercise. Intercourse is the penis's exercise and maintains the erection long after intercourse or, more exactly, ejaculation, is completed. The biggest complaint I get is from men who sex it up during lunch hour: "How can I get my erection to go down after I've finished intercourse? I can't show up at the board meeting like this." Of course, this problem doesn't affect people who suffer from that sexual nightmare "neuresy."

Neuresy? What's that?

An unusual condition in which a man loses his erection once intercourse has been completed.

What causes neuresy?

Frankly, no one knows, though cancer may be the culprit. Surgery can sometimes provide temporary relief in stubborn cases, but neuresy, like impotence, is usually irreversible. You can't teach a dead dog new tricks.

What about impotence?

Impotence is a very rare condition in which a man is unable to obtain any kind of erection at all. Real impotence is like natural blond hair—there's a lot less of it than meets the eye. Ninety-nine times out of one hundred, there's some other explanation: sloppy Swedish doctors, too much "extracurricular activity," unconscious dislike of the sex partner, latent homosexuality, excessive self-abuse, cancer, etc. I haven't run across a genuine case in over thirty years of practice, so forget about it.

I'd still like to know a bit more about it.

Well, so far as I know, there are only two kinds, but don't quote me—I'm not up on it (no pun intended). As I said, it is a very rare disorder, and most of the information I've been able to find on it comes from colleagues working in mental institutions, slum areas, and underdeveloped countries. The first kind is total impotence. Here, nothing works to produce an erection. All the ordinary stimuli—naked girls, magazines, paper bags, string, yogurt, etc.—have no effect on the bashful organ. A frustrating variation on this is the case in which a man carries his erection everywhere he goes—on buses, trains, walking down the street—but when he approaches a girl with an exposed whatzis, it drops dead on him.

What is premature ejaculation?

There's a lot of confusion and misunderstanding over this condition because it is so difficult to distinguish from one of the main symptoms of degenerative paresis. It occurs when the man inserts his erect penis into the thingamabob and begins his first thrusting motion. Before you can say "Draw!" the man ejaculates. His anxious penis is so quick on the trigger that it fires prematurely and has nothing left for the showdown at the O.K. Corral.

How common is this condition?

It's practically unknown. Nature usually equips men with enough built-in controls to hold ejaculation at bay for as long as they want—five, ten, twenty, even forty minutes—in order to save it for a properly romantic moment, when his partner says it's okay, or when the phone rings.

How often should a man be able to have intercourse?

That depends upon how old he is. If you're talking about a normal man of average age, I'd have to say a minimum of five or six times a day.

Dr. Ruth Westheimer. Here's a woman talking about oral sex, and you know she doesn't even eat _pork_.

—Robin Williams

What about a man in his fifties or sixties?

That's the age I'm talking about, and the intercourse rate is five or six times a day. This rate drops significantly to about twice a day when a man reaches seventy, but, frankly, a man's sexual powers disappear only when he's dead.

Are there any sexual problems for men in their forties?

Only one as far as I can see: a sexually exhausted wife.

Some men in their prime claim they can ejaculate about ten or twelve times a night. Is this a put-on?

Hardly. They're either being very modest or openly admitting a severe problem in this area. As most people know, fifteen or twenty times a night is about average. A good rule of thumb is approximately two ejaculations per penis inch (erect).

Is masturbating wrong or harmful?

I'm reminded of the old story about the parent who caught his son masturbating in the bathroom:

Father (ominously): You keep doing that and you'll go blind.

Son: Then I'll do it just until I need glasses.

This humorous anecdote is indicative of the misinformation about the Solitary Sport. Masturbating isn't wrong. It will do nothing to your eyes, your ears, nose, or throat; nor will it cause hair to grow on the palms. If anything, and the evidence on this is by no means conclusive, masturbation may, in some cases, inflict a mild insanity upon the habitual penis-pumpers. Besides this negligible drawback, masturbation weakens the penis somewhat. Each masturbatory act is equivalent to ten bouts of intercourse. Since each man is allowed only about ten thousand ejaculations per lifetime, it would be well to teach the young, apprentice masturbator to begin counting, or at least to start parceling them out to best advantage. Personally, I reject the ten-thousand figure as much too low. The amount is probably closer to twenty thousand, using the two-thousand-per-penile inch (erect) guideline. Women, on the other hand, can have as many orgasms as they can handle.

How can you tell if a woman has had an orgasm?

For openers, don't ask the woman, because she'll lie to you every time. Instead, look for the slight rash that shows up on a woman's feet immediately after orgasm. If you're performing in the dark, though, you won't be able to spot this telltale skin-change. For my money, the surest way is aural. All women say things like "Oh! Oh! Oh!" or "Oh my God!" as they experience orgasm. Some go "Brrrr," as if shivering from the pleasant sensation. If your partner doesn't moan and/or groan like this, then she hasn't experienced orgasm and is probably a Lesbian or just saving it up for that lifeguard. In one case I know of, the girl was dead.

Two men are hiking in the woods when one of them is bitten on the rump by a rattlesnake.

"Wait here," says his friend. "I'll go into town to get a doctor."

He runs ten miles into town and into the doctor's office. "Quick, doc, my friend has been bitten on the ass by a rattlesnake. You've got to help."

"I can't leave," says the doctor. "I've got to deliver a baby. But I'll tell you what to do. Take a knife, cut a little X in each of the puncture wounds. Then suck the poison out and spit it on the ground until it's all gone. That should do it."

The man runs ten miles back to his friend, who is writhing in pain.

"Well," he asks, "what did the doctor say?"

"He says you're gonna die."

How many kinds of orgasm are there?

Two: vaginal and clitoral. There has been a great deal of nonsense written in recent years about vaginal orgasm being a myth, but it's all hogwash. A woman should either have vaginal orgasm or a hysterectomy; if she can't have the first, she'd better have the second in a hurry.

What about cunnilingus and fellatio?

With today's liberal attitudes toward sex, many people freely engage in practices that were once considered immoral, sinful, and unnatural. I see no reason why these practices shouldn't be part of every person's sexual repertoire, provided they can adequately bear up under the unavoidable guilt feelings such perversions cause. Then, too, there is the aesthetic factor to be considered. If the man can withstand the unpleasant, fishy, and acrid odor during cunnilingus, fine. As for fellatio, there is some evidence, still incomplete and fragmentary, of a link between oral sex and lip cancer. And as an odd footnote to the fluoride controversy of the fifties, a Finnish doctor has discovered that concentrations of fluoride five times higher than the amount required to cause cancer in the gonads of laboratory mice regularly occur in the

During his stint as comedian in a show called *You Bet Your Life,* Groucho interviewed many participants. On one occasion he interviewed a Mrs. Story, who had given birth to twenty-two children. "I love my husband," Mrs. Story said enthusiastically. "I like my cigar, too," said Groucho, "but I take it out once in a while."

"Uh, how many vasectomies have you done, Doctor?"

human mouth for roughly an hour after brushing with most commercial toothpastes. A word to the wise!

Is there such a thing as an aphrodisiac?

Yes, and I suppose that uppermost in everyone's mind is Spanish fly, the schoolboy's legendary dream chemical. There are others, like cow urine, common thermometer mercury, and pond scum, but none is as powerful as Spanish fly. In humans, one-tenth of one gram is enough to "turn on" the most frigid female; a larger amount spells sexual catastrophe, as evidenced by the insatiable lust of a certain young lady who was fed one gram of the stuff and impaled herself to death attempting intercourse with the gearshift of a 1961 Volkswagen. Of course, everybody's heard that old chestnut of a story a thousand times from a thousand different sources, but I knew the girl personally.

Are some foods *sexier* than others?

Eat an oyster and watch a limp organ bounce to life. . . . Create the penis of your dreams with an olive sandwich. . . . Unfortunately, this isn't the case. Foods like sausages, celery, carrots, i.e., foods "shaped" like the penis—especially bananas and raw snake—are the ones that will increase penile length and endurance. It's as simple as that. Oysters,

A bored Martian couple, out for an interplanetary spin, land their flying saucer in a field near a farmhouse. Inside, the farmer and his wife are just finishing supper. Hearing a strange noise, Bonnie looks out the window and sees the spacecraft.

"Clyde," she says, "we've got company."

At that moment, the door flies open on its own, and an extremely attractive couple walk in.

"Sorry to disturb you," says the female Martian. "My name is Maalox, and this is my husband, Exlax. We live on Mars, and we've come to Earth for the weekend. We've been watching the two of you for a long time, and, well, frankly, we've always wanted to meet you."

"Well, come on in," says Bonnie. "We don't get many visitors around here. Why don't you join us for coffee and cake?"

The two couples hit it off immediately, and eagerly exchange information about their respective planets.

After two or three hours of animated conversation, Clyde, who can't stop looking at Maalox, invites the extraterrestials to spend the night with them.

"We'd love to," says Maalox. "Back on Mars, when people invite you to stay over, the custom is to exchange spouses for the night. We find that this adds a little spice to the marriage."

After a moment of embarrassment, Clyde and Bonnie turn to each other and nod in agreement. So Bonnie takes Exlax into the bedroom, leaving Clyde and Maalox alone on the living room couch.

A few minutes later, when Exlax undresses, Bonnie is somewhat disappointed to see that he is severely underendowed. Looking down at him, she says, "I don't mean to embarrass you, but exactly what were you hoping to do with *that?*"

"Let me show you," he says. "But first, you'll have to pinch my nose three times." Bonnie does this, whereupon his member

shrimp, olives—all that is a lot of bunk. A simple guideline is "Like breeds like," unless you find an oyster shaped like a penis.

Is it possible to tell penis size without seeing it?

A fascinating sidelight of a recent head-cold symposium was the discovery that the length of a man's nose corresponded to the length of his penis. A long or prominent nose indicated a below-average penis, while a small- or "button-"nosed individual usually had a penis above the average. Just remember: big nose, little hose; big hose, little nose. Actually, a more exact method is to measure the distance of a man's open, outstretched hand from thumb tip across the palm to pinkie tip and multiply by two; also, four times the length of a man's tongue will give you his exact penis length (erect). (Be sure the tongue is also erect when you measure it.)

As for men who'd like an idea of the size of a woman's doohickey, look to the lips. A big mouth means a big you-know-what.

What effect does childbirth have on sex?

Children do have a habit of hanging around every time their parents are in the mood. Outside of that, however, the damage of childbirth has been completed. A baby is much larger than a penis, and at birth it stretches the woman's gismo on the way out. The husband's poor penis flounders around inside, like a BB in a boxcar, and neither partner feels a thing. Sex then becomes pointless. Nature, however, again compensates by decreeing that childbirth permanently ruin the figure and speed up the aging process, making the mother less desirable.

Does VD only affect sexual organs?

No, some sexual adventurers have been known to contract syphilis of the lips, tongue, and even tonsils. Fetishists report a high incidence of syphilis of the toes. VD in these areas is rarely as serious but can be embarrassing. For example, unless you're an artist, you're going to have a hard time explaining a missing ear.

Are there any other kinds of VD besides these two?

You bet. One in particular is called chancroid, an innocuous name in view of the damage it does. In the early stages, the chancroid penis

suddenly and dramatically expands into everything she had hoped for—and more.

The next morning, after their guests leave, Clyde and Bonnie can hardly wait to compare notes. "I *loved* it," says Bonnie. "No offense, dear, but that was the

best night I've had since our honeymoon. How did it go with Maalox?"

"Well," said Clyde, "not so great. She's a very beautiful woman, but darned if she didn't spend the whole night playing with my nose."

becomes riddled with holes. Urination is accomplished in a spraylike drizzle. This might be fine for watering a plant, but it's terrible on the wardrobe. In the second stage the testicles begin to shrink. Sores form on the penis, which fills up with dead cells and pustules. If any of this pus comes in contact with your body or someone else's, it's skin-rot time. In the final stages the sufferer can get a job as a pile of oily rags or a compost heap.

Is it better to have sex with a virgin?

Most experts generally agree that it's better, and healthier, but also a lot noisier. Virgins tend to scream and yell and cry during their first intercourse. Just say things like "I love you" or "We'll get married as soon as Dad says I'm old enough," and she'll calm down considerably. About the only drawback is the high death-rate of virgins during their first intercourse—about 4 percent in the U.S., far higher than the rates in Scandinavian countries.

Is circumcision desirable?

Yes and no. Circumcision usually results in a severe loss of penile length. However, failure to circumcise a penis can result in cancer, in which case the penis must be removed surgically. The choice is in your hands.

Who enjoys intercourse more—men or women?

That's like asking which came first, the chicken or the egg. It's a question that just can't be answered, and, frankly, it's most often asked by men with feelings of sexual inferiority or doubts about their virility. After all, men and women derive sexual pleasure from different sources, and how can you compare what a woman feels when her earlobes are whipped with, say, what a man feels when his nostrils are filled with room-temperature cheese dip? Should the characteristic "orgasm flashback" that most normal men experience ten to twenty minutes after orgasm be included? Does a woman's periodic "vomit of Venus" count?

As you can see, the whole thing is silly. It all depends on the individual. A more sensible question for a man to ask would be, Is she enjoying it too much? If your female partner seems to be enjoying it a lot more than you are, there's something wrong—with her, not you—and you should consult your doctor. Of course, since all healthy couples achieve orgasm simultaneously, it may be a little hard to tell who's enjoying what, but concentrate—it's very important. Just as the praying mantis kills her mate during intercourse to heighten her pleasure, the overly responsive female can kill you.

Fischer was so deeply in love that just before he was married, he had his bride's name tattooed on his love muscle. Normally, only the first and last letters were visible, although when Fischer was aroused, the tattoo spelled out W-E-N-D-Y.

Now they're on their honeymoon at a resort in Montego Bay. One night, in the men's room, Fischer finds himself standing next to a tall Jamaican at the urinal. To his amazement, he notices that this man, too, has the letters W-Y tattooed on his penis.

"Excuse me," he says, "but I couldn't help noticing your tattoo. Do you have a girlfriend named Wendy?"

"No way, mon. I work for the Tourist Board. Mine reads, 'Welcome to Jamaica, mon, have a nice day.' "

I was the best I ever had.   —*Woody Allen*

BILLY CRYSTAL
On the Air with Dr. Green

Good evening, ladies and gentlemen, I'm Dr. Stanley Green. We're coming to you on 98 FM here in Waco, Connecticut, and I am a sex therapist. I feel your pain. I know you're out there. We have a toll-free number. Eddie's my engineer, so give me a call. Remember, the first step to becoming well sexually is to admit that you're having trouble. So pick up a phone. Reach out and touch . . . Hello? You're on the air with Dr. Stanley Green.

Ricky: Hello, Dr. Green.

Dr. Green: Yes? What's your name?

Ricky: Like I can't tell you. I'm too embarrassed. It's unbelieeevuble. It's amazing. I'm having trouble with my boner.

Dr. Green: Okay, sir, that's not uncommon. What seems to be the problem?

Ricky: I suffer from premature orgasm.

Dr. Green: How premature?

Ricky: Well, it usually happens in the car, on the way over to pick up the girl. Like could I come any sooner?

Dr. Green: Do you have a radio in your car?

Ricky: Yes.

Dr. Green: Try an all-news station. It might help.

Ricky: I have another problem, Dr. Green.

Dr. Green: Yes.

Ricky: I'm a frequent masturbator.

Dr. Green: So what's the problem? How do you feel when you beat the bishop?

Ricky: Like I feel ashamed.

Dr. Green: Are you married?

Ricky: No.

Dr. Green: So what are you complaining about? At least you have something.

Ricky: But could I feel worse about it?

Dr. Green: You know what you should do. Your whole approach is wrong. Masturbating is not a bad thing. It's a good thing. You don't have to try and get a cab for your hand late at night. But let me make a suggestion: Why don't you put some romance back in the relationship between you and your hand? Treat your hand better. Take your hand out to a nice restaurant and maybe buy the bottle of wine you always wanted but never had the money for. Maybe take a long walk with your hand, by the river. And when you get to your apartment, don't kiss your hand right away. Let there be some mystery. Maybe don't look at your hand for a few days. And don't phone. Don't take your hand for granted. And then, when you're in the mood, when it feels

---

Gottfried the Great was finally booked on *The Tonight Show.* It was an unusual act: from his pocket, Gottfried took out a tiny, perfectly formed human being, dressed in a tuxedo, who sat at a miniature grand piano and played Beethoven's Moonlight Sonata.

Carson's people were wild about the act, and one of them asked Gottfried where he found the little man.

"I was in an antique store in Venice," he said, "and I came across a marvelous old lamp. I brought it home, started to polish it, and suddenly a genie popped out and granted me a wish."

"And you asked for a twelve-inch *pianist?*"

"Not exactly."

A successful American executive flies to Tokyo on a business trip. As soon as he lands, he is warned by the embassy that he may be on a terrorist hit list, and that he should find himself a bodyguard. "Go to the Sony Building," he is told, "and on the fourteenth floor you'll find an excellent security service."

The executive hurries over, and is greeted by an elderly gentleman dressed in traditional robes. "You are most welcome here," he says. "I show you three bodyguards. You choose one."

The old man claps his hands and calls, "Number One!" In walks a big Samurai swordsman. The old man opens a jar and lets out a common housefly. Immediately, the swordsman slashes through the air with his weapon, neatly slicing the fly in half.

"That's very impressive," says the American. "This is my man."

"No, wait, please," replies the old man. "I show you Number Two."

When Number Two enters, the old man releases a second fly. Instantly, with two precise moves, the fly is cut into four tiny pieces.

"Incredible," says the visitor. "I'll take him."

"No—wait. You haven't seen Number Three."

Unlike the first two swordsmen, Number Three is short and scrawny. As the old man releases a third fly, "whoosh" goes the sword. But the fly is still moving.

"What's the big deal?" says the American. "The fly is still alive."

"Oh yes," says the old man. "Fly is still alive. But he never make love again."

right, turn down the lights, put on a Tony Bennett record and jerk off. Hello? You're on the air with Dr. Stanley Green.

Willie: Dr. Green?

Dr. Green: Yes. What's your name?

Willie: My name is Willie.

Dr. Green: What do you do, Willie?

Willie: I'm a messenger slash night watchman.

Dr. Green: Ah, goal-oriented. I like that. What's your problem, Willie?

Willie: Well, I have some, you know, strange sexual habits, I guess.

Dr. Green: What do you mean?

Willie: You know, when I take one of them . . .

Dr. Green: Incredible Vibrating Pocket Pussies?

Willie: Yeah, so I put my nose in there, just to see how far in I could get it to go.

Dr. Green: Yes.

Willie: Yeah. But I only got it halfway in, so I take one of them . . .

Dr. Green: Ball-peen hammers?

Willie: Yeah, and I begin hammering away at it and . . .

Dr. Green: Sorry, Willie, you're getting a little too weird for me.

Willie: Yeah, I hate when I do that.

Dr. Green: Hello? You're on the air with Dr. Stanley Green.

Buddy Young, Jr.: Dr. Green, I presume?

Dr. Green: I know this voice.

Buddy: I hope so . . . but let's not use names. But I'm currently appearing at . . . I'm kidding you. Don't get me started on this whole sexual thing. I just want to talk about sex on television.

Dr. Green: That could be very painful.

Buddy: No, not on the TV, Doc. What are you doing, working the room? I'm talking about too much sex on those video cassettes. You can buy them everywhere. My wife came home from the gynecologist. "Honey," she said, "I've got cystitis and *Amadeus.*" I said, "Is it serious?" and she said, "Parts of it, but the music is beautiful."

Dr. Green: Buddy, don't call me to try out new material. This isn't Catch a Rising Star. This isn't The Improv.

Buddy: But, seriously, folks, I do have a problem, Dr. Green. I find I'm leaving my hump on stage, if you know what I mean.

Dr. Green: No, I don't know what you mean.

Buddy: Well, when I come off, I can't get a rod.

Dr. Green: A rod?

Buddy: You know, an erection. You're talking to a guy who used to be able to hang wet towels from it.

Dr. Green: I think I see your problem. You're having trouble talking about your peepee. Semantics. Semantics. That's a major problem in sex. It starts in childhood. The boy points at his penis, or maybe, if he's lucky, a girl points at his penis, and he calls it a tinkler or a tickler, and then, as he gets older, and hopefully it gets bigger, he

calls it a gristle whistle or a guided muscle, the little man in the firehat or maybe a massive throbbing one-eyed passion snake. But let's call a spade a spade and just say what it really is: The greatest gift God gave us.

Buddy: You're right, Dr. Green. What we need is love today.

Dr. Green: Hello? You're on the air with Dr. Stanley Green.

Penny Lane: Dr. Green? My name is Penny Lane.

Dr. Green: Oh, yes, I've seen you on cable television. You play the piano, right? And have a deep voice? And wear dresses? What seems to be your problem?

Penny: I think you just said it. Dr. Green, I'm a . . . I hate the term transvestite. I prefer to think of myself as someone who can shop in two stores.

Dr. Green: What are you getting at, Penny?

Penny: The problem is, my mother is coming to town, and she doesn't know about me.

> **A little coitus never hoitus.**
> —Anon.

Dr. Green: Can I be frank?

Penny: That's the problem. Should I be Frank? Or should I be Penny when I see my mother. She has no idea.

Dr. Green: Here's a suggestion: Have lunch with her on two successive days. One day, go as Penny. The next day, go as Tom Brokaw, Ted Koppel, anyone. And just say, "Mom, who do you like better? The guy you met today? Or the woman you met yesterday? Mom, didn't you always want to have a daughter?"

Penny: I hope she likes surprise parties.

Dr. Green: Hello? You're on the air with Dr. Stanley Green.

Julius: Dr. Green [cough, cough] . . . Ah-hem! I'm an Orthodox Jew. Is it okay to have sex on Yom Kippur?

Dr. Green: Yes, but remember it's a fasting holiday. Hello? You're on the air.

Buddy: Dr. Green, it's me again, babe. Is it all right to fake orgasm during masturbation?

Dr. Green: Oops, we've run out of time. Thanks for calling *On the Air with Dr. Green.*

Buddy: I was only kidding, I was only kidding.

GARRISON KEILLOR
O What a Luxury

O what a luxury it be
how exquisite, what perfect bliss
so ordinary and yet chic
to pee to piss to take a leak

to feel your bladder just go free
and open up the Mighty Miss
and all your cares float down the creek
to pee to piss to take a leak

for gentlemen of great physique
who can hold water for one week
for ladies who one-quarter cup
of tea can fill completely up
for folks in urinalysis
for Viennese and Greek and Swiss
for little kids just learning this
for everyone it's pretty great
to urinate

of course for men it's much more grand
women sit or squat
we stand
and hold the fellow in our hand
and proudly watch the mighty arc
adjust the range and make our mark
on stones or posts for rival men
to smell and not come back again

women are so circumspect
but men can piss to great effect
with terrible hydraulic force
can make a stream or change its course
can put out fires or cigarettes
and sometimes
laying down our bets
late at night outside the bars
we like to aim up at the stars.

DON MARTIN

ONE FINE DAY IN FLORENCE

CALVIN TRILLIN
Alice, Let's Eat

A man goes into a bakery and orders a German chocolate cake.

"I'm very particular," he tells the baker. "The cake must be in the shape of the letter *B*. Can you do that for me?"

"It won't be easy," the baker says. "I'll have to make it by hand and it will take three days. But I'm sure you'll be happy with it."

Three days later the man returns. But when he sees his cake, his face falls. "I'm sorry," he says. "It's not your fault, but I can't accept this cake. I guess I forgot to mention that it has to be in the shape of a lower-case *B*, rather than a capital *B*. I'll pay you anyway, but would you please try again?"

"It's your money," says the baker with a sigh. "It'll take another three days, but I want my customers to be happy."

Three days later the customer returns. "The cake looks wonderful," he says. "It's exactly what I wanted."

"Great," says the baker. "Let me put it in a box for you."

"That's all right," the man says. "I'll eat it here."

Now that it's fashionable to reveal intimate details of married life, I can state publicly that my wife, Alice, has a weird predilection for limiting our family to three meals a day. I also might as well admit that the most serious threat to our marriage came in 1975, when Alice mentioned my weight just as I was about to sit down to dinner at a New Orleans restaurant named Chez Helène. I hardly need add that Chez Helène is one of my favorite restaurants in New Orleans; we do not have the sort of marriage that could come to grief over ordinary food.

Without wanting to be legalistic, I should mention that Alice brought up the weight issue during a long-distance telephone call—breaking whatever federal regulations there are against Interstate Appetite Impairment. Like many people who travel a lot on business, I'm in the habit of calling home every evening to share the little victories and defeats of the day—the triumph, for instance, of happening upon a superior tamale stand in a town I thought had long before been completely carved into spheres of influence by McDonald's and Burger King, or the misery of being escorted by some local booster past the unmistakable aroma of genuine hickory-wood barbecuing into La Maison de la Casa House, whose notion of "continental cuisine" seems to have been derived in some arcane way from the Continental-Trailways bus company. Having found myself on business in New Orleans—or, as it is sometimes expressed around my office, having found it my business to find business in New Orleans—I was about to settle into Chez Helène for a long evening. First, of course, I telephoned Alice in New York. I assumed it would give her great pleasure to hear that her husband was about to have enough sweet potatoes and fried oysters to make him as happy as he could manage to be outside her presence. Scholars of the art have often mentioned Chez Helène as an example of what happens when Creole blends with Soul—so that a bowl of greens comes out tasting of spices that the average greens-maker in Georgia or Alabama probably associates with papists or the Devil himself.

"I'm about to have dinner at Chez Helène," I said.

"Dr. Seligmann just told me today that you weighed a hundred and eighty pounds when you were in his office last week," Alice said. "That's terrible!"

"There must be something wrong with this connection," I said. "I could swear I just told you that I was about to have dinner at Chez Helène."

"You're going to have to go on a diet. This is serious."

It occurred to me that a man telephoning his wife from a soul-food restaurant could, on the excuse of trying to provide some authentic

atmosphere, say something like "Watch yo' mouth, woman!" Instead, I said, "I think there might be a better time to talk about this, Alice." Toward the end of the second or third term of the Caroline Kennedy Administration was the sort of time I had in mind.

"Well, we can talk about it when you get home," Alice said. "Have a nice dinner."

I did. It is a measure of my devotion to Alice that I forgave her, even though my second order of fried chicken was ruined by the realization that I had forgotten to tell her I had actually weighed only a hundred and sixty-six pounds. I always allow fourteen pounds for clothes.

I must say that Alice tempers her rigidity on the meals-per-day issue by having a broad view of what constitutes an hors d'oeuvre. That is not, of course, her only strong point. She is tenacious, for instance—having persisted for five or six summers in attempting to wheedle the recipe for the seafood chowder served at Gladee's Canteen, in Hirtle's Beach, Nova Scotia, out of the management. She is imaginative—a person who can turn a bucketful of clams into, on successive evenings, steamed clams, clam fritters, clams in white wine sauce, and a sort of clam billi-bi. I can testify to her restraint: on the Christmas I presented her with a Cuisinart food processor, not having realized that what she really wanted was a briefcase, she thanked me politely, the way an exceedingly courteous person might thank a process server for a subpoena. ("Well," I finally said. "I thought it might be good for mulching the Christmas tree.") She is generous—the sort of wife who would share even the tiniest order of, say, crawfish bisque with her husband, particularly if he had tears in his eyes when he asked. Alice has a lot of nice qualities, but when someone tells me, as someone often does, how fortunate I am to have her as my wife, I generally say,

There was a young man of Calcutta
Who had a most terrible stutta,
He said: "Pass the h . . . ham
And the j . . . j . . . j . . . jam,
And the b . . . b . . . b . . . b . . .
**   b . . . b . . . butta."**

"Yes, she does have a broad view of what constitutes an hors d'oeuvre."

I don't mean that her views on this matter are as broad as the views held by our friend Fats Goldberg, the New York pizza baron and reformed blimp, who, in reporting on the semiannual eating binges in Kansas City he still allows himself, often begins sentences with phrases like "Then on the way to lunch I stopped at Kresge's for a chili dog." A Kresge chili dog, it seems to me, reflects a view of hors d'oeuvres that has strayed from broad to excessive. (It also reflects the fact that Fats Goldberg in binge gear will eat almost anything but green vegetables.) What I mean is that if we happen to be driving through Maine on our way to Nova Scotia, where we live in the summer, Alice does not object when, ten miles from the lobster restaurant where we plan to stop for dinner, I screech to a halt in front of a place that has the look of a spectacular fried-clam stand. "It'll make a nice hors d'oeuvre," she says.

While I'm speaking in Alice's defense, I should also say that I consider her failure with the children half my own: no one person could be responsible for engendering in two innocent little girls a preference for frozen fish sticks over fish. In fact, in Nova Scotia I have seen Alice take a halibut that was on a fishing boat an hour before, sprinkle it ever so slightly with some home-ground flour, fry it for a few seconds until it is covered with a batter whose lightness challenges the batter on a Gladee's fishball, cut it into sticklike slices, and present it to her very own little girls—only to have them pick at it for a few minutes and gaze longingly toward the freezer.

Oddly enough, both of our girls have shown, in quick, maddening flashes, indications of having been born with their taste buds intact. Once, while we were visiting my mother in Kansas City, Abigail, our older daughter, looked up at me during breakfast and said, "Daddy, how come in Kansas City the bagels just taste like round bread?" Her father's daughter, I allowed myself to hope—a connoisseur of bagels before she's five. By age nine she'll probably be able to identify any bialy she eats by borough of origin: she'll pick up some change after school working at Russ & Daughters Appetizer Store as a whitefish taster. On trips to Kansas City, her proud father's hometown, she'll appear as a child prodigy on the stage of the concert hall, lecturing on the varieties of the local barbecue sauce. Not so. At nine, offered anything that does not have the familiarity of white chicken or hamburger or Cheerios, she declines with a "No, thank you" painful in its elaborate politeness. This is the daughter who, at the age of four, reacted to a particularly satisfying dish of chocolate ice cream by saying, "My tongue is smiling." How quickly for parents do the disappointments come.

Abigail's younger sister, Sarah, has a palate so unadventurous that she refuses to mix peanut butter with jelly. I have often told her that I hope she chooses a college rather close to home—New York University, perhaps, which is in Greenwich Village, just a few blocks from where we live—so that when I show up every morning to cut the crusts off her toast I won't require a sleepover. For a couple of years, Sarah refused to enter a Chinese restaurant unless she was carrying a bagel in reserve. "Just in case," she often explained. More than once, Alice and Abigail and I, all having forgotten Sarah's special requirements, started to leave for a family dinner in Chinatown only to hear a small, insistent voice cry, "My bagel! My bagel!"

One night, in a Chinese restaurant, Sarah became a fancier of roast squab. We were at the Phoenix Gardens, a place in Chinatown that happens to have, in addition to excellent roast squab, a dish called Fried Fresh Milk with Crabmeat, which tastes considerably better than it sounds, and a shrimp dish that is one of the closest New York equivalents to the sort of shrimp served in some Italian restaurants in New Orleans. Just why Sarah would decide to taste roast squab still puzzles historians, since it is known that three months were required for Abigail, perhaps the only human being she completely trusts, to persuade her that chocolate ice cream was really something worth trying. Sarah herself has always treated her passion for a single exotic foodstuff as something that requires no explanation—like a mortgage officer who, being sober and cautious and responsible in every other way, sees nothing peculiar about practicing voodoo on alternate Thursdays. During lunch once in Nova Scotia, the subject of favorite foods was brought up by a friend of ours named Shelly Stevens, who is a year or two older than Abigail and is known among gourmets in Queens County mainly for being just about the only person anybody has ever heard of who eats banana peels as well as bananas. Sarah looked up from her peanut-butter sandwich—hold the jelly—and said, "Squab. Yes. Definitely squab."

It is not really Alice's fault that our girls are subject to bad influences. One morning, while I was preparing lunches for them to take to P. S. 3, I unwrapped some ham—some remarkably good Virginia ham that Alice had somehow managed to unearth in a store around the corner otherwise notable only for the number of hours each day the checkout counter clerk manages to spend doing her nails. Sarah said she didn't want any ham. It turned out that she had trouble eating a ham sandwich for lunch because a little girl with a name like Moira would always sit next to her and tell her how yucky ham was—Moira being a strict vegetarian, mung-bean and bean-sprout division.

"The people who warned us about sending our children to public school in New York were right," I said to Alice. "Now our daughter is being harassed by a mad-dog vegetarian."

Alice was opposed to my suggestion that Sarah attempt to place Moira under citizen's arrest. At the least, I thought Sarah should tell Moira that bean sprouts are the yuckiest food of all except for mung beans, and that carrot juice makes little girls pigeon-toed and bad at arithmetic. As it happens, health food does disagree with me. I tend to react to eating one of those salads with brown grass and chopped walnuts the way some people react to eating four or five fried Italian sausages. (I, on the other hand, react to eating four or five fried Italian sausages with a quiet smile.) Alice claims that what bothers me is not health food but the atmosphere of the health-food restaurants in our neighborhood—some of which seem modeled on the last days of a

LICENTIOUS LIMERICKS

The limerick packs laugh
    anatomical
Into space that is quite economical
  But the good ones we've seen
  So seldom are clean
And the clean ones so seldom are
    comical.

(These verses are all somewhat
    "blue"
And might be offensive to you
  So if you're in doubt
  You can just tear them out
Or not look—which is harder to
    do.)

A young violinist in Rio
Was seducing a lady named Cleo
  As she took down her panties
  She said, "No andantes;
I want this *allegro con brio.*"

There was a young lady of Exeter,
So pretty that men craned their
    necks at her,
  And one daring young knave
  Even ventured to wave
The distinguishing mark of his sex
    at her.

particularly unsuccessful commune. It's a neat theory, but it does not account for the time in Brunswick, Maine, when—during a festival whose atmosphere was absolutely splendid—I was fed something advertised as "whole foods for the multitudes" and immediately felt as if I had taken a very long journey in a very small boat. Fortunately, someone at the festival had mentioned hearing that a diner just outside of Brunswick served chili spicy enough to charbroil the tongue, and just a small cup of it turned out to be an antidote that had me feeling chipper enough to order some more. I had realized I was at the right diner even before I sat down: a sign on the door said, "When you're hungry and out of work, eat an environmentalist."

MORE LICENTIOUS LIMERICKS

There was a young fellow called
    Lancelot
Whom his neighbors all looked at
    askance a lot;
    For whenever he'd pass
    A delectable lass,
The front of his pants would
    advance a lot.

There was a young man from
    Australia,
Who painted his ass like a dahlia;
    The color was fine,
    The painting, divine,
But the aroma—ah, that was the
    falia.

A lady while dining at Crew,
Found an elephant's wang in her
    stew.
    Said the waiter, "Don't shout,
    Or wave it about,
Or the others will all want one
    too."

310   **MATTERS OF TASTE**

Norton drives up to the country to see his cousin the farmer.

As he pulls into the driveway, he is stunned to see a pig with what appears to be a wooden leg.

When his cousin comes out to greet him, Norton says, "Does that pig really have a wooden leg?"

"Let me explain," says the farmer. "That's Ed. He's probably the smartest pig in the whole county. Three years ago, he surprised us all by publishing a small book of poems. And for the past few months, he's been writing a financial column for our local paper."

"That's hard to believe," says Norton.

"Wait, there's more," says the farmer. "Why, just two weeks ago my little granddaughter was playing in the barn when the building caught fire. Old Ed broke out of his pen, ran into that barn, and dragged that little girl out. He actually saved her life."

"That's fantastic," says Norton. "I've never heard of a pig like this before. But I still don't understand: How did Ed end up with a wooden leg?"

The farmer laughs. "Well," he explains, "a pig like that you don't eat all at once."

Now and then—when Alice mentions, say, the nutritional value of brown rice—I have begun to worry that she might have fallen under the influence of the Natural Food Fanatics or the Balanced Diet Conspiracy. Once they learned of her fundamentalist views on Three Meals a Day, after all, they might have figured that they had a foot in the door. Could it be, I wonder in my most suspicious moments, that Moira's mother has been sneaking in for missionary work—waiting until I'm out of town, then clunking over in her leather sandals from her food co-op meeting to talk up the health-giving properties of organically grown figs? In calmer moments I admit to myself that Alice's awareness of, say, the unspeakable destruction wrought by refined sugar is probably just another example of knowledge she seems to have absorbed from no immediately ascertainable source. Occasionally, for instance, we have come home from a party and I have said, with my usual careful choice of words, "What was that funny-looking thing whatsername was wearing?" Then Alice—the serious academic who teaches college students to write and explains foreign movies to her husband, the mother of two who still refers to those rich ladies who swoop through midtown stores as "grownups"—tells me who designed the funny-looking thing and how much it probably cost and which tony boutique peddled it and why some people believe it to be chic. At such moments I am always stunned—as if I had idly wondered out loud about the meaning of some inscription on a ruin in Oaxaca and Alice had responded by translating fluently from the Toltec.

I admit that Moira's mother has never been spotted coming out of our house by a reliable witness. I admit that the girls do not show the vulnerability to Natural Food propaganda they might show if their own mother were part of the conspiracy. Sarah, in fact, once left a summer nursery program in Kansas City because the snacktime included salad. "They gave me salad!" she says to this day, in the tone a countess roughly handled by the customs man might say, "They searched my gown!"

All in all, I admit that Alice is, in her own way, a pretty good eater herself. The last time she failed to order dessert, for instance, was in the spring of 1965, in a Chinese restaurant that offered only canned kumquats. I have been with her in restaurants when she exulted over the purity and simplicity of the perfectly broiled fresh sea bass she had ordered, and then finished off the meal with the house specialty of toasted pound cake covered with ice cream and chocolate sauce. I suppose her only serious weakness as an eater—other than these seemingly uncontrollable attacks of moderation—is that she sometimes lets her mind wander between meals. I first began to notice this weakness when we were traveling in Italy just after we got married. ("It all shows up on the honeymoon," the wise heads used to say when the subject of marriage came up at LeRoy's Waldo Bar in Kansas City.) There we were in Italy, and Alice was devoting a good hour and a half right in the middle of the morning to inspecting a cathedral instead of helping me to comb the Michelin guide for the lunch spot most likely to stagger us with the perfection of its fettucine. I tried to explain to her that marriage is sharing—not merely sharing one's fettucine with one's husband if he is gazing at it adoringly and is obviously having second thoughts about having ordered the veal, but sharing the burden of finding the fettucine restaurant in the first place.

Since then, Alice has, as they say, grown in the marriage—and so, in another way, have I. Still, there are times when, in a foreign country, she will linger in a museum in front of some legendary piece of art as the morning grows late and I become haunted by the possibility that the restaurant I have chosen for lunch will run out of garlic sausage before we get there. "Alice!" I say on those occasions, in a stage whisper that sometimes fails to get her attention even though the museum guards turn to glare in my direction. "Alice! Alice, let's eat!"

A PLAY BY MICHAEL O'DONOGHUE

The Tip

(Hotel guest gives bellboy what appears to be a dollar bill.)

Bellboy: Thank you.

(Bellboy realizes that what he thought to be a one-dollar bill is actually a ten-dollar bill.)

Bellboy: THANK YOU!

(Bellboy realizes that he has again been in error and that what he thought was a ten-dollar bill is, in reality, a million-dollar bill.)

Bellboy:

Drawing by M. Stevens. © 1987 The New Yorker Magazine, Inc.

YOU!!!

(Curtain)

RUSSELL BAKER
Francs and Beans

As chance would have it, the very evening in 1975 Craig Claiborne ate his historic $4,000 dinner for two with thirty-one dishes and nine wines in Paris, a Lucullan repast for one was prepared and consumed in New York by this correspondent, no slouch himself when it comes to titillating the palate.

Mr. Claiborne won his meal in a television fund-raising auction and had it professionally prepared. Mine was created from spur-of-the-moment inspiration, necessitated when I discovered a note on the stove saying, "Am eating out with Dora and Imogene—make dinner for yourself." It was from the person who regularly does the cooking at my house and, though disconcerted at first, I quickly rose to the challenge.

The meal opened with a 1975 Diet Pepsi served in a disposable bottle. Although its bouquet was negligible, its distinct metallic aftertaste evoked memories of tin cans one had licked experimentally in the first flush of childhood's curiosity.

To create the balance of tastes so cherished by the epicurean palate, I followed with *a pâté de fruites de nuts of Georgia,* prepared according to my own recipe. A half-inch layer of creamy-style peanut butter is

314

troweled onto a graham cracker, then half a banana is crudely diced and pressed firmly into the peanut butter and cemented in place as it were by a second graham cracker.

The accompanying drink was cold milk served in a wide-brimmed jelly glass. This is essential to proper consumption of the pâté, since the entire confection must be dipped into the milk to soften it for eating. In making the presentation to the mouth, one must beware lest the milk-soaked portion of the sandwich fall onto the necktie. Thus, seasoned gourmandisers follow the old maxim of the Breton chefs and "bring the mouth to the jelly glass."

At this point in the meal, the stomach was ready for serious eating, and I prepared beans with bacon grease, a dish I perfected in 1937 while developing my *cuisine du depression.*

The dish is started by placing a pan over a very high flame until it becomes dangerously hot. A can of Heinz's pork and beans is then emptied into the pan and allowed to char until it reaches the consistency of hardening concrete. Three strips of bacon are fried to crisps, and when the beans have formed huge dense clots firmly welded to the pan, the bacon grease is poured in and stirred vigorously with a large screwdriver.

This not only adds flavor but also loosens some of the beans from the side of the pan. Leaving the flame high, I stirred in a three-day-old spaghetti sauce found in the refrigerator, added a sprinkle of chili powder, a large dollop of Major Grey's chutney and a tablespoon of bicarbonate of soda to make the whole dish rise.

Beans with bacon grease is always eaten from the pan with a tablespoon while standing over the kitchen sink. The pan must be thrown away immediately. The correct drink with this dish is a straight shot of room-temperature gin. I had a Gilbey's 1975, which was superb.

For the meat course, I had fried bologna *à la Nutley, Nouveau Jersey.* Six slices of A & P bologna were placed in an ungreased frying pan over maximum heat and held down by a long fork until the entire house filled with smoke. The bologna was turned, fried the same length of time on the other side, then served on air-filled white bread with thick lashings of mayonnaise.

The correct drink for fried bologna *à la Nutley, Nouveau Jersey* is a 1927 Nehi Cola, but since my cellar, alas, had none, I had to make do with a second shot of Gilbey's 1975.

The cheese course was deliciously simple—a single slice of Kraft's individually wrapped yellow sandwich cheese, which was flavored by vigorous rubbing over the bottom of the frying pan to soak up the rich bologna juices. Wine being absolutely *de rigueur* with cheese, I chose a 1974 Muscatel, flavored with a maraschino cherry, and afterwards cleared my palate with three pickled martini onions.

It was time for the fruit. I chose a Del Monte tinned pear, which, regrettably, slipped from the spoon and fell on the floor, necessitating its being blotted with a paper towel to remove cat hairs. To compensate for the resulting loss of pear syrup, I dipped it lightly in hot dog relish which created a unique flavor.

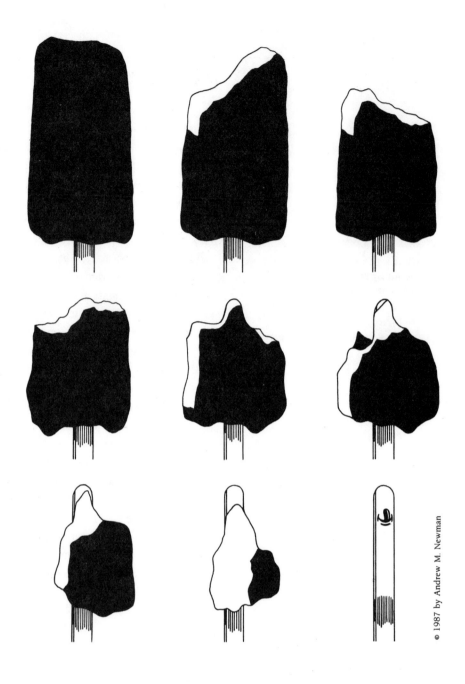

© 1987 by Andrew M. Newman

With the pear I drank two shots of Gilbey's 1975 and one shot of Wolfschmidt vodka (nonvintage), the Gilbey's having been exhausted.

At last it was time for the dish the entire meal had been building toward—dessert. With a paring knife, I ripped into a fresh package of Oreos, produced a bowl of My-T-Fine chocolate pudding which had been coagulating in the refrigerator for days and, using a potato masher, crushed a dozen Oreos into the pudding. It was immense.

Between mouthfuls, I sipped a tall, bubbling tumbler of cool Bromo-Seltzer, and finished with six ounces of Maalox. It couldn't have been better.

MEL BROOKS & CARL REINER
Two Thousand Year Old Man

Sir, could you give us the secret of your longevity?

Well, the major thing is that I never ever touched fried food. I don't eat it, I wouldn't look at it, and I don't touch it. And I never run for a bus. There'll always be another. Even if you're late for work, you know, I never run for a bus. I never ran, I just strolled, jaunty-jolly, walking to the bus stop.

Well, there were no buses in the time of . . .

No, in my time . . .

What was the means of transportation then?

Mostly fear.

Fear transported you?

Fear, yes. You would see . . . an animal would growl, you'd go two miles in a minute. Fear would be the main propulsion.

I think most people are interested in living a long and fruitful life, as you have.

Yes. Fruit is good, too, you mentioned fruit. Yeah. Fruit kept me going for a hundred and forty years once when I was on a very strict diet. Mainly nectarines. I love that fruit. It's half a peach, half a plum, it's a hell of a fruit. I love it! Not too cold, not too hot, you know, just nice. Even a rotten one is good. That's how much I love them. I'd rather eat a rotten nectarine than a fine plum. What do you think of that? That's how much I love them.

A gourmet restaurant in Cincinnati is one where you leave the tray on the table after you eat.

—Anon.

P. J. O'ROURKE

An Intellectual Experiment

Recently I performed an intellectual experiment. I read one issue of the *New York Review of Books* (Vol. XXXI, No. 7, April 26, 1984), then watched one evening of prime-time network television (Monday, April 23, 1984, 7:30–10:00 P.M.). The comparison would, I hoped, give some clue to an ancient puzzle: Which is worse, smart or stupid?

The experiment seemed fair. The *New York Review of Books* is undeniably intelligent, and television is famously thick-headed. I'm impartial. I'm bright about some things. I don't watch television or read the *New York Review*. About other things, I'm rather dim.

RAW DATA

I began reading the *New York Review* at 3:00 in the afternoon. The lead article was by Harold Bloom, Sterling Professor of the Humanities at Yale. It was a review of *Walt Whitman: The Making of the Poet* by Paul Zweig, though that book was hardly mentioned. Mr. Bloom took some five thousand words to say Walt Whitman is a very, very important poet who masturbated a lot.

The piece had many phrases like ". . . the true difficulties of reading Whitman begin (or ought to begin) with his unnervingly original psychic cartography," and contained such Whitman quotes as:

> O great star disappear'd—
> O the black murk that hides the star!
> O cruel hands that hold me powerless—
> O helpless soul of me!

Mr. Bloom said, "Only an elite can read Whitman." This may be why I always thought the poet was a self-obsessed ratchet-jaw with an ear like a tin cookie sheet. "How," asked Bloom, "did someone of Whitman's extraordinarily idiosyncratic nature become so absolutely central to nearly all subsequent American literary high culture?" Beats me.

There were eleven other articles in this issue of the *New York Review* and one poem. Some of the articles deserve brief summaries:

Neal Ascherson reviewed *A Warsaw Diary, 1978–1981* by Kazimierz Brandys and *The First Polka* by Horst Bienek. Mr. Brandys was a communist but got over it. After twenty years in the Polish Communist Party he decided that communism, at least when it has Russians in it, is not a good idea. Nonetheless the Solidarity movement caught him by surprise. Now he lives in New York and writes books about being confused.

The First Polka is a novel about life in Upper Silesia. Upper Silesians were troubled because they couldn't decide if they were Polish or German. Then came World War II.

Gabriele Annan reviewed *Colette* by Joanna Richardson and *The Collected Stories of Colette* edited by Robert Phelps. I gather Colette used language beautifully but didn't have anything to say. Ms. Annan had a great deal to say (one hundred column inches). *The Collected Stories of Colette* includes all the dirty stuff but leaves out *Gigi*.

Milan Kundera contributed an essay titled "The Tragedy of Central Europe." Mr. Kundera, who used to live in Central Europe, thinks the little countries there are swell. At least, they were swell before communism with Russians in it. If somebody doesn't get the Russians out of Central Europe (and/or communism) the culture in these countries is going to disappear. Culture is a hard thing to define, said Mr. Kundera, and it seems to be disappearing everyplace else, too.

Gerald Weales reviewed *All Faithful People: Change and Continuity in*

Middletown's Religion (a group effort). From 1976 to 1981 a group of social scientists studied Muncie, Indiana. Muncie is the "Middletown" where Robert and Helen Lynd did their pioneering sociology work in 1929. Despite oodles of staff, piles of money, help from computers, and time to spare, contemporary sociologists are not doing as good a job as the Lynds. Mr. Weals said *All Faithful People* should be taken with a grain of salt (and some lime and some tequila, suggests this writer).

Some of the articles do not deserve brief summaries:

The Wandering Jew by Stefan Heym was reviewed by D. J. Enright. It sounded like an interesting novel, but by the time I'd finished reading Mr. Enright's exhaustive praise, I was too bored to even consider buying the thing. Michael Wood reviewed two books about Alfred Hitchcock and proved that some people are unable to experience even the slightest of life's pleasures without being thrown into frenzies of analysis. And Howard Moss's critique of the Martha Graham Dance Company's performances at Lincoln Center was a powerful argument that people who like dancing should shut up and dance.

One article I could not comprehend. Charles Rosen reviewed Julian Rushton's *The Musical Language of Berlioz*. When writing contains such asides as "This is how Schönberg is able to reconstruct the effect of dissonance and consonance rhythmically within a nontonal system," I am out of my depth. However, I gathered Mr. Rosen's thesis was that Berlioz's music either stinks or it doesn't.

One other article I could comprehend too well. It was called "Reagan's Star Wars" and in it nine experts from the Union of Concerned Scientists argued that a space-based missile defense system would be expensive as all get out, would make the Russians hopping mad, and wouldn't save us from getting blown up anyway. The experts presented a great number of facts and figures and many long passages of thoughtfulness to support their arguments. But it seemed to me that by using common sense and inductive reasoning based on the history of defensive weapons the same arguments could have been made in two hundred words.

The poem, by Patricia Storance, was called "Illegitimacy." It did not rhyme. The text implied illegitimacy is an uncomfortable state.

Among all this intelligence there were a couple things of interest. Irvin Ehrenpreis reviewed the forty-eight volume Yale Edition of *Horace Walpole's Correspondence* edited by W. S. Lewis. Walpole, fourth Earl of Oxford, was a creature of the Enlightenment and a vivid and hilarious letter writer who roundly damned the world about him. Mr. Ehrenpreis called it a "style of ironic recoil" and quoted liberally. Ehrenpreis did not, however, address some important questions. What manner of man makes his living by editing forty-eight volumes of somebody else's bread-and-butter notes? Who, at a cost of $2,700, buys a set of books like this? Where do they put them? Did Mr. Ehrenpreis really read them all? And how did he find the time?

Robert O. Paxton's review of Don Clark's de Gaulle biography was also worthwhile. Mr. Paxton argued that de Gaulle had a perceptive and

MORE LICENTIOUS LIMERICKS

There was a young lady named
    Alice
Who peed in a Catholic chalice.
    She said, "I do this
    From a great need to piss,
And not from sectarian malice."

There was an old Bey of Calcutta
Who greased up his asshole with
    butter.
    Instead of the roar
    Which came there before
Came a soft, oleaginous mutter.

There was a young lady of
    Wheeling
Who professed to lack sexual
    feeling
    'Til a cynic named Boris
    Just touched her clitoris
And she had to be scraped off the
    ceiling.

A mathematician named Hall
Has a hexahedronical ball.
    And the cube of its weight
    Times his pecker, plus eight,
Is his phone number—give him a
    call.

PANDERING TO INTELLECTUALS

pragmatic vision of world politics and that his behavior during the sixties was not inspired by anti-Americanism or egocentricity. Instead, said Paxton, de Gaulle was very sensibly putting distance between France and the American penchant for turning every CARE package and UN vote into A Great Crusade.

It took about three hours to read the *New York Review of Books*. I lay down for a while with a cold compress on my forehead and then began watching television.

Seven-thirty is the official beginning of "prime time." I had a choice of *Entertainment Tonight* on ABC, *Wheel of Fortune* on CBS, or *Family Feud* on NBC. *Entertainment Tonight* seemed to be the name of the thing I was looking for rather than the thing itself. *Wheel of Fortune* sounded a little *too* stupid. I chose *Family Feud*. It turned out to be a fascinating show. Two perfectly normal American families dressed in go-to-church/second marriage/get-a-bank-loan clothes were pitted against each other. They were asked questions but instead of answering them they had to predict the answers that a hundred other perfectly average Americans gave. "Know thyself," said the ancient Greeks. "Know thy neighbor," say the more practical Americans.

The first question was "Name the most time-saving invention." "Washing machine" was the winning answer, and a good one too. Clean clothes are the hallmark of civilization. But "microwave" came in second. Ugh. Delicious food is the other hallmark of civilization. "Car" and "airplane" ranked only third and fourth—possibly an indication of latent provincialism. "Dishwasher" followed in fifth place and "telephone" in sixth. It's a sign of American folk wisdom, this ambiguous attitude toward the telephone. There aren't many Horace Walpoles in this generation.

I could have pondered all this for hours—minutes, anyway—but another question was already posed. "What should athletes *not* do when in training?" "Smoke cigarettes" came in first, reasonably enough. But down the list in fifth place was "have sex," which doesn't hurt athletes a bit. Was this some recrudescent puritanism seeking a fitness-era excuse for itself? Unfortunately at this point I was interrupted by that dubiously time-saving device the telephone. (I suppose I should get a VCR, but the only thing I like about television is its ephemerality.) I was forced to give *Family Feud* only partial attention but did glean that 35 percent of Americans consider pink the most popular nightgown color. By the time my caller hung up, the contestants were playing a word game ("Things used for transportation in the city: . . . bus . . . feet . . .") interrupted by a farty buzzer sound. This was of no interest. But it was disturbing to see American quiz-show contestants applaud themselves when they won. What happened to humble disclaimers and mumbled thanks to third-grade teachers? By the way, does anyone blush anymore?

At 8:00 I had to choose among CBS's *Scarecrow and Mrs. King,* which I feared might be about Stephen King's mother, ABC's *That's Incredible,* which I was sure wouldn't be, and NBC's *TV's Bloopers and Practical Jokes.* This seemed too horrid to pass up, and it was. The hosts were Dick Clark. *American Bandstand*'s master of ceremonies during this century's worst period of popular music, and Ed McMahon, who has some ill-defined role on *The Tonight Show.* They talked to each other a good deal. I believe some of the time they were making jokes.

The "bloopers" were outtakes from television shows where actors and actresses made mistakes. Some mistakes were amusing. An actress named Deidre Hall had a prolonged struggle with syllable #3 in "infinitesimally." The point seemed to be that the famous make mistakes just like the rest of us. The "practical jokes" were all played on well-known people (at least the show claimed they were well known). I was perplexed. The beauty of a practical joke is vengeance. What reason was there to wreak vengeance on these supposed celebrities? Has fame replaced wealth as a criterion of class division? Is being unknown the modern equivalent of being oppressed? Are fameless people therefore justified in rising up against the better-publicized?

One practical joke, however, was telling. Some actress I'd never heard of was escorted into a "butcher shop" to buy steaks for a barbecue. The butcher brought out a live cow, showed the actress where the steaks would be sliced out, then led the cow into a back room. A shot was heard, followed by the sound of a meat saw. The

---

This guy was a terrible burglar. He didn't even take our TV. He just took our remote control. Now he drives by every once in a while and changes channels on us.
—Brian Kiley

actress was horrified and the audience convulsed. How far we've come from our agrarian heritage.

The rest of the show was simply junk, mostly in the form of old television commercials shown for their alleged amusement value. Another, particularly idiotic segment had the nighttime collegiate-humor-show host David Letterman tour an inventors' convention and sneer at people. A Mexican man had created a device to detect signs of life in a casket. Mr. Letterman and the audience thought this hilarious. It may not be such a good joke in a country with poor medical care and no embalming. A black woman had developed a heated chair cushion to keep people warm in chilly homes. Letterman thought this, too, was risible. I'm glad his home is so well heated. I've used a similar item in duck blinds and found it a godsend. The audience laughed whenever foreigners were on the screen. A number of the inventors were Oriental and the audience seemed to find that extremely funny. I hope the audience finds waiting in unemployment lines as amusing.

TV's Bloopers and Practical Jokes lasted an hour—remarkable content mileage. Incidentally, whenever any of the befuddled victims said, "Oh, my God," "God" was bleeped out.

At 9:00 NBC and ABC were showing movies, so I watched something on CBS called *Kate and Allie*. As best I could figure, the situation in this situation comedy is that Kate and Allie are two divorced women who've set up house together with one in the role of housewife and the other as breadwinner. There are a number of children. The atmosphere is faintly homoerotic but with references to dating men. In the episode I saw, the breadwinner (I couldn't determine which was Kate and which was Allie) lost her job and the housewife began making money by baking cakes at home. In the end, as per a long-established rule of situation comedy, everything returned to *status quo ante*. The message seemed to be that housewifery and job-holding have equally valid rewards. And some people hate to clean house, and some people hate to have jobs. People should do what they like best, within reason—a fair-minded thesis and utopian in a friendly, middle-class American way.

The movies were still on at 9:30, so I watched CBS's *Bob Newhart Show*. This also dealt with woman's place in society. The character played by Mr. Newhart has moved to a small town in Vermont. The people there are very backward. At a potluck supper all the men ate in the dining room while the women ate in the kitchen. The wife of Mr. Newhart's character took umbrage at this and convinced the women to rebel and eat their potluck in the dining room. They did so but ended up at a separate table away from the men.

I've lived in northern New England for years and have never seen such behavior. But maybe this is what potluck suppers are like in Los Angeles, where situation-comedy writers live.

To be fair, I suppose I should have watched one more half hour of television. But after careful, objective consideration of the evidence, gathered thus far, I decided: Screw it.

ANALYSIS

In the two lists below I have attempted to summarize the information gathered from one issue of the *New York Review of Books* and one evening of network television.

Information from *New York Review*	Information from Network Television
1. Walt Whitman is an important poet.	1. Washing machines save more time than jet planes or telephones.
2. He masturbated a lot.	2. Athletes shouldn't smoke cigarettes.
3. He was a hard guy to figure.	3. Maybe they shouldn't have sex either.
4. Communism is bad when Russians have anything to do with it.	4. Pink is a popular color for nightgowns.
5. Upper Silesians couldn't decide if they were Polish or German, then most of them died.	5. Americans do not blush to congratulate themselves.
6. War is bad.	6. Dick Clark and Ed McMahon are entertaining.
7. Colette's French was good.	7. Actors are human.
8. Colette was a self-obsessed ratchet-jaw.	8. It's fun to trick others.
9. The Farrar, Straus and Giroux edition of *The Collected Stories of Colette* doesn't have *Gigi* in it.	9. Meat comes from dead animals.
10. Central Europe's culture is disappearing.	10. Old television commercials are silly.
11. Russians are bad.	11. We're more sophisticated than we used to be.
12. Everybody's culture is disappearing.	12. Foreigners are funny.
13. Sociology isn't what it used to be.	13. Orientals are particularly funny.
14. Stefan Heym has written a novel of genius but it's complicated.	14. David Letterman is funny too.
15. Alfred Hitchcock was a hard guy to figure.	15. You can't say "God" on television unless you mean it.
16. The Martha Graham Dance Company isn't what it used to be.	16. Traditional male and female social roles are both rewarding.
17. The Martha Graham Dance Company's costumes are too la-di-da.	17. A little lesbianism is cute as long as you date men.
18. Berlioz's music either stinks or it doesn't.	18. People should do what they like best, within reason.
19. A space-based missile defense system will be expensive.	19. Men and women should be equal.
20. It will make the Russians mad.	20. Small-town folks are behind the times.
21. It won't work.	21. Some things never change.
22. Atomic war is very bad.	

CHARLES McGRATH & DANIEL MENAKER
Is There No End to PBS Culture?

[The following is a glimpse of the new British television series "The Saga of Culture," soon to be aired on our own Public Broadcasting System, with an introduction for American audiences by Joe Garagiola.]

INTRODUCTION

Joe: Hey there, I'll bet there's a lot of things you don't know. There were sure a lot of things I didn't know until I met Sir Arbiter Soup, Kenelm Digby Professor of Physics and Lapinology at Magdalen College, Oxford, and a heck of a nice guy. For the next 13 weeks, Sir A is going to talk to us about what's been going on around here for the last 5000 years. We call it *(cut to titles; Purcell's "Trumpet Voluntary" in background)—The Saga of Culture.*

EPISODE 1

Sir Arbiter (sitting before a fire and stroking a cat; dressed in a blazer, cricket whites and boater): Where did it all begin? How did we get where we are? *(Pauses, takes out pipe, lights it.)* Where do we go from here? *(Fetches decanter, pours sherry, sniffs, sips, drains glass, banks fire and puts out cat.)* Does a flush beat a straight? *(Refill on sherry.)* Not easy questions. One might almost say hard questions—perhaps even stumpers. But if you will share these evenings with me, perhaps together we can stumble upon some answers, or at least pick up a couple of bimbos. *(Another refill; lets cat back in.)* In this first hour we shall be, as it were, skipping hither and yon, establishing the general lines of our inquiry. We call this hour *(strains of "There's No Business Like Show Business" in background)* "The Dogs of Change."

(Dissolve on Sir A, swigging from decanter, and cut to him sitting in a shopping cart in the parking lot of the Food Fair in Yaphank, Long Island.)

Sir A: Some say that our long climb out of the primordial soup may have begun here *(stretches arms wide; Mantovani can be heard, faintly)* in the Olduvai Gorge . . . *(Looks around, takes nervous pull from hip flask. Cut to Olduvai Gorge.)* Here in the Olduvai Gorge. Some say that the climb began elsewhere, possibly in Jersey City. Whatever. In any event, five years ago Dr. Louis Leakey unearthed here a pocket comb and the keys to a 1917 Hispano-Suiza. *(Close-up of comb and keys,* back-lit.) From this the chap deduced that Australopithecus may well have been the first to comb his car. Poppycock! What matters most to the Saga of Culture, don't you see, is the change from the nomadic life to a fixed agrarian society . . .

(Cut to farm in Somerset, England; Sir A, wearing bib overalls, feeding slops to swine.)

Sir A: I'm here at the farm of Thomas Shandy, which to my mind represents the culmination, the apogee, the peak, if you will—or even if you won't—of English bucolic life. (*Puts down slop bucket, takes long swig from hip flask, saunters over to where Farmer Tom is pitching hay.*) The English yeoman farmer, like all his brethren since the time of the metamorphosis of man the hunter (*Homa venator*, in the Latin) to man the cultivator (*Homo agricola*), draws sustenance and wisdom from his native ground (*terra naturalis*). From the roots, herbs and kohlrabi he gathers . . .

Farmer Tom (*shouldering Sir A aside and peering into the camera*): Is this for the telly, then? Are you here for the UFOs? Poor Alf, they carried him off last night. All yellow and pink they was, with a tuft of hair growing out the back. I says to the missus, I says, "It's petrol they're after. They use it to make their beer. They suck it up with long hoses, see . . ." (*Large hook appears camera left, moves horizontally, engages Farmer Tom by the neck, and drags him off.*)

Sir A: Quite. (*Takes nervous pull from flask; weaves uncertainly toward farmhouse, camera right; bends over, snatches up a chicken and tucks it under his arm.*)

(Cut to Jeu de Paume museum, in Paris, and Sir A, wearing beret and artist's smock, standing in front of Manet's "Le Déjeuner sur L'Herbe.")

Sir A: Over the centuries, artists have been fascinated with the pastoral ideal. Edouard Manet took this theme and, in this famous painting, transformed it into a nice piece of cheesecake. The very first thing we notice about this masterpiece is that it is vaguely rectangular in shape and, *mirabile dictu!*, suspended from a wall. How convenient, for if it lay upon the floor we should have to crane. Note here the fruitful volumes, the irregular—one might almost say jaunty—disposition of the figures, the dynamic interplay of light and shadow, the volumetric modeling of the pectoral areas. Note, finally, the expression of the woman in the right foreground. Who is this woman who regards us with such bemusement? What does her half smile suggest about the level of dentistry in the late 19th century? What, finally, is she saying to us today? "Will you still respect me in the morning?" Or is her expression as unreadable as the blank enigma that confronts us here . . .

(Cut to Easter Island and Sir A, wearing Bermuda shorts and flowered sport shirt, standing beside one of the heads. "Also Sprach Zarathustra" thunders in background.)

Farmer Brown buys twelve pigs at an auction, only to discover that they are all female. He immediately calls Farmer Jones to ask if he can bring them over to mate with Farmer Jones's male pigs.

"Sure," says Farmer Jones.

Farmer Brown gathers his twelve pigs and loads them into the truck. When they get to the Jones farm, the pigs jump out and spend the rest of the day mating with the males. Before he leaves, Farmer Brown says, "By the way, I've never had pigs before. How will I know if they're pregnant?"

"Well," says Farmer Jones, "look for signs of unusual behavior. That's usually how you know."

The next morning, Farmer Brown looks out his window and sees nothing unusual. So he loads the pigs up and brings them to the Jones farm again.

The following morning, the pigs are still behaving normally, so once again he takes them to the Jones farm.

The next morning he feels too discouraged to look out the window. "Honey," he says to his wife, "would you mind telling me if our pigs are doing anything unusual?"

"Well," she says, "eleven of them are in the back of the truck, and the twelfth one's honking the horn."

Sir A (*shouting*): The meaning of these great stone heads has puzzled generations of archaeologists and telephone repairmen, and theories of their origin are as numerous as wogs in the Punjab. Professor Schliemann, who never saw them at all, held that they were weathercocks. Levi-Strauss has argued that they are early, somewhat oversized examples of dashboard statuary. And Leakey thinks they are all that remain of the South Pacific Professional Bowlers' Hall of Fame. Whatever the case may be, we can say one thing with certainty: they have no arms or legs!

(*Cut to blast furnace in a steel mill in Scranton, Pa.; Sir A, wearing helmet and goggles, holding a can of beer. Nearby, a steelworker, stripped to the waist, opens grate and stokes roaring flames.*)

Sir A: It was here in the West—though not notably in the indolent Mediterranean areas—that man, through the machine, began to tame his environment. Steel mills like this one provide some of the essential materials for such wonders of technology as the Saturn rocket, the cyclotron, and the Kitchen Magician, which chops, slices, dices, peels, shreds, mashes, hashes and juliennes. And for a limited time only, for $3.59 ($4.59 for stereo tapes) extra, includes an album you cannot buy in any record store—"100 Great Songs of the Korean Conflict Sung by Rosemary Clooney and Vic Damone."

(*Cut to Sir A, again sitting before fire in smoking jacket, sipping sherry, stroking cat*).

Sir A: There you have it, then. A preliminary, panoptic look at some of the subjects we shall be investigating in detail over the next twelve Tuesday evenings. (*He rises, sways unsteadily and sits down.*) I hope you can join me here next week for an episode we call (*"Trumpet Voluntary" wells in background*) "Problem Dandruff and the Waning of the Middle Ages."

EPILOGUE

Joe: Pretty interesting, huh? If you liked that, you'll want to stay tuned. In just a few minutes Anthony Hopkins will interview Alistair Cooke about why there's always an Oriental-rug backdrop for BBC interviews. In the meantime, this is Pledge Week . . .

No matter when I look, all I ever see on PBS is one of four shows: (1) Insects making love. (2) A lion walking along with a dead antelope in its jaws. (3) Some spiffily dressed, elderly Englishman sitting in a tall-backed chair in a room that is paneled in dark wood. (4) A station announcer talking about what great shows they have and urging us to send more money.
—Mike Royko

Detroit is Cleveland without the glitter.   —*Anon.*

GERALD SUSSMAN

Not Quite TV Guide

Sunday
MORNING

5 AM **8** FEED THE PIGS
9 START THE SOUP
11 RELIGIOUS FANATIC HOUR
21 STOREFRONT GOD
5:30 **4** JESUS & CO—Cartoon
7 BREAKFAST WITH THE PROPHETS
6 AM **2** FELIX THE PRIEST—Clerical Cartoon
5 MOVIE—Adventure
"Assault on Bloomingdale's." (1982) Communist-dominated Latin-American team tries to capture Bloomingdale's department store in New York City and hold all its customers and staff hostage. Fernando Rey, Henry Silva, Jay Silverheels, Rita Moreno. (4 hrs.)
7 AM **2** CAPTAIN KOALA—Children
A visit to a whiskey distillery in Kentucky.
7 LOU GRANT'S TOMB
12 HAVE COFFEE WITH CHRIST
8 AM **2** BLACK WONDER WOMAN
6 POPEYE, WOODY WOODPECKER, AND THE HOLY GHOST—Religious Cartoon
ERN RABBI JOSH MEETS FATHER BOB
JON MEDICINE BALL CHAMPIONSHIPS
Live, from Boca Raton, Fla.
CDN EARLY MORNING FATIGUE
9 AM **5** ZOO POLICE IN ACTION
9 N.Y. TIMES REPORT
Ex-New York City Mayor John Lindsay reads the entire Sunday edition of the *New York Times.*
11 PENIS BOY—Cartoon
10 AM **7** DISCO CHURCH
11 AM **7** FIRST NOVELS
Aspiring novelists read from their works.
CDN TOOTH DECAY CHARTS
SOB MOVIE—Fantasy-Adventure
"Island of Lost Keys." (1978) Scientist with enormous magnet attracts people's housekeys to his island, leaving thousands locked out of their homes. Burt Lancaster, Rhonda Fleming, Gladys Knight. (8 hrs.)
ERN PROTESTANTS, CATHOLICS, AND JEWS, BUT NO MOSLEMS
11:30 **BLT** SOFT CHEESES
Noon **2** LITTLE PEOPLE TRY TO BE HEARD
ECN INCREDIBLY GREAT PERFORMANCES
Leonard Bernstein leads the New York Philharmonic, the Boston Symphony, and the Philadelphia Orchestra in Beethoven's Fifth, Seventh, and Ninth symphonies simultaneously.
1 PM **8** WASHINGTON BULLSHIT
11 INCREDIBLE BULK
1:30 **7** MOVIE—Adventure
"Captain Swashbuckle." (1938) Captain Swashbuckle (Humphrey Bogart) preys the seven seas in search of voluptuous women with low-cut blouses and flaring skirts. With Maria Montez, Barbara Stanwyck, Andy Devine, Eddie ("Rochester") Anderson. (6 hrs.)
11 WALL STREET FAILURES

42 ADVENTURES OF BLACK BEAUTY—Lena Horne
2 PM **5** GOLF
The Glenfiddich Classic from Aberdeen, Scotland. Alcoholic champions compete for $3,000,000 worth of single malt whiskey.
8 BOXING
World Fruitweight, Micro-Weight, Bantam-Cock Weight, and Bruiser-Weight Championships, officially commissioned by the WBA, WPA, AFL, CIO, and CIA Boxing Commissions. Alfredo Bonito vs. Benny Barbone; Sugar Bob Johnson vs. Hector Spector; Cornelius Castaneda vs. Gabriel Garcia Marquez.
CDN INCURABLE SYPHLIS CASES
3 PM **5** WORLD WIDE WORLD OF WEIRD SPORTS
Lippizaner scallions from Vienna; hunting for wild veal in Montana; hair-pulling competitions from a girls' boarding school in New Zealand.
11 MOVIE—Suspense Drama
"The Man from Somewhere." (1976) Mysterious man materializes from somewhere and makes everyone in small midwestern town very nervous. Meryl Streep, Lionel Stander, Terry Moore. (5 hrs.)
HMS PRINCE CHARLES'S PERSONAL LIFE
His morning toilette, the choosing of the day's wardrobe, his favorite morning cartoons.
BLT TREATING WOK COOKING INJURIES
3:30 **7** AMERICAN SPORTY MEN
Former President Richard Nixon and wife, Pat, poach wild stag on the estate of King Juan Carlos of Spain; Burt Reynolds searches for his brother in the Canadian Rockies; Paul Newman breaks world land-speed record for a car—6,000 miles an hour.
4 PM **78** BULGARIAN SHOE FESTIVAL
HPN OUT ON A LIMB
Panel discussion: "Artificial arms or hand hooks, which is better?"
4:30 **4** AUTO BODY AND FENDER RACING
From Fort Lauderdale, Fla.
5 PM **12** PROPAGANDA REPORT FROM INDIA
13 HARMONY AND NEEDLEPOINT
Music and sewing for the hard of hearing.
21 MUCHACHAS, MUCHACHAS, MUCHACHAS
78 LITTLE CRIMINALS
Missing house pet roundup.
SOB WARM ICE CAPADES
Daredevil skaters on warm, slightly melted ice. Featuring the Flying Albinos, Smokey the Whitefish, and Arlene Dahl.
6 PM **2** CATCH-UP NEWS
4 OPEN WOUND
Paramedic show.
7 MOVIE—Musical
"Grease 3." (1984) Same cast as "Grease

Sunday

EVENING

2," now in college, getting more liberated and almost going all the way. (6 hrs.)

⑬ REGGIE JACKSON MAKES FUDGE

㉑ CITIZENS' ARRESTS

ⓔⓢⓟ SOMETHING'S GOING ON

6:30 ⑫ FOREIGNERS SPEAK OUT

7 PM ② 120 MINUTES

④ VOYAGE TO THE END OF YOUR NOSE

Children's science fantasy show about everyday things we take for granted. Alastair Cooke and Mamie Van Doren.

⑦ EATING ALONE

⑨ ADOLF HITLER: HIS INFANCY—Documentary

Part I of the new documentary series, with many baby pictures, never seen before.

8 PM ② SMILE PRECINCT—Drama

Storefront dentists fight crime and tooth decay in a slum neighborhood. Tonight: An ex-con goes berserk and steals a high-speed drill. Stars: David Soul, Susan St. James, Flip Wilson. Guest stars: Albert Finney and Henny Youngman.

④ SHASHLIK AND JAMIE—Adventure-Drama

Ivan Shashlik is a Russian double agent also working for the CIA, who is hired as a butler by a mysterious twelve-year-old international financier, code-named "Jamie." Jamie also has a sexy, full-grown mistress named Fiona. Together, they wipe out the world of international crime. Shashlik: Chad Everett. Jamie: Charles Nelson Reilly. Fiona: Catherine Deneuve.

⑦ THORNS IN MY SIDE—Comedy

Fred Thorn is a widower with fourteen rambunctious children, nine of whom possess ESP and telekinetic powers. The other five are a concert cellist, a consumer's rights advocate, a filmmaker, a laundromat owner, and a vampire. Fred: Gary Crosby.

㉑ BANCO POPULAR

9 PM ② THE WASHINGTONS

When Tom's long-lost Uncle Zack from Australia shows up claiming he is a millionaire, everyone gives him a blow-job. Tom: Berry Gordy. Pam: Pearl Bailey. Uncle Zack: Marvin Gaye.

④ POCKY AND PIZZAFACE

Pocky (Tracy Nelson) and Pizzaface (John Stamos) are a pair of outcast teenagers with terrible skin problems. But they have each other and a pet rhino who protects them from bullies. Tonight: Pocky and Pizzaface send off for a mail-order skin cream that nearly kills them.

⑦ I NEED ALL I CAN GET

⑬ HUNGARIAN HEEL CLICKING

ⓂⓉⓂ INSIDE DAVID BOWIE'S

close up

10 PM ⑧

THE THORNBERGS

Rosamund Pike's epic 5,000-page best-selling novel finally comes to the screen in this 39-week maxi–mini-series. The story of Israel Thornberg, an Australian-Jewish sheepherder, rabbi, and patriarch, and his long, forbidden love with Rebecca, his blue-ribbon sheep, has already captured the hearts of millions. Set against a background of raging family conflicts, uncontrollable lust and the vicious, cutthroat competition of the garment industry in Sydney, *The Thornbergs* has all the necessary ingredients for a very special Special.

Lord Olivier plays Israel Thornberg, torn between his love of Rebecca and the beckoning wiles of Goola (Victoria Principal), the aborigine who sets her eyes and the rest of her body on the Thornberg fortune. Israel must battle his own son, Barry (Barry Manilow), who leaves the sheep ranch to set up his own garment business and attempts to stifle his father. Israel's only loyal ally is Rebecca, the sheep (Dustin Hoffman), who leads the Thornberg flock to Sydney to vote in a heated stockholder's meeting (5,000 sheep, also stockholders).

Also stars Mark Hamill, O. J. Simpson, Susan St. James. Directed by Francis Ford Coppola. (9 hrs.)

FRANK GANNON
Vanna Karenina

Happy, perky faces are all the same. Unhappy, unperky faces are all different.

It was clear to Vanna as she looked at the contestants that they were a hideous, loathsome lot. There was nothing for anyone to be happy or perky about. Vanna thought about all these things and bubbled and smiled.

An accountant from Encino got "Free Spin." Vanna thought that it would be interesting to ask him just what he thought all this meant. Could it save him from his miserable life as an accountant in Encino? Did he actually think that? She stared at him and clapped as she had these thoughts.

Vanna thought to herself as she strode across the letter platform in a green flounce drop-shoulder gown by Mackie. She turned around and turned the lighted letter, which turned out to be an *R*.

R, she thought. *Why R we born?* She could not conceive of a position in which life would not be a misery. *We all must suffer,* she thought, *that is the condition of life, yet we never acknowledge that, we just go on living our futile lives. Yet, when one sees the truth. who is one to tell? What is one to do?*

Walk over to the puzzle platform and turn a letter around. And that is just what Vanna did.

She thought of the many people in her life: SER __ __Y IV __ __ __VITCH, KATA __ __ __OV, KOZN __ __ __EV. They had all meant so much before, when they had won the right to come back. Some of them had come back for an entire week! Now Vanna could feel nothing for them. They were just like other pathetic, hopeless human wretches, like so much patio furniture with large price tags.

Vanna had seen so many contestants: teachers, doctors, lawyers, housewives, hoe-down announcers, city cops. Vanna seemed to see all their history, and all the crannies of their souls, as it were turning a light on in their innermost beings. She knew everything. She had seen everything that there was to see about humanity: how some would keep their extra money on account even though there was an attractive curio cabinet still available, how some would have the puzzle solved and yet continue to spin the wheel out of sheer naked human greed. Greed, mendacity, really bad taste in clothes, bad spelling, she had seen it all. She had looked deep into the bowels of evil, smiled broadly and bubbled.

She thought of the first day she had met VR __ __SKY. How foolish she had been. How could she love a man who wouldn't even tell her all the letters in his name? She had been such a fool, but now she knew what she must do. It was as inevitable to her as the bonus round at the end of every show. She beamed a winning smile, clapped her hands together, walked off the letter platform and stood next to the wheel.

She stood motionless before the swiftly turning wheel. A feeling such as she had never known came over her. She crossed herself. Then she clapped her hands together and jumped up and down, squealing with excitement. Her life came flooding back to her. She saw her childhood. She was sitting over a steaming bowl of alphabet soup, lost in revery. She was standing in front of a full-length mirror at Gramps's house, practicing being perky. She had so many thoughts, so many memories.

Yet she did not take her eyes off the turning wheel. Suddenly she dove, face forward onto the wheel, impaling herself between "Lose a Turn" and "$450." As she felt her life ebb out, a life filled with so many troubles, so many falsehoods, so much sorrow, so much evil, so many of the glitziest gowns this side of dream date Barbie, she lifted her head, looked straight into the camera, smiled and waved "Bye-bye."

It seems like only yesterday that my daughter spoke her first words. My wife and I were having breakfast, and she was in the den watching Mr. Rogers. From three rooms away we heard, "I'm not your fucking neighbor!" Apparently it was building up.
—Jonathan Katz

MR. ROGERS PAUSES FOR STATION IDENTIFICATION

WALKER PERCY
The Last Donahue Show

The Donahue Show is in progress on what appears at first to be an ordinary weekday morning.

The theme of this morning's show is Donahue's favorite, sex, the extraordinary variety of sexual behavior—"sexual preference," as Donahue would call it—in the country and the embattled attitudes toward it. Although Donahue has been accused of appealing to prurient interest, with a sharp eye cocked on the ratings, he defends himself by saying that he presents these controversial matters in "a mature and tasteful manner"—which he often does. It should also be noted in Donahue's defense that the high ratings of these sex-talk shows are nothing more nor less than an index of the public's intense interest in such matters.

The guests today are:

Bill, a homosexual and habitué of Buena Vista Park in San Francisco

Allen, a heterosexual businessman, married, and a connoisseur of the lunch-hour liaison

Penny, a pregnant fourteen-year-old

Dr. Joyce Friday, a well-known talk-show sex therapist, or in media jargon: a psych jockey

Bill's Story: Yes, I'm gay, and yes, I cruise Buena Vista. Yes, I've probably had over five hundred encounters with lovers, though I didn't keep count. So what? Whose business is it? I'm gainfully employed by a savings-and-loan company, am a trustworthy employee, and do an honest day's work. My recreation is Buena Vista Park and the strangers I meet there. I don't molest children, rape women, snatch purses. I contribute to United Way. Such encounters that I do have are by mutual consent and therefore nobody's business—except my steady live-in friend's. Naturally he's upset, but that's our problem.

Donahue (striding up and down, mike in hand, boyishly inarticulate): C'mon, Bill. What about the kids who might see you? You know what I mean. I mean—(Opens his free hand to the audience, soliciting their understanding)

Bill: Kids don't see me. Nobody sees me.

Donahue (coming close, on the attack but good-naturedly, spoofing himself as prosecutor): Say, Bill. I've always been curious. Is there some sort of signal? I mean, how do you and the other guy know—help me out—

Bill: Eye contact, or we show a bit of handkerchief here. (Demonstrates)

Studio Audience: (Laughter)

Donahue (shrugging [Don't blame me, folks], pushes up nose-bridge of glasses, swings mike over to Dr. J.F. without looking at her): How about it, Doc?

Dr. J.F. (*in her not-mincing-words voice*): I think Bill's behavior is immature and depersonalizing. (*Applause from audience*) I think he ought to return to his steady live-in friend and work out a mature, creative relationship. You might be interested to know that studies have shown that stable gay couples are more creative than straights. (*Applause again, but more tentative*)

Donahue (*eyes slightly rolled back, swings mike to Bill*): How about it, Bill?

Bill: Yeah, right. But I still cruise Buena Vista.

Donahue (*pensive, head to one side, strides backward, forward, then over to Allen*): How about you, Allen?

Allen's story: I'm a good person, I think. I work hard, am happily married, love my wife and family, also support United Way, served in the army. I drink very little, don't do drugs, have never been to a porn movie. My idea of R & R—maybe I got it in the army—is to meet an attractive woman. What a delight it is, to see a handsome mature woman, maybe in the secretarial pool, maybe in a bar, restaurant, anywhere, exchange eye contact, speak to her in a nice way, respect her as a person, invite her to join me for lunch (no sexual harassment in the office— I hate that!), have a drink, two drinks, enjoy a nice meal, talk about matters of common interest—then simply ask her—by now, both of you know whether you like each other. What a joy to go with her up in the elevator of the downtown Holiday Inn, both of you silent, relaxed, smiling, anticipating— The door of the room closes behind you. You look at her, take her hand. There's champagne already there. You stand at the window with her, touch glasses, talk—there's nothing vulgar. No closed-circuit TV. Do you know what we did last time? We turned on LA BOHÈME on the FM. She loves Puccini.

Donahue: C'mon, Allen. What are ya handing me? What d'ya mean you're happily married? You mean *you're* happy.

Allen: No, no. Vera's happy, too.

Audience (*mostly women, groaning*): Nooooooo.

Donahue: Okay-okay, ladies, hold it a second. What do you mean, Vera's happy? I mean, how do you manage—help me out, I'm about to get in trouble—hold the letters, folks—

Allen: Well, actually, Vera has a low sex drive. We've always been quite inactive, even at the beginning—

Audience (*groans, jumbled protests*): Nooooo.

Donahue (*backing away, holding up placating free hand, backing around to Dr. J.F.*): It's all yours, Doc.

Dr. J.F.: Studies have shown that open marriages can be growth experiences for both partners. However—(*groans from audience*)— *However:* it seems to me that Vera may be getting the short end here. I mean, I don't know Vera's side of it. But could I ask you this? Have you and Vera thought about reenergizing your sex life?

Allen: Well, ah—

Dr. J.F.: Studies have shown, for example, that more stale marriages have been revived by oral sex than any other technique—

Donahue: Now, Doc—

A stranger shows up in Las Vegas during the annual Jerry Lewis Telethon, and arrives at the studio with two enormous valises. "I'm carrying a million dollars in cash for Jerry's kids," he says. "But I insist on giving it to Jerry personally, on the air."

"A million dollars?" says the producer. "That's a lot of money. Let's have a look."

Proudly, the visitor opens one of the valises, which contains twenty thousand fifty-dollar bills.

"I've never seen that much cash," says the producer. "How did you raise it?"

"It wasn't easy," says the stranger. "For the past six months, I've been visiting public men's rooms all across the country. I stand beside them at the urinal, and I say, 'You better give me a hundred dollars for Jerry's kids, or I'll cut off your family jewels with a knife.' I did this for eight hours a day, and that's how I raised the money."

"That's unbelievable," says the producer. "A million dollars in cash. And what's in the other bag?"

"Well," says the donor, a little sheepishly, "some don't give."

"What's the matter, Lassie . . . is Timmy in trouble?"

Dr. J.F.: Other studies have shown that mutual masturbation—

Donahue (eyes rolled back): We're running long, folks, we'll be right back after this—don't go away. Oh boy. *(Lets mike slide to the hilt through his hand, closes eyes, as camera cuts away to a Maxithins commercial)*

Donahue: We're back. Thank the good Lord for good sponsors. *(Turns to Penny, a thin, inattentive, moping teenager, even possibly a preteen):* Penny?

Penny (chewing something): Yeah?

Donahue (solicitous, quite effectively tender): What's with you, sweetheart?

Penny: Well, I liked this boy a lot and he told me there was one way I could prove it—

Donahue: Wait a minute, Penny. Now this, your being here, is okay with your parents, right? I mean let's establish that.

Penny: Oh, sure. They're right over there—you can ask them. *(Camera pans over audience, settling on a couple with mild, pleasant faces. It is evident that on the whole they are not displeased with being on TV)*

Donahue: Okay. So you mean you didn't know about taking precautions—

Dr. J.F. (breaking in): Now, that's what I mean, Phil.

Donahue: What's that, Doc?

Dr. J.F.: About the crying need for sex education in our schools. Now if this child—

Penny: Oh, I had all that stuff at Ben Franklin.

Donahue: You mean you knew about the pill and the other, ah—

Penny: I had been on the pill for a year.

Donahue (scratching head): I don't get it. Oh, you mean you slipped up, got careless?

Penny: No, I did it on purpose.

Donahue: Did what on purpose? You mean—

Penny: I mean I wanted to get pregnant.

Donahue: Why was that, Penny?

Penny: My best friend was pregnant.

Audience: (Groans, laughter)

Dr. J.F.: You see, Phil, that's just what I mean. This girl is no more equipped with parenting skills than a child. She is a child. I hope she realizes she still has viable options.

Donahue: How about it, Penny?

Penny: No, I want to have my baby.

Donahue: Why?

Penny: I think babies are neat.

Donahue: Oh boy.

Dr. J.F.: Studies have shown that unwanted babies suffer 85 percent more child abuse and 150 percent more neuroses later in life.

Donahue: (striding): Okay, now what have we got here? Wait. What's going on?

There is an interruption. Confusion at the rear of the studio. Heads turn. Three strangers, dressed outlandishly, stride down the aisle.

Donahue (smacks his forehead): What's this? What's this? Holy smoke!

Already the audience is smiling, reassured both by Donahue's comic consternation and by the exoticness of the visitors. Clearly, the audience thinks, they are part of the act.

The three strangers are indeed outlandish.

One is a tall, thin, bearded man dressed like a sixteenth-century reformer. Indeed, he could be John Calvin, in his black cloak, black cap with short bill, and snug earflaps.

The second wears the full-dress uniform of a Confederate officer. Though he is a colonel, he is quite young, surely no more than twenty-five. Clean-shaven and extremely handsome, he looks for all the world like Colonel John Pelham, Jeb Stuart's legendary artillerist. Renowned both for his gallantry in battle and for his chivalry toward women, the beau ideal of the South, he engaged in sixty artillery duels, won them all, lost not a single piece. With a single Napoleon, he held off three of Burnside's divisions in front of Fredericksburg before being ordered by Stuart to retreat.

The third is at once the most ordinary-looking and yet the strangest of all. His dress is both modern and out-of-date. In his light-colored double-breasted suit and bow tie, his two-tone shoes of the sort known in the 1940s

"I had a couple of strange dreams this week," Fred told his therapist. "On Monday, I dreamed I was living in a wigwam. Then, on Wednesday, I dreamed I was living in a tepee. What do you think?"

"Obviously," said the therapist, "you're two tents."

as "perforated wing-tips," his neat above-the-ears haircut, he looks a bit like the clean old man in the Beatles movie A Hard Day's Night, a bit like Lowell Thomas or perhaps Harry Truman. It is as if he were a visitor from the Cosmos, from a planet ten or so light-years distant, who had formed his notion of earthlings from belated transmissions of 1950 TV, from watching the Ed Sullivan Show, old Chester Morris movies, and Morey Amsterdam. Or, to judge from his speaking voice, he could have been an inveterate listener during the Golden Age of radio and modeled his speech on that of Harry Von Zell.

Donahue (backpedaling, smacking his head again): Holy smoke! Who are these guys? *(Beseeching the audience with a slow comic pan around)*

The audience laughs, not believing for a moment that these latecomers are not one of Donahue's surprises. And yet—

Donahue (snapping his fingers): I got it. Wait'll I get that guy. It's Steve Allen, right? Refugees from the Steve Allen Show, *Great Conversations?* Famous historical figures? You know, folks, they do that show in the studio down the hall. Wait'll I get that guy.

General laughter. Everybody remembers it's been done before, an old show-biz trick, like Carson barging in on Rickles during the C.P.O. Sharkey taping.

Donahue: Okay already. Okay, who we got here? This is Moses? General Robert F. Lee? And who is this guy? Harry Truman? Okay, fellas, let's hear it. *(Donahue, an attractive fellow, is moving about as gracefully as a dancer)*

Stranger (speaks first, in his standard radio-announcer's voice, which is not as flat as the Chicagoans who say, Hyev a hyeppy New Year): I don't know what these two are doing here, but I came to give you a message. We've been listening to this show.

Donahue (winking at the audience): And where were you listening to us?

Stranger: In the green room.

Donahue: Where else? Okay. Then what do you think? Let's hear it first from the reverend here. What did you say your name was, Reverend?

Stranger: John Calvin.

Donahue: Right. Who else? Okay, we got to break here for these messages. Don't go 'way, folks. We're coming right back and sort this out, I promise.

Cut to Miss Clairol, Land O Lakes margarine, Summer's Eve, and Alpo commercials.

But when the show returns, John Calvin, who does not understand commercial breaks, has jumped the gun and is in mid-sentence.

Calvin (speaking in a thick French accent, not unlike Charles Boyer): —of his redemptive sacrifice? What I have heard is licentious talk about deeds which are an abomination before God, meriting eternal

---

MORE LICENTIOUS LIMERICKS

There was a young man of
    Devizes,
Whose balls were of different
    sizes;
    The one that was small
    Was of no use at all,
But the other won several prizes.

On the chest of a barmaid in Sale
Were tattooed the prices of ale,
    And on her behind,
    For the sake of the blind,
Was the same information in
    Braille.

A lady of features cherubic
Was famed for her area pubic;
    When asked of its size,
    She said with surprise,
"Are you speaking of square feet,
    or cubic?"

There was a young man of
    Dumfries,
Who said to his girl: "If you
    please,
    It would give me great bliss,
    If, while playing with this,
You could give some attention to
    these."

---

damnation unless they repent and throw themselves on God's mercy. Which they are predestined to do or not to do, so why bother to discuss it?

Donahue (gravely): That's pretty heavy, Reverend.

Calvin: Heavy? Yes, it's heavy.

Donahue (mulling, scratching): Now wait a minute, Reverend. Let's check this out. You're entitled to your religious beliefs. But what if others disagree with you in all good faith? And aside from *that* *(prosecutory again, using mike like forefinger)* what's wrong with two consenting adults expressing their sexual preference in the privacy of their bedroom or, ah, under a bush?

Calvin: Sexual preference? *(Puzzled, he turns for help to the Confederate officer and the Cosmic stranger. They shrug)*

Donahue (holding mike to the officer): How about you, sir? Your name is—

Confederate officer: Colonel John Pelham, C.S.A., commander of the horse artillery under General Stuart.

Penny: He's cute.

Audience: *(Laughter)*

Donahue: You heard it all in the green room, Colonel. What 'dya think?

Colonel Pelham (in a soft Alabama accent): What do I think of what, sir?

Donahue: Of what you heard in the green room.

Pelham: Of the way these folks act and talk? Well, I don't think much of it, sir.

Donahue: How do you mean, Colonel?

Pelham: That's not the way people should talk or act. Where I come from, we'd call them white trash. That's no way to talk if you're a man or a woman. A gentleman knows how to treat women. He knows because he knows himself, who he is, what his obligations are. And he discharges them. But after all, you won the war, so if that's the way you want to act, that's your affair. At least, we can be sure of one thing.

Donahue: What's that, Colonel?

Pelham: We're not sorry we fought.

Donahue: I see. Then you agree with the reverend, I mean Reverend Calvin here.

Pelham: Well, I respect his religious beliefs. But I never thought much about religion one way or the other. In fact, I don't think religion has much to do with whether a man does right. A West Point man is an officer and a gentleman, religion or no religion. I have nothing against religion. In fact, when we studied medieval history at West Point, I remember admiring Richard Coeur de Lion and his recapturing Acre and the holy places. I remember thinking: I would have fought for him, just as I fought for Lee and the South.

Applause from the audience. Calvin puts them off, but this handsome officer reminds them of Rhett Butler–Clark Gable, or rather Ashley Wilkes–Leslie Howard.

Donahue (*drifting off, frowning; something is amiss but he can't put his finger on it. What is Steve Allen up to? He shakes his head, blinks*): You said it, Colonel. Okay. Where were we? (*Turning to Cosmic stranger*) We're running a little long. Can you make it brief, Harry—Mr. President, or whoever you are? Oh boy.

The cosmic stranger (*stands stiffly, hands at his sides, and begins speaking briskly, very much in the style of the late Raymond Gram Swing*): I will be brief. I have taken this human form through a holographic technique unknown to you in order to make myself understood to you.

Hear this. I have a message. Whether you heed it or not is your affair.

I have nothing to say to you about God or the Confederacy, whatever that is—I assume it is not the G2V Confederacy in this arm of the galaxy—though I could speak about God, but it is too late for you, and I am not here to do that.

We are not interested in the varieties of your sexual behavior, except as a symptom of a more important disorder.

It is this disorder which concerns us and which we do not fully understand.

As a consequence of this disorder, you are a potential threat to all civilizations in the G2V region of the galaxy. Throughout G2V you are known variously and jokingly as the Ds or the DDs or the DLs, that is, the ding-a-lings or the death-dealers or the death-lovers. Of all the species here and in all of G2V, you are the only one which is by nature sentimental, murderous, self-hating, and self-destructive.

You are two superpowers here. The other is hopeless, has already succumbed, and is a death society. It is a living death and an agent for the propagation of death.

You are scarcely better—there is a glimmer of hope for you—but that is of no interest to me.

If the two of you destroy each other, as appears likely, it is of no consequence to us. To tell you the truth, G2V will breathe a sigh of relief.

The danger is that you may not destroy each other and that your present crude technology may constitute a threat to G2V in the future.

I am here to tell you three things: what is going to happen, what I am going to do, and what you can do.

Here's what will happen. Within the next twenty-four hours, your last war will begin. There will occur a twenty-megaton airburst one mile above the University of Chicago, the very site where your first chain reaction was produced. Every American city and town will be hit. You will lose plus-minus 160 million immediately, plus-minus 50 million later.

Here's what I am going to do. I have been commissioned to collect a specimen of DD and return with it so that we can study it toward the end of determining the nature of your disorder. Accordingly, I propose to take this young person referred to as Penny—for two reasons. One, she is perhaps still young enough not to have become hopeless. Two, she is pregnant and so we will have a chance to rear a DD in an environment free of your noxious influence. Then perhaps we can determine whether your disorder is a result of some peculiar earth environmental factor or whether you are a malignant sport, a genetic accident, the consequence of what you would have called, quite accurately, in an earlier time an MD—*mutatio diabolica,* a diabolical mutation.

Finally, here's what you can do. It is of no consequence to us whether you do it or not, because you will no longer be a threat to anyone. This is only a small gesture of goodwill to a remnant of you who may survive and who may have the chance to start all over—though you will probably repeat the same mistake. We have been students of your climatology for years. I have here a current read-out and prediction of the prevailing wind directions and fallout patterns for the next two weeks. It so happens that the place nearest you which will escape all effects of both blast and fallout is the community of Lost Cove, Tennessee. We do not anticipate a stampede to Tennessee. Our projection is that very few of you here and you out there in radio land will attach credibility to this message. But the few of you who do may wish to use this information. There is a cave there, corn, grits, collard greens, and smoked sausage in abundance.

That is the end of my message. Penny—

Donahue: We're long! We're long! Heavy! Steve, I'll get you for this. Oh boy. Don't forget, folks, tomorrow we got surrogate partners and a Kinsey panel—come back—you can't win 'em all—bye! Grits. I dunno.

Audience: (Applause)

"Thanks. We had a wonderful time, and so did you."